THE BLUE AND THE YELLOW STARS OF DAVID

THE BLUE AND THE YELLOW STARS OF DAVID

The Zionist Leadership in Palestine
and the Holocaust
1939–1945

DINA PORAT

Harvard University Press
Cambridge, Massachusetts
London, England
1990

This book is a revision of *Hanhaga be-milkud,* published in 1986 by Am Oved, Tel Aviv. Translation of the original Hebrew text was done by David Ben-Nahum

Publication of this book was assisted by a grant from the Lucius N. Littauer Foundation.

This book is printed on acid-free paper, and its binding materials have been chosen for strength and durability.

Library of Congress Cataloging-in-Publication Data

Porat, Dina.
    The blue and the yellow stars of David: the Zionist leadership in Palestine and the Holocaust, 1939–1945 / Dina Porat.
        p. cm.
    Translation of: Hanhaga be-milkud.
    Includes bibliographical references.
    ISBN 0-674-07708-3 (alk. paper)
    1. Holocaust, Jewish (1939–1945)   2. World War, 1939–1945—Jews—Rescue.
3. Jews—Palestine—Politics and government.   4. Zionism—History.   I. Title.
D804.3.P6713   1990
940.53′18—dc20   89-26778
                                                                                      CIP

ACKNOWLEDGMENTS

My thanks are first due to Daniel Carpi, the incumbent of the Benjamin and Chaya Schapelski Chair of Holocaust Studies in Tel Aviv University, who skillfully guided me through a doctorate on a subject that is an open wound in Israel. For their help and patience while I collected material, I thank the staffs of the Central Zionist Archive and the Yad Vashem Archives in Jerusalem, the Labor Party Archives and the Histadrut Archives in Tel Aviv, and the American Joint Distribution Committee Archive in New York.

No less am I indebted to my colleagues in the 1984–85 group at the Institute of Advanced Studies at the Hebrew University in Jerusalem: Yehuda Bauer (who headed the group), Saul Friedlander, Yisrael Gutman, Dov Kulka, Michael Marrus, and Bernard Wasserstein. Aryeh Dvoretzky, director of the Institute at the time, and his staff provided an ideal working environment for me to produce a book in Hebrew.

It gives me great pleasure to thank Yosef Hayim Yerushalmi, the director of the Center for Israel and Jewish Studies at Columbia University, where during a sabbatical in 1988 I was able to complete a first English draft. My deep gratitude goes also to David Ben-Nahum, for his translation of that draft; to Haya Amin, the first editor, for her original ideas; to Judith LaFemina, who carefully revised and typed the manuscript; to Dorothy Harman, who brought the manuscript to Harvard University Press; to Ann Hawthorne, who edited the final draft, for her observant eye; and most especially to Margaretta Fulton for her sensitive and clever guidance.

I thank Mrs. Miriam Dolan and the late Mr. Moshe Kol for having allowed me to use material in their possession.

I am grateful to the American Friends of Tel Aviv University for their financial support.

Finally, I give special thanks to the rescue activist who spent hours trying to make me understand a painful event in history.

This book was written under the auspices of the Benjamin and Chaya Schapelski Chair of Holocaust Studies in Tel Aviv University. The Chair was donated by David and Nathan Shapell of Los Angeles in memory of their parents:

Benjamin Schapelski, killed in Wolbrom, 1942

Hela Schapelski, killed in Auschwitz, 1943

CONTENTS

FOREWORD

Saul Friedlander

Dina Porat's book deals with a particularly difficult and sensitive chapter of contemporary Jewish history that has hitherto evaded systematic inquiry. Beyond its intrinsic scholarly importance, this remarkable study should be understood within its context.

During the Yom Kippur War of October 1973, as on the eve of the Six Day War of 1967, an atmosphere of impending catastrophe, accompanied by a sense of isolation from the rest of the world, permeated the Israeli collective. The vision of potential destruction led to a new remembrance of the extermination of European Jewry—a clear indication of how close to the surface in Israeli minds was the unmastered past.

With the passage of a decade, other events and themes came to dominate the life of the Jewish state: the ongoing occupation of Arab territories and its sequels; the unease from within, which reached a new height with the 1982 Lebanon War; the intense questioning of some of the basic tenets of Zionist ideology. All of these factors—by sensitizing the issue of victims and oppressors, as well as by making use in an unprecedented way of a rhetoric linked to the *Shoah*—intensified this revisiting of the Jewish catastrophe in Israeli consciousness. This heightened awareness was particularly striking among the post-1948 generation. Thus, paradoxically, with the exception of the survivors themselves, it was the generation who did not live through the events of World War II and did not partake in the struggle for the establishment of the Jewish state, who were and are living through an existential confrontation with the extermination of European Jewry. And it is the current Israeli scene that fuels their investigations and gives power to their reflections.

Within this context a new authenticity and urgency began to emerge through the historiography, the literature, and the arts dealing with the fate of the Jews of Europe. The new generation has looked at issues previously avoided or merely used as political weapons, and brought them into the sphere of artistic expression and serious discussion.

Dina Porat's study stands out among the historical works published by the scholars of this post-1948 generation, because of both the highly controversial subject it addresses and the standard of scholarly research as well as intellectual honesty it attains. During the early years of the State of Israel, the themes dealt with by Dina Porat were, in notable instances, the object of fierce polemics; no attempt was made to reach substantiated historical evaluation. Porat's conclusions, as free as possible from ideological stances, do not pretend to be definitive, demonstrating the author's sensitivity to the issues discussed. By enlightening us in a remarkably nuanced way about the attitude of the Yishuv's leadership toward the events in Europe, by helping us to understand rather than to judge, Dina Porat's book represents a major contribution to the history of the Jewish catastrophe and of the Jewish community in Palestine during World War II.

THE BLUE AND THE YELLOW
STARS OF DAVID

Introduction

Ever since the end of the Second World War, the Israeli public has been traumatized by feelings of guilt concerning the Holocaust. The prevailing opinion has been that the Yishuv—the Jewish community in Palestine in the pre-state 1940s—failed to do what could have been done to rescue Jews in Nazi-occupied countries. Especially since the Yom Kippur War, in 1973, art, journalism, and literature have reflected both the increasing influence exerted by the Holocaust on Israeli society and politics and an intensive questioning of Zionism.

This bitter, self-critical, continuing public debate addresses four major issues. First, when did the Yishuv and its leadership grasp the fact that the Nazis were undertaking the systematic killing of all European Jews? Second, once this fact was understood, what financial and human resources were allocated and how much effort was expended? Third, what rescue plans were devised, and to what extent were they carried out? Fourth, what role did European Jewry play in the evolution of Zionist policies and ideology?

The issue of information and interpretation, perhaps more than the others, involves questions about the exercise of leadership in the Yishuv and especially by the Jewish Agency Executive, which in the late 1930s served as the operative organ of the World Zionist Organization and in the 1940s was already considered by the 470,000 Jews then living in Palestine to be "the government of the state-in-the-making." These questions about the role of the JAE include: Did it establish independent sources of information, or did it rely on reports from others? Was the information sufficiently reliable to provide a true picture? Was it sufficiently up-to-date to be useful in planning rescue operations? Was the information shared with the public, or was there a deliberate attempt to prevent disclosure? How did leaders analyze and evaluate the situation, and at what point did they grasp its full meaning?

These questions open up still deeper and more complex problems, related to the fact that people who undergo different experiences attribute different meanings to the same words. For example, the Hebrew term *Shoa*—*Holocaust* in English, *Churban* in Yiddish—is universally accepted today as the synonym for the systematic killing of the Jews in Nazi-occupied Europe. It was used at least as early as December 1938 at a meeting of the inner circle of Mapai, or the Labor party, the dominant party in the Yishuv, in discussing the events of Kristallnacht, or Night of the Broken Glass, on November 9–10, 1938. On that occasion party leaders spoke of the Shoa that had befallen the Jews of Germany and Austria, of the great tragedy of their "annihilation," and of the need to find "avenues of rescue" for them.[1] Yet the Nazis' operational plans for the mass murder of the Jews did not take shape until the spring of 1941. Surely the Mapai speakers did not have in mind what we think of today as the Holocaust. They were, rather, looking for appropriate words to describe the mass arrests, sporadic killings, humiliation, and abuse that culminated in the events of Kristallnacht.

Thus, when evaluating the response of the Yishuv, the historian must first address the meaning of the terms used by Jews sending information out of occupied Europe, both to the senders and to the recipients in Palestine. This issue of interpretation transcends the particular context of the Zionist leadership in Palestine facing the Holocaust in the early 1940s. It pertains to any context in which humans strive to grasp unprecedented events and phenomena while they are occurring, before they are incorporated in personal, national, and universal experience.

PART ONE

Grasping the Unprecedented

1

First Warnings: September 1939 through 1940

The outbreak of war in Europe in 1939 disrupted communications with Palestine but did not end them. In September and October the war was waged only in Poland; in western Europe there was a "phony war," with no actual fighting. Nonetheless, the Yishuv and the Jewish Agency Executive (JAE) in Palestine felt cut off from the theater of operations. David Ben-Gurion, then chairman of the JAE, complained that "our colleagues" at the Zionist office in London, a central office headed by Chaim Weizmann, then president of the World Zionist Organization (WZO), "are at the front and know what's going on better than we do" but had failed to transmit the information to Palestine.[1]

Ben-Gurion and his colleagues could not afford to be cut off from the scene of events: the task of the Jewish Agency, as defined in 1922 when the League of Nations confirmed the British Mandate over Palestine, was to represent the Jewish people to the British mandatory authorities and to cooperate with them in order to implement the Balfour Declaration of November 1917 that "His Majesty's government view with favor the establishment in Palestine of a national home for the Jewish people." Hence the Jewish Agency, through its various departments, directed immigration, land purchase, settlement, the raising and investment of funds. Most of the Agency's Executive members lived and worked in Jerusalem; they maintained close contact with the branches of the World Zionist Organization in many countries, especially with the two important offices in London and New York. Formally, the JAE was subordinate to the Zionist Actions Committee (ZAC), the supreme authority between congresses, in which the different Zionist parties were represented. Actually, it spearheaded the political struggle of both the Yishuv and the WZO.

There were also difficulties in maintaining contact with the "Pales-

tine Offices" throughout Europe, which had served, for all practical
purposes, as embassies of the Jewish Agency. Before the war, they had
been in charge of distributing the immigration certificates allocated
and issued by the British mandatory government. They had also provided information about the situation in Europe in general and the
Jewish communities in particular, in addition to the regular information supplied by the press and news agencies, particularly the Jewish
Telegraphic Agency (JTA) and Palestine Correspondence (PAL-
COR), the Agency's own official news service. Contacts were also disrupted between the Agency's European offices and those in America,
South Africa, and Australia, threatening the continued flow of funds
and political support from Zionist organizations in the Anglo-
American world and of immigration from Europe—the lifeline of the
Yishuv's future. Finally, the mandatory government imposed increasingly strict censorship on the press and postal services in Palestine,
and the British high commissioner, Sir Harold MacMichael, saw to it
that the regulations were enforced. By the end of 1942, newspapers
were allowed to quote only the bulletin of Reuters, the British news
agency; and even its reports were censored in Palestine. The Yishuv
managed to circumvent this situation by listening to radio broadcasts
of various European stations, especially the BBC. Its members also
founds ways to publish information in the daily Hebrew press, such
as including news in editorials and other commentaries.[2]

In October and November 1939, to overcome these problems the
JAE decided, first, to establish a Jewish Agency office in Geneva (in
neutral Switzerland), to be run by Richard Lichtheim, a veteran German Zionist; second, to set up a network of couriers to Europe for
transmitting information and instructions; third, to dispatch a non-
Jew to the occupied central part of Poland, which was called the "General Government" area by the Germans and which came to include
most of the main ghettos formed after the outbreak of war. (Later,
toward the end of 1941 and during the spring and summer of 1942,
most of the extermination camps were built within the boundaries of
the General Government.) For weeks there had been hardly any news
of what was happening to the Jews there, and the urgency of getting
information overruled fears that this strategy might be construed as
an illegal act and a breach of loyalty to the Allies, who forbade contacts with the occupied areas.[3]

From the beginning of the war, Geneva served as a center for the
gathering and exchange of information from areas under German
occupation. Representatives of several Jewish organizations were already there, including Gerhard Riegner and Abraham Silberschein

on behalf of the World Jewish Congress (founded in Geneva in 1936 by Stephen S. Wise and Nahum Goldmann to represent worldwide Jewry and to fight for its rights); Shmuel Scheps, head of the Palestine Office, and his colleague Chaim Posner (later Pazner); Chaim Barlas, head of the Immigration Department of the Jewish Agency; and Nathan Schwalb (later Dror), a delegate of Hechalutz (The Pioneer), a Zionist youth movement that educated its 100,000 members for a life of physical labor in settlements in Palestine and formed part of Mapai, the Labor party. Lichtheim, Schwalb, and Silberschein regularly sent detailed summaries of the situation to Palestine. These reports were based on the testimonies of refugees who passed through Geneva, on evaluations by officials, and on any mail that reached them from Poland (in 1939 and 1940 the Jews there were still allowed to communicate with the outside world, although their mail was subject to strict censorship) and other occupied areas. After September 1940, when Barlas moved from Geneva to Istanbul, mail from occupied Europe started arriving there as well.

News also reached Palestine directly from individuals, youth movements, Zionist party offices, and community centers in Europe. All such information was shared among recipients. Translations of letters and abstracts of conversations with refugees that arrived at the Tel Aviv offices of the World Union of Mapai—run by its political secretary, Melech Neustadt (later Noy)—were sent to the JAE, to the secretariats of all the kibbutzim and youth movements in Palestine, and, when relevant, to the new-immigrants' associations. These recipients, in turn, forwarded their news to the World Union. Only Agudat Yisrael and the Revisionists kept their correspondence and news to themselves. Agudat Yisrael, the ultra orthodox, anti-Zionist party, refused to be included in the Yishuv's institutional framework: the Jewish Agency and the General Council of the Jewish Community in Palestine, most often called the National Council (Vaad Leumi), which was in charge of strictly domestic, nonpolitical, issues. The right-wing Revisionist party, founded by Ze'ev Jabotinsky, was included in the National Council but left the World Zionist Organization in 1935 to become the main opposition to the dominant Labor party, as well as the General, Liberal, and Religious Zionist parties of the Yishuv and the WZO.

Toward the end of 1939, the JAE established what became known as the Committee for Polish Jewry, sometimes also called the Committee of Four, consisting of Moshe (later Moshe Chaim) Shapira, Eliyahu Dobkin, Emil Schmorak, and Yitzhak Gruenbaum, one of the most prominent Jewish leaders in Poland in the 1920s, as chairman. All four were also members of the JAE. At the beginning of 1940 the committee set up a center to collect and disseminate information. Much of this information came from Ignacy Schwarzbart, a member of the Polish National Council in London, which was in contact with occupied Poland, and later with the Polish underground. Poland's consul in Tel Aviv, Henrik Rosmarin, allowed the committee to use the diplomatic pouch to send news between London, Istanbul, and Palestine, thus bypassing British censorship. Also included in the pouch was news from the local and German presses in occupied Europe. Although this material was subject to German supervision and therefore had to be treated with suspicion as propaganda, it was an important source of details about life under enemy domination.[4]

Jewish workers in the Office of the British Censor also helped get news out of Palestine to neutral centers by wording material nonexplicitly and by stamping letters as if they had been checked by the censor. In addition, much information was conveyed in person by emissaries going abroad on public or private missions. In charge of contacts both with the censor's office and with those going abroad was Eliyahu Golomb, prominent leader of the Labor movement and commander of the Haganah (Defense), the main clandestine military organization of the Yishuv, whose tens of thousands of members undertook various national missions, such as taking care of illegal immigrants.[5]

Through these various channels of communication, adapted to changing conditions throughout the war, the JAE "received comprehensive information every week."[6]

One of the first evaluations of the situation in Poland reached Palestine in October 1939 from Chaim Weizmann, president of the WZO, in London. His informant, a man who had escaped from Warsaw, reported in detail the abuses perpetrated there, including the murder of hundreds of Jews by drowning and starvation. The informant believed the Germans' motive was to punish the Jews for their heroic resistance during the invasion of Poland. His explanation left room for hope that the situation would improve once the Germans had stabilized their position there.[7] But another report at the same time, from Lichtheim in Geneva, was more pessimistic. He predicted that two million Jews would be annihilated by the Germans as cruelly as the Armenians had been by the Turks in 1915–1916. Lichtheim's report was received in Palestine, then, at the very beginning of the war, as a gloomy forecast that was not fully substantiated by facts.

In December 1939 Lichtheim sent a report based on the testimony of a Swiss Red Cross official, who detailed the isolation of the Jews in

Poland and their suffering from typhoid and hunger. Jews who had escaped from Poland to Geneva reported to Lichtheim about thousands of victims of bombings, robbery, hunger, and kidnaping and described the preparations under way for moving all Jews into ghettos. Lichtheim also provided details about the situation in the former Czech region of Bohemia-Moravia, now a German protectorate. The Jews there had been ruined economically; many had been arrested; and thousands had been deported to the Lublin area in Poland, where they were suffering from disease, cold, hunger, and violence. The report ended with a plea to the Jewish world for help: "Do something! Don't ever forget the children here!"[8]

Lichtheim, Schwalb, and Silberschein continued to submit such eyewitness reports throughout 1940. By the beginning of that year, additional information was reaching Palestine from Lithuania, where about 15,000 refugees—including many leaders—from occupied Poland maintained contact with family members and colleagues who had remained behind. Because it was possible to telephone, telegraph, or write from Lithuania to the free world, these refugees were an important and reliable source of information until the Russian invasion in June. Thousands of them proceeded to Palestine by way of western Europe or Odessa and Turkey. Thousands of others arrived by way of Rumania or Italy. In all, about 4,500 legal and 3,800 illegal immigrants arrived during 1940.[9]

Among the leaders who reached Palestine from Poland through Lithuania were Apollinary Hartglas, former president of the Zionist organization there; and Moshe Kerner, a former delegate to the Polish parliament. They reported to the JAE in February 1940, and what they said was consistent with the information from Switzerland. Later that year their report was published in a booklet titled *The Shoa of the Jews in Poland,* together with a survey of the condition of Polish refugees in Hungary, Slovakia, Rumania, Lithuania, and the Soviet Union. This was the most comprehensive summary of the situation of European Jews during the first year of the war, and it was prepared by the people whose discretion and judgment were held in high esteem. Hartglas' major conclusion was that

> the [Jewish] population of Poland is being mercilessly and cruelly annihilated . . . by the barbaric use of physical and moral terror and sadistic abuse: mass murder, starvation, exposure to epidemic, and the suppression of any will to live. Polish Jewry's three and a half million are dying in the areas under occupation. If the war does not end soon, if there is no miracle, all that will be left on Polish soil is one gigantic Jewish graveyard.[10]

Hartglas was, then, the first to refer explicitly to physical extermination. He did so even before the Germans actually decided on such a course of action. That decision did not come until the following spring, on the eve of Germany's invasion of the Soviet Union. Hartglas was also the first to ascribe a general purpose and a method to German actions. Other refugees already in Palestine viewed the same events much less pessimistically. In their opinion, Jewish suffering was a side effect of the war and the brutality of the lower echelons of the occupying German army and of the anti-Semitic Polish population. In fact, older Polish Jews remembered favorable German treatment during the First World War.

Although some refugees referred to the situation in Poland as a Shoa, they did not use the word in the same way that Hartglas did. For them it meant the worst hardship, destruction, and abuse they could then imagine. The Yishuv leaders, too, spoke in 1940 about a Shoa, as they had in 1938, after Kristallnacht. But now they used it to refer to the dispossession and uprooting of millions of people who, it was feared, would be very hard to resettle after the war. Then "hundreds of thousands, maybe millions, will be suspended between heaven and earth." [11]

The first serious disruptions of communications channels occurred in mid-1940. Germany occupied Belgium, the Netherlands, and much of France; Italy joined the war; the Mediterranean was closed to civilian vessels; the Soviet Union invaded the Baltic states. Mail from the Balkans continued to arrive regularly in Palestine; contact with Geneva continued by way of London; and PALCOR, the Agency's news service, could still telegraph to Britain, the United States, and South Africa. However, civilian air service ceased, and civilians could travel on military aircraft only if their business was assigned a high priority. A journey from Palestine to London sometimes took weeks. Strict British censorship of mail continued; transportation difficulties and British immigration regulations reduced the number of immigrants reaching Palestine. As a result, consultations among the Zionist offices in London, New York and Jerusalem became exceedingly complex, and each office had to act independently in urgent matters.

After a five-week journey from London to Palestine by way of South Africa and Egypt, Mapai leader Dov Hoz in early August 1940 reported to his colleagues "with pain and indignation toward the Zionist movement that news of the destruction of the people of Israel in many countries reached the Zionist office in London . . . but . . . the London center has not become . . . a center of information that would break through all barriers and establish contacts with those centers of

Jewry in danger of total annihilation." Hoz suggested doing some-thing "daring and involving great sacrifices . . . an adequate attempt [to get more firsthand information] has not yet been made."[12] It was true. Neither the courier service nor the dispatch of a non-Jew to Po-land—decisions taken almost a year before—had been implemented.

It is noteworthy that Hoz reported to the Mapai Center on a matter of national importance. Mapai, a socialist party, controlled about 50 percent of all the institutions in the Yishuv, and 75 percent of the workers' union. Its various committees discussed and largely deter-mined, though unofficially, the policy of the Yishuv. Yet the growing concentration of power in its hands was accomplished by a constant bitter struggle with the Revisionists. Mapai was also continuously en-gaged in ideological disputations with other more radical left-wing parties and groups within the Labor movement.

Hoz's report, which like the others described the "destruction of the people of Israel in many countries," was not discussed formally by any institution of the Yishuv. During the second half of 1940, it was men-tioned briefly at JAE meetings about other crucial but mostly local subjects. Why did neither the JAE nor any other important body of the Yishuv hold a thorough closed discussion about the situation of European Jews since they now possessed comprehensive and reliable information? And why did neither the Agency nor any other central Yishuv organization make this information public? The bulletins and summaries of information reaching Palestine were not published there. Nor did the Jewish Agency either confirm or deny newspaper reports. Most editors of daily papers, regardless of partisan affiliation, later testified that the Agency never sought to influence their publi-cation or interpretation of information from Europe.[13]

These questions are hard to answer, because there are no written records of any deliberations, in any of the Yishuv's central institu-tions, on the situation of European Jewry or on whether to make more information about it available to the public. Later in the war, the com-mon feeling in the Yishuv was that the Agency should have encour-aged newspapers to pay far more attention to such an important issue, and some publicly accused its members of deliberately suppressing information.

It is unlikely that fear of British censorship prevented public circu-lation of such news. Although public discussion of other issues, such as settlement, defense and illegal immigration, was forbidden, both the press and Yishuv leaders found ways to disseminate information. News was often spread by word of mouth; the Yishuv was a small com-munity, and relations among most people were very informal. Many

thousands volunteered for various missions, so they were both involved and informed.

Hoz's remarks provide one clue. Until the summer of 1940 the Yishuv, including its political leadership, did not consider itself to be a
center of information about the Jews of Europe. London was the
headquarters of the Allied powers and the seat of most governments-
in-exile, which maintained contact with their respective countries and
thus supposedly had direct access to news from them. Accordingly,
the London office of the WZO was regarded as the appropriate center
for information about European Jewry. Moreover, the Yishuv saw itself as a small community at the margins of the war. This physical
remoteness made it impossible to undertake the task of helping the
Jews of Europe. According to Ben-Gurion, "This work should not be
managed from here"; it was an assignment better suited for the newly
founded World Jewish Congress; for the American Jewish Joint Distribution Committee (JDC), the most important Jewish welfare and
support organization since its foundation in 1914; and for American
Jewry as a whole. All of these were closer to the centers of political
influence and had the financial means to provide effective help.[14]

Nonetheless, Hoz's plea that the Yishuv take action was not without
effect. Despite the opposition of Ben-Gurion, there were those who
agreed with Hoz. Their agreement marked the beginning of the process whereby the Yishuv ultimately decided to assume responsibility
for the fate of the Jewish people as a whole and to become a center
for activity aiding Jews under Nazi rule.

Another line of thought within the Yishuv, though never articu-
lated explicitly, was apparently as follows: The situation is serious, but
the Jewish Agency Executive is aware of it and has appointed a committee to deal with it. There are representatives in Geneva to keep an
eye open. The fact that the news has been more or less the same since
the beginning of the war seems to indicate a more or less stabilized
situation, so perhaps this is as far as the Germans intend to go. Moreover, the measures taken by the Germans in Western Europe are more
moderate than those taken in Poland; so far, they are directed against
rights and property, not against life itself. Perhaps, then, German policies are determined by local factors rather than by a general plan.

A more basic reason for the lack of discussion—public or in closed
meetings—of the situation of European Jews during 1940 was the fact
that it was already common knowledge. Nazi persecutions since January 1933 had turned many Jews into refugees; their urgent needs
were known all too well to the Jewish Agency. The resulting conflict
between Jewish migration to Palestine and British regulations had

brought a progressive deterioration in relations between the Yishuv and the British mandatory authorities.

In fact the deterioration had started during the 1920s, at the beginning of the Mandate period, when the British authorities set a "schedule," or quota, for immigration certificates, issued twice a year to Jewish individuals living in any country without financial resources. Other categories, such as "capitalists," who could invest in Palestine or who owned more than a certain sum; "pupils" whose maintenance was guaranteed by local organizations; and "dependents" or relatives, were allowed in without restrictions. (In contrast, there were no restrictions on the number of Arabs allowed to immigrate to Palestine.) The size of the quota was dependent upon what the British defined as the current "economic absorptive capacity" of Palestine and was never high enough to accommodate the number of refugees. Thousands of Jews entered Palestine by sea with a tourist visa or by fictitious marriage to a certificate holder; others crossed the Lebanese or Syrian border on foot.[15] Thus the first stage of what the British called illegal immigration, and what the Yishuv called the Ha'apala (the struggle to "climb up" to the Land of Israel) or Aliya Bet (Immigration B), started through individual initiative.

During the 1930s, pressure for more certificates grew in tandem with persecutions in eastern and central Europe. During this period the situation of Jews in Poland and Rumania seemed at least as severe as in Nazi Germany. The second, organized stage of Aliya Bet started in July 1934 with the arrival of a ship carrying 350 people from Poland, Latvia, and Lithuania. A month later, a second arrived. The third was turned away by the British coast guard and, after being refused entry to several Mediterranean ports, returned to Poland. At that point, in November 1934, Aliya Bet ceased until 1937.[16]

Jewish legal immigration reached unprecedented numbers after the Nazis came to power: 30,000 in 1934, 42,000 in 1935, 62,000 in 1936. From 1933 to 1939, 55,000 Jews immigrated to Palestine from the Reich (Germany, Austria, and Czechoslovakia) as a result of an agreement called the Ha'avara between the Jewish Agency and the German government that permitted each immigrant to take about £300 and encouraged German export at the same time. (The agreement was vehemently opposed by the Revisionists and especially by American Jews, who favored a conclusive ban on Germany and German products.) In the same period, 74,000 came from Poland. In all, about 250,000 arrived. The Jewish population in Palestine doubled to about 470,000 , while the Arab population reached a million.[17]

The Arabs, increasingly concerned about the volume of Jewish immigration and its economic repercussions, retaliated violently from April 1936 until the outbreak of the war in September 1939, in what Arab and British historians call the Arab Revolt. About 600 Jews were killed, thousands were wounded, and attacks on settlements and transportation lines caused severe damage. The Yishuv responded by establishing fifty-two new settlements and by reorganizing and reinforcing the Haganah.

A British royal commission headed by Lord William R. Peel convened in November 1936 to devise a solution. Its recommendations, published in July 1937, were to split Palestine into three parts: a Jewish state in the Galilee, the valley of Jezrael, and along the coast; an area comprising the holy places, a corridor of access to them, and Eilat, all to remain under British control; and an Arab state everywhere else. This was the first time a Jewish state had been considered by non-Jewish authorities, and in response the Arabs renewed their attacks—this time against both the Jews and the British.

The British crushed the attacks militarily but appeased the Arabs politically. The threat of war in Europe made stability in the Middle East an urgent necessity, to keep British supply lines safe and troops free for combat at the front. Whitehall officially abandoned the partition plan and announced a new policy in the White Paper published in May 1939 by Malcolm MacDonald, secretary of state for colonial affairs. The purchase of land by Jews was to be limited, and immigration restricted to 75,000 over the next five years, with illegal immigrants to be deducted from that number, to ensure that the Jewish population in Palestine remained at one-third of the total. Immigration after 1944 would be dependent upon Arab consent.[18]

The Yishuv viewed the White Paper as a disaster for Zionism and as a betrayal by Britain. The Jewish Agency issued a statement that "it is in the darkest hour of Jewish history that the British Government proposes to deprive Jews of their last hope . . . The Jews will never accept the closing to them of the gates of Palestine nor let their national home be converted into a ghetto."[19] The leadership organized demonstrations and violent clashes with British forces, who reciprocated with a massive search for illegally held weapons and stronger measures against Aliya Bet boats.

Aliya Bet resumed in April 1937 as a result of continuing pressure from Europe. This third stage was initiated by the Revisionists, who were soon joined by kibbutz movement emissaries and private individuals and groups in Europe. Regardless of affiliation, the organizers rejected the formal Zionist line that Aliya Bet would further worsen relations with the British and thus imperil legal immigration, and that

Britain would abandon its pro-Arab policy once its political needs changed.

After Kristallnacht in November 1938 and the MacDonald White paper, Yishuv leaders supported Aliya Bet unanimously. Shaul Meirov (later Avigur), a well-known Haganah leader, was appointed to head the organization, or Mossad, for Aliya Bet. From then until its abrupt termination in November 1940, Aliya Bet gained impetus. From April 1937 to September 1, 1939, forty-five sailings brought about 22,000 people from European ports. The vessels were mostly old, even unseaworthy, and almost always overcrowded and ill-equipped. Two ships sank. Two were captured by the British and returned to Europe. The rest managed to anchor at night, outside the territorial waters of Palestine. People were brought to shore in small boats by local Jews alerted by Haganah members, who organized the landings. The newcomers were hidden in homes for a while. Those discovered by the British were taken to the Atlit detention camp, near Haifa, and kept there for months. Their number was deducted from the quota of 75,000.[20]

With the outbreak of the war, Chaim Weizmann declared that all parts of the Yishuv, even the Irgun Zvai Leumi (Etzel for short), the anti-British Revisionist armed underground, were prepared to enlist in the British army, fight the Nazis, and support Britain in every possible way. Ben-Gurion declared that "we must fight the war as if there were no White Paper and we must fight the White Paper as if there were no war."[21] Recruitment started immediately, and 6,500 men and women joined the British army in 1939–40.[22]

In February 1940, however, the mandatory government specified new regulations that prohibited the purchase of land by Jews in two-thirds of Palestine, allowed purchase in almost all of the other third with authorization from the high commissioner, and made land free in only 5 percent of the territory. The Yishuv reacted again with large-scale violent demonstrations and a general strike. Ben-Gurion resigned from the chairmanship of the JAE, claiming that British policies would result in a ghetto for the Yishuv.

The swiftness of German conquests in western Europe in the spring of 1940, the formation that May of a new British government under Winston S. Churchill, who was known to be pro-Zionist, and the beginning of the Battle of Britain all gave rise to hopes for a change in Britain's Middle Eastern policies and even for military cooperation between the British army and the Yishuv. The latter became part of the front when the Italian air force bombed the Palestinian coast during the summer and about 200 people were killed.[23]

In the meantime, Aliya Bet continued. By then it was clear that most countries were closed to any more refugees, and British and American plans to settle Jews in remote parts of the world had proved chimerical. Seven more ships came, some of them carrying more than 1,000 refugees. One sank; one was caught. From September 1939 to October 1940, 8,500 newcomers arrived, and the British decided to put an end to it. They exerted diplomatic pressure on countries from which the ships left for Palestine. They drastically reduced the legal immigration quotas (in nineteen of the first thirty-nine months of the war, no quota application was approved) on the grounds that Axis agents might be planted among Jewish refugees (although this claim was used repeatedly throughout the war, no such agent was ever found). Finally, armed British coast guard boats attacked refugee ships. The irony of the situation was that German policy from 1939 to the spring of 1941 was one of expulsion of Jews, not of extermination, and thus was in accord with the Aliya Bet effort.

In November 1940 three ships carrying 3,500 refugees from Germany, Austria, and Czechoslovakia anchored near Tel Aviv. The British announced that they would send them, and all others caught henceforth, to their colony of Mauritius, in the Indian Ocean. Yishuv leaders decided to attract world attention, especially in the United States, with one dramatic act. An explosive was attached to the *Patria* to prevent its sailing to Mauritius. But the ship sank immediately, and 200 people drowned; 1,645 refugees were forced to board another ship and were sent to Mauritius until the end of the war. Aliya Bet virtually ceased. Ships were hardly available. And once the Nazis adopted a policy of extermination, it became too difficult for Jews to get out. From November 1940 to March 1944 two more ships sank and two more got through, bringing the number of illegal arrivals since the beginning of war to 18,000.[24]

This chain of events best accounts for the Jewish Agency's response to the news that reached it from Europe in 1940. The Yishuv was engaged in its own urgent problems. The peril threatening Europe's Jews needed no clearer demonstration than the fact that so many were ready to risk their lives in old ships and face so many hardships to escape. Perhaps the Jewish Agency felt no need for public or internal discussion at that stage. The tragedy was known. It was knocking at their gates.

The leaders of the Yishuv had detailed information, but they did not realize that 1940 marked the beginning of a chapter different from any previous one in the Jews' long history of persecution. There was certainly no apprehension of any plan aimed at the Jewish people as a whole, to which the events of 1939–40 were but a preamble.

2

A Semblance of Stabilization: 1941

In the spring of 1941 Britain's military position deteriorated both in Europe and in the Middle East. Bulgaria joined the Axis; Yugoslavia was occupied. The British had to withdraw from Greece and from Crete and were faced with a rebellion in Iraq. Field Marshal Rommel was advancing in North Africa. The Yishuv perceived a German invasion of Syria and then Palestine as a real possibility. Had Hitler decided to take the Middle East first and postpone the invasion of Russia, Palestine would have been crushed in a pincer movement from Syria in the north and Egypt in the southwest.

The Jews in Palestine responded by enlisting in greater numbers in the British army and by strengthening their military power at home. The British mandatory government allowed the formation of a specially trained elite unit of the Haganah for guerrilla warfare behind enemy lines. The Haganah's own goal, undisclosed to the British, was to get in touch with European Jewry. In the meantime, under the shadow of the threat, new settlements were established, forty-seven of them during the war. Wartime industry gave a boost to the economy in 1941, and cultural life flourished.

In February 1941 Ben-Gurion returned to Palestine after ten months in Britain and the United States meeting with influential leaders. In his view, the most vital task of the Zionist movement was to crystallize a political program that would bring about the establishment of a Jewish state after the war and, in the meantime, overcome the prevailing mood of failure in the Yishuv because the national home was not being built quickly enough to offer a haven to European Jews.

Upon his return Ben-Gurion expressed astonishment at the apparent complacency in Palestine toward the war in Europe and the destruction of Jews there. "Information about all this is certainly available here," he said, but "the matter is not a central fact in the life of the Yishuv."[1] To remedy the problem, Ben-Gurion proposed intensifying the sense of "Zionist urgency and brotherhood" and reinforcing activities both between the Zionist movement and the Yishuv and between the Yishuv and European Jewry. The immediate goal should be to establish a Jewish state ready to receive millions of Jews after the war. "This," he said, "is what present-day Zionism and the problems of the Jewish people are all about."[2] Thus Ben-Gurion's concentration on postwar goals shifted attention away from the present plight of European Jews and reinforced the current perception that although their suffering was unprecedented, a substantial number would survive.

In discussions held in Yishuv institutions and the Agency in the spring of 1941, Ben-Gurion's thesis prevailed. As Yitzhak Gruenbaum expressed it, anything Hitler did could be undone after the war ended "save the uprooting of large parts of Jews from the European economy."[3] This was the considered opinion of the head of the Committee of Four, who had more access than most others in Palestine to the news from Europe. Apparently the Committee of Four concurred. *The New Deep Mire* (a reference to Psalms 69:3), a thorough compilation and analysis of Jewish, Polish, and German source material sponsored by the committee and published in the first half of 1941, reviewed the situation of the Jews in Poland and concluded that there was no method in the German actions. They were trying "to turn . . . millions of Jews in Poland into penniless beggars while the Jews were fighting for their dignity with all their strength, refusing to give up."[4] This was accepted as an accurate evaluation of the situation.

News continued to arrive from Europe despite disruptions in communication and the reduction in the number of refugees reaching Palestine. In February 1941 there was news of ferocious, unprecedented pogroms in Rumania; in April and May, of the deteriorating situation in Slovakia and the deportation of thousands from Germany. Eyewitnesses, whose descriptions were repeated in letters and in the press of the free world, reported the situation of Jews in forty ghettos in Poland and warned that, if the present situation continued, none would survive.

In 1941, with the Mediterranean blocked and the Balkan states reduced to German satellites (though not actually occupied), Istanbul's importance as a source of information increased. Lithuania's importance ceased with its annexation by the Russians in June 1940. Hungary, on the other hand, which was still independent, was considered a haven for Jews from Poland and Slovakia. The escapees passed on information to Hungarian Jewish leaders. Their reports on the political situation in Hungary and the state of Jewish communities and Zionist groups in occupied Europe were relayed to Palestine in two stages. First, reports were sent to Istanbul with Hungarian intelligence agents, diplomats, businessmen, and various officials and, although it was not entirely reliable, through the regular mail. Second, Yishuv emissaries carried material from Istanbul to Palestine. Similar contacts were developed in western Europe. For example, Abraham Silberschein in Geneva and Yitzhak Weissman, the representative of the World Jewish Congress in Portugal, communicated through diplomats and double agents.[5]

In June 1941 Germany invaded the Soviet Union, and the murder of hundreds of thousands of Jews, from the Baltic states to the Crimea, began. Four *Einsatzgruppen* ("special operation units"), together with other German units and local collaborators, rounded up and shot entire communities. Hundreds of thousands were killed in a few months. News of these atrocities did not leak out immediately because there were few survivors, because they were carried out at the front, and because the perpetrators were sworn to secrecy.

In Palestine it was assumed that the Jews in Nazi-occupied Soviet territories would be subjected to the same treatment as those in Nazi-occupied Poland. Leaders felt they had only to wait for news from the refugees who would start to arrive or "to reread all those chapters in the chronicles of destruction [in *The New Deep Mire*] . . . from the stories of wandering and mass deportations to the mass killings and punitive acts which took the lives of hundreds of Jews."[6] Mass killings, apparently, were still thought of in terms of hundreds. A few days after the invasion, the Mapai Secretariat discussed possible scenarios. Those who feared the worst proposed sending emissaries immediately to Turkey and Iran to direct the stream of refugees to Palestine. During a discussion two weeks later, following the rapid retreat of the Red Army, Ben-Gurion said: "What many of us, including me, were so afraid of is now a fact: The terrible problem of European Jewry after the war is not just that of five million Jews in Europe, excluding the Jews of the Soviet Union. On the front between the Nazis and the Russians . . . millions of Jews . . . are now subject to destruction." Moshe Shertok (later Sharett), head of the Agency's Political Department, expressed the view that the suffering "was one of the inevitable evils created by the war, rather than a problem demanding a solution, and one cannot look now for an immediate positive constructive solution"; the full extent of the destruction could be known only after the war.[7]

Both Ben-Gurion and Shertok, then, considered the Jews' experiences to be a result of their being at the front, in the line of fire. Only a military victory could end this form of suffering, and the Yishuv could not possibly know the extent of their hardships or do anything about it. The words *Shoa, destruction,* and *catastrophe* were now used with harsher connotations than before, but those meanings still did not correspond to reality. The gap between what was actually happening and what the Yishuv perceived to be happening had become abysmal.

The events of July 1941 demonstrate how great this gap was. Shertok informed his Mapai colleagues about a pogrom in Baghdad at the beginning of June: 500 were reported dead. At first the report was questioned; the figure seemed too high to be trusted. But Jews in Baghdad who had sent word to Palestine in June about hair-raising brutalities feared that in fact 1,000 were dead. The Mapai leaders expressed shocked disbelief: "Such atrocities were not committed even in Nazi Germany." A similar report on a pogrom in Jassi, Rumania, at the end of June, claiming that thousands were dead, was questioned as well.[8] The scale of German actions at this time in the Soviet Union was still unknown.

Nor did the Mapai leaders know that in February 1941, three months before the attack on the Jews in Baghdad, Haj Amin el-Husseini, the mufti of Jerusalem and leader of the Palestine Arab Higher Committee, had submitted to Hitler the following proposal for a German declaration: "Germany and Italy recognize . . . the right of Palestine and other Arab countries to solve the question of Jewish elements in Palestine and in other Arab countries . . . in the same way as the Jewish question in the Axis lands is being solved." The riots in Iraq were, perhaps, a first attempt at such a solution.[9]

The British censor forbade publication of the news about the violence in Iraq. The front had moved away from Palestine in the second half of 1941, but British control in the Middle East was not secure: the Arabs continued to lean toward the Axis. Wide coverage of the riots in Iraq would not only damage Britain's prestige in the Middle East; it might also rouse Arabs elsewhere, most notably in Palestine, to attack the Jews. Indeed, John S. MacPherson, the secretary of the mandatory government, believed that even news from Europe might prompt Arab violence. After confiding to Gershon Agronsky (later Agron), editor of the *Palestine Post* (the leading English-language daily, in the summer of 1941 that British intelligence believed the death toll among the Jews of Europe was far higher than had been made public, he suggested that Agronsky and other editors refrain from publishing such information, not only because it might hinder the Jews' war effort but also because it might encourage the Arabs "to start an all-out assault on the Jews of Palestine." [10] Less than two years had passed since the end of the Arab Revolt, and the Yishuv was still feeling its effects. There is no written evidence that Agronsky consulted with the leadership on this issue of voluntary self-censorship, but the fact remains that they decided to abide by British regulations and keep the information secret.

In the second half of 1941 the situation seemed to get worse. Richard Lichtheim sent word that there were hardly any Jews left in Zagreb. A Polish refugee who reached Palestine in September said that people were dying every minute in the streets of the ghettos, mainly from hunger, and that, if the war continued another two years, no Jews would be alive to witness the victory. Toward the end of the summer the press started reporting on the situation in the occupied Soviet areas: more ghettos established; "specialists for Jewish questions" following the German army; people being loaded into vans. By October the press was covering the deportations from central Europe to the east and quoting Hungarian officers' vivid descriptions of horrors on the front line. Chaim Barlas, in Istanbul, got word from Hungary at the same time about *Einsatzgruppen* atrocities in the Ukraine, reported by Jews who had escaped. In November Eliyahu Dobkin told the JAE about the cruel expulsion of Jews from Bukovina and Bessarabia to Transnistria. He then reported that in June 7,800 Jewish men had been shot to death in one day in Jassi. "The Shoa surpasses everything we've heard so far," he concluded. The figure of 7,800 in one day was met with disbelief. The JAE appointed a committee, headed by Gruenbaum, to look into the matter further. [11] (Apparently, either the Committee of Four was no longer functioning, or it concentrated only on matters related to Polish Jewry.)

In December Nathan Schwalb sent a detailed report from Geneva describing extreme suffering in all countries under Nazi occupation, and the JAE held its first full discussion of the situation of Jews in Europe. Although the news from different places and sources seemed to be consistent and seemed to be getting consistently worse, the full truth had not yet been grasped: "mass slaughters" were still mentioned as a possibility rather than as a reality. Members of the Executive confessed: "None of us knows what to do to help." [12]

In the face of this news, from September 1941 until January 1942 the JAE continued to seek encouragement from more heartening reports: "an increase in the training of thousands of pioneers in centers in Poland, Czechoslovakia, and Germany, who needed help"; sporadic Jewish self-defense in various places; and continuing high morale among the Jews in Europe. Yishuv leaders still believed that the sufferings of the Jews were incidental to the German occupation. Thus it was that in September the Agency granted recognition to the platform of the Council of Polish Immigrants in Palestine, which demanded civil equality and full rights for the Jews of Poland after the war as well as the right to immigrate to Palestine. Thus it was that Ya'acov Chazan, leader of the left-wing pioneering movement Hashomer Hatzair, demanded that the JAE prepare a practical plan for helping the hungry masses in Europe after the war and denounced the pessimists who had warned that "the Diaspora was being subjected to a rapid death." [13]

Not much had changed in 1941. The feeling of isolation persisted. There were no more discussions of the situation of the Jews of Europe in the leading organs of the Yishuv than there had been in 1939–40. Between August and December the Mapai Central Committee did not discuss the subject once. There were fewer headlines about it than there had been the year before. Toward the end of 1941, a fuller picture began to emerge. Yet, there was still hope that the gravity of the situation was exaggerated.

3

The Beginnings of Change:
January–August 1942

In January 1942 a letter from the soviet foreign minister, Vyacheslav Molotov, was publicized in London. The letter, which had been distributed to foreign ambassadors in the USSR, listed crimes committed by the Nazis and included a short description of their special cruelty toward the Jews. At the end of the month the Mapai Central Committee heard a report about photographs that had been circulated in London, showing Jews in eastern Poland being herded out of towns by the Germans and murdered. The committee did not discuss either the Molotov letter or the report; instead, it continued a previous discussion about the position of the British left toward the Soviet Union.[1]

At this time numerous stories were appearing in the Palestinian press about the Jews of Europe, including the high death rate in Warsaw; the dwindling population of the ghettos of Łodz and Vilna; the murder of Jews in various parts of Poland; the murder of children and elderly people and the rape of young girls in the Nazi-occupied areas of Russia, as reported by the Soviet Jewish writer Ilya Ehrenburg; and the expulsion of Jews from Czechoslovakia. Neither the Jewish Agency nor any Mapai committee discussed these topics. On February 1 Emil Schmorak of the Committee of Four told the JAE of a report "that some special gas was tried on four hundred Jews from Holland and they all died from it." This was the first time that gas had been mentioned as a means of extermination. The news had been reported only in the London *Jewish Chronicle*, since no other paper had believed the information could be true; and it did not elicit any comment from the JAE. Schmorak went on to complain that the committee elected in November 1941 for the purpose of "clarifying and improving the state of the Jews in the areas under Nazi occupation" was not functioning. Gruenbaum, admitting that the committee had not yet met even once, promised to convene it as soon as possible and asked those who had complaints to make practical suggestions instead.[2]

In February 1942 the SS *Struma,* an old cattle boat packed with 770 refugees, including 70 children, sank in the Black Sea. Only one person survived. After two months of negotiations between the Jewish Agency and the mandatory government, the *Struma* had been refused entry to Palestine and then had been turned away by the Turks into the open sea, in spite of the sign hoisted with the words "Save Us!" This incident illustrated not only the gravity of the situation in Europe but also the Yishuv's helplessness. Rage against the British reached a new high; posters bearing the picture of Sir Harold Mac-Michael, "known as High Commissioner for Palestine, WANTED FOR MURDER of 800 refugees," appeared on many walls. The dead were collectively mourned, protest meetings were held, and all the Yishuv institutions discussed at length how the Yishuv should react. At a special session of the Assembly of Representatives, an affiliate of the National Council, Hitler's "war of extermination against the Jewish people" was described in great detail. The Assembly demanded international action to help the persecuted and open the gates of Palestine to the survivors. Money was collected to help the refugees, and a petition was circulated demanding "a shelter for the wanderers and for Jewish refugees in their national home, their homeland."[3]

Most of the subsequent discussion in the Yishuv focused on immigration to Palestine as a solution, the Yishuv's right to fight the Nazis under its own flag, and its relations with the British. Little attention was given to the actual plight of the Jews of Europe.

In mid-March the daily press in Palestine published information provided by Bernard Jacobson, the Joint Distribution Committee's representative in Budapest: Hungarian soldiers returning from the front reported that 250,000 Jews had been murdered by the Gestapo in the Ukraine, among them Jews expelled to that area from central Europe. Also published were an official letter to the U.S. government from Molotov and eyewitness testimonies collected by the American legation in Moscow. According to these reports, every few days another few thousand Jews were murdered in the occupied Soviet areas—some by shooting, others by the use of explosives. Altogether, at least 100,000 had already been killed.

This information differed from any received so far in three respects. First, it pointed to a connection between the expulsion and subsequent murder of Jews from central Europe and thus implied the existence of a plan. Second, the JDC and the American legation could be considered reliable sources, whereas Soviet sources were usually suspected of releasing anti-Nazi propaganda. Third, this was the first time that official sources claimed that tens of thousands of Jews had been murdered within a short time in the same area.

The day this information was published, a delegation of party members from the Jordan Valley came to the Mapai Secretariat in Tel Aviv. The historian Ben-Zion Dinaburg (later Dinur), acting as their spokesman, expressed the anxiety of many in the Yishuv over the "death and expulsion of Jews, unprecedented in world history." He analyzed the growth of anti-Semitism—even in countries now fighting the Nazis—and noted that although many in the Yishuv felt despair and embarrassment, those feelings had not yet turned into public anxiety. He theorized that people confronted with a dangerous situation often allow themselves to become preoccupied with minor questions in order to avoid the real issues, which they cannot face. This, he believed, might explain the proliferation of political and intramural squabbling at just that time in the Yishuv.

Other members of the delegation urged the party to greater activity and more intensive dissemination of information to the public. Their position was that the entire Jewish people—the Yishuv included—was being threatened, not merely the Jews of Europe. Therefore, it was the Yishuv's responsibility to lead the struggle for the survival of the people as a whole.

A delegation from the youth movements also appeared before the Secretariat that day. One of its spokesmen, Aharon Meged, declared, "We are quite shocked by the disaster of the *Struma* and by the disaster of the Jews in general, the disaster of Jewish exile. The ground is burning under our feet, but we lack a program for transforming our wishes into deeds, and this is why we feel permanently disgraced. Assign duties to us and you will discover reservoirs of devotion and self-sacrifice that still exist among the youth of the Yishuv." Another speaker, Yehuda Braginsky, one of the heads of Aliya Bet, criticized the leadership more harshly: "Discussions—there are none. A place to clarify matters doesn't exist. When news comes, the reaction is always 'let's wait for more; maybe it's not true.' When a suggestion is made to do something, it is turned down. We have not even tried to do everything in our power. This muteness, this lack of will, this lack of courage must cease."[4] After hearing these statements, the Secretariat went on to discuss a variety of marginal issues.

Criticism of Gruenbaum and his various committees was also voiced that month by members of the World Jewish Congress in Tel Aviv. In their opinion, the Committee of Four had failed to fulfill the task for which it had been appointed—gathering in one place all information available about the Jews of the occupied countries. At the end of March, in another expression of lack of confidence in the functioning of the Agency's committees, the council of Polish Immigrants in Palestine sent a summary of all information in their hands to the Polish government-in-exile in London and demanded that it sound the alarm and mobilize world public opinion for rescue operations.[5]

But despite these explicit and implicit criticisms, and despite a change in the attitude of some members of the Yishuv toward the situation in Europe, the voices were raised only sporadically and were still those of a minority. They lacked sufficient leverage to persuade the JAE or the Mapai Central Committee to take immediate practical action.

News came in with increasing regularity. In April and May the Yishuv was informed of the murder of 90,000 Jews in Minsk; the liquidation of Estonian Jewry; the continued expulsion of Jews from the Reich and their murder in the east; the deaths of three-quarters of the Jewish population of Vilna; the liquidation of the Kovno ghetto; further experiments with gas on the Jews of Holland; confirmation of the news that 52,000 Jews had been killed within a few days in Babi Yar, near Kiev. The press also quoted warnings from the Jewish Anti-Fascist Committee, established by the Soviet government in 1942 to enlist Western support for the Soviet war effort, that the ultimate goal of all these acts was the annihilation of the Jewish people.

All newspapers in the Yishuv, regardless of political affiliation, cautioned their readers that there was an element of exaggeration in the descriptions of the killing methods other than by shooting—the use of explosives, the burning and burial of living people, and the burial of children alive in the presence of their parents. Since much of the news came from Soviet sources, the press in general tried to explain it as part of a propaganda war between two former allies—the Soviet Union and Nazi Germany. Indeed, the report of children's being buried alive came from *The Red Star*, the Red Army paper.

The news agencies were accused of blowing out of proportion "any rumor about the spilling of Jewish blood." Comparisons were made with the atrocity propaganda disseminated during the First World War and later discovered to have been grossly exaggerated. Journalists seized upon every contradiction or denial—and, as could be expected, contradictions and denials abounded, as did the verification of nonevents. In most cases the truth eventually emerged, but in the meantime editors had to rely on their own interpretations and intuition. One editor, for example, explained in the following way the news that only 20 percent of the Jews living in Riga prior to the occupation were left: "This means that, with the help of the Soviet government, 80 percent have been taken out and saved. The percentage of survivors from the smaller towns is probably similar."[6]

In contrast, Jewish Agency representatives in Geneva and Istanbul seldom questioned the credibility of the catastrophic news they sent to Yishuv leaders. And this information was not made public. Thus, whereas the Jewish press in Palestine and the general public relied on news agencies and the foreign press and were constantly warned that their credibility was suspect, the leadership possessed its own sources of information, which was assumed to be correct by those who sent it.

At the end of May 1942 the Mapai Central Committee addressed the question of the Polish refugees in the Soviet Union. Eliyahu Dobkin told the committee that he had numerous reports from Teheran, including one from the Polish consulate there, and others from Polish refugees who arrived in Palestine via Teheran, to the effect that a million Jews had been saved by escaping to Russia. It was already known that hundreds of thousands had fled from Poland to Russia upon the outbreak of war in 1939 and that more had been transferred by the Russians from areas bordering Germany on the eve of the German invasion in June 1941. In August and September 1941 the Yishuv had received information that "masses of Jews" were in Tashkent, Samarkand, and other parts of Uzbekistan. In April 1942 Wladyslaw Sikorski, the premier of the Polish government-in-exile, had announced that there were 650,000 Jews among the Polish refugees in the Soviet Union. Now, according to Dobkin, the number being given general credence was a million, maybe even more.

This figure was encouraging, for it meant that one-third of Polish Jewry was safe. Dobkin warned, however, that because chaos prevailed in Russia the figures were unlikely to be accurate. He also warned—and this was the crux of his remarks—that "these Jews are about to be wiped about, although in different ways," since they were suffering from terrible want, hunger, and disease.

It was Dobkin's opinion that this information should not be publicized in Palestine or abroad even if the censorship permitted it: "Such publicity would hurt our rescue operations, which are the only thing we must concentrate on." Publishing testimony of the suffering and high death rate of Jews in Russia might be construed as criticism of the Soviet Union itself. In reaction, the regime might thwart efforts to get the Jews out of the Soviet Union, or it might adopt a harder line toward Zionism and Jews in general. Now, when public opinion in the West and in Palestine was so sympathetic to the Soviet Union for its courageous resistance to the Nazis, was no time for such disclosures.

Dobkin was careful to distinguish between the one million Polish Jews who were endangered by wartime conditions but not subjected to a deliberate scheme to end their lives and the other two million under Nazi occupation. The plight of the latter, he assumed, was well known to members of the Central Committee; there was no need to elaborate on "the atrocities that are now being inflicted upon them."

Dobkin ended his remarks with what he called "self-flagellation": the members of the Central Committee were not interested in fulfilling their duty toward the Diaspora; they were, at most, prepared to listen to tales of woe on the radio. They had never applied themselves to a serious discussion of the problem; it had often been "the nineteenth item on the agenda." Leaders who were approached to join in the effort or were asked to free volunteers of current responsibilities in order to undergo training for missions in the Diaspora replied that "this was not the time." Dobkin explained this apparent lack of interest in terms of a confession of his own response: "I don't know how the others feel," he said, "but I feel a strange barrier between myself and new immigrants coming to Palestine ... six [other officials] who visited newcomers arriving [from Poland via the Soviet Union] through Teheran, in the camp at Atlit [near Haifa], were unable to find a common language with these Jews who, despite everything [they underwent in the Soviet Union], have not experienced the same atrocities being inflicted on tens of thousands of other Jews [under Nazi occupation]." He was referring, of course, not to a language barrier, but to a psychological one.

Some of his listeners, such as David Remez, secretary general of the Histadrut, the General Federation of Jewish Workers in Palestine, felt unjustifiably rebuked: "I am among those who, for some reason, had never been told about many of these things ... Maybe there was too much conspiracy in the whole matter, too much whispering about. The information seems to have evaporated between the mouth and the ear. I am shocked to hear that it has been impossible to raise these questions at the Central Committee [of the Histadrut]." The Histadrut was the most important economic institution in the Yishuv, with the broadest educational and social welfare networks. It was also the home base of the Haganah. The Histadrut gave Mapai its broad socioeconomic base and the Agency its political power. It is striking that Remez, a leader in such a pivotal position, had not received up-to-date information on so crucial an issue.

The discussion ended in general agreement that both people and means would be forthcoming to deal with this issue. The participants agreed to try, in the very near future, to discuss concrete means toward "a major rescue effort" (as Dobkin phrased it) in a responsible forum, either the Central Committee or the JAE. That forum would also discuss another question: Should the details of the situation be made known to the public at large? In the meantime, it was decided, a way must be found to ensure that "the facts will be made known to the people in charge."[7]

Not long afterward Dobkin himself went to Teheran and returned two months later, in August 1942, with the opinion that "all the information that has reached us so far is baseless." The Polish Jews in Russia were scattered all over, wandering from one place to another or held in detention camps, unaware of each other's existence. Their number, he estimated, was between 300,000 and 400,000. Most of them were broken in spirit, having gone through terrible suffering, and were living on garbage. It was doubtful that they could survive for long. According to official Polish sources, the death rate among refugees in general was about 25 percent; in the camps, almost 50 percent.

The discrepancies in information about the situation and numbers of refugees in the Soviet Union reinforced the position of the skeptics, who claimed that large numbers—for good or for bad—should not be believed before being checked, preferably by someone from the Yishuv. The news in general, however, was depressing. If the condition of the Jews in the Soviet Union was desperate, then the plight of the Jews in Nazi-occupied Europe was probably hopeless.[8]

Dobkin's mission to Teheran contrasted sharply with another one, undertaken by Melech Neustadt, a month earlier. Neustadt had gone to Istanbul on behalf of the Histadrut to try to contact members of the Zionist pioneering movements in the Nazi-occupied countries. He had left Palestine feeling that he could do no more than "pay a moral debt and calm our conscience." A few weeks later, however, he returned convinced that contacts were possible without the dispatch of Palestinian couriers. He had been able to correspond with all the occupied areas except Łodz and some regions in Nazi-occupied Russia. Those answering his letters had provided such diverse details as the price of bread in certain Polish towns and the number of Jews in Theresienstadt. The assumption prevailing in the Yishuv, that it was impossible to establish direct contact, was, in his opinion, "the only possible excuse for the fact that we have done nothing, or hardly anything, for so long." He believed that there was a "possibility for safe, efficient help."[9]

Neustadt urged the Histadrut and the World Jewish Congress to open offices in Istanbul. In June 1942 he himself established—and headed—the Committee for Alleviating the Distress of Our Comrades in the Diaspora. It consisted of representatives of all the parties in the Histadrut who were in touch with their members, particularly their youth movements, in occupied Europe.

Just as Dobkin's mission reinforced the skeptics, Neustadt's endeavors reinforced an optimistic view persistent in the Yishuv since 1940—namely, that the Zionist movement in Europe was alive and active and being led by young people; the Jews were adjusting to the difficulties of the war; and, even though the Nazis wanted to exterminate the Jews, they also needed them as a work force and this might save large numbers from extinction. In short, the Jews were living up to the injunction of Ezekiel 16:6: "In your blood live."

Neustadt's optimism was short-lived. At the end of May 1942 the Polish government-in exile received a detailed report from the Bund, the large left-wing Jewish workers' party in Poland, asserting that the Nazis had started the physical extermination of the Jewish population of Poland. The murder was spreading from the occupied areas of the Soviet Union to eastern Poland and the General Government area. About 700,000 people had already been killed, mainly by shooting but also by poison gas pumped into sealed trucks. The information in this report was made public through the initiative of Szmul (Arthur) Zygielbojm, a Bund member of the Polish National Council in London. It was broadcast by the BBC three times in June, published in a white paper by the Polish government-in-exile, and sent to all the Allied governments and parliaments. It was presented at a press conference attended by the British minister of information, Brendan Bracken, and at a World Jewish Congress conference in London. It was reported in the *Daily Telegraph* and in the Jewish press. For the second time that year, an Allied government gave credence to the idea that there was a methodical plan to exterminate the Jews. On June 30, 1942, the World Jewish Congress announced on the American broadcasting networks that at least one million had already been killed. This figure, which was closer to the truth than the Bund's, was immediately publicized in Palestine.[10]

That same day, the JAE met. The topic of discussion was whether or not German Jews in Palestine had the right to publish a German-language newspaper at a time when Germany was synonymous with a lexicon of murder. During the discussion Gruenbaum mentioned "the atrocities and the murder of hundreds and thousands of Jews by the Germans." Not only does such a topic seem completely out of keeping with events at the time; but Gruenbaum's mention of "hundreds and thousands" was in marked contrast to the figure of 700,000 to one million dead already circulated in England and the United States and published in Palestine.[11]

From the end of June until the middle of October 1942, the destruction of European Jewry was discussed only tangentially, in relation to concerns nearer home. In North Africa the Axis armies were advancing toward Egypt, and for the third time since the outbreak of war the Yishuv was in danger. The fall of Palestine seemed highly possible. The British high commissioner informed Yitzhak Ben-Zvi, the chairman of the National Council, that if Alexandria fell the British would evacuate the Middle East. The message originated from Whitehall and was delivered officially.[12]

It was obvious that if the German army invaded Palestine, it would enlist the help of the Arab population in destroying the Jews, much as it had enlisted the help of the Ukrainians, Lithuanians, and Poles. The mufti of Jerusalem, Haj Amin el-Husseini, had already declared publicly that he considered the German solution to the Jewish problem appropriate for the Arabs. Thus, in the months immediately following publication of reliable information on the systematic extermination of the Jews of Europe, the immediate question for the Yishuv was not whether it could save the Jews of Europe but whether it could save itself. The Jews of Europe were not an object of rescue for the Jews of Palestine but an object for comparison.

Various options for meeting the crisis were discussed: evacuating women and children to a neutral or allied country; concentrating the entire Yishuv in Jerusalem in the hope that the Germans would not bomb the Holy City; acquiring prisoner-of-war status for the entire population; enlisting wholesale in the British army, withdrawing with it, and participating in a later reconquest of Palestine. Others suggested surrendering to the Germans and working for them while organizing a resistance movement, as had been done in many of the occupied countries in Europe. Individuals began looking for places to hide their children—in monasteries or with Arab friends. Others equipped themselves with poison. It was suggested that a number of leaders leave the country to establish a government-in-exile, and one Hasidic rabbi informed Shertok that his followers in the United States insisted that he save his own life. Shertok answered that no leader was leaving the country, that all would remain with the people "for better or for worse."[13]

Many of these ideas—particularly the evacuation of women and children—were discussed at emergency meetings of the Histadrut and the Haganah command. It seemed suicidal for the Yishuv to try to defend itself against the Germans, who had so far proved invincible, and especially after a British withdrawal and in the midst of a hostile Arab population double its size. Nevertheless, the Yishuv unequivocally rejected all other courses and immediately began preparing to defend the territory, with its "back against the wall."[14]

At a meeting of the JAE, two divergent attitudes were expressed. Gruenbaum felt that the Yishuv must embark upon a heroic course that would at least leave for posterity "the legend of Masada"—of fighting to the last man rather than living "the life of a whipped dog" like the Jews of Germany and Poland. Moshe Shapira differed. If ghettos were established for the Jews of Palestine, he said, there would still be hope that the remnant that survived would be able to regenerate the House of Israel.[15] There is a striking parallelism between the reactions of these two leaders in the new Jewish community in Palestine to the possibility of German conquest and those of some leaders of the Jewish communities in Europe, on the one hand, and of the youths who organized the revolts in the ghettos, on the other.

From June until October, when Rommel's forces withdrew after the Battle of El Alamein, the Yishuv acquired arms and military training, built up reserve stores of food and equipment, and established communications with the outside world. During the same period there was a steady flow of news from Geneva and Istanbul and from the few refugees who managed to reach Palestine. Most of it was published in the local press. At the beginning of July, information was received about the deportation of the Jews of Paris, Belgium, and Holland as well as the deportation of all the Jews left in Czechoslovakia and Germany. On July 22 the deportation of the Jews of Warsaw to Treblinka began, and 6,000 people were taken daily from the ghetto. This was made public in Palestine a few days later, and on July 30 in Tel Aviv Gruenbaum led a protest meeting of Polish-born residents.

The beginning of August brought news of murders in Lublin and the use of gas in the Bełzec death camp in Poland. From the Soviet Union came eyewitness reports of *Einsatzgruppen* atrocities in the Crimea and in Minsk. The Soviet Ministry of Information published a "black paper" in Yiddish summarizing the casualties in the Soviet Union and Poland.

In July and August Jewish organizations in America began organizing protest marches and appeals. A mass protest took place in New York in the middle of July to which Churchill and Franklin D. Roosevelt sent telegrams expressing their own and their governments' sympathy. In Britain, representatives of various organizations and of the Allied governments-in-exile appealed to the British government and to the American ambassador, John G. Winant, to provide practical help for the Jews and punishment for the war criminals. The Swiss press printed a similar appeal by Swiss intellectuals and quoted a tough anti-Nazi speech by Churchill that evoked a broad response. Thus, the summer of 1942 saw the beginning of international reaction to the murders taking place behind enemy lines.[16] Even so, a crucial change in the perception of the situation had yet to take place.

4

The Turning Point:
End of 1942

At the beginning of August 1942, a Jewish representative in Geneva received information from a German source whose reliability was confirmed by Swiss mediators that a plan had been discussed at Nazi headquarters to exterminate 3.5 to 4 million Jews in the fall. They would be brought from all parts of Europe to the east, where the extermination would be carried out by various means, including the use of prussic acid.

This was the first time that information had been provided by a reliable German source indicating the time, place, and methods for the annihilation of millions.[1] The news was passed on to the other Jewish representatives in the city. Chaim Posner and Richard Lichtheim cabled Chaim Barlas in Istanbul to forward it urgently to Palestine. Gerhard Riegner, head of the World Jewish Congress office in Geneva, cabled Stephen Wise, the president of the WJC in New York, who was thought to have access to President Roosevelt, and M. P. Sidney Silverman, the organization's representative in London. But despite the reliability of the source, Riegner ended the cable with the qualification: "We send this information with due reservation since we cannot confirm its accuracy."[2] The U.S. State Department asked Wise not to publicize the contents until they could be further verified. During September and October, American agents checked the details. In November, Undersecretary of State Sumner Welles informed Wise that documents received from the American legation in Bern "confirm and justify your deepest fears" and, consequently, the information could be made public.[3]

Lichtheim spent two weeks corroborating the information through another reliable German source before cabling details to Jerusalem at the end of September. He noted both that he had verified the news independently and that it corresponded to what he had described "in a hundred previous reports." At the beginning of October Gruenbaum answered him: "Shocked your latest reports regarding Poland which despite all difficult believe stop Haven't yet published do everything possible verify cable." Apparently Gruenbaum understood the cable as referring to Poland only, and not to Europe in general. Lichtheim replied that the information had already been verified by two independent sources, a difficult task in itself since "for obvious reasons there are no eyewitnesses and the figures are not known." Therefore, he added, "do not publicize in writing." In his next cable he wrote that "it is easy for me to understand that you do not want to believe the report."[4]

In October Enschel Reiss, an active member of the Polish-Jewish organizations in Palestine, received several cables from Abraham Silberschein of the World Jewish Congress in Geneva about mass murders carried out in specially designed installations, after which the fat and bones of the dead were used for industrial purposes. Reiss later recalled that "the contents of the cables were so horrible that officials in Palestine doubted their veracity and did not want to publish them." News arrived from Stockholm to the effect that "a great number of people have recently been murdered by gas," but it was not specified where this had happened. At the end of October Barlas returned to Palestine with further details that he himself had gathered as well as additional material from Posner and Lichtheim.[5]

Information concerning the methodical extermination of the Jews of Europe thus reached Palestine from the end of September 1942 on. The news was both sent and received with certain doubts despite the facts that it had been verified by different sources and that it corroborated previous reports. It soon became evident to the informants in Europe that the recipients in Palestine had greater reservations than they themselves. As a result, in October and November their letters and reports became longer, more assertive, and more detailed.

Leaders of the Yishuv, indeed, received the news with disbelief. Stories of death factories and commercial use of the dead seemed even more incredible than previous stories about the monstrous methods employed in mass killings, and had the effect of further discrediting the previous information.

At a JAE meeting in October on a range of matters, Gruenbaum reported on his correspondence with Lichtheim while requesting an allocation to carry out verifications of the news. "It seems," he said, "that the information is exaggerated"; yet he had asked a variety of sources to clarify the "rumors" about the murder of Jews, and all had replied that the Jews "were being sent to forced labor camps and disappearing."[6] Gruenbaum's choice of words indicates that he was still unprepared to accept the harsh truth.

Other members of the JAE reacted in a similar way. Ben-Gurion vacillated between hope and despair. On the one hand he said: "He who does not see what the Jewish people is now facing is blind . . . they can all be murdered. I don't know if any Jews will be left after Hitler." But two sentences later he was speaking about "several millions, at least two million Jews, bereft of home and property, who will have to be transferred immediately to Palestine." Moshe Shapira maintained that there was "a certain degree of exaggeration" in all the information. Moshe Shertok asserted that the only reliable centers of information were London and New York, ignoring the fact that the same news that had reached London and New York had reached Palestine as well. At the end of the discussion Eliezer Kaplan, the treasurer of the Agency, allocated fifty Palestinian pounds to Gruenbaum for cables, although Gruenbaum has requested a hundred.[7]

In the middle of November a group of sixty-nine Yishuv members who had been caught in Europe at the outbreak of the war, most of them women and children, arrived home. They had been exchanged for a group of Germans held by the Allies. The arrivals were taken first to the new immigrants' camp at Atlit, where they were questioned individually and at length by the members of the JAE. Dobkin and Shapira brought detailed reports. Each exchangee brought information of a different sort—deportations, drowning, burying people alive—and about different places: the death camps in Sobibor and Treblinka (Auschwitz was mentioned too, but as a hard labor camp); various ghettos; communities in western and central Europe. Their accounts complemented and corroborated one another and confirmed earlier ones. These people could not be "filed away" like a cable or a letter, as Barlas was to say later, embittered by the fact that his and his colleagues' reports went unheeded. Among the exchangees were members of kibbutzim and sabras, so that there was no barrier between them and Yishuv or Agency officials. The alienation that had been felt at earlier meetings with survivors was absent here.[8]

The exchange group, as they came to be called, felt they owed a debt of honor to those they had left behind. They tried to pay that debt by repeating over and over again the scenes of hardship and horror. But again, their reports generated more shock than belief.

Ya'acov Kurtz, a member of the exchange group from Tel Aviv who had formerly been a prominent citizen in his Polish town, wrote later: "People did not believe me. They said I was exaggerating. I was interrogated as if I were a criminal trying to put something over on people.

They asked me how I could know what was happening in some place while I was locked into a ghetto. 'How could you know what happened to the Jews who were deported if you weren't there?' They went to great lengths to weaken my credibility so that even I would doubt the truth of what I knew." Kurtz, however, was able to understand the reaction in Palestine because of his own experience in Poland. There Jews had seen crowded trains full of Jews from western and central Europe pass before their very eyes and yet refused to understand the significance. They heard that masses of Jews had been killed in neighboring areas and refused to believe what their own eyes had not seen.[9]

One of the women from the group met with Dobkin at the home of Fischel Schneerson. Schneerson was one of the leaders of the tiny protest group of intellectuals called Al Domi (Do Not Be Silent), which was trying to arouse public opinion in the Yishuv over the plight of European Jewry. At the end of their conversation, Dobkin asked her if she was not exaggerating. The woman stood up, slapped him in the face, and left. Even Dobkin, who devoted a lot of time and energy to dealing with the news, was incapable of accepting forms of human brutality for which he had no existing frame of reference. It was especially hard to believe that the first to be murdered were always children, the elderly, and the infirm. "I admit," Shertok cabled to London in November, "that had I not heard it myself from people who had been there, I would not have believed it." Ben-Gurion expressed a similar feeling.[10]

On November 22, 1942, the JAE for the first time since the war had begun devoted a meeting almost exclusively to European Jewry. Dobkin reported on his talks with the exchange group and expressed the opinion that one had to accept the facts as true although he doubted whether all the members of the Executive really believed them. The next day the JAE published the following announcement in the local press:

> The Jewish Agency Executive in Jerusalem has received from authoritative and reliable sources detailed information regarding the acts of murder and slaughter committed against the Jews of Poland and the Jews of central and western Europe deported to Poland.
>
> According to this information, following the June visit to Warsaw of Gestapo Chief [Heinrich] Himmler, the Nazi authorities in Poland began the systematic extermination of the Jewish population in Polish towns and cities. A specially appointed government committee travels around the country and directs extermination operations. Jewish children up to the age of twelve have been ruthlessly executed en masse. Elderly people have been killed as well.

Able-bodied Jewish men were registered and sent in groups to un-known destinations and have not been heard of since. In various places, Jewish women were assembled by the Nazi authorities and also sent away . . .

Information from the ghettos of Warsaw and Łodz points to an appall-ing reduction of the Jewish population there in recent months.

According to information from the same sources, there are mass de-portations of Jews from the cities of central and western Europe. There are only 28,000 Jews left in Berlin.

The Jewish Agency Executive discussed this information at its meeting yesterday and decided on a series of activities and appeals abroad re-garding the situation of the Jews of Europe. A special committee was elected to carry out these activities.

The Agency announcement did not mention the death factories in Sobibor or Treblinka, reported by the exchange group. Nor did it al-lude to the fate of those who disappeared. People could thus still hope that the missing would ultimately survive. The announcement re-ferred to the "appalling reduction" of the population of the Warsaw ghetto but failed to report that out of 380,000 Jews only 50,000 were left. The massacre of more than a million Jews in the Nazi-occupied area of Soviet Russia was not mentioned, nor was it indicated where the Jews of central and western Europe were being sent.

The testimonies of the exchange group seem to have shocked the Agency members enough to compel them to issue a public formal an-nouncement in the press, the first to address the situation of Euro-pean Jewry. Yet the wording of the announcement confirms Dobkin's contention that despite everything they had been told, leaders—him-self included—were still reluctant to believe the worst. It may be that the Agency did not want to generate a climate of wholesale despair in the Yishuv. There is some evidence that a few members of the exchange group were requested to give their details only in closed forums.[11]

It is quite likely, though hard to prove, that Gruenbaum, as head of the Committee of Four, formulated the announcement. Its tone re-flects his reservations. Of all the people on the Executive, his skepti-cism and refusal to face reality seem to have been the most tenacious. The fact that he, who had been an admired leader of Polish Jewry, was now watching its destruction from a safe place surely increased his inability to accept the bitter news at face value. Another reason, surely, was the knowledge that one of his sons, Eliezer, had been deported, probably to the camp in Buchenwald or in Birkenau (which was not yet known to be the worst part of Auschwitz).

Even though the announcement did not reflect the full severity of the situation, the Yishuv was shocked and dismayed. What had been considered doubtful or exaggerated was now revealed to be true. Reactions varied between self-reproach and harsh accusations against members of the Jewish Agency.

Shneur-Zalman Rubashov (later Shazar), a Mapai and Histadrut leader, asked rhetorically: "Who gave us permission not to know what was happening . . . to refuse to listen? Who gave us permission to delude ourselves?" He was dismayed to realize that the Zionist movement, "which professes to shoulder responsibility for the destiny of the nation," could have been guilty of such negligence. This view was expressed frequently both in newspapers—in letters to the editor and in articles—and in heated conversations.[12]

Accusations came primarily from the Revisionists, that is, from the opposition, but also from Mapai members. Gruenbaum, head of the Committee of Four, was the chief target. He was accused of keeping the cables from Geneva secret for months. Meetings at which he was scheduled to speak were canceled. The press was vehement. The Revisionists declared that they would not sit together with the man who had "concealed the catastrophe of Polish Jewry." (Like Gruenbaum, they did not refer to European Jewry as a whole.) The controversy lasted for weeks. Gruenbaum retorted that the public had been well informed but had been reluctant to believe the information. Furthermore, Rommel's advance in North Africa had diverted public attention from the issue.[13] His assertions, which were quite true, only generated even harsher accusations against him.

Ben-Gurion and others who defended Gruenbaum expressed conviction that the public had known the general picture even before the latest news arrived. At a meeting of the Histadrut Executive in which Agency members were attacked, Dobkin countered: "I participate in all meetings of the Jewish Agency Executive, and I tell you that we did not know any more than anyone else in the Yishuv. But if I read to you what you too have known, I think you will be as frightened as the rest of us." To prove his point, he read out the headlines of *Davar*, the Labor newspaper, from June, July, and August and then asked: "How could we have read all this and then continued to eat our meals calmly, without sounding the alarm?" This, he continued, "was our collective psychological state" until the arrival of the exchange group. "We did not pay attention [to what we read] nor did we believe it."[14]

Apparently members of the JAE were not aware of the fact that there was an essential difference between the news that the public had received from the press and the steady flow of information that had reached them exclusively; nor did they seem to feel any special obligation, stemming from their position as leaders in the Yishuv, to pay special attention to the news.

The end of November 1942 marks the first time the Jewish Agency confirmed the news that had appeared in the press to the effect that a calculated, systematic extermination of the Jews of Europe was being carried out. The news was published simultaneously in the United States, with government approval. On December 17, 1942, the Western media published a joint statement by the Allied governments condemning the Nazi extermination of Jews. The extermination was acknowledged as a verified fact and was given extensive coverage in the Jewish and general press—at least during the first few months of 1943.

5

The Ebb of the Tide:
1943–1944

After the announcement by the Allies, the British eased press censorship on the subject, and newspapers in Palestine could publish more news.[1] Furthermore, the dispatch of additional emissaries from the Yishuv to Istanbul resulted in the establishment of a more elaborate communications network with occupied Europe. More general information, as well as letters and reports, now reached Palestine both from the areas under occupation and from Geneva, by way of Istanbul. Nonetheless, very little changed in the way in which the news was received and processed in Palestine.

First of all, the Yishuv still felt remote from events and lacking in a comprehensive picture of the situation. In May 1943, for example, Melech Neustadt declared that "there is no reliable information available to us or to our people either in Geneva or in Istanbul. There is no clear news about anything." More than a year later, in June 1944, Ben-Gurion told the JAE that "we don't know what the real situation in Poland is."[2]

In fact from the beginning of 1943 all entrance to and exit from the General Government area had been denied to both Jews and non-Jews, so less information was available about the ghettos and camps there. Even less was known about the situation in the Baltic states and in German-occupied areas in the Soviet Union. Moreover, lines of communication, even those between Geneva and Istanbul, were broken from time to time.

Second, the condition of the Jews in Europe became a subject of central concern to the Yishuv in late 1942 and early 1943. After the spring of 1943, however, less time and space were devoted to it. Like the disaster that befell Polish Jewry with the outbreak of the war, the extermination ceased to command special attention once the details had become familiar. It was a known fact, publicized in the press; it had been discussed by the national institutions from various perspectives. Only when some extraordinary event occurred—such as the revolt in the Warsaw ghetto or the extermination of Hungarian Jews—did the issue return to the headlines and to center stage.

Third, leaders still commonly looked for ways of reducing the enormity of the tragedy, such as using contradictions between one piece of evidence and another. Fragments of one story were added to fragments of another to produce a third and different one. For example, in January 1943 Gruenbaum informed his colleagues that there had been a halt in the exterminations and that the remnant of the Jews had been concentrated in fifty-five ghettos. In fact the only halt had been in the flow of information between Poland and Geneva.[3] On the other hand, bits of incorrect information were sometimes given credence and became a source of despair. This was the case when news of the destruction of the Warsaw ghetto reached Palestine in February 1943, two months before the uprising. The source reported the death of two of the ghetto's best-known leaders, Tossia Altman and Zivia Lubetkin. The latter had became a symbolic mother figure ("Die Mameh" in Yiddish) to Polish Jewry. The destruction of the largest ghetto in Europe, which enclosed a community of utmost importance to the Jewish world, provoked no mourning assemblies. Perhaps it is easier to respond fully to the death of a person whom one has known than it is to internalize the collective death of hundreds of thousands or even millions of anonymous individuals.

Fourth, the Jewish Agency made no changes in the way it disseminated the information it did receive. Emissaries in Geneva and Istanbul warned against publication of details that might fall into the hands of the Germans and impede rescue operations. Thus, information-collecting centers continued their more or less monthly publication of bulletins that summed up the news about European Jewry, distributing it not to the public but rather to functionaries and institutions. In the interest of security, most of the information was at least a few weeks old, and significant details were omitted. Occasionally the press was given the particulars of certain rescue operations or fundraising campaigns or of the arrival of survivors in Palestine, but it was left free to decide how the news should be presented to the public.

During 1943 the Al Domi group suggested that the Jewish Agency establish a large office of information that would employ experts to compile and disseminate material for both the Yishuv and the world at large. The material would explain the nature of the Holocaust, its origins, and the damage it was inflicting on all of humanity. The JAE rejected the idea and continued to support the publication of memoirs of refugees, collections of letters from Europe, and the like.[4] As a result of this policy, most Jews in Palestine had access only to information furnished by the press or passed by word of mouth. A full and open public debate on the subject was never conducted.

There was no one decisive moment during the war when everyone understood that the Jews in Europe were being systematically annihilated. The absorption and assimilation of the facts started at the end of 1941, was resisted in 1942, and continued in 1943 and even in 1944. It was a slow process, strengthened by the gradual accumulation and corroboration of information from various parts of Europe. It was a personal process, too, not one determined by party affiliations or by opinions held before the war. It is even possible that the process was not necessarily intensified for a person who was in charge of contacts with European Jewry and was not on the decline for someone who concentrated on other occupations. Melech Neustadt and Eliyahu Dobkin are good examples. Some public figures who later wrote memoirs or gave interviews said that news of the extermination reached Palestine only in the middle of 1943; others moved the date as far up as 1944.[5] What they actually referred to was the approximate date they started to grasp the news they had long possessed.

Sometimes, even people who were aware of the facts vacillated between accepting and rejecting them. The same Apollinary Hartglas who predicted in 1940 that, if the Germans continued in their methodical way, there would not be a Jew left in Poland, refused to believe the refugees who confirmed his prediction. And in November 1942, when Chaim Barlas arrived in Palestine and told him about the systematic extermination, he said, "If I believed everything you say, I would commit suicide."[6] As late as January 1944, two refugee Zionist activists arrived from Poland after passing through Slovakia and Hungary. Members of the Histadrut, who had a fairly good knowledge of the events, asked behind the refugees' back: "Aren't they exaggerating? Aren't they being somewhat hysterical?"[7] Yet the information the refugees provided only confirmed what had already been received. Golda Myerson (later Meir) later wrote in her autobiography: "In a certain way, I suppose, it should be chalked up to the credit of normal, decent men and women that we could not believe that such a monstrously evil thing would ever actually happen."[8]

The Holocaust was an acute deviation from the collective experience of humanity. Even in the history of such long-suffering people as the Jews, it was unprecedented and, therefore, unthinkable. People who managed to crawl out of mass graves and return to the remnants of their communities encountered total disbelief. New arrivals at concentration camps could not credit what the experienced inmates told them. People had difficulty in believing their own eyes, and today survivors find it difficult to believe their own memories. The partisan and poet Abba Kovner, himself a survivor, wrote: "When visions of what happened *there* rise up before my eyes, I am completely stunned, horrified. Did what happened really happen?"[9]

Certainly people remote from the scene, living under conditions of normalcy—however relative this term may be during wartime—were hard pressed to understand what had happened, what was happening. And indeed, to this day, much of the reserve of the survivors toward people "who were not there" stems from a suspicion that their stories are not always believed. Perhaps the currency given to denials today that the Holocaust ever took place has its roots in that same incapacity to grasp such a phenomenon.

The meaning of the word *Shoa* itself underwent a metamorphosis during the period. In 1938, after Kristallnacht, it meant abuse, arrest, murder. In 1940 it referred to the ghettos, hunger, crowded living conditions, disease, death. In 1941 it described the escape of penniless masses of Jews from the east, where conditions were insufferable. Only from 1942 on did the word become synonymous with the systematic annihilation of millions.

The original, biblical, meaning of the word *shoa* is sudden destruction or ruin, a sudden or unexpected blow of the mights of nature. The very use of this word in Palestine from 1938 on for the horror and the accompanying feeling of helplessness may have embodied some collective apologetic mechanism: If this was a sudden blow, something that could not have been foreseen, it also could not be prevented or resisted. The historian, with the advantage of hindsight, can see the Holocaust as the culmination of complex processes that emerged over several generations. But while it was actually happening, it seemed a catastrophe that descended, suddenly, unexpectedly, on the Jewish people, and the status that the word *Shoa* gained is perhaps a reflection of that perception.

The letters that reached Palestine from Europe during the Holocaust are among the most beautiful and moving documents that survived from that period. This is so, not only because they are a reflection of the agony of a people at the time of its greatest calamity; or because they were written to Palestine, which stood as a sanctuary, one ray of light in otherwise total darkness; or because they reflected a desire to go on living, though not at the expense of moral values. The most moving feature of these letters is the coding employed. The conditions under which they were written and dispatched precluded any advance agreement on the code. Yet the common experience that binds Jews beyond time and place provided a clear and unambiguous code.

The word *stephen* meant dollars, after the famous American rabbi and leader Stephen Wise; *b'nei brith* or *kaplans* meant Palestinian pounds because Kaplan was the treasurer and because *brith* means the covenant—the bond with the Land of Israel; *zivia* equaled Polish zlotys and Poland in general because she was "the Mama" of Polish Jewry. Calques were used, such as *kahalski,* in which the Hebrew word for community was joined to a Polish suffix. The term *Ashkenazim* referred to the Germans—as it had in medieval Hebrew. Everyone knew that Namirov was a town in Russia in which the Jews had fortified themselves during the pogroms of the seventeenth century and fought until they were overcome; so it could stand for an uprising. A sentence claiming that "Mr. Amos Twelve fulfilled his promise of 5.3" required no further explication. It was a quotation from Amos, one of the twelve minor prophets, 5:3: "The town that marches out a thousand strong shall have a hundred left, and the one that marches out a hundred strong shall have but ten left to the house of Israel." The destruction of European Jewry echoed down the corridors of time.

That all these references and many others would be understood by any Jew, secular or religious, was taken for granted. But the painful irony is that this was not enough to transmit the real plight of the writers. Joel Palgi, who was parachuted behind enemy lines during the war, tried upon his return to Palestine to convey to his listeners what he had experienced in Europe—in vain. "We all use the same words," he said, "but their meaning is entirely different." [10]

PART TWO

Reaction and Self-Mobilization

6

Public Response

Once the reality of the Holocaust had been grasped, the Yishuv was confronted with the question of what to do. A public debate, which lasted from 1943 through 1944, dealt with issues such as the proper response (demonstrations? petitions? of what nature?), the establishment of rescue organizations (of what scope? manned by whom?), and rescue funds (what sums? allocated from which budget?). Soon the debate gained a dynamic and characteristics of its own, with the public and some leaders pressing for more efforts and the Jewish Agency trying to remove the pressure and to act cautiously.

The first issue to be addressed by both the Agency Executive and the public was that of the organized response of the Jews in Palestine to the events in Europe. On November 22, 1942, the JAE considered ways of expressing public concern. Moshe Shapira of the Mizrachi, the Religious Zionists, suggested a day of mourning, fasting, and prayer, during which all work would cease and the public would be urged to attend rallies similar to those held in response to the White Paper of May 1939. The JAE decided to have a day of mourning without rallies and asked the Committee of Four—Shapira, Eliyahu Dobkin, Yitzhak Gruenbaum, and Emil Schmorak—to find appropriate ways of channeling public grief.[1]

The political implications of rallies such as those suggested by Shapira troubled members of the Agency. They needed a way to express forcefully the Yishuv's anxiety over the Holocaust, thus putting pressure on the British to ease restrictions on immigration, and to devote major efforts and resources to rescuing the Jews of Europe—all without hurting the war effort. It was the same dilemma Ben-Gurion had raised at the beginning of the war when he had distinguished between fighting the war and fighting the White paper. The meeting took place less than one month after the Battle of El Alamein. During the summer of 1942, when there had been a real danger that the Germans would conquer Egypt and Palestine, the Yishuv had cooperated with the British on military matters. After the German defeat in North Africa, it was feared (justifiably, as it turned out) that continued cooperation would be short-lived. The JAE had to consider whether that moment, at the end of November, was the right time to renew the confrontation.

These questions were not discussed very thoroughly at the meeting of November 22. Executive members had not yet clarified for themselves how, and how much, the news from Europe would change their attitude toward the mandatory government and the White Paper. In the meantime they maintained their traditional positions: the moderates tipped the balance against taking action harsh and forceful enough to bring the Yishuv into conflict with the British.

The next day a majority of the National Council supported the Agency's decision not to endorse strikes and rallies. But no clear idea emerged about how to organize a day of mourning. A joint committee of the JAE and the National Council was formed to plan the day's events and to work with representatives of Agudat Yisrael so that the organized response would involve the Yishuv in its entirety.[2]

It was also on November 23 that the Agency's official announcement of the systematic extermination of the Jews of Europe appeared in the press. Several days later the National Council decided, in conjunction with the Agency, to declare not one but three days of "alarm, protest, and outcry," beginning on November 30.

This change was prompted by the extent of public reaction to the Agency announcement. Until the end of the year the press was filled with letters and articles demanding immediate action to stop the murders and to take revenge on the war criminals. Headlines cried: "Do not be silent!" "The Yishuv will not rest!" "Every hand in Israel will be raised in revenge!" "Protest, Rescue, Revenge!" Soldiers sent letters to the newspapers and came to the Jewish Agency's recruiting offices demanding "an increase in the size of the Jewish fighting force" within the British army. They called for the immediate establishment of "ghetto demolition squads" in order to save the remnant. It would have been impossible for the Yishuv institutions to ignore such public response; after all, three-quarters of the immigrants since the First World War were of European origin, and 90 percent of the 250,000 who had immigrated during the 1930s had come from Europe, and most of those from Poland.[3]

On the first of the three scheduled days of mourning and protest, a special session of the Assembly of Representatives convened in Jerusalem. After the prayers and speeches, the session adopted a resolution in the name of the Yishuv as a whole, calling on the Allies and on world Jewry to take action to save the Jews and to take revenge on the guilty. The resolution ended with a vow not to remain passive nor to let the world remain passive. The following day there were assemblies throughout the country. The third day was devoted to fasting and prayer; at noon, public transportation and all work not essential to the war effort ceased for the day. All public entertainment was canceled.[4]

Although the joint committee extended the scope and duration of the response, the kind of events scheduled did not permit the public to turn the mourning into a spontaneous demonstration against the continued British restrictions on immigration. The three days of mourning and protest did, however, turn into a spontaneous demonstration of unity.

> A hundred thousand people participated in the processions—children, old people, women, artisans, teachers and students, workers and store-keepers, porters and draymen, rabbis and yeshiva students, members of all communities . . . The enormity of the grief and shock was expressed by people carrying Torah scrolls at the head of each procession . . . Wherever the scrolls were seen, people broke out crying.[5]

These three days marked a watershed in the wartime consciousness of the Yishuv. "What happened in this country last week was something extraordinary," Ben-Gurion commented, apparently referring to the atmosphere of unity in the Yishuv. He suggested that such activities be continued, not only to allow people to vent their feelings but also to facilitate organization of actual rescue operations. A few days later the JAE proposed two main areas of action: raising funds for rescue work and coordinating public protest with Jews throughout the free world, particularly in the United States and Britain. The Agency hoped to create a chain in which each link would activate the next: the Yishuv, free world Jewry, the non-Jewish public in the democratic countries, and their governments.

To this end the JAE suggested that a delegation be sent to the United States and, if possible, to Britain and South Africa. Ben-Gurion made a counterproposal that representatives of all free world Jewry be brought to Palestine for a Zionist convention to discuss the imminent danger to the European Jews and, by extension, to the Zionist enterprise as a whole. Both suggestions were accepted, and a joint committee of the JAE and the National Council was appointed to choose the Yishuv delegation.[6]

After protracted negotiations among the various political parties, the committee realized that it would be impossible to choose a united delegation representing the Yishuv. It therefore decided to send Gruenbaum alone. In the end, with the exception of Rabbi Meir Berlin, who went to the United States on behalf of the Mizrachi in January 1943, no one went. Although the idea of the delegation occasionally came up, as Shertok admitted in May 1943 it remained just "a proposal on the agenda of the Executive." Likewise, Zionists in the United States proved unable to choose a delegation to send to Palestine.[7]

At this point Ben-Gurion observed, "We are in a terrible situation because of the lack of contact and communication among the members of the Executive scattered around the world."[8] Contacts among the Jewish communities throughout the world were, indeed, difficult to maintain on a regular basis. Yet Ben-Gurion's statement must give pause. First of all, only a few weeks before, in October, he had returned from a second long journey to the United States, where he could have discussed the question of coordination with Stephen Wise, Nahum Goldmann, and other American Zionist leaders. Second, more than anything else, disputes within the Zionist movement had prevented the dispatch of the two delegations. Thus, if there was a "terrible situation," the JAE, including Ben-Gurion, was at least partly responsible.

Meanwhile news of the extermination of the Jews of Europe continued to reach the West, rousing the American and British public. Jewish, Christian, and nonsectarian individuals and organizations began exerting pressure on their governments to take measures in response. On December 17, 1942, Britain's foreign secretary, Anthony Eden, read a statement in Parliament on behalf of the twelve Allied governments and committees. It declared that the attention of the Allies had been directed to the extensive information coming out of Europe, according to which the German authorities intended to annihilate the Jewish people. The Allies condemned this barbaric policy and promised to take action to punish the criminals. Parliament rose to its feet in silent solidarity. The declaration was published that day by all the Allies.[9] Its effect on the public was much like that of the Yishuv three days of mourning: it marked the point at which the extermination was officially recognized for what it was.

In Palestine the Allied declaration was portrayed as an effect of the three days of mourning. A joint communiqué by the Agency and the National Council announced: "The outcry of the Yishuv in the three days of mourning and protest broke through the wall of silence and suppression surrounding the horrible slaughter ... arousing the leaders of humanity in the free countries." The communiqué also pointed out that the declaration had, however, made no mention of rescuing Jews or of opening the gates of Palestine to the survivors.[10]

The wording of the communiqué must also give pause. Since the beginning of 1942, reports had been published and broadcast in the West, especially during May and June, about the great numbers being killed. A rally had been held in New York in July to which Roosevelt and Churchill sent telegrams of support. Public pronouncements had been made by Jews and non-Jews in various parts of the world. Neither newspaper reports in Palestine (which relied heavily on the Allied press) nor public reaction to them had been stronger or more frequent than in other countries. Indeed, it was in Palestine that the authenticity of the information had been doubted and had not been formally addressed by the institutions until November. Thus, although it would be hard to detect any deliberate Allied attempt to expose the murder of the Jews, it could scarcely be said that the Yishuv had been the first to break through the "wall of silence and suppression."

In mid-December information reached Palestine to the effect that Himmler had ordered the liquidation—by January 1, 1943—of all remaining Polish Jews and of all Jews left in Austria, Germany, and Czechoslovakia. It was clear that time was not just short but had practically run out. Emotions in Palestine surged again. On December 17, the day of the Allied declaration, the National Council, in consultation with the Jewish Agency, declared another mourning period, this time of thirty days—from December 18, 1942, to January 16, 1943. "The whole way of life of the Yishuv," said the statement, "should express mourning and outrage, as well as a demand from ourselves and from others to save what can still be saved." Everyone was asked to refrain from celebrations, the press and the schools to give prominence to the topic, and rabbis to recite special prayers in the synagogues.[11]

In Britain the church, the press, Parliament, and the trade unions criticized the Allied declaration for contenting itself with an expression of sympathy rather than proposing any real action. Eden responded that as a result of public pressure the government would try to do everything in its power, even though "huge difficulties" lay in the way. These developments received extensive coverage in the press in Palestine. It was generally believed in the Yishuv that public opinion in Britain was more sensitive to the fate of the Jews of Europe than in the United States.[12]

The Jewish Agency may have missed an opportunity to put pressure on the British government when it was vulnerable to public opinion. A reaction stronger than a declaration of mourning, such as a mass demonstration or a general strike supported by public opinion in Britain, might have dissuaded the mandatory government from engaging in a confrontation with the Yishuv on the issue of rescue and immigration. But it remains an open question whether the combined pressure could have forced the British government to make real concessions.

The emphatically religious nature of public mourning itself proved controversial within the Labor movement. Many of the socialist-secular leaders felt that the *Galuth* (Diaspora) style of fasting and lamentations, with rabbis leading processions and holding Torah scrolls aloft, was out of place and time. They considered fasting to be nothing more than "an expression of weakness . . . a very nice Messianic gesture." In Ben-Gurion's view, the days of mourning lacked "adequate Zionist character," by which he apparently meant that there was not enough emphasis on Palestine as the new center of Jewish life. He also believed that organized mourning would become a noncommittal substitute for real action and would work against a sober view of the situation.[13] On the other hand, some of the nonreligious Labor members—particularly those who exerted spiritual and moral leadership, such as Yitzhak Tabenkin and Berl Katznelson—felt that traditional forms were more capable of uniting everyone in the Yishuv than was Zionism, which still lacked shared frameworks and patterns of public life. In times of trouble, they said, it was preferable to stress the common elements rather than the differences between the religious and the secular or between the Yishuv and the Diaspora.[14]

Although the minutes of its meetings do not include an explicit decision to that effect, later developments indicate that the Agency decided to entrust the Chief Rabbinate and the National Council with religious and general expressions of mourning while it sought more useful and practical means of expression.

The month of mourning proved to be too great a burden on the public. Yitzhak Ben-Zvi, chairman of the National Council, admitted, "We tried but failed." Every Thursday was supposed to be a day of fasting, prayer, and study, but it was implemented only once. Appeals by the National Council to the public to demonstrate and not to use the day for outings appear to have been based on experience. People in the entertainment business complained that their livelihood was being threatened; thousands of allied soldiers were passing through Palestine after the retreat of the Germans in North Africa, and they were starved for fun. Consequently, the National Council decided to allow the cinemas and theaters to operate. However, music and dancing "in prominent contradiction to the feelings of the Yishuv" was not permitted. The vagueness of the injunction enabled whoever wished to do so to circumvent the ban.[15]

There was a minority, indignant at the business-as-usual atmosphere, who not only favored public mourning but even tried to pressure the national bodies into continuing a mourning regime after the month was over. Prominent among them was the Al Domi group, which felt that saving the Jews of Europe should have priority over all other matters. Many others, however, thought that the month of mourning was organized public hysteria and a demand for payment of lip service that could not be constantly met. They urged the Yishuv to demonstrate a firm spirit in the face of the disaster. In a letter to the press someone coined the phrase: "Not 'Al Domi' but 'al dema' [do not weep]."[16]

The debate was never resolved. It continued as a month of mourning neared its end and ways were considered for concluding it. The Revisionists and Agudat Yisrael were opposed to repeating the old scenario and advocated stronger, more dramatic forms of action—mass rallies, work stoppages (even on British army bases), or a mass sitdown strike in Jerusalem in front of the offices of the government and the high commissioner.[17]

The Histadrut Executive also demanded more militant action "that would carry the Diaspora [in this case, Jewish communities in the free world] with it. Its members felt that American and British Jewry needed to be given an example to follow. "We in Palestine," said David Remez, "are different from the people in America . . . with regard to demonstrations." He was referring to the repeated delays in holding a giant rally in New York. The "Stop Hitler Now!" rally that eventually took place in Madison Square Garden on March 1, 1943, was attended by 75,000 Jews, and there were signs that the public was looking for a stronger way to express its feelings. Indeed, Histadrut leaders cited members of the Yishuv "who cry out . . . and demand action," and criticized the national institutions for doing "actually nothing."[18] The Jewish Agency did not change its policy, however, and the month of mourning faded away without a public event to honor its termination.

In January and February 1943 the news from Europe confirmed the regular and systematic transportation of Jews from various countries to the camps in the east. A feeling of depression prevailed in the Yishuv. None of its rescue proposals (see Part Three) had yet produced any results, and the Allies had done nothing since their declaration at the end of December. On February 2, 1943, the Assembly of Representatives convened for two hours "to commemorate the victims whose numbers have been increasing daily and to express before the entire world our disappointment at the do-nothing policy of the democratic countries." Statements were made on behalf of the Chief Rabbinate and Agudat Yisrael. Ben-Gurion and Gruenbaum spoke. During the session every place of business was closed down and all work stopped, including work on British army bases. All entertainment was canceled that night. The Assembly's statement reflected the Yishuv's feeling of helplessness in the face of the free world's apparent indifference to the catastrophe afflicting the Jewish people. The only threat they could direct at the Allies was that "the blood of the People of Israel, being spilled in vain, will never let you rest." [19]

This session of the Assembly was similar to those that had opened the three days of mourning and the month of mourning, but a certain weariness with the subject was already apparent, both in its brevity and in its organization; as members of the National Council complained, it required coordination among at least nine bodies. Since Ben-Gurion was speaking, Gruenbaum also demanded the floor; if the Ashkenazi chief rabbi spoke, then so would the Sephardic chief rabbi; if Agudat Yisrael made a statement, the Revisionists would have to do the same; finally, the women's organizations also wanted to be heard. The list of demands seemed endless. This weariness was even more marked in the Assembly's next session, held on March 24, 1943, and devoted primarily to economic issues and to the problems of enlistment in the British army—4,350 men and women had volunteered in 1941, and 8,980 in 1942. The situation of the Jews of Europe was discussed only at the opening, when Gruenbaum analyzed the information accumulated so far. The statement issued was even more desperate than the previous one. [20]

In the four months that had elapsed since the Agency's November 22 announcement, the Yishuv had participated in four public events protesting the Holocaust—all of them similar in form and substance. The general public feeling was that a static model of reaction had developed and was losing more of its impact with every repetition. "The same stoppage of work, the same fast," the same speeches by the rabbis, and the same declarations. "We have become tired of assemblies. There is nothing to say that we haven't already said. The rallies are just a show." Since each leader held to his own position on the best way of expressing protest, there was also nothing new in the debates about it. A parallel "pattern for a regular protest ritual" developed among American Jews as well. [21] Public response seemed to be waning, gradually disappearing from the national agenda. Two events, however, rekindled the debate. Both began on April 19, 1943: the Bermuda Conference on refugees and the revolt in the Warsaw ghetto.

At the Bermuda Conference, Great Britain and the United States were supposed to discuss solutions to the problem of the European refugees in general, and cautious hope was roused that help would be forthcoming for the Jews as well. In Palestine, debate on the subject had already begun in March. The Jewish Agency was convinced that the conference would result in nothing and that any public effort to affect its outcome was therefore a waste of time and energy. But the Revisionists again proposed more militant action, suggesting a mass demonstration in Jerusalem. This time they were supported not only by Agudat Yisrael but also by the leftist parties of the Histadrut, Hashomer Hatzair and Left Poalei Zion, which felt it desirable that news reach the outside world over friction in Palestine "between the government and the Jewish population because of a demonstration against the disaster of the Diaspora." Representatives of new immigrant organizations demanded a large rally in Tel Aviv. A meeting of representatives from the settlements and local councils unanimously supported demonstrations. Ben-Zvi warned the National Council that "if *we* don't do something on a mass scale, others will." Gruenbaum and Shapira conveyed the same kind of warning to the Jewish Agency.[22]

Thus urged by public pressure, the National Council started preparations for another public assembly on the eve of the Bermuda Conference. But members of the Histadrut Executive, most notably David Remez and Golda Myerson, proposed that a petition be circulated by the Assembly of Representatives and signed by every Jew. The national institutions would cease all other activity for two days and devote themselves exclusively to the petition. First, signing the petition would give every individual a sense of participation and would dispel some of the prevailing depression. Second, the public would see that the leaders sympathized with them in their agony. Remez declared: "Our children will remember these two days when their parents were imbued with a different spirit." Myerson hoped that the petition could also be signed by Jews and non-Jews in the United States, Britain and South Africa. Two to three million signatures, she thought, could be used to exert effective pressure on the Allied governments.[23]

Most members of the JAE and some members of the National Council opposed the idea of a petition, arguing that it would be a waste of time and effort. Ben-Zvi doubted that it would be possible to reach an agreement on the wording. Only after lengthy debates and under pressure from Remez did the National Council finally decide to appoint a committee to look into the matter. Thus the Bermuda Conference opened without any preliminary public event in Palestine.

The conference ended a week later, and its resolutions were kept secret. The news did reach Palestine, however, that all proposals submitted by the Jewish Agency and by the Rescue Committee had been rejected. On May 3, 1943, the Assembly of Representatives expressed the Yishuv's deep disappointment with the results and issued an appeal to "everyone with a human conscience" to do everything possible to rescue the remnant of the Jewish people. Myerson felt that the Yishuv was partly to blame. "What do we want from the Gentiles," she asked, "if the Yishuv itself has not yet tried to move heaven and earth?"[24]

On Passover Eve, April 19, 1943, the Warsaw ghetto revolt broke out, and news of it filled Jews throughout the world with pride and agony. Those in Palestine pressed for some way to express their willingness to extend help and make sacrifices. On May 6 the Histadrut called a special conference and proclaimed seven days of fundraising "to encourage the defenders of the ghettos." The Zionist Actions Committee (ZAC)—the supreme Zionist authority—proposed organizing a contribution from the Yishuv as a whole. Representatives of the towns and settlements and the Histadrut Executive pressured the National Council to have, if not a demonstration—to which the Agency still objected—at least a one-day strike that would involve workers both in industry and in the army camps; rallies would be held, preceded by the signing of a petition to establish an unprecedented "Warsaw Day." The JAE objected to the petition but had to give in: it had itself entrusted the National Council with this aspect of the matter and had to abide by its own decisions.

The general strike and the petition were supposed to reflect a united Yishuv, but Agudat Yisrael and the Revisionists did not consider these activities commensurate with so decisive an event as the Warsaw ghetto revolt. The two parties announced that they would neither support the activities sponsored by the National Council nor urge their public to sign the petition. On the other hand, they also would not interfere in any way.[25]

Meanwhile critics in Britain had pressured the government to schedule a debate in Parliament on the results of the Bermuda Conference and its refugee policy. The date was set for May 19. The Zionist Actions Committee convened the day before. Representatives of various parties expressed their disapproval that no appropriate public action had been organized in Palestine either before or after the Bermuda Conference. They accused members of the JAE of having rejected almost all proposals put to them, both from fear of the consequences and from disbelief in the Yishuv's ability to implement them. The JAE was further accused of showing no consideration for public feeling and of belittling the value of public action, which could have reinforced world sympathy once the pitiful results of the Bermuda Conference became known.

The ZAC declared a need—especially if the parliamentary debate failed to produce results—for "a mass public reaction against the lack of action in the area of rescue." This was the resolution that the opponents of the prevailing policy had hoped for—an appeal by the highest Zionist authority for a forceful public response.[26]

As expected, the debate in the British Parliament failed to produce any practical results. By June 15, 1943, more than 250,000 adults and close to 60,000 children in Palestine had expressed disapproval by signing a petition demanding immediate action from the Allies. It was submitted together with a memorandum specifying practical suggestions for rescue to the high commissioner and to all the consuls and representatives of the Allies and the neutral countries in Palestine and in London. "What can I, you, or His Majesty's Government do?" the high commissioner, Sir Harold MacMichael, asked Ben-Zvi, who handed him the petition. "Everything depends on Germany."[27] It is doubtful whether the petition had any effect on rescue operations, but the Jews in Palestine may have found some relief in signing it. It was a form of "mass public reaction," and it stressed their anxiety for the fate of the Jews of Europe. But this was not the militant reaction that the controversy was about—rallies, demonstrations, strikes.

By the second half of 1943 the JAE had three more arguments against taking stronger action, in addition to its conviction that demonstrations and outcries were devoid of practical value. First was the constant anxiety that mass demonstrations would give the Arabs a pretext for rekindling the 1936–1939 riots, especially in the mixed cities—first and foremost Jerusalem. Second, at the beginning of 1943 leaders in Palestine had thought that organized reaction by the Yishuv would serve as a model for American and British Jewry, rousing them to action. After the Bermuda Conference, however, the Yishuv felt that the Jews of New York, London, and other Jewish centers had lost their sense of outrage and returned to their own affairs and their own intramural controversies. It was high time to recognize the fact that a strike or demonstration in Palestine received no more than two or three lines of foreign coverage.[28] Third, such rallies and strikes could easily lead to an open confrontation with the British, which would serve as a pretext for a forceful suppression of the Yishuv now that Britain had recovered its position in the Middle East. Recent actions against the Yishuv had included searches for arms and ensuing trials, the closing of recruiting offices, and a refusal to establish a Jewish brigade in the British army.

Conflict with the mandatory government was to be avoided both for its own sake and because of the tension that would result between the parties of the Yishuv and the Revisionists. The Agency feared that "the provocative elements," "the unrestrained among us"—namely, the Revisionists—might take over the streets. Bitterness toward the British was mounting, and the Agency was afraid it might lose control of the situation. Mapai leaders were determined to prevent such a development. They considered the Revisionist insistence on violent action a political maneuver and not merely an expression of pain over the plight of the Jews. As Eliezer Kaplan put it, "The Revisionists want to make political capital out of the Jewish disaster, and it is our duty to warn people that Jewish life cannot be played with. Of course, we have to do everything we can, but we cannot allow ourselves to be carried away by empty shouting."[29]

After the Bermuda Conference, members of Etzel—the Revisionists' underground military organization—stepped up its activities in the United States. They founded the Emergency Committee for the Rescue of European Jews, headed by Peter Bergson (Hillel Kook's pseudonym). The committee tried to direct the attention of the American public to the fate of the Jews of Europe in order to push the Roosevelt administration to establish a governmental committee. It used high-powered public relations methods—full-page newspaper advertisements, large rallies, and a dramatic pageant titled "We Will Never Die," a cooperative effort by well-known American artists that was performed in the major cities. Over 100,000 Americans witnessed it, including Eleanor Roosevelt and hundreds of public figures who supported the committee.[30] The Jewish and Zionist establishments believed that Etzel's activities, though stemming from sincere concern, had a divisive influence. Ben-Gurion referred to the committee as "a gang of reckless Etzel members" who, for the sake of publicity, "are desecrating the name of Israel among the Gentiles."[31] The Jewish Agency was not willing to allow a similar situation to develop in Palestine. It did not want a vociferous minority inciting the public to action contrary to the policies of the authorized leadership.

In December 1943 the head of the Revisionists in Palestine, Aryeh Altman, proposed initiating deliberately violent confrontations with the British. Gruenbaum warned against the proposal, calling its likely efficacy "illusory." The spilling of so much Jewish blood all over Europe had not yet moved the Allies to save the Jews. Shertok added his opinion that, considering the number of British dead and wounded or taken prisoner in the war, a few more British dead in a confrontation with the Yishuv in Palestine would have no effect whatever.[32]

At this point the debate between the Revisionists and the Zionist leadership, both in the United States and in Palestine, went beyond the issue of how to respond to the inaction of the Allies and became part of the decades-long bitter ideological struggle over the question of how Zionism would be realized. The Labor movement adhered to Chaim Weizmann's famous dictum, "One more goat, one more acre," which in this case meant one more immigration permit and one more refugee saved. Mapai members advocated effective hard work and objected to what they considered vain eloquence and empty slogans.

The majority of the public adhered to the Labor policies on the main political issues, but the case of the Holocaust proved different. The Jewish Agency, preoccupied as it was with its responsibility for the development of the national home, may have failed to notice the growing gap between its policies and public sentiment regarding the fate of the Jewish people. As logical and politically realistic as its arguments may have been, the public did not want to listen. The scope of the catastrophe and the close personal and organizational ties with the Jews in Europe produced a highly emotional reaction. "Our Zionism is an outcry"; "We cannot remain silent; Jewish history will never forgive us; our brothers' blood cries out to us"; bitter experience has shown that "response as such is futile . . . but, is simply a violation of human dignity, of both the living and the dead, that hundreds of thousands of Jews are being trampled under, like weeds, without a cry or an appropriate reaction." Leib Jaffe, an emissary from Palestine, voiced the same explicit criticism against American Jewish leaders: they "are making a great mistake by adopting a position opposed to the will of the people and viewing the popular protest movement as unnecessary."[33]

Nevertheless, debate over the proper public response faded away in 1944. From the beginning of that year, with the exception of the Revisionists, those who had advocated strong public protest came to support the position of the JAE. This was especially true of members of the Histadrut Executive. First of all, they realized that the Allies had no intention of sacrificing, as Gruenbaum put it, "even a fraction of their own interests" in order to save Jews.[34] Second, the Allied invasion of western Europe opened up new possibilities for helping survivors in the liberated countries. The non-Jewish public in the West became less attentive to the situation of the Jews still under Nazi control. The Yishuv's fear that after the war there might not be anything left to salvage was ignored.

During 1944 most public efforts in the Yishuv went into raising funds for rescue operations. Only with the German invasion of Hungary in March 1944 was the issue of public protest raised again—for the last time. When news reached Palestine that preparations were under way for transporting the Jews of Hungary to death camps, Melech Neustadt and Zalman Aharonovich (later Aranne), another Histadrut and Labor leader, demanded that the National Council declare a "Hungarian Jewry Day" to raise the alarm immediately all around the world. Without world action, they said, there would be nothing left to do but mourn these Jews after their extermination. At the same time, they themselves doubted if such a demonstration would prove useful. Gruenbaum made a similar proposal to the JAE and was told by Ben-Gurion that the matter "did not belong to the Jewish Agency but to the Yishuv, namely, to the National Council." [35]

Within a few weeks, beginning in the middle of May, 430,000 Hungarian Jews were sent to Auschwitz. The Yishuv stood by helplessly, stunned at the rate of the transports, the efficiency of the extermination apparatus, and the number of victims. June 5, 1944, was appointed a "Day of Alarm for the Rescue of the Remnant." As Neustadt and Aharonovich had warned three months earlier, there was nothing left to do but mourn. It was a day of work stoppage, fasting, and public assemblies. A stern warning was issued to the governments of Rumania and Bulgaria, where there were still Jews left, that the day of judgment was near. The Allies were entreated to make rescue and immigration possible. [36]

At the beginning of December 1944 the Assembly of Representatives appealed to the Allies to save the surviving remnant. An appeal was also issued to members of the underground forces and to churches and relief organizations throughout Europe to help return Jewish children who had been hidden with Christians to Jewish hands. In the second week of March 1945, when the war in Europe was at an end and the scale of the disaster became known to all, the Yishuv held a full week of mourning that concluded with a day of fasting, a work stoppage, and another demand to save the remnant. [37]

The issue of the Yishuv's organized public reaction to the annihilation of European Jewry is still an open wound. In Palestine daily life continued, scarcely affected by the war; indeed, the war accelerated economic development: after 1942 the British army placed large orders locally, and the throngs of soldiers passing through Palestine were another source of profit. The Yishuv lived its life, construction continued, business was conducted. There were even celebrations. In the summer of 1943 the kibbutz movements revived the Daliah Folk Dance Festival and convened thousands of young people for a choral meeting in Ein Harod. Students at the Hebrew University of Jerusalem held a Purim festival. None of these events was a lavish affair, since simplicity ruled public life. Most people did not consider them an affront in the face of destruction of European Jewry, but rather a manifestation of new Jewish vitality. Also, agony was a part of daily life, and when the news was particularly bitter, expressions of pain multiplied. But public attention was not sustained, and life would return to normal for weeks or months, until the next shocking event.

7

The Joint Rescue Committee

After the Agency's official announcement on November 23, 1942, that Europe's Jews were being systematically exterminated, the Jewish public in Palestine began to press for a wider and more representative body than the Committee of Four, one that would have greater authority and reflect the Yishuv's real concern to expedite rescue operations. The Jewish Agency began long-drawn-out negotiations on the subject with other organizations in the Yishuv.

Ben-Gurion and Gruenbaum were determined not to allow "the founding of new firms." The JAE therefore decided to add Dov (Bernard) Joseph, the legal adviser of the Agency's Political Department, to the Committee of Four; to name the new, five-member organization the Action Committee; and to make it the nucleus of a wider body. Ben-Gurion would invite representatives of Agudat Yisrael and the National Council to join; the latter would, in turn, invite the Revisionists, who had left the World Zionist Organization in 1935 but were represented in the National Council. The new, wider body was to operate under the aegis of the Agency and by its authority. After discussions with Ben-Gurion, Agudat Yisrael agreed to the proposal even though it meant that the new partners would have to accept a lesser status.[1]

Gruenbaum led negotiations with the Revisionists in an atmosphere of mutual recrimination. The Revisionists considered the older Committee of Four "chiefly to blame for the suppression of news and the absence of any action." They were referring to the alleged suppression of information received from reliable German sources in Switzerland in the summer of 1942 about the planned annihilation of three to four million Jews. The Agency, on the other hand, feared that the Revisionists, rather than helping in rescue operations, would simply use their presence on the committee to criticize what was being done and to incite the public against the JAE. Nevertheless, the Revisionist delegate at the negotiations, Joseph Klarman, accepted Gruenbaum's proposal, declaring that he had been convinced that the National Council sincerely wanted them to join the committee. The lack of any similar reference to the sincerity of the JAE was not fortuitous: suspicion was mutual.[2]

The discussions ended in the middle of January, and a committee of twelve was appointed. It consisted of the five members of the Action Committee; Benjamin Minz and Rabbi Yitzhak-Meir Levin of Agudat Yisrael; three members of the National Council—Yitzhak Ben-Zvi, Shlomo-Zalman Shragai of the Religious Zionists, and Yehoshu'a Suprasky of the General Zionists; and two Revisionists, Klarman and Herman Segal. Gruenbaum was elected chairman.

There were also tortuous deliberations regarding an appropriate name; each group sought one that would adequately reflect its presence. The name finally chosen, the Committee for the Jews of Occupied Europe, was deliberately neutral. Later the committee was also referred to as the United Rescue Committee of the Jewish Agency or the Rescue Committee. The new body satisfied the Jewish Agency: it was not quite a "new firm," it represented all sectors of the Yishuv, and it remained under Agency supervision. The public, too, was satisfied for the time being and hoped that the new organization would prove to be an effective tool for rescue operations, worthy of both its name and its sponsors.[3]

Satisfaction was not unanimous, however. The new-immigrants' associations and other public and economic organizations had been given only indirect representation, through the National Council. The JAE believed that the presence of too many small interest groups—there were some forty immigrants' associations alone—would reduce the committee's effectiveness. Gruenbaum thought that it would be sufficient to invite their representatives for briefings from time to time and entrust them with the care of the refugees arriving in Palestine.

The immigrants' associations, however, were not willing to step aside. They maintained contact with their countries of origin, with various international agencies, and with governments and were *au courant* with the situation of the Jews in each place. They demanded that the Rescue Committee, which threatened to make them redundant, incorporate all of them.

But the new immigrants' associations were only part of the problem. When the scope of the extermination first became known in the Yishuv, rescue committees sprang up everywhere. Thus the Women's

International Zionist Organization, the Committee of Refugee Rabbis, the Women Workers' Council of the Histadrut, the Chamber of Commerce, and the Sephardic Association, among other organizations, all demanded at least one representative on the Rescue Committee. The JAE's solution was to establish a public council, in conjunction with the committee, on which the various associations and organizations would be represented. In this way the JAE hoped to retain control while giving such groups a sense of involvement.[4]

This, however, was not the end of the matter. The structure of the Rescue Committee immediately came under attack first in the National Council on January 17, 1943, and in the Zionist Actions Committee the following day. These were the first meetings at which either body concerned itself exclusively with the plight of European Jewry.[5]

The National Council began its meeting with criticism of the Action Committee. Though appointed at the end of November, the committee had met very seldom. According to Shragai, it "didn't exist," "had no head," and lacked a plan for action. Once every two weeks Gruenbaum passed on secondhand information received from Geneva and Istanbul, and Shragai doubted whether committee members even read the material. Given the obvious failings of the smaller body, how could the new, more cumbersome Rescue Committee possibly be more efficient?

According to Suprasky, the Action Committee's faulty functioning stemmed from the fact that it consisted of "people who had a thousand commitments that consumed all their time." "If they want to be members of the Action Committee and at the same time keep up their jobs and departments," said another, "then woe unto us, what a terrible responsibility we will bear toward the Jewish people, towards Zionism, towards the future." Others, however, argued that the problem was that "the roads to rescue are blocked." David Remez remarked that the disaster was "of such fantastic proportions that it is hard to convince ourselves that there is a way." In other words—although Remez was not so explicit—perhaps the whole idea of rescue was futile, however good the organization.

The National Council demanded a special rescue institute granted wide authority by the Agency, headed by "a person acceptable to the whole Yishuv," and manned by people of stature who would do nothing else for at least three months—the clear implication being that Gruenbaum did not meet these requirements. However, the Council agreed that the Agency should remain responsible for the political issues associated with rescue.

A committee elected at this meeting convened the next day with

Ben-Gurion and the Action Committee to formulate a "proposal for reorganization" of the Rescue Committee. But the resulting proposal was contrary to the wishes expressed at the meeting: it built on the existing Rescue Committee, with the addition of several activists who would devote themselves exclusively to the body, plus the public council, to be convened once a month. The head of the committee would be required to devote himself to it full-time for a certain period.

At the meeting of the Zionist Actions Committee later the same day, Gruenbaum presented a summary of the news from Europe and requested approval of the proposal formulated a few hours before. He immediately encountered a barrage of criticism. The ZAC attacked the idea of adding a public council to the Rescue Committee: it would be merely a cumbersome, inefficient "parliament." Most speakers demanded a rescue institute with wide authority, although they divided over whether it should be part of the Jewish Agency or a separate body. Those who favored the latter did so on the grounds that it would often have to conduct clandestine or illegal activities and therefore could not afford an open connection with the Agency, whose work had to be aboveboard. Gruenbaum, hurt by the wording of the proposal, with its implication that he was not "a person acceptable to the whole Yishuv," threatened to resign. After a long and heated debate (the minutes cover about a hundred pages), the ZAC approved the joint "proposal for reorganization" prepared that morning. Again, the outcome was contrary to the speakers' explicit opposition to perpetuating existing bodies.

Why did Ben-Gurion and the Action Committee succeed in imposing their will in this matter twice in one day? There are two possible explanations. First, it may simply have been more expedient to keep the Rescue Committee, with all its shortcomings, than to enter into lengthy negotiations about the composition, powers, and responsibilities of a new body. The Action Committee included the two de facto heads of the Immigration Department—Eliyahu Dobkin and Moshe Shapira—who had been handling related issues since the beginning of the war (when Chaim Barlas, director of the department, decided that his work should be done abroad, on the spot). Dov Joseph, as legal adviser of the Agency's Political Department, had been dealing with governments and international agencies since 1936. Forming an entirely new organization would have entailed loss of time and a duplication of work already done by the Agency's departments. Second, discussions not recorded in the minutes may have tipped the balance: the JAE promised that if certain large-scale rescue plans then being considered proved to be feasible, it would act immediately to fund and implement them.[6] In any case the outcome attests to the JAE's prestige and strategic powers. Indeed, some of the participants left the meeting feeling they had been outmaneuvered in some way that they could not quite fathom.[7]

The result was that Gruenbaum would remain as chairman; there would be a coordinating secretariat of three (Apollinary Hartglas, Gruenbaum's friend from the time of their joint Zionist work in Poland, as political secretary; Avraham Haft, experienced in fundraising, as financial secretary; and Joseph Kleinbaum, as technical secretary); an executive consisting of the twelve people elected two weeks earlier to serve as the Rescue Committee executive or presidium; a "plenum" of twenty-five to thirty people, including the executive; a council of fifty to sixty people, including members of the plenum.

On January 31, 1943, the new Rescue Committee began operating, and an announcement to that effect was published by the JAE in the local press and forwarded to Jewish organizations in Britain and the United States.[8]

The Rescue Committee's authority and areas of responsibility were never defined. The Agency's departments continued operating as before, and foreign policy—including contacts with the mandatory government—remained the sole responsibility of the Agency's Political Department. Even travel by an emissary required the approval of the mandatory authorities and was granted only after a request by the Political Department. The Immigration Department continued to handle the acquisition and distribution of immigration permits, contacts with all training groups and youth movement in the occupied Europe, and contacts with Yishuv representatives in neutral countries. The organization of public events had already been delegated to the National Council. Nor did the committee have any financial power: it could not initiate a special fundraising drive without giving priority to existing funds and appeals. The JAE decided, with Gruenbaum's concurrence, that money collected for rescue would be deposited with the Agency's treasury and disbursed only with its approval.

Although the Rescue Committee produced a monthly bulletin in Hebrew and English, which it distributed in Palestine and abroad, it did not retain exclusive control even over the collection and publishing of information. These tasks were performed by the Neustadt committee of the Histadrut, by the secretariat of the Mapai World Union, and by other movements, parties, and immigrants' associations.

It is not surprising that the members of the committee felt themselves to be redundant. "The committee's wings have been clipped, and it is not capable of any important action," complained Gruenbaum. Suprasky was even harsher: "The public is being deceived . . . Nothing is ever done or will be done, except making plans." Minz and Rabbi Levin, of Agudat Yisrael, were the most explicit: "In the first few weeks after the committee was established we saw that . . . [it] had only decorative value, and had no possibility of operating, since the departments of the Jewish Agency considered its operation an infringement of their own jurisdiction."[9] Members of the Rescue Committee, especially those who were not also members of the JAE, concluded that it was neither an Action Committee, since it could not act, nor a forum for coordinating action, but merely an advisory body, proposing ideas that it was not authorized to carry out. They complained that they spent most of their time reading reports and letters from Europe, listening to descriptions and analyses of the situation from Gruenbaum or from emissaries visiting Palestine, and putting together proposals for action, based on what they had read and heard. Before the body was given an official name, it was casually referred to as "the Committee for Formulating Proposals in Connection with the Disaster of the Jews of Europe," a name that clearly reflected its members' own view of its role.[10]

Even as an advisory body the Rescue Committee wielded little influence. The JAE devoted little time to its suggestions; Ben-Gurion relegated them to the end of meetings and sometimes cut Gruenbaum short. He would summarily push proposals through the Executive, often in opposition to Gruenbaum's opinion. The committee was not consulted in matters considered the province of the JAE and sometimes not even in matters that were eminently its own—such as illegal immigration or related political issues. Its prestige was so low that an emissary sent to Turkey at its behest coordinated his mission only with the Political Department and neither informed the committee of his departure nor reported to it upon his return. On another occasion the Agency launched a special fundraising campaign for rescue work while Gruenbaum was abroad and without any prior consultation with him.

This state of affairs probably reflected to some extent the relationship between Ben-Gurion and Gruenbaum. The two had different political backgrounds and more than once took opposing positions on central issues. Ben-Gurion derived his power from the Labor movement and particularly from the pioneering settlement movement, in which he had been active in Palestine for close to thirty years. Gruenbaum belonged to the General Zionist party, which was centrist. He had come to Palestine from Poland only in 1933 and was now cut off from his power base there. The high point in his life had been the period he had served in the Polish parliament, where he had become an eloquent public speaker defending the rights of the Jews. Ben-Gurion despised parliamentary mannerisms and hyperbole and did not refrain from faulting Gruenbaum on this score. People who worked closely with both were unequivocal in their view that "Ben-Gurion could not stand Gruenbaum."[11]

Gruenbaum found himself between a hammer and an anvil. He had to represent the Rescue Committee at meetings of the JAE, and the Agency at meetings of the Rescue Committee. He had to present the committee's proposals to the JAE and try to get them accepted and then explain at meetings of the Rescue Committee—which included the Revisionists and Agudat Yisrael, both ardent opponents of the Jewish Agency—why he had failed. This dual role was later defined by one of the Revisionist representatives, Eliezer Shostak (who replaced Herman Segal), as "Gruenbaum's tragedy." Klarman and Shostak felt that Gruenbaum's attitude to rescue matters was closer to theirs than to the JAE's. In any event, the members of the Rescue Committee were convinced that the JAE flagrantly disregarded them and their chairman.

The Rescue Committee itself was poorly organized. During the two years of its existence, its various forums—executive, plenum, and council—met perhaps a total of twice a month. Because meetings were not regularly scheduled, members found it difficult to make proper preparations and even to attend. Sometimes notification arrived after the meeting had taken place. A further impediment was the fact that the composition of both the executive and the plenum changed from time to time. The inevitable result was confusion: proposals made at one meeting and summed up at another were discussed by different participants. It was also cumbersome to have to refer proposals first to parent bodies for approval. Finally, members of the original Committee of Four usually met before meetings of the executive and the plenum to discuss topics that they were reluctant to air in the presence of the Revisionists and Agudat Yisrael. The paradoxical result was that the officially defunct Committee of Four discussed more topics than the executive, which in turn handled more issues than the plenum, while the council was, for all intents and purposes, nonexistent.

The Rescue Committee had no permanent premises and operated haphazardly. Minutes were taken in pencil, and copies were not made. Members who missed a meeting found it difficult to find out exactly what had happened. Criticism of these shortcomings was harsh and chronic, and suggestions for change came from all quarters. The Revisionists and Agudat Yisrael consistently felt ignored; representatives from the National Council were indignant. All partners to the Rescue Committee except the JAE considered it improperly managed and directed their complaints at the JAE members, especially the chairman. Gruenbaum also came under attack from other organizations and in public forums. There were recurring demands from all quarters to replace the head of the Rescue Committee with someone of greater prestige and influence, someone who would enjoy the full backing of the JAE, primarily of Ben-Gurion and of the Labor movement—someone like Berl Katznelson, Yitzhak Tabenkin, or even Chaim Weizmann.[12]

Gruenbaum might have defused some of the criticism had he resigned from his numerous other positions and announced publicly that he was devoting his time exclusively to rescue work. As the revered leader of Polish Jewry, he seemed to many the most natural choice for the position. And as Remez said, stressing his work in the Committee of Four since the beginning of the war: "If there is one person entitled to head this activity and worthy of it, this person is Gruenbaum." But Gruenbaum did not resign from anything. Moreover, when demands were made that at least some leaders of the committee quit their other jobs, he replied that they "would go crazy because there are no opportunities for action." And Gruenbaum was famous for hard work and devotion to duty.[13] A critical question is whether the chairman of the Rescue Committee believed that rescue was at all possible.

8

Rescue Fund Allocations
from the Yishuv

The debate that began in the JAE at the end of 1942 over the allocation of funds for rescue can be understood only in the larger context
of the Yishuv's economic situation as a whole and the financial resources available to the Agency at the time.

The economy of Palestine had been badly hurt at the beginning of
the war—particularly in citrus exports, construction, tourism, and
banking (many people withdrew their savings). Unemployment rose;
by late 1940 it had reached 26,150, affecting approximately one out
of six heads of families. But recovery began in mid-1941 and continued through the end of the war. Orders from British army bases in
the Middle East stimulated industry and trade; soldiers passing
through the country were in need of various services; and the con-
sumption of local products instead of imported ones spurred new
economic and agricultural developments. From 1942 on there was an
increased demand for manpower as a result of enlistment in the British army and the halt in immigration; an increase in bank deposits—
from about 22 million Palestinian pounds (equal in value to the British pound throughout the mandatory period) in 1939 to about 91 million at the end of 1944—from monies paid for goods and services by
the mandatory government and the import of Jewish capital; and a
positive balance of payments. On the other hand, prosperity induced
inflation: prices tripled from 1939 to the end of 1942.[1]

The standard of living of Jewish workers rose faster during the war
than in the years before, but it did not keep pace with the general
acceleration of the economy. There were several reasons for this. The
Jews paid taxes both to the mandatory government and to the National Council, as well as numerous indirect taxes for, and voluntary
support of, various funds. Rents were high, and the progressive de-

valuation of the Palestinian pound gradually lowered buying power. Inflation also increased the gap between wage earners and the well-to-do, especially those who had acquired their wealth as a result of the war. Thus, although the economy as a whole was experiencing recovery and growth, most individual workers lived very modestly, even frugally. People earned, on the average, between seven and ten pounds a month in 1939 and, with inflation, between seventeen and twenty-five in 1945. (One Palestinian pound was equivalent to $27.60 in 1989.) Most of the Jewish capital brought into Palestine during the period remained in private hands and did not serve public needs.[2]

The Jewish Agency's budget at the end of 1942 was based on the income of three funds. Two of these, the Foundation Fund and the Jewish National Fund (JNF), collected some money in Palestine but much more among Jewish communities around the world. The Foundation Fund, established in 1920 to rebuild the land of Israel, was the main financial resource of the Zionist movement and the Jewish Agency. During the war it provided 5.5 million Palestinian pounds for immigration, new settlements, housing construction, and related activities. During the same period the JNF, founded in 1901 at the beginning of the Zionist movement to purchase land in Palestine, spent 6 million Palestinian pounds on land acquisition and reclamation. For the Zionist movement, intensive land purchase and settlement were the highest priorities, to assure the Yishuv's postwar existence and development.[3]

More and more Jews in Palestine joined the British army as the Germans advanced in North Africa in the summer of 1942; by the end of that year their number reached 20,000. (By the end of the war they numbered close to 30,000 and constituted about 15 percent of all Jewish breadwinners in Palestine.) In July the national Institutions announced another tax, for the newly established third fund, the Mobilization Fund, to support soldiers' families, to improve training, and to acquire ammunition for defense in Palestine. At the same time the taxation system was streamlined and compulsory rates were imposed—as compulsory as was possible, given that institutions lacked formal state authority. All workers had to pay 4 percent of their wages to the Mobilization Fund, and employers had to match the sum. Tax rates for the self-employed and the wealthy were based on estimated income from one workday per month. These revenues were divided among the central bodies dealing with defense, security, and soldiers' families.[4]

The Mobilization Fund raised about 2.1 million Palestinian pounds by the time the war ended. It was a prestigious enterprise, and even the Revisionists gave up their own fundraising operations and joined the effort, receiving an allocation for their mobilization offices.[5]

Three main funds, then, financed JAE activities: the Foundation Fund, the Jewish National Fund, and the Mobilization Fund. When the Agency was faced with the need to allocate money for rescuing the Jews of Europe, it had to decide whether to use existing funds or to find other sources. Because resources were limited, it was necessary to decide which had priority, rescue efforts or building the country. This decision required a comprehensive discussion of Zionist goals.

In the meantime the Agency tried to deal with two other issues. At the end of 1942 the Jewish Agency had appealed to the mandatory government to allow the 29,000 unused immigration permits remaining from the 75,000 White Paper quota to be used for children in Nazi-occupied countries. The Agency's treasurer, Eliezer Kaplan, assured the government that the Agency would allocate any funds necessary for their absorption in Palestine.

For the time being, however, the Agency decided not to initiate a significant fundraising campaign or to announce the allocation of a large sum for bringing children to Palestine. First, its members were not yet convinced that large-scale rescue was possible; they were waiting for concrete ideas from the emissaries in Geneva and Istanbul. Second, the transfer of money to areas occupied by the Germans would have been in violation of Allied regulations, specified in the summer of 1942, which forbade sending any material aid to enemy territory. Even if it were possible to get money out of Palestine without the permission of the authorities, it would still be hard to transfer it to neutral countries (especially Turkey, where foreign currency regulations were very strict), and even harder to get it from there to Jews in the occupied countries. Jews no longer had permanent addresses, and they faced risks by making contact with the outside world. If the money were entrusted to free-lance, non-Jewish couriers, the Agency could never be sure it would reach its destination.

Nevertheless, the issue of the absorption of children reached the public, and a spontaneous collection of money began at the end of December 1942. The JAE, fearing that this effort might trigger a spate of partisan fundraising, immediately decided to allow the Rescue Committee to coordinate unpublicized fundraising. At the same time, the Agency Executive and the National Council decided on a campaign to increase contributions to the Mobilization Fund and to social services.[6]

Another subject discussed in January 1943, both by the Agency and by the Zionist Actions Committee, was the allocation of money to help Zionists in occupied areas. It was decided to begin with the modest sum of 10,000 pounds but to increase the amount "if there are possibilities of extending aid to the movement in the occupied Diaspora." The Histadrut Executive had made a similar allocation for the same purpose.[7]

Help had been extended to Zionist officials and members of the pioneering movements since 1939. But now, in late 1942, it had become clear that all help was a matter of life or death. A package of food or money for a bribe or a forged document could save a life. The Zionist organizations considered themselves obligated to help their own members before helping those who turned to Palestine only in calamity. In the 1930s and 1940s, ideological and partisan affiliations were often stronger than family ties, determining one's priorities, one's behavior, and one's spiritual world. Moreover, because the Zionist movement was small, the activists and officials of one organization or party were familiar with their counterparts in other groups as well as with their own membership. Moreover, mass rescue was a task that no one knew how to address. "Let us not delude ourselves," Eliyahu Dobkin warned at the ZAC meeting on January 10. "It is not in our power to save the millions, since we cannot get to them. We also cannot raise the tens of millions of pounds needed for that. We have only very limited possibilities for helping our comrades in the Diaspora."[8]

In mid-January 1943 the JAE was sharply criticized for its lack of real initiative, its failure to conduct a thorough discussion of the task of Zionism in such times, and its failure to allocate money for large-scale rescue operations. At a meeting of the Histadrut Executive, Melech Neustadt, who had just returned from Istanbul, where he had gone again to examine rescue possibilities, reported that the Jews of Europe were crying out for help from the Yishuv and that the emissaries in Istanbul believed there were ways to help, however speculative. The meeting passed a unanimous resolution calling for "special concerted efforts to discover ways of rescue" to offset the Agency's ineffectualness. The National Council also demanded that the Agency immediately allocate 250,000 pounds to investigate rescue possibilities. Mention was made of a bitter discussion with Kaplan, who had refused to allocate "one penny" for the time being—saying that, if and when money was needed, the Yishuv would be willing to collect it. The Zionist Actions Committee expressed amazement that JAE members had claimed that rescue was not the Agency's responsibility and that it was constrained from becoming involved in any way by the regulations governing its activities.[9]

The Agency's critics maintained that it had done things backwards. Funds should have been allocated to save several groups while the situation was being investigated. The money might have created possibilities that could not have been explored otherwise. If the Executive waited for suggestions from Istanbul or Geneva before beginning to raise money, opportunities would be missed. The JAE had to be convinced that rescue *was* its responsibility and that action must be on a scale commensurate with the size of the catastrophe.

At the next meeting of the ZAC, in mid-January 1943, Gruenbaum argued that money from the Foundation Fund should not be used for rescue operations: "No, and I say it again—no! This tendency to consider Zionist activities secondary must be resisted"; Zionism was "the central point in every period—in times of catastrophe as in normal times," and the building and development of Palestine could not be halted. The Diaspora had entrusted the Yishuv with this task, and the Jewish Agency had to fulfill its trust. The struggle for redemption of the land did not "readily fit with activities for the benefit of the Diaspora, and this is our tragedy." But if a choice had to be made between the two, then "Zionism comes first." Funds for rescue operations had to come from other sources.

Gruenbaum's position, similar to that of other members of the JAE, was no secret. He had made numerous pronouncements before, and one newspaper had already called him "an anti-Semite." Nevertheless, when he finished, there was an uproar. Leaders insisted that saving the Jews of Europe was the primary goal of the Zionist movement at that moment, and that a few hundred thousand pounds could be allocated from the Agency's 1,150,000-pound budget for that year. Even rescue plans that appeared to be fantastic should be approved, they said; losing money had to be considered a calculated risk. "This is what Zionism is all about now." They also suggested a large-scale fundraising campaign—for rescue and not just for absorption of children, and for all Jews, Zionist or not. Other ZAC members, however, stopped short of such extreme recommendations. Although they spoke fervently of rescue as a Zionist duty and demanded funds for it from the general budget, the sums they mentioned were small. The resolution passed at the end of the meeting urged the new Rescue Committee to look into ways of funding the exploration of rescue possibilities.[10]

The Agency refused to allocate money for rescue from its budget, but it promised to honor any financial obligation incurred by others in such enterprises. The emissaries and activists of Aliya Bet were frequently told, "Do what you can—the Agency is behind you. If you find a way or a boat, money will not be the problem." [11] Such commit-ments, though quite explicit, could also be construed as ducking re-sponsibility and as an admission that the Agency itself had no idea how rescue could be implemented; moreover, it could always back out if the plan was not realistic enough.

The Histadrut Secretariat was not prepared to let the matter rest. To prevent inroads into the Mobilization Fund, it proposed that the Foundation Fund triple the sums it collected in Palestine and devote two-thirds of them to rescue. In the meantime, it offered the Agency 50,000 pounds to get started and asked it to match the figure. A dele-gation of central members went to Jerusalem to convince the Mapai members in the Agency—Ben-Gurion, Shertok, and Kaplan, the trea-surer—to accept the plan. The JAE rejected the offer; before any money was allocated, it had to be proved that rescue was somehow possible. [12]

At the next meeting of the JAE, on January 24, Kaplan explained in detail the difficulties of allocating Foundation Fund money for res-cue. First, he said, "we are only the trustees of this money, which has been donated . . . for the purpose of building the land, and we are not allowed to use it for anything else." Second, Agudat Yisrael's repre-sentatives on the Rescue Committee were likely to refuse to partici-pate in the fundraising efforts of a Zionist organization such as the Foundation Fund. Instead, they might start their own fundraising op-eration, and the Rescue Committee's hard-won unity would be shat-tered. Third, when the Mobilization Fund was established, it had been decided not to allow any other fundraising campaigns. Last, but not least, Kaplan said, he did not see much possibility of using large sums of money to aid the Diaspora, since the possible avenues of help were getting narrower daily.

Despite Kaplan's arguments, the JAE decided that the Foundation Fund would organize, as part of its regular campaign for 1943, a spe-cial drive to collect money for the refugee children from Europe. In the meantime the Executive would advance a 15,000-pound loan—instead of the 50,000 the Histadrut had demanded—to the unpubli-cized campaign being conducted by the Rescue Committee. [13]

The Histadrut Executive received the Agency's decision with indig-nation. As one member said, "It is the result of being preoccupied with daily problems to the point of being unable to see beyond them. It happens to all of us. I am sure that each one in the Agency Execu-tive feels the pain of the Diaspora as acutely as we do . . . but they miscalculate. They are being shortsighted about what can be done." The Histadrut Executive decided to appeal the decision. [14]

The Agency was not only shortsighted; it had been out of touch with public sentiment ever since the news of the Holocaust had been verified. Many Jews in Palestine were prepared to donate large sums for rescue; individuals and settlements frequently appealed to officials, asking how they could help or, simply, where to send their money. They wanted action, slim as the chances might be. The Histadrut warned that if the Agency continued to ignore popular sentiment, the result would be spontaneous, uncoordinated acts of assistance that might hurt the Agency's own fundraising activities.[15]

The matter was raised again in the ZAC at the beginning of February. Although only two weeks had passed since its last meeting, the atmosphere was now graver. News about the accelerated pace of extermination had reached Palestine in January. Every day the newspapers reported expulsions and killings in the Balkans, the Netherlands, Belgium, Germany, and even Norway. The ghettos, they wrote, were in fact death traps; the U.S. State Department had confirmed that Hitler's plan was to annihilate five million Jews; Joseph Goebbels had announced that nothing would keep Germany from killing every Jew in Europe, and Himmler had ordered the murder of all Polish Jews by the beginning of 1943.

At the opening of the meeting Gruenbaum read a telegram that had just arrived from Istanbul, saying (mistakenly) that there were no more Jews left in Warsaw and that "something horrible is about to happen in Rumania." "We are at a dead end," he said.

> To my great regret, I have to say again that I don't believe we can really do anything. I don't believe that the governments will do anything of consequence. And it is hard for me to believe that the German Government, that Hitler would let the Jews out. We certainly cannot abstain from any action. We should do all we can . . . but our hopes are infinitesimal. Let me tell you, I know my remarks aroused objections. I think we have only one hope left—and I would say the same thing in Warsaw— the only action, the only effort that provides us with hope, that is unique, is the effort being made in the Land of Israel.

Gruenbaum later explained that he had come to this conclusion not through ignoring the plight of the Diaspora, as he was accused, but rather through "a bitter calculation": saving the Jews of Europe was impossible, and Palestine, "this little niche," was all that was left. Moreover, he was sure that many in the Yishuv had reached the same pessimistic and cruel conclusion but did not dare voice it and risk attack as he had.[16] It is an open question whether Gruenbaum had moved from one extreme—of rejecting the news and denying its veracity— to another—of accepting it and totally despairing.

After Gruenbaum's remarks the ZAC discussed the 1943 budget of the Agency Executive. It proposed appropriating 250,000 Palestinian pounds for new settlements; another 250,000 for agricultural development; and tens of thousands for the water system, for commerce and industry, and so on. A loan of 15,000 pounds was earmarked for rescue activities, in addition to the money already being raised for the absorption of children. Suprasky alone spoke against the budget proposal, suggesting an appropriation of 100,000 pounds for rescue. Three weeks earlier, he had suggested 250,000; perhaps the news caused him to modify his request. No one seconded his proposal, and Suprasky had to withdraw it. The budget was passed by majority vote.

As a response to the spontaneous contributions for the rescue of children at the end of December, the Agency had decided to entrust unpublicized fundraising to a special subcommittee of the Rescue Committee, also headed by Gruenbaum. In January 1943 the Agency and the Histadrut each appropriated 15,000 pounds as a loan, to be returned once the campaign succeeded. The National Council, the Revisionists, and Agudat Yisrael (as members of the Rescue Committee) were also asked to advance loans. The Rescue Committee decided to use the money for rescue of all Jews, not just of Zionists.

The subcommittee compiled lists of several hundred wealthy potential donors in the hope that they would quickly contribute large sums. Leaders such as Ben-Gurion, Moshe Shertok, Golda Myerson, and David Remez went to talk to them, and emissaries from Istanbul reported on their on-the-spot work. The initial response was tremendous: in small gatherings in private homes, thousands, even tens of thousands of pounds were sometimes collected in one evening. Encouraged by this success, the subcommittee set its goal at 100,000–120,000 Palestinian pounds.[17]

At the beginning of February Menachem Bader, an emissary in Istanbul, returned to Palestine and demanded more funds from the Histadrut Secretariat to undertake certain rescue attempts proposed by Jewish leaders in Slovakia and Rumania. Like Neustadt before him, Bader tried to convey that there were opportunities for action but that time was running out: "I came to tell you that our hands are empty and that money is necessary in order to try and buy with it some respite for our brothers who are faltering in their desperate race against inexorable time and death's reaper." The risk of losing tens of thousands of pounds was trivial compared with the plight of European Jewry, which was "impaled on the ram's horn." The fear that money from Palestine would indirectly help the enemy seemed to him ridiculous in a war that was costing each side billions; the small sums given by the Yishuv could make a difference only to the Jews of the Diaspora; they could not tip the balance.

In response to Bader's report, the Histadrut Secretariat tried again to move the JAE to action—this time with a threat. If the Executive did not immediately appropriate 25,000 pounds for rescue work, the Histadrut would collect money independently and send it to Istanbul with no conditions attached. A committee was elected, with Myerson as chairman. The committee pledged to devote a week to negotiations with the Agency and the Mobilization Fund board and to start fundraising in organizations affiliated with the Histadrut. The purpose was "to move things out of a situation in which no one knows why nothing gets done." [18] The minutes make clear the participants' frustration.

Three days later Myerson's committee called a meeting of the National Council and the Mobilization Fund board to discuss the relation between the Mobilization Fund and the secret campaign of the Rescue Committee. Aharon Bart, chairman of the Mobilization Fund, said openly that a separate campaign was unacceptable because it would damage the Mobilization Fund. Still, the Mobilization Fund would add money to the sums advanced as loans by the Jewish Agency and the Histadrut to investigate possible means of rescue. "If these attempts prove justified and can be pursued further, we will then decide if we can handle the financing of these activities as part of our fund's work."

Bart's cautious remarks and the hint that he planned to deprive the Rescue Committee of a task it was successfully accomplishing angered Gruenbaum: "I am the person who said that Zionism is above everything, but if we are able to do something without hurting essential Zionist interests, then we should do it." Remez simply blew up. "We are ashamed of ourselves . . . Some of our comrades cannot sit in their offices any more, cannot eat their bread . . . I will disobey any organization, even if I am censured . . . We have to change the way we think about this matter." He demanded that the secret campaign be intensified and announced that the Histadrut was increasing its advance from 15,000 to 25,000 pounds and making it an outright grant, not a loan. He appealed to the JAE and the Mobilization Fund likewise to increase their advances and turn them into contributions and stressed that the money raised by the Histadrut was in addition to all the other funds and campaigns that the Histadrut had pledged to support.

The JAE and the Mobilization Fund finally gave in. After two and a half months of discussion, the JAE allocated 75,000 pounds for rescue attempts—but as loans; a joint committee of the Rescue Committee, the Mobilization Fund, and the Histadrut would continue soliciting donations from the well-to-do.[19]

To get a clearer view of the situation, the JAE sent Kaplan to Istanbul. When he returned a month later, at the end of March, his attitude had changed, perhaps as a result of more direct contact with the rescue work and the echoes of suffering in Europe. Kaplan now supported the claim by the emissaries in Istanbul that, with systematic action and appropriate financial support, results were possible even though the rescue of thousands could not be assured. Kaplan announced that he had approved the expenditure of 80,000 pounds for special programs in Istanbul and in Geneva, in addition to the regular budget of 10,000 pounds a month for the emissaries. Energized by Kaplan's announcement, the Histadrut Executive and Rescue Committee decided to raise 250,000 pounds, to draft Kaplan as a speaker, and to make an appeal to Jews overseas even without the Mobilization Fund.[20]

But Kaplan was not yet ready to touch the national funds. Instead, he insisted on merging the unpublicized fund with the Mobilization Fund. The Rescue Committee protested, but it was a weak body in comparison with the MF. In mid-April 1943 its fundraising was absorbed into the Mobilization Fund, which became the Mobilization and Rescue Fund (MRF). The united appeal was to raise 50,000 pounds a month and to use 80 percent of it for mobilization and security, 20 percent for rescue, effective until January 1944. The partners would discuss the distribution of any surplus. The Jewish Agency ratified the agreement only after it was satisfied that the allocation of money for rescue could not undercut security needs or support for the 20,000 soldiers' families. Later in April, at a session of the Assembly of Representatives, the board issued a formal declaration that the Mobilization Fund had been assigned "the additional task of helping the Diaspora in its self-defense and rescue" and had become the Mobilization and Rescue Fund.[21] But no one in the JAE questioned whether rescue work might suffer as a result of the agreement, except Gruenbaum, who finally gave in.[22] The Rescue Committee and the Mobilization Fund remained two different organizations, each with its own board or presidency and its own tasks.

The agreement met with sharp criticism, largely because there had been a perceptible increase in rescue activities in March and April. Ze'ev Shind, another emissary in Istanbul, arrived in Palestine and reported to the Histadrut Executive new possibilities for help and rescue operations. He requested an increase in the regular budget for emissaries from 10,000 to 20,000 pounds a month and another 50,000 pounds for illegal immigration. The emissaries in Istanbul had found more ways of transferring money to Europe (especially to Poland), and the Mossad for Aliya Bet was hoping to extend its activities in the Balkans and was about to purchase a vessel for that purpose.

But the most important news at that time came from Warsaw. A rebellion against the Nazis was being organized, and the Yishuv was called upon to help with funds. The news came in a coded letter, using Hebrew words with Polish suffixes to speak about the coming nuptials of "Ami" (my people) with "Miss Harigevitch" (death) at the apartment of "Aunt Haganaska" (defense). Would "Mr. Hatsalska" (rescue) like to send a greeting card? "If he does, he must hurry." Five thousand pounds were sent to Warsaw immediately, but despite Myerson's urging, there was no emergency fundraising campaign.[23]

At the end of April 1943 cables reached Palestine from the National Jewish Committee in Warsaw notifying the Yishuv that the ghetto revolt had begun, the ghetto was burning, and money was urgently needed to buy arms and to exchange Zionist activists, or at least to keep them from starving. The Jewish Agency was asked to send at least 25,000 pounds immediately. The cables were read at an emotionally charged meeting of the Histadrut Secretariat, and, although the pleas were addressed to the Jewish Agency, the Histadrut decided to help, especially since most of the rebels seemed to belong to the Zionist pioneering movements.

The Secretariat asked the Agency to appropriate 50,000 to 60,000 pounds for help and rescue operations, and another 40,000 to 50,000 for illegal immigration. It also decided to increase wage earners' regular payments to the MRF from 4 to 5 percent, or at least to 4.5 percent, or to raise Histadrut dues by a penny. Some members were enraged by the discrepancy between this proposal and the tragedy that was taking place in Warsaw. "Our answer to those carrying on the revolt is going to be half a percent?!" "Half a percent for the rescue is a disgrace!" "This is not a matter for pennies or tax raises!" They demanded that a separate, urgent fundraising campaign be held in the next week or two, that Myerson devote an entire month to collecting money for the rescue, and that the merger between the Mobilization Fund and the secret Rescue Committee fund be reexamined.[24]

As a result, the Histadrut held a workers' conference at the beginning of May. Members of the Histadrut Executive stressed the gap between the rate of the extermination and the slim successes of rescue efforts and emphasized the duty of Jewish workers to contribute to the rescue of their brethren. The conference closed calling for a week dedicated to donations during which each worker would contribute one day's wages.

The results were disappointing. No JAE member attended the conference. Some workers evaded paying, some tried to reduce the sum they had to pay, and some demanded proof that the money would indeed reach the Jews in the ghettos. And factional quarrels in the Histadrut and deliberate disruptions were said to have hurt the project. About 27,000 pounds was collected, only two-thirds of the target. Some blamed the failure on a dearth of advertising, but Myerson replied that such an issue needed no advertisement. Collection of donations was to continue until the target sum was reached.[25]

The Histadrut Executive wanted the contribution of one day's wages to go entirely to rescue operations. The MRF demanded that the money go into its joint account because not all workers had contributed 4.5 percent. The Histadrut considered this demand unjustified, even "deceitful," since the MRF had not allowed separate rescue appeals to the public. The debate lasted from mid-May to mid-June, and the Mobilization and Rescue Fund seems to have prevailed.[26]

Meanwhile, the emissary from Istanbul was still waiting for a decision that would enable the work to continue. Once again a Histadrut delegation went to the Agency, this time to offer Kaplan a loan so that the emissary could leave with at least 30,000 pounds. The Rescue Committee and the Zionist Actions Committee demanded that funds for rescue be collected separately, outside the framework of the MRF, or at least that the share allocated for rescue be increased to 50 percent of the united fund. Gruenbaum proposed that the ZAC obligate the JAE to provide the emissaries with whatever they needed. This was a very unconventional proposal, coming as it did from a member of the Executive itself. Kaplan gave in to the mounting pressure and promised that the emissary would be able to go back with instructions providing for "quite extensive activity." The JAE also agreed to conduct an internal investigation of rescue needs on the basis of written information to be provided by Gruenbaum.[27]

At the end of July Shaul Meirov, who headed Aliya Bet operations, asked the JAE to allocate for illegal immigration an additional 25,000 pounds from funds collected abroad. He received a flat refusal. "We could not convince them . . . All our demands . . . were to no avail . . . Distressed, we decided to turn to the Histadrut." The Histadrut Secretariat agreed to the request on the spot and harshly criticized the JAE for its inaction: the Agency was beginning to think that it did not need either a planned budget or fundraising activities for rescue, because "the Histadrut is there and will come to the rescue at the last minute."[28]

The internal probe never took place, either in the Agency Executive itself or jointly with the Histadrut or in any other important forum. Nor did any of these bodies ever unequivocally resolve to rescind the merging of rescue and mobilization into one fund. Either the JAE vanquished the opposition or else members were wary of harming the mobilization needs. It is probable that the strongest critics, who were Mapai leaders, preferred to try to convince Ben-Gurion, Kaplan, and Shertok through informal, friendly conversations. They certainly did not want to join forces with Agudat Yisrael or the Revisionists to push through a formal resolution against their own comrades. The party had just been through one painful ideological split with its left wings. During the second half of 1943 relations were also difficult with both the British and the Revisionists.

At the end of August 1943 Venia Pomerantz (later Ze'ev Hadari), an emissary in Istanbul, came to Palestine, described the situation in Europe, stressed the importance of every package of food or medicine sent to the occupied areas, and, like the emissaries before him, asked permission to risk Yishuv money. At the beginning of September the Histadrut persuaded the Agency to organize a onetime appeal for 250,000 pounds, to be called "Diaspora Month."[29]

In the summer of 1943 the regular fundraising of the merged Mobilization and Rescue Fund, which had been conducted since April, badly needed stimulation, for two reasons. First, the farther the Allies advanced into previously occupied areas, the more possibilities there were to extend help. On the other hand, as the Allies came closer to victory, the satellite countries, Hungary, Bulgaria, and Rumania, began to explore the possibility of shifting their allegiance, and fear increased that Germany would invade them and annihilate the Jews still there. Yishuv leaders foresaw such an eventuality as early as September 1943 and suggested again and again that a million pounds be collected in preparation for it.

Second, the income of the MRF had declined; in the spring and summer of 1943 it had failed to achieve its monthly quota of 50,000 pounds. A year had passed since it had been founded, and the Germans were no longer at the door of Palestine. (Only 2,900 enlisted in the British army in 1943, compared with almost 9,000 in 1942.) Despite devoted efforts by the fund's workers, routine had taken over and public fervor had cooled. The MRF needed new impetus. Dobkin and Kaplan defined the situation openly. "The idea of rescue is coming to the aid of the mobilization. If it weren't for it [rescue], the [Mobilization and Rescue] Fund would be in big trouble. The success of this new project [Diaspora Month] depends, to a great extent, on people's knowing that a special effort will benefit the rescue."[30]

However, there was a difficulty in scheduling Diaspora Month. The Foundation Fund and the Jewish National Fund usually opened their annual campaigns in October, close to the Jewish New Year's Eve. Shertok and Ben-Gurion favored holding Diaspora Month first and the other campaigns afterward. Shertok reflected that, from a Zionist point of view, nothing could be "more urgent and more necessary and better reflect the responsibility of the Yishuv as the center of the Jewish people than such a project." Ben-Gurion agreed. "The rescue of the Jews of Europe has not only a financial side but a moral side too. It is now one of the central issues. It is not merely a question of helping the Jews of Europe; it is raising the stature of Palestine and the Zionist funds. The fact that Palestinian Jewry has taken the lead in rescue operations is an important Zionist asset." In other words, Shertok and Ben-Gurion were interested both in successful fundraising for rescue operations and in the prestige those operations would bring to the Zionist enterprise. The Yishuv would be seen as the savior of the people. The JAE approved their proposed timing of Diaspora Month from mid-September until Yom Kippur, the Day of Atonement, 1943.[31]

Diaspora Month, the Yishuv's first comprehensive fundraising effort for rescue, was launched at a special session of the Assembly of Representatives, attended by most religious and political leaders. Workers were asked to pay "a true quota," that is, the full sum for which each was assessed. Everyone else was asked to give a special donation, which would be "entirely devoted to saving our brethren." Door-to-door collections included institutions and businesses. At the end of the month, on "Diaspora Day," badges were distributed that read "The Voice of Our Brothers' Blood," an allusion to God's accusation against Cain: "The voice of your brother's blood is crying to me from the ground" (Genesis 4:10).

Ben-Gurion was drafted to address an assembly of industrialists and businessmen. He asked that everyone present contribute generously, since the Yishuv was enjoying economic prosperity—"a little too much, maybe more than should be permitted." He said that because Jewish communities in the free world were doing much less than their share, the Yishuv had to make up for their shortcomings. Thirty thousand pounds were raised that evening.[32]

It soon became clear that the campaign would not reach its original goal, and the target was reduced to 150,000 pounds. In the end, less than 80,000 pounds came in. The Histadrut consequently reduced its commitment to 20,000 pounds, donating a sum in proportion to what had actually been collected. After deductions for the mobilization's share (80 percent) and payment on loans, 32,000 pounds remained for rescue work.

Why was Diaspora Month a failure? The organizers offered a number of answers. First, the mandatory government had recently implemented a personal income tax. Second, the Agency had approved the project only three days before it was to begin, and it was a complex operation. But the main reason lay elsewhere. Public enthusiasm had waned, especially among merchants and the well-to-do. About 10,000 households contributed nothing. Some factories consistently evaded payment—both workers and employers discreetly looked the other way. The quota of 4.5 percent was seldom met. Not everybody was prepared to attend lectures on the Jews of Europe unless a brilliant speaker was scheduled. It seemed to some that "the Yishuv has fallen into an atrophy."[33]

One reason for the decline in interest may have been the fact that rescue operations had to be conducted in complete secrecy, because the publication of details might have jeopardized plans. Even the emissaries had written that "if the money cannot be obtained without publicity we would rather do without it." As a result, people began to doubt that rescue activities were being conducted at all or that the money was reaching its destination and actually helping. Furthermore, only a few hundred survivors had reached Palestine after almost a year's investment of time and effort. It was not unusual to hear such comments as "For the time being . . . we have not seen even one surviving child" or "everything is so conspiratorial, there's a feeling that nobody is taking care of the matter."[34]

After Diaspora Month, the question remained how to find money for rescue. The only regular income was the 10,000 pounds a month received from the MRF. Chaim Barlas, the senior representative of the Jewish Agency in Istanbul, arrived in Palestine and asked for at least 50,000 pounds a month. The Rescue Committee threatened a separate fundraising campaign if income from the MRF continued to decline. After all, as Rabbi Yitzhak-Meir Levin put it, "the Mobilization Fund exploited the slogan of rescue" while prohibiting the Rescue Committee from appealing directly to the public. Suprasky suggested "getting out on the streets for the money." But not even the harshest critics of Agency policy, such as Myerson and Remez, who had originally objected to the fund merger, wanted to jeopardize the mobilization needs.[35]

In the absence of any other solution, the Histadrut Executive decided to continue the activities of Diaspora Month until the original target sum was collected. It again suggested appealing urgently to Jews abroad to help raise the 250,000 pounds, so that Barlas could return to Istanbul with enough money for three or four months' activities.[36]

The total amount spent for rescue in 1943 was about 320,000 pounds (the equivalent of about $8.6 million in 1989). The Jewish National Fund spent more than three times as much that year for reforestation and land purchase, as did the Jewish Agency for its own range of activities in Palestine. The MRF spent 500,000 pounds for defense purposes and for the support of soldiers' families.[37]

At the beginning of 1944 two Zionists from Poland, Joseph Korniansky and Eliezer Unger, reached Palestine via Slovakia and Hungary. Their reports to various Yishuv organizations were published in the newspapers and aroused public reaction again. "Two people came out of hell and shook our conscience to its roots," said Joseph Sprinzak, a labor leader. "Something must be done." The refugees reinforced the emissaries' request for a budget of 50,000 pounds a month. They made it clear that, despite all the risks and the losses, most of the money sent by the Yishuv was reaching those in need. But money was also needed, they said, for unexpected rescue possibilities—"an iron fund." They emphasized that little time was left for preparations: in their estimation, the Germans would invade southeastern Europe within two or three months.[38]

The Zionist Actions Committee promptly called for a special campaign to raise 250,000 pounds for rescue and for an intensive worldwide fundraising effort, to be launched by a Yishuv delegation in the United States two weeks hence, in mid-January. When Kaplan and Bart continued to hesitate, their colleagues attacked them. Remez claimed that 1944 would be blessed with "an abundance of money and work"; Dobkin and Gruenbaum argued that the recently approved 1944 budget of 2.1 million pounds for defense, land reclamation, and settlements could spare a substantial sum for rescue; Eliyahu Golomb warned that tens of thousands of Jews who would come out of that hell alive would ask if everything had been done to save them. Gruenbaum again threatened to resign and reminded members of the Mobilization and Rescue Fund that it owed the Rescue Committee a considerable sum of money. Remez warned the MRF board not to miss "a unique opportunity . . . to make a real appeal to the Jews of the Diaspora . . . and to ignite a spark in the heart of the Yishuv." The board finally accepted the ZAC appeal to raise 250,000 pounds in one month through the concerted effort of all sectors of the Yishuv, and in mid-February a detailed agreement on the matter was reached between the Rescue Committee and the MRF.[39]

While the issue was being discussed, Meirov arrived from Istanbul and reported on preparations for Jewish armed resistance in Rumania, Hungary, Slovakia, and southern France. Warning that "what can be done today won't be possible tomorrow," he asked for 100,000 pounds to arm the future fighters. His information gave additional impetus to the special campaign.[40]

Preparations for the special campaign took place throughout March. The Industrialists' Association, the Chamber of Commerce, contractors, and transportation organizations decided to contribute considerable sums beyond their regular monthly quotas. Many settlements had already donated large amounts, and the public employees in another had decided to donate one month's wages even before the campaign began. To reach as many people as possible and to promote a sense of public involvement, Jewish Agency and Histadrut employees were to spend three half-days going from door to door, selling stickers for each contribution of from four shillings to a pound.[41]

The Histadrut Secretariat again had a long-drawn-out debate over shillings, tag-day, a new entertainment tax, and other ways to raise the 50,000 pounds. Even the price of eggs came under discussion. Zalman Aharonovich interrupted in protest: "We are all living with a great big accepted lie . . . as far as the rescue goes." He said that the Yishuv had 45 million pounds in the banks (in fact at the time it had more than 53 million) and that the economic enterprises of the Histadrut had a basic capital of 10 million pounds. He suggested that 5 percent of this capital be given for rescue and that the Jewish Agency give one million pounds. The fact that such sums had not yet been donated and that there was haggling over pennies instead was, in his eyes, "the disgrace of the generation." The Histadrut Secretariat decided to discuss his proposal in a few days.[42]

In mid-March the Nazis invaded Hungary. Fear mounted also for the Jewish communities of neighboring Bulgaria and Rumania. Barlas sent an urgent demand for 100,000 pounds to purchase a large Turkish boat for transferring refugees from the Balkans to Palestine. Meirov appeared again before the Histadrut Secretariat to support this request and reported that a clear, though unofficial, order had been sent from Palestine not to hesitate: Kaplan had agreed to lend the emissaries 100,000 pounds for the purchase or rental of ships. The sum would be returned to the Agency out of the proceeds from the special MRF campaign. At the same meeting Melech Neustadt read a cable from the National Jewish Committee in Warsaw:

> We appeal to you at the last moment, before the remnant of Polish Jewry is annihilated . . . Jews are suffering in the ghettos and in the camps . . . hiding in the woods and in Aryan neighborhoods . . . and death is lurking everywhere . . . The money received from you is a drop in the bucket. We have just received your last dispatch of 10,000 Palestinian pounds . . . We appeal to you to increase your financial aid tenfold . . . The remnant of Polish Jewry is waiting for you to save them.

Aharonovich again demanded that 5 percent of the Histadrut's capital be appropriated for rescue and accused his colleagues of not discussing his proposal because the urgency of the situation "has not yet sunk into the minds of the members of the Histadrut."[43]

The special campaign, called "The Yishuv to the Rescue," finally got underway at the beginning of April 1944. By the end of May, 110,000 pounds had been raised; the door-to-door sticker sale, conducted in the three major cities during Passover, netted another 20,000 pounds. Over the summer the total reached 200,000 pounds. Despite debates about which section of the Yishuv failed to fulfill its duty there was a general feeling that the campaign was the most successful yet.

The Jewish Agency continued to advance loans. From March to mid-June it gave 200,000 pounds, of which 70,000 was an outright grant. But the Histadrut Secretariat did not consider this amount adequate. The emissaries were reporting that 4,000 people could be saved and that boats were waiting in the Rumanian port of Constantza until another 250,000 pounds could be found. Once more applying pressure to the Yishuv and world Jewry, the Histadrut Secretariat threatened to adopt Gruenbaum's 1943 suggestion that the ZAC compel the Jewish Agency to raise the money. The Agency provided the 250,000 pounds and promised to consider similar requests.[44]

From the beginning of 1944, the Yishuv was further embroiled in disputes with the Revisionists about rescue. The Revisionists' daily, *Hamashkif*, condemned as a public deception "the vague demand" to collect money for rescue. In the Revisionists' view, money was not the solution, but direct action against the British that would force them to change their policy on matters of immigration and rescue.

In the summer of 1942 the Revisionists had agreed to fulfill their commitments to the Mobilization Fund and to limit any separate fundraising to their own members and supporters. In addition, they had pledged that Etzel, their armed underground, would not benefit from the allocation they received from the Mobilization Fund; that money would be used only for their mobilization office and soldiers' families.[45] They had renewed this agreement in February and again in October 1943. However, their dissatisfaction with the situation deepened. March 1944 would mark the fifth anniversary of the White Paper. In February Etzel detonated explosives in the immigration offices of the mandatory government and in the police headquarters in Jaffa. Several British policemen were killed. The government reacted by refusing to issue entry permits for refugees, and there was an uproar in the Yishuv.

Opinions in the JAE were divided. Some members demanded that the Revisionists be excluded at once both from the MRF and from the Rescue Committee and that all contacts with them be severed. Gruenbaum, however, argued: "The man in the street will say that they are fighting for immigration while we are defending the British Government. It is very easy to blame us for the failures of rescue. The real culprits are out of reach, and it would be to the Revisionists' advantage to incite the public against us." Furthermore, said Gruenbaum, if the Revisionists were excluded from the Rescue Committee, Agudat Yisrael might leave as well; then the committee would fall apart, and there would be disastrous repercussions in occupied Europe. He suggested that rescue matters be kept out of the Yishuv's internal quarrels. Even if all contact with the Revisionists were severed, he pointed out, it would be impossible not to save anyone affiliated with them; in that case they would be getting the benefits of the rescue work without sharing the responsibilities.[46]

Ben-Gurion rejected all proposals for arbitration and refused even to meet with the Revisionists. At the same time, *Hamashkif* revealed that the Revisionists had founded a separate rescue fund, called Shivat Tzion (Return to Zion). Its main purpose was to finance the activities of Joseph Klarman, their representative on the Rescue Committee, who had started separate rescue operations in Istanbul in addition to his work with the other emissaries. Although the Revisionists refused to give up their rescue fund, they also fought bitterly to remain on the Rescue Committee. Gruenbaum was finally forced to issue a public statement that Revisionist participation in the Rescue Committee had been terminated. As a result of the dispute, the MRF's income declined after midsummer.[47]

Early in June 1944 the Allies invaded Europe, and late that month it became clear that 430,000 Hungarian Jews had already been transferred to Auschwitz. This tragic chapter marked a turning point in the Yishuv's approach to events in Europe. From that time on, there was less talk about saving Jews in the occupied areas; the focus shifted to survivors in the areas being liberated by the Allies.

At the end of July the JAE considered appealing to the Soviet Union to transfer aid to Poland, which was being liberated. In September the Executive started to discuss postwar policy. Should it aim to rehabilitate the communities that had been destroyed? But surely such a non-Zionist approach would reinforce the continued existence of the Diaspora. How could the Yishuv help in a way that would still be in keeping with Zionist principles? Who would the Agency's partners be? How should it cooperate with non-Zionist groups such as the American Joint Distribution Committee? What about compensation for lost Jewish property? By October the JAE had concluded that its problem was no longer rescue but rather immigration.[48]

In 1944 the Yishuv spent 858,000 pounds on rescue (equivalent to $23,690,000 in 1989). This money came from two sources: 315,000 pounds from the Mobilization and Rescue Fund (which collected 862,000 pounds that year) and the remainder from Jews abroad, including the JDC (see Table 1). The Jewish National Fund spent 1,766,000 pounds that year (over half of it collected in the United

Table 1. Rescue expenses in relation to total expenses, Jewish Agency and Mobilization and Rescue Fund, February 1, 1943–June 1, 1945

	February 1–December 31, 1943		1944		January 1–June 1, 1945	
	1000s of Palestinian pounds	%	1000s of Palestinian pounds	%	1000s of Palestinian pounds	%
Mobilization and Rescue Fund						
Total income	702	—	862	—	?	?
Allocation for rescue	218	31	315	36.5	114	?
Jewish Agency						
Total income	1150	—	3350	—	?	?
Allocation for rescue	320	24.8	858	25.6	147	?

Note: Data for 1945 are incomplete because of the difficulty in differentiating between expenditures in the first half in occupied countries and in the second half in the liberated areas.

States) on its traditional tasks, reforestation and land reclamation; the Foundation Fund spent 3,350,000 pounds on immigrants' absorption, settlement, and industrial development, allocated in the Jewish Agency's budget (2,100,000 pounds plus a loan of 1,250,000 pounds from Lloyds).[49]

An analysis of the Rescue Committee's monthly balance sheets shows that from February 1, 1943, to June 1, 1945, the Yishuv spent 1,325,000 Palestinian pounds on rescue: 645,000 from the Mobilization and Rescue Fund, 510,000 from the JDC, and 170,000 from Jewish communities in the free world.[50] The money was spent on two major efforts: 523,500 pounds on Aliya Bet in 1943 and 1944 (which received a total of 693,300 pounds between November 1941 and September 1945), and the remainder to save Jews in Nazi-occupied Europe.[51] During this period the average per capita donation in the Yishuv was about 1.3 pounds (the 1989 equivalent of about $38) for rescue.

Given the harsh criticism leveled at both the JAE and the MRF, as well as the JAE's persistent fear that the Zionist enterprise would be hurt, one should evaluate the amounts spent on rescue in relation to the sums spent for other major items such as defense, settlement, and immigrant absorption. Table 1 shows that from February 1, 1943, to June 1, 1944, rescue allocation was equivalent to 25 percent of the Jewish Agency's total expenditures and amounted to 34 percent of the MRF's. Rescue was in fact the single largest item for the MRF and one of the major expenditures in the Yishuv, together with settlement, labor, housing, and preparations for future financial and industrial development.

It is also clear, however, that fundraising in the Yishuv probably could have been handled more effectively. In 1943 and 1944 the Yishuv's economic situation improved considerably, and many were willing to contribute to rescue. Moreover, the Yishuv institutions knew that direct material aid was the most effective way of helping Jews in the occupied areas—more so than political or military negotiations. The fact that almost three-fifths of the Yishuv's rescue funds were spent in Europe attests to this awareness.

Because the JAE claimed that it was not the body responsible for rescue, the Histadrut became the center of discussions on rescue and rescue funds, especially with regard to illegal immigration.

The Histadrut remained the harshest critic of the JAE. In November 1943 David Remez voiced a typical view: "The Agency Executive has made a grave error by not making unlimited sums available for rescue efforts right from the start. If the Executive had taken a ten-year million-pound loan on which it had to pay interest, the Yishuv and world Jewry would know that no opportunity for rescue has been overlooked." Most critics, however, were wary of diminishing the Zionist budget or of eating into funds for defense. Nor did they want an open confrontation with the JAE, which they considered to be the supreme political authority, entrusted with carrying out Zionist policy. The result was that the harshest critics of the JAE became its propelling force. "[The Histadrut] did the Zionist movement and Zionist Executive a great service—by taking the initiative and forcing the Agency Executive to follow suit, the Histadrut Executive saved the Agency's honor." [52]

9

Rescue Fund Allocations
from Free World Jewry

From the beginning of rescue operations, the Yishuv considered itself responsible for setting the example for the rest of free world Jewry, "so that history will exonerate us."[1] But it was clear that the Yishuv could not shoulder the entire burden of helping European Jewry.

That free world Jewry would be able and willing to participate in the Yishuv's rescue efforts was a foregone conclusion. The success of the appeal depended on coordination and contacts, which were not easy to maintain during a world war. In addition, the Jewish world had to accept both the Yishuv's leadership in the handling of rescue activities and its Zionist policy in general. Since the members of the Zionist movement on the eve of the war had not composed more than 10 percent of all Jews it was doubtful that such acceptance would in fact be forthcoming.

Ben-Gurion advocated approaching the Jews of the United States, primarily the American Joint Distribution Committee. "The JDC has millions," he said, "and nothing to do with them." He believed that if the Yishuv came up with a feasible plan for rescue, it could demand these millions, and that if the Yishuv raised 250,000 Palestinian pounds, the JDC would match it three times over. Kaplan and Gruenbaum were dubious: "The JDC is over there—in America."[2] JDC representatives in the occupied areas, including Poland, had found ways of continuing their operations, primarily by taking loans from local banks with the promise of repayment after the war. But JDC aid to the Jews of Europe had stopped in the summer of 1942. It was doubtful whether it could be prevailed upon to renew its activities, first and foremost because American Jews were Allied citizens. Regulations forbidding the transfer of money and materials to the occupied areas came into effect in December 1941 and were spelled out in detail the following summer. Thus, at the very time when the world learned about the systematic extermination, the JDC's elaborate apparatus and resources stopped being fully utilized in Nazi-occupied Europe. In August 1942 the organization's secretary-general in New York, Moses A. Leavitt, had informed the Agency that because of the Allied restrictions the JDC could no longer transfer assistance across enemy lines.[3]

Ben-Gurion suggested a cooperative effort; the Yishuv was willing to take risks, even to break the law, to continue rescue efforts, and the JDC could supply funds. The central problem was that the JDC was, by definition, a nonpolitical, neutral relief organization, whereas the Jewish Agency was a political body par excellence. If the JDC put its resources at the disposal of the Jewish Agency, the latter would receive the credit for any accomplishments. The JDC was unlikely to relinquish voluntarily its prestigious, exclusive, decades-long position as the helper and savior of Jews in need. A "hard debate with the JDC," as Kaplan put it, was sure to follow, and it did.[4]

In the spring of 1943 the Jewish Agency requested money from Judah-Leib Magnes, the JDC's senior representative in Palestine and the president of the Hebrew University. Magnes turned down the Agency's request, both because of the illegal nature of the operations in Istanbul and because of JDC principles: the Diaspora was the province of the JDC and Palestine the province of the Zionist movement, and this prewar separation of functions should continue. The Yishuv, which depended on financial support from world Jewry, should spend its money not in the Diaspora but for the development of Palestine. As one Mapai member put it, "It is more than just the ocean that separates us and America."[5]

Chaim Barlas, Melech Neustadt, and others involved in rescue activities and in Aliya Bet defended the JDC's position. In their experience, the JDC had rarely refused to fund operations that seemed feasible and were in accordance with their policies, including those related to Aliya Bet. They had to be approached not with requests for declarative statements but with practical plans. Moreover, after his meeting with Agency members, Magnes defined the crucial issue in a letter to Paul Baerwald, chairman of the JDC in New York: if the rescue of large groups could be achieved, "would the JDC be willing to contribute"? Baerwald's reply was yes.[6]

In June 1943 Dobkin and Gruenbaum reported to the Zionist Actions Committee that Magnes had announced the JDC's willingness to participate in the rescue operations of the Yishuv with matching funds. They informed the press that an agreement had been reached, that a joint committee had been established to extend help to refugees from Poland in the USSR on the same half-and-half basis, and that the Yishuv was simply awaiting formal approval from JDC headquarters and the imminent arrival of the JDC representative from New York.[7]

The Agency, however, had acted too soon in releasing this news. Perhaps keeping the negotiations secret, so as not to embarrass the JDC, would have been a better policy. In August 1943 Joseph Schwartz, chairman of the JDC's European Executive Council, arrived in Palestine. He was welcomed as the first representative of organized American Jewry to come to Palestine since the war had broken out—but with the implication that such a representative should have made an appearance a good deal sooner.

At a formal meeting with the National Council, Schwartz defended the policy of his organization. Had the JDC begun to operate illegally, it would have endangered its extensive legal activities as well as its agreements with governments and other official bodies regarding loans that would be returned only after the war. Such operations were being carried out all over the world—from Shanghai to Portugal, including Poland, Italy, and Yugoslavia. The JDC had to keep enough money in reserve to repay those loans after the war.

Schwartz corroborated Barlas and Neustadt: the JDC had been in close contact with the Jewish Agency and had helped generously whenever there was a problem of paying for the transportation of survivors to Palestine, which "was much more important to us than sending them to some remote islands." Most of the expenses of youth immigration, immigration from Aden, and immigration through Turkey had been funded by the JDC; and it was about to fund immigration from Portugal and from the Balkans as well. All of this was in addition to maintaining refugees in Spain, Switzerland, Shanghai, North Africa, and other parts of the world, not to mention the transfer of 100,000 people from Europe to the Americas.

Schwartz explained that all these activities were being carried out in the face of growing anti-Semitism in the United States. This fact put the JDC in a difficult position vis-à-vis public opinion and the U.S. government because it was responsible for an influx of refugees and the expenditure of American money abroad. Schwartz commended the Yishuv's actions to raise large sums to be sent to occupied Europe and asserted: "We are willing . . . to go on giving money in order to bring over any Jew who can be saved from Europe, as far as we can." In other words, the JDC offered to continue help in funding immigration and transportation, but there was no mention of Baerwald's consent to contribute funds for rescue from occupied areas.[8]

When he met with the Histadrut Secretariat and the Rescue Committee, Schwartz encountered harsh rebukes. Golda Myerson said that although the Yishuv should have risked much more money, "we sent comrades on the basis of slim hopes. We did anything possible and even the impossible—things that were forbidden, or things that anyone with sound judgment would have considered absurd." American Jewry, on the other hand, could also have done a good deal but did not because it was concerned primarily with itself. "For the Jews of the world, there are no laws or borders now," she continued. "There is really only one law. Millions of Jews are being annihilated while large powerful countries enact special laws to protect themselves. No one is lifting a finger to save these Jews. If we don't do it—no one will."

Myerson—like Shneur-Zalman Rubashov, Joseph Sprinzak, and David Remez, who spoke in the same vein—did express appreciation for the JDC's activities. Rubashov, however, protested that most of the aid from the JDC was reaching those who had already been saved rather than those whose lives were still threatened. The Yishuv could not understand the distorted patriotism of American Jews. He suggested, as Ben-Gurion had before him, that if American Jews could not overcome their fears of infringing their government's regulations, they should "let us be their emissaries. Let them supply us with the means, and we will do the work. We have nothing to fear." Both meetings ended with a resolution to seek ways of cooperating with the JDC.[9]

The JDC was prepared to cooperate—its way. Late in August, Schwartz cabled his headquarters in New York: "All formal relations with Jewish Agency severed. We shall continue [to] cooperate with them and consult [on] matters as occasion requires but will set up no joint committees and [the] one already in existence [in] connection [with] Teheran package service dissolved." The Jewish Agency, Schwartz concluded, found the arrangement satisfactory.[10]

Indeed, Schwartz continued on to Istanbul and reached an agreement with the emissaries there that would keep the JDC formally not involved while informally financing activities, much to the satisfaction of the Jewish Agency. The JDC would continue to fund immigration to Palestine; more important, it would allocate 20,000 Palestinian pounds a month to the emissaries. This regular income, which began in October 1943, represented almost half of the emissaries' monthly budget at that time. Officially, the money was earmarked for transportation and for the absorption of refugees in Palestine rather than for rescue and aid, but there is little doubt that Schwartz knew what the money was being used for. Menachem Bader, who was in charge of the illegal disposal of funds in Istanbul, criticized this state of affairs, which put the whole onus of illegality on the Yishuv. Kaplan knew, however, that any explicit reference to what was actually being done could only cause damage. He may also have liked the idea that the Jewish Agency would be more strongly identified than the JDC with rescue operations.[11]

At the end of 1943 the U.S. Treasury authorized arrangements with European banks that legalized financial aid to the occupied areas. At that point the JDC began objecting to the Yishuv's operations in Europe and in other places, such as Aden and Teheran, where Jewish refugees from the Soviet Union gathered. Now that the JDC could legally support operations in enemy territory, it wanted to return to the prewar division of labor: "Helping the Diaspora is the sole responsibility of the JDC," and the World Zionist Organization should use its money for the development of Palestine.[12] But the leaders of the Yishuv, persuaded that the JDC was undermining Zionist activities in the Diaspora, sought a new arrangement. Late in 1943 several members of the Histadrut Secretariat, led by Dobkin, suggested that the Jewish Agency establish a world Jewish relief organization that would include the JDC, the Board of Deputies of British Jews, the World Jewish Congress, the United War Appeal of South Africa, the Rescue Committee in Palestine, and other Jewish organizations that were extending aid to the Jews of Europe. The organization would consolidate and coordinate relief operations both during and after the war. It had other goals as well: to end the monopoly of the JDC and turn relief operations into a general Jewish undertaking, to bring more immigrants to Palestine, and to gain prestige for the Yishuv and for the Zionist movement.

The proposal prompted Yishuv leaders to discuss whether the new organization would do more harm than good in the event that the JDC refused to cooperate and an open breach resulted. They acknowledged that the JDC had carried out "a gigantic historical enterprise in helping Diaspora Jews" and that any open conflict would injure the Jewish world, particularly in that most important area—the extension of aid. "Damned be any Jewish quarrel if it hurts the needy," was Sprinzak's view. Myerson differed: it was unacceptable that the JDC should continue presenting itself as the savior of the Jewish people. Zalman Aharonovich warned that the anti-Zionists in the JDC might carry the day against the pro-Zionists and thwart cooperation. Dobkin predicted that the clash would reach the occupied areas as well, although the difficult conditions there "require an approach that the JDC cannot handle." In other words, the JDC would oust the Yishuv from rescue operations in the occupied areas but would be unable to manage them alone because it lacked the appropriate tools and the necessary experience.[13]

The issue at stake, then, was not simply rescue work but who would represent Diaspora Jewry before European and international authorities and gain credit for the efforts. Zionists and non-Zionists were competing for the support of Jews during the war and—no less important—afterward. The Jewish Agency reached a clear position on the matter. It was not going to let the JDC overshadow it or conduct any aid or rescue operations without it. The JDC might be unwilling to cooperate directly with the Agency, but it could hardly refuse Dobkin's suggestion for a worldwide, united Jewish body without appearing factious. The JDC, however, did refuse. "Glad you gave Shertok no encouragement . . . clearly we cannot tie up and must remain independent," was Leavitt's answer from New York to Schwartz after the latter's meetings with Shertok. Moreover, the JDC threatened that "fundamental change and new assumption by Jewish Agency would have definite repercussions in fundraising situation" in the United States. In other words, the JDC threatened to publicize that the Jewish Agency was using for rescue funds collected for Zionist construction.[14]

Friction increased between the JDC and the JAE. At the beginning of 1944 the War Refugee Board (WRB) was established in the United States with the support of the president and the secretary of the Treasury. The board not only gave the JDC permission to transfer money to the occupied areas but also provided it with a legal and authoritative American channel for doing so. It was feared in Palestine that the possibilities opened by the establishment of the WRB would strengthen the JDC and increase its reluctance to cooperate with the Jewish Agency. It was also feared that willingness to contribute to rescue would decrease in Palestine.

In the spring and summer of 1944 relations with the JDC deteriorated further. Each organization continually accused the other of trying to take the credit for its own efforts and achievements and for publishing incorrect information in the Jewish press.[15] In June the emissaries in Istanbul sent word that the JDC was preparing to start separate operations there, and that relations were already "at sword's point." Using Russian expletives and flaming rhetoric, the Histadrut Secretariat accused the JDC of "sabotaging aid and rescue," warned that it would fight the JDC openly in the United States, and demanded that the JDC send a delegation to Palestine to review its pol-

icy. In the meantime it called an official meeting with JDC representatives in Palestine in order "to prevent matters from continuing to
take the wrong course."[16] Putting the problem in unambiguous terms,
the Secretariat's delegation persuaded Magnes of the need to cooperate, particularly at that time, when there were real possibilities for immigration from the Balkans. Magnes left for Istanbul with Kaplan to
press the JDC not to renege on its commitments. The public saw this
move as proof that differences could be overcome where rescue was
concerned.[17]

The meetings in Istanbul in July 1944 brought improved relations.
On his return Kaplan reported that "by and large, the attitude of
these comrades reflected both willingness to cooperate and loyalty to
the Jewish Agency in Istanbul." The JDC agreed to provide 75 percent of the money needed for boats for 7,000 immigrants. While
awaiting approval of this arrangement in the United States, the JAE
instructed its emissaries to continue operations without worrying
about money. The JDC would continue to operate independently out
of Geneva and Lisbon and to help smuggle refugees out of the occupied areas. Its operations from Istanbul would continue in cooperation with the Jewish Agency. The JDC would send 85,000 pounds a
month to the occupied areas in addition to the 20,000 pounds a
month for the emissaries; all monies would be disbursed from Istanbul rather than from Geneva in order to avoid duplication. Any activities involving armed resistance would be handled solely by the
Agency. The JDC also committed itself not to act without consulting
the Jewish Agency.[18]

This was the substance of Kaplan's report, which included much
praise for Schwartz. But the internal JDC correspondence shows that
for the JDC the agreement did not represent a fundamental change
in policy; rather, it was an attempt to regulate the work of and to keep
a suspicious eye on the Jewish Agency: "We must be over careful concerning our contacts and agreements with the Jewish Agency and we
here [in New York] have no relationship at all with the actual work
that goes on, in and through the Agency."[19]

The agreement lasted only from July through October 1944; in
mid-October the JDC canceled it effective as of November 1. Two reasons were given. First, the Allies' advances gave rise to hopes that direct relief work would soon be possible, and so the JDC decided to go
on helping Jews independently rather than through the Agency,
which was more active and independent than the JDC was ready to
allow. Second, there was serious disagreement about the Mossad's
methods in connection with Aliya Bet. Its activists claimed that the

unpredictable situation in the Balkans rendered rescue so urgent that there was no point in obtaining safe-conduct permits for the ships or in waiting for the approval of the JDC in New York in each case. The JDC strongly objected to endangering the lives of the passengers and terminated its financial participation, although it was "prepared to consider such participation in every future boat . . . on its own merits, and only if we approve each project before [it is] carried out." [20]

The JDC's announcement upset Jewish communities around the world and reduced their willingness to work with the Agency. The Agency declared that it would continue rescue operations on its own and would try, independently, to cover all expenses of immigration. It expressed hope that other Jewish bodies would cooperate with it now, especially to save the remnant of Hungarian Jewry. [21]

One cannot avoid the thought that the Jewish Agency was better off without the agreement with the JDC—and knew it. The JDC continued financing transportation to Palestine as promised, and the Jewish Agency got the credit for the continued rescue operations since it was known throughout the Jewish world that the JDC had terminated its financial support.

Jewish organizations in South Africa had refused to allocate funds for rescue operations since the beginning of the war for fear of violating Allied regulations. Most Jews in South Africa had come from Poland and Lithuania, so they preferred to donate parcels for the Polish and Lithuanian Jewish refugees in the Soviet Union instead. They also promised to contribute 40,000 Palestinian pounds for the transportation of refugee children to Palestine once they had escaped from the occupied areas. Although the Zionist movement in South Africa had grown stronger in the 1940s, not all the influential Jewish organizations there were eager to see rescue operations coordinated from Palestine. Gruenbaum believed that the position taken by South Africa's Jews reflected not just a legalistic attitude but also a lack of understanding. [22]

Gruenbaum went to South Africa in August 1943. He discovered that the leaders of the United War Appeal, the emergency committee established to help European Jewry, knew a good deal more than he had thought. The South Africans had many pertinent questions. Why wasn't the JDC participating in the Yishuv's rescue operations? Was the Rescue Committee in Palestine sure that the money it collected was indeed being spent for rescue purposes? Was there discrimination in the allocation of aid to Zionists and non-Zionists? How could help be extended to Jews in Lithuania or Poland?

Gruenbaum did his best to answer these questions and to convey the urgency of the rescue needs. After negotiations, a written agreement was drawn up and signed by Gruenbaum on behalf of the Rescue Committee and by the United War Appeal on behalf of the Jewish organizations of South Africa. Under the agreement, the latter promised 30,000 pounds for rescue, in addition to the 40,000 pounds promised earlier for refugee children, under the following conditions: the money would be distributed regardless of affiliation; the Yishuv would continue to give money on its own; the Rescue Committee would inform the Jews of Europe that it was getting money from South African Jewry—that is, not only "the JDC and the Zionists" were helping; and a representative of South African Jewry would be entitled to check the accounts of the rescue operations. The money would be sent without delay.[23]

By the time Gruenbaum left South Africa, the United War Appeal had collected 500,000 pounds. But because the South African community assumed that the war would end at the beginning of 1944, it kept most of the money for postwar rehabilitation, and the Rescue Committee in Palestine was not promised more than 70,000 pounds in all. The agreement with Gruenbaum was ratified in Jerusalem, although Yishuv leaders protested the attempt of Diaspora Jews to determine the use of their contributions and deplored the fact that South African Jewry had decided to keep most of the money for postwar purposes.[24]

South Africa's Jews, however, insisted on standing by the original terms of the agreement. When Nicolai Kirschner, chairman of the Zionist Federation of South Africa, came to Palestine toward the end of 1943 for an extended visit, he met with the Rescue Committee. Gruenbaum tried to convince him to give at least some of the 40,000 pounds earmarked for the immigration of children to rescue operations. "Rescue is also immigration," he told Kirschner. Gruenbaum actually wanted the money in order to smuggle people out of Poland to Hungary. Kirschner praised the Yishuv's rescue operations and the devotion of the emissaries, but he was unable to dispose of the 40,000 pounds differently: "You may ask [for the funds], but I cannot promise." To the members of the committee, this reply implied that the Yishuv was a pauper begging at the door of rich Jewry for its own needs and not for the rescue of other Jews. Rabbi Yitzhak-Meir Levin quoted a letter sent by Jews from occupied Europe declaring that Hitler was not the only one to blame for the murder of the Jews; so were "the Jews of the world who could help and don't." Barlas suggested that Kirschner return with him to Istanbul and see for himself what was being done there. That would convince him to give the 40,000 pounds solely for rescue.[25]

In January 1944 the South African Jews requested a release from their previous commitments on the grounds that the Jewish Agency was not fulfilling its part of the agreement. In their opinion, copies of the correspondence between the Rescue Committee and the emissaries, sent to South Africa as part of the agreement, clearly indicated discrimination in favor of Zionists in the distribution of aid and in decisions regarding who would immigrate to Palestine. The South Africans returned the correspondence with a list of potential beneficiaries for aid and a request that a full explanation be returned by airmail; until such an explanation was received and found satisfactory, no more money would be forthcoming.[26]

Apparently the explanation was not sent, for early in 1945 the United War Appeal was still asking Kaplan for a detailed report of expenses and activities funded by their contributions until then. Their suspicions that the money was used only for Zionist purposes were reflected in their questions. Why had the JDC stopped funding operations of the Jewish Agency in October 1944? Was the Agency continuing by itself? What proportion of its operations went to extending help regardless of whether or not it involved immigration to Palestine? Gruenbaum had been asked similar questions a year and a half before. Neither the South African Jewish community's faith in the Jewish Agency nor its willingness to help unconditionally seem to have grown during that time.

Altogether, the Jews of South Africa sent not 70,000 but 57,000 pounds to Palestine for rescue attempts (see Table 2), most of it between September 1943 and January 1944. The agreement with the Rescue Committee was not renewed, and it appears that not all of the 40,000 pounds earmarked for children was sent. In the spring of 1945 the Rescue Committee sent several reports about the ways the funds had been spent. Their ironic wording implied that the South Africans failed to understand that rescue operations during wartime could not be conducted according to the letter of Anglo-Saxon niceties.[27]

In the 1940s Zionist activity in Egypt was still far from organized, and, despite the country's proximity to Palestine, Egyptian Jews felt very little interest in the life of the Yishuv. There was, however, a good deal of partisan fundraising by representatives of various Yishuv organizations. When Ruth Klieger-Eliav was sent to Egypt in February 1943 on behalf of the Mossad for Aliya Bet to collect money for res-

Table 2. Rescue Committee's income and expenditures for rescue, February 1, 1943–June 1, 1945

	1000s of Palestinian pounds
Income	
Mobilization and Rescue Fund	517
South Africa	57
Egypt	55
American Joint Distribution Committee	433
Australia	12
Foundation Fund (Britain)	37
British Fund	5
Other countries	17
Total	1133
Expenditures	
Poland	76
Slovakia	100
Hungary	135
Rumania	165
Expenses in Istanbul	23
Western Europe	160
Parcels	10
Total	669

Source: Rescue Committee, balance sheet 2, file S26/1268, Central Zionist Archive, Jerusalem.

cue, she was in competition with all the other efforts. The Yishuv had a reputation as "a money-squeezing association." Even more troubling, Egyptian Jews were not aware of what was happening in Europe. What was needed was not only organization but a good deal of public education.[28]

Once concerted efforts were made, the Foundation Fund, the Jewish National Fund, and the Prisoners' Redemption Fund (for rescue) collected a record 140,000 pounds from Egypt's Jews by the end of 1943. This responsiveness, especially to the Prisoners' Redemption Fund, surprised Yishuv leaders. "We have reached Jews who until now could not be influenced," said Kaplan, "and as a result many people have come closer to our ideas." "The Jews of Egypt, alienated as they may be," said Myerson, "have now given money for a boat and for rescue. No one dreamed that we could collect anything there."[29] She was referring specifically to the purchase of small boats in which Jews were taken from Greece to Istanbul with the help of the Greek underground. The fact that many Jews in Egypt were from Greece might explain their high motivation in helping save Greek Jews.

But like their counterparts in South Africa, Jewish leaders in Egypt attached conditions to their contributions: most of the money should be used solely to move children from Europe to Palestine, and it would be made available only when the children were already on their way. The money for the boats—30,000 pounds—was given to the Rescue Committee and not to the Jewish Agency; when Gruenbaum went to Egypt to try to get the rest of the money, he was told that the 110,000 pounds would be given "only for actual rescue, that is to say, for transferring Jews from the Diaspora to Palestine." Gruenbaum explained that rescue was not just a matter of moving Jews to Palestine, which was now almost impossible, but mainly of helping Jews in the occupied areas, which was possible. But he failed to convince his listeners. Remez was outraged. "I do not understand the Jews of Egypt, who have money but insist, 'Show us the Jews!' . . . I don't know what language they speak, but it is not a Jewish language." Most of the money collected for rescue apparently remained in Egypt. Only 55,000 pounds had reached the Rescue Committee by the end of the war (see Table 2).[30]

Negotiations between the Jewish Agency and the Jews of Great Britain were the most difficult of all, and their results, in relative terms, among the poorest. By the end of 1943 only a few thousand pounds, raised by non-Jewish members of the labour party in England in a special "British Fund," had reached Palestine (see Table 2). Zionists in Britain discussed at great length how much money should be allotted to rescue, but no more money reached Palestine by the spring of 1944. The JAE described the response as "a disgrace to Zionism."[31]

At a meeting of the Zionist office in London in April 1944, attended by Chaim Weizmann, it was decided not to establish a special rescue fund but instead to allocate for rescue 10 percent of the proceeds of the Joint Palestine Appeal (which combined collections for the Foundation Fund and the Jewish National Fund). The JPA's board of governors, headed by Sir Simon Marks, objected, as did representatives of the Jewish National Fund. The members of the Zionist office thought that the objections stemmed from an unwillingness to break the law. "Until the government announces that it has no objections, they will not allocate money from the JPA for rescue." They suggested that the money from England be spent exclusively on the absorption of refugees in Palestine—which would not infringe the law. Marks offered his own compromise: 10 percent would be allocated for rescue by the JAE in Palestine and not by the Joint Palestine Appeal in London. Eventually the Agency decided to instruct the Jewish National Fund in Jerusalem to tell its London branch to allocate the requested 10 percent. If this was not acceptable, the JAE would be forced to announce a separate fundraising campaign in England for rescue, which would make inroads into the Joint Palestine Appeal campaign.[32]

Gruenbaum sent the threat to London by cable and followed it up with a long letter to Marks on June 8: it was the obligation of the Yishuv, as the representative of the world Zionist movement, to help its brethren in Europe; because the Joint Distribution Committee had refused to become involved in important aspects of rescue work, the Yishuv had taken this task upon itself and, from modest beginnings, had achieved substantial results. The main rescue work at the time, he wrote, was bringing Jews out of Rumania to Turkey and from there to Palestine in small boats. At that very moment five boats were waiting in Constantza to transfer 3,800 people. The more money available, the more Jews could be saved. "It is great Zionist work," he continued, "and one can say that [while] rescuing Jews we are working at the same time for Palestine. It is the very task for which the [JPA] was created." In conclusion, Gruenbaum asked Marks to reconsider his decision.[33]

Gruenbaum's plea seems to have succeeded. Money began reaching the Rescue Committee from London, including 10 percent of the proceeds of the Foundation Fund. The Jewish National Fund in England, however, refused to allocate any of its income for rescue. The total amount from Britain shown in the records of the Rescue Committee is 37,000 pounds (see Table 2).[34]

In 1943 and 1944 the Joint Distribution Committee transferred to the Yishuv and its emissaries 510,000 Palestinian pounds. A little less than half of this sum (216,300 pounds) was sent to Europe in monthly allocations of 20,000 pounds. Most of the balance was used to finance the passage of legal and illegal refugees from occupied Europe to Turkey and from there to Palestine; thus the JDC financed three-fifths (or 300,000) of the 523,500 pounds spent by the Aliya Bet activists. In June 1944 Barlas expressed his gratitude to the JDC, "the Jewish financial instrument," for its generous help in transferring 15,000 refugees to Palestine since the beginning of the war. By the end of the war, the JDC's share of the Yishuv's total expenditures for aid and rescue came to 38.6 percent.[35] The rest of the Jewish communities in the free world—Egypt, South Africa, and Britain (along with the Jews of Australia, who sent 12,000 pounds, and the World Jewish Congress and South America, which made small contributions)—gave the Yishuv about 170,000 pounds for rescue, 12.8 percent of the Yishuv's rescue expenses. Together with the JDC, they provided 680,000 pounds, about half the money spent by the Yishuv.

This state of affairs reflects the attitude of the Jewish communities toward the Yishuv as well as some of their own problems. Most of the communities established emergency committees for the aid of European Jewry. These committees included representatives of various Jewish organizations. The fact that they were not all Zionist made cooperation with the Yishuv difficult. Furthermore, except for the British, they were far from the arena of conflict, both geographically and psychologically.

Most of the organizations in the large Jewish communities refused to violate Allied regulations despite the fact that the situation was one of life and death. Perhaps these Jews still lacked confidence in their own countries. Apparently, they were not yet as fully integrated or as powerful as the Yishuv leaders thought. The smaller communities were usually divided into groups according to their countries of origin in Europe. This fact did not facilitate concerted action, but it did strengthen the motivation of each to help Jews from their own countries, a motivation parallel to the Yishuv's willingness to save Zionists—a priority harshly criticized by the leaders of the Jewish communities.

The Allied restrictions led the JDC to operate mainly in nonbelligerent countries or liberated areas, helping those who had managed to escape from the occupied areas. For the same reason, small Jewish communities allocated money mainly for the transfer of children. This emphasis ignored the urgent necessity of keeping alive the Jews in the occupied areas and moving them to safer places, in hiding or in other countries in occupied Europe. Getting out of Europe was the last stage, and very few, including children, reached it. As a result, most of the money remained in the communities' coffers.

The Jewish communities' and organizations' fear of violating Allied regulations, their suspicion of the Zionist leadership, and their concern about their image as rescuers in the eyes of the Jews of Europe during and after the war resulted in a strange ambivalence toward the Yishuv's rescue activities. Though suspicious that it was using rescue operations to advance Zionist interests, they blamed the Yishuv for not using the money it received exclusively for the development of Palestine. They also rejected the JAE's argument that priority should be given to rescue over immigration. This attitude contrasted painfully with the hopes and faith of European Jews in the Jewish Agency and the Yishuv and directly harmed rescue efforts.

Neither the Jewish Agency nor the World Zionist Organization was considered the appropriate center for directing rescue operations. A worldwide Jewish committee for rescue was not established, and the JDC, whose prestige, professionalism, and financial resources would have made it the natural core of such a committee, preferred to maintain its independence. The Jewish Agency did seek the participation and cooperation of free world Jewry in rescue operations, as in Egypt and in South Africa, and it repeatedly approached JDC representatives in Palestine and in Europe in the hope of bypassing JDC headquarters in New York. But no Yishuv organization ever sent a prestigious delegation to the United States or any other country, despite repeated resolutions by the Jewish Agency, the ZAC, the Histadrut, and the National Council to do so. Such a step might have shown free world Jewry the importance the Agency attached to rescue and led to more concerted action.

The JAE refused to use the Zionist budgets for rescue, preferring to solicit additional, separate contributions from the Yishuv and from Jewish communities. At first glance, its appeals appear to have been successful: the Jewish communities' contributions amounted to about half the rescue expenditure of the Yishuv. However, the Yishuv numbered about half a million, whereas American Jews numbered about five million and the rest of free world Jewry about three million more; proportionally, free world Jewry could have contributed sixteen times as much. Yishuv leaders frequently expressed both disappointment in the sources and pride (laced with Zionist rhetoric) in the Yishuv's own attitude: "It [the Yishuv] came to help—it was the first to understand the situation, the first to send rescuers, the first to give money for rescue work. We undertook great fundraising projects . . . People said that what gave them the strength to go on was the support from Palestine." The Yishuv considered its fundraising for rescue "a shining page in the history of the Yishuv" and a disgraceful one in the history of the other Jewish communities, which "remained calm and unperturbed and did not assist in the rescue of our brethren."[36]

The Yishuv as a whole felt doubly isolated—both from a hostile or indifferent Gentile world and, even worse, from an unresponsive Jewish world, which, because of self-interest, suspicion, and considerations of prestige, left the Jews of Europe to their fate and the Yishuv to shoulder the risks and burdens of rescue.

PART THREE

Rescue Efforts

10

Rescue Operations
in Neutral Countries

The Yishuv's planning and implementation of operations to save European Jews began for the most part at the end of 1942 and continued through 1943, fading away toward the end of that year. Only a few plans developed in 1944. In this and the following chapters each plan will be traced separately, from conception through conclusion. But because they unfolded at the same time, they affected one another: the leaders in Palestine and the emissaries abroad regarded them as one general effort in which the failure or success of one part necessarily affected the chances of another.

The Yishuv's delegates in neutral countries were the links between the Yishuv and European Jewry. They were the ones who transmitted ideas for rescue plans between Europe and Palestine; they also attempted to find means of rescue on their own and to convince the Yishuv that such means existed.

Once Germany had occupied or extended its influence throughout most of Europe, only five nations on the continent remained neutral: Spain, Portugal, Sweden, Switzerland, and Turkey. In these countries, the Jewish Agency and other Jewish organizations established delegations or operations centers manned mostly by emissaries from Palestine or Jewish representatives from the Zionist office in London, who maintained contact with the occupied areas and with the satellites.

THE IBERIAN PENINSULA

With the outbreak of war in September 1939, and particularly after the occupation of western Europe in the spring of 1940, many Jewish refugees, most of them penniless, began reaching Spain and Portugal.

They took a risk, not knowing how the regimes there were going to treat them, since both countries, though neutral, were fascist and known to be sympathetic to the Axis.

At the end of 1939 Nahum Goldmann suggested that a center for immigration and refugee aid, sponsored by the Jewish Agency and with the financial support and participation of the American Joint Distribution Committee and other Jewish organizations, be established in Lisbon. Although refugees kept arriving by the thousands and Goldmann reiterated the idea throughout 1940 and 1941, with similar proposals made by Yitzhak Gruenbaum, Chaim Barlas, and Shlomo Shmuelevich (later Shamgar) of the local Zionist organization in Lisbon, the Agency did not consider possibilities of rescue to the Iberian peninsula until November 1942.[1] In that month, when the Agency started discussing the organization of rescue operations in general, three developments forced attention to the area: the Germans' occupation of southern France, which until then had been controlled by the Vichy government, threatened both the local Jewish population and the refugees who had gathered there; the Allies invaded North Africa; and Spain agreed to leave the Pyrenees passes open for Frenchmen who wanted to joint the Free French Army. Jews, too, could thus take advantage of this route.

Moshe Shertok approached the U.S. and British governments for help in convincing Spain, Portugal, and Switzerland to accept more Jewish refugees. He also undertook, on behalf of the Agency, to transfer to these neutral countries the immigration permits that had been allocated to France. Despite its Axis sympathies, from September 1939 to November 1942 Spain had granted about 30,000 transit visas to Jews and allowed the JDC and other organizations that operated there illegally to transfer refugees to North and South America. Furthermore, despite depressed conditions as a result of the recent civil war, Spain did not limit the number of refugees or the duration of their stay. Although it refused to let Jewish organizations operate formally within its territory, Spain also granted certificates of protection to several thousand Jews of Spanish origin in the occupied areas.[2]

Travel between the Iberian peninsula and the Middle East was difficult, because the Mediterranean was closed to civilian traffic, and North Africa was a war zone. The JAE therefore asked the Zionist office in London to send an emissary to Lisbon and promised to equip him with as many immigration permits as possible. After many delays, Wilfred Israel, a member of a prominent Jewish family in London, left England in April 1943 for a short stay in Portugal. He was to organize the immigration to Palestine of 400 refugees and to investigate ways of getting children out of the occupied areas into neutral countries.[3]

Israel tried to convince the Agency in Jerusalem of the immediate "technical and moral need" to open an office in Lisbon, manned by Yishuv emissaries with appropriate experience and adequate means for smuggling people out of France, Belgium, and the Netherlands to Switzerland and Spain. Similar requests had reached Palestine from France and from the emissaries in Istanbul. All of them clearly considered smuggling people over the borders more urgent than the distribution of the 400 permits.[4]

In June 1943 Israel was killed in a plane crash. Apparently he had made no progress in getting children out, and the immigration permits had not arrived from Palestine. The emissaries of the youth movements in England, most of them kibbutz members from Palestine, urged the Agency to reinforce its delegations in the neutral countries without losing any more precious time. However, not until October 1943 did Fritz Lichtenstein (later Peretz Leshem) arrive in Lisbon from London to ascertain how much Israel had accomplished. His other assignment was to convince all Jewish organizations there to cooperate fully with one another, particularly the JDC and the representative of the World Jewish Congress, Yitzhak Weissman.[5] Lichtenstein wrote later:

> My mission on behalf of the Jewish Agency was limited in time and specific in terms of its goals. I was assigned the job of sorting out the refugees in Spain and Portugal and getting them to Palestine. All other tasks—checking possibilities of rescue, increasing the flow of refugees or organizing them on the southern side of the Pyrenees—were not my responsibility and seemed impractical to London. They did not object, however, to any emissary doing these things "on the side," to the extent that time would permit but without spending any money or undertaking any commitments whatsoever.[6]

He tried in vain to convince the JDC to help him finance illegal rescue activities. The JDC paid for the subsistence of refugees in the Iberian peninsula and their travel expenses to the free world but refused to be involved in illegal contacts or rescue operations. Lichtenstein sent reports to Palestine and to London stressing that rescue opportunities were being missed because there was no permanent Agency representative in Spain. At that very time, he added, many Jews, especially children, were again being deported from France to the extermination camps.[7]

At the end of 1943 Shlomo Steinhorn and Joseph Croustillon, two representatives of the French Jewish underground organization, the

Armée Juif, reached Lisbon through the Pyrenees and met with Lichtenstein. They wanted both financial assistance and authorization from the Jewish Agency to start smuggling people out of France on a larger scale than before. Although Lichtenstein agreed with their overall ideas and considered them his "natural allies," he had neither the means nor the authority to work with them. He may also have hesitated through lack of trust: emissaries from the free world tended to be wary of the extreme measures proposed by underground activists in the occupied areas. Lichtenstein regarded Steinhorn and Croustillon as dangerous "for Palestine and likely to join the Etzel [the Revisionists' armed underground, which advocated, and used, violence against the British in Palestine]." Steinhorn and Croustillon were deeply disappointed. Nevertheless, they sent a detailed report on their organization and its operations to the Jewish Agency in Jerusalem.[8]

In January 1944 Lichtenstein succeeded in hiring a ship for the refugees and received the long-awaited permits. The SS *Nyasa* sailed to Haifa with 756 people on board. Among them were other underground activists from France who, upon arriving in Palestine, handed Eliezer Kaplan and Eliyahu Dobkin an additional detailed report on the Armée Juif and the possibilities of rescue from France. The information they supplied might have been what finally moved the Agency to open an office in Lisbon and to allocate a small monthly budget for its operation. In April 1944, about a year before the end of the war, shortly before the invasion of Normandy and the liberation of western Europe, a year and half after the subject had been put on the JAE agenda, and more than four years after the idea had first been raised, the Jewish Agency opened an office in the Iberian peninsula. Lichtenstein continued his work in cooperation with other Jewish organizations. A second ship, the SS *Guine,* was financed by the JDC and left for Palestine in November with 434 immigrants on board; and another two left in the middle of 1945. Although he worked with Weissman to save children and adults from France as well as Greek Jews of Spanish origin, his rescue operations were quite limited.[9]

Dobkin left for Lisbon in June 1944 and returned two and a half months later. The Armée Juif's independent and elaborate operations—which included transferring thousands of people through the Pyrenees, smuggling orphans and refugees into Switzerland, forging documents, and hiding Jews—had impressed him deeply. In a long, detailed report to the JAE he stated that the Iberian peninsula was a "somewhat new corner" for him and that the Armée Juif was "a great discovery . . . it was a great shock to find out that this movement existed." [10]

Dobkin's assertion of ignorance again raises questions about the Jewish Agency's use of the information it was given. It had been apprised of rescue possibilities through the Iberian peninsula at least since the end of 1942. There had been letters from Wilfred Israel and from Lichtenstein in 1943, as well as reports by the Armée Juif representatives and the testimonies of the *Nyasa* immigrants in 1944. Could all this information simply have been filed away? Dobkin himself admitted that it "went unnoticed." Perhaps in the few cases in which its attention was directed to Spain and Portugal, the Agency believed the reports about rescue possibilities to be exaggerated: "We did not think it was possible to do any work from there." [11]

Only after his visit to Spain did Dobkin realize that "in this corner, as in others, there were many possibilities for saving Jews" that were not being utilized. He put most of the blame on the Allies but also some on the Agency's long-term reluctance to send emissaries and to attempt unconventional action: "If we had gone and done things . . . earlier—how much more we could have achieved." Dobkin reported that while he was in Spain he and Weissman organized the transfer of several hundred children from France and reached an agreement with the Spanish government to accept 3,000 more children from Hungary, to grant 1,600 more transit visas for adults from Hungary, and to extend Spanish protection to 900 more Jews of Spanish origin. Dobkin also reached an agreement with the Portuguese government to grant visas to any Jews who claimed that their ancestors had once lived in Portugal; proofs would have to be supplied only after the Jews were already in the country. Certainly the approaching end of the war facilitated matters for Dobkin, but it is also obvious that many rescue opportunities had indeed been missed.

Thanks to Lichtenstein's good relationships with all the Jewish organizations during his visit Dobkin also got representatives of the JDC and the World Jewish Congress, after years of friction between them, to sign an agreement with the Agency to establish a joint rescue committee. The agreement was signed in July 1944 in the presence of representatives from the U.S. and British embassies. [12]

In the second half of the war, 11,500 Jews were saved through the Spanish and Portuguese rescue routes. Several factors account for the failure to save many more: the strained relations between the JDC and the WJC, the JDC's refusal to become involved in illegal rescue operations, the delays in sending an emissary to Portugal from London, and the Jewish Agency's scant attention to the situation in France and Spain. The Agency was unresponsive to reports and requests about the possibilities that had been created, and it did not establish a strong, permanent delegation there. Instead, representatives came for short periods, became entangled in local disputes, and spent most of their time distributing immigration permits rather than organizing rescue operations.

The JAE may have been a captive of its own prejudices, namely, that these Catholic "fascist or semi-fascist countries" would certainly not help in the rescue of Jews. Ironically, it was through Spain, Portugal, and especially Italy that tens of thousands of Jews were saved during the war. The attitude or their general populations and of most army and police officers, officials, and lower clergy toward the persecuted Jews contrasted sharply with the official position of their regimes. "I plead guilty," said Dobkin. "In this corner, we were late." [13]

SWEDEN

In February 1943 the Agency Executive in Jerusalem financed a trip from London to Stockholm by Shlomo Adler-Rudel, who was experienced in organizing youth immigration. He had a threefold assignment: to investigate the possibilities in Sweden of helping the Jews of Denmark and Norway, to establish contacts with the Baltic states, and, most important, to convince the Swedish government to give shelter to 20,000 children from the occupied areas. Although, according to Adler-Rudel, most local Jewish leaders greeted this mission with skepticism, he soon got in touch with the Swedish minister of relief, Gustav Moeller, who promised to discuss the question of the children with the prime minister. Moeller also made an immediate commitment that any Danish Jews who reached Sweden would be welcome and that his government would do everything in its power to help the refugees. [14]

While he awaited the Swedish government's reply concerning the children, Adler-Rudel worked with young Zionist refugees from Denmark to organize the escape of all Danish Jews. Within a few weeks, with the cooperation of some local Zionists, enough money was collected to purchase a boat. This was later used by Danish Jews in their escape to Sweden. Adler-Rudel also took the initiative in setting up a joint committee of almost all Jewish organizations in Sweden. This committee played a key role in establishing ties with the Danish underground in preparation for the escape, in sending Raoul Wallenberg to Hungary in 1944, and in appealing to Heinrich Himmler, head of the S.S., in April 1945 in an attempt to save the Jews who remained in the concentration camps.

Adler-Rudel kept the press informed about the situation of the Jews of Europe and met regularly with public figures in Sweden, notably the American and British ambassadors. He maintained regular contact with representatives of the Jewish Agency in New York. As a result of the New York representatives' lobbying, Secretary of State Cordell Hull authorized the U.S. ambassador in Stockholm to look into ways of alleviating "the plight of these unfortunate people." [15]

In April 1943 the Swedish government approved the entrance of 20,000 Jewish children, and the American and British ambassadors promised to help obtain funds from their governments for maintaining the children in Sweden and transferring them to Palestine after the war. Although there were already 150,000 non-Jewish refugees in Sweden, the Swedish government repeated its offer to provide a haven for Jews. [16]

At this point the success of the plan to rescue children seemed to hinge on fulfillment of the promise given by the U.S. and British ambassadors. Adler-Rudel returned to London at the end of April and there, together with officials from the Jewish Agency offices in London and New York, appealed repeatedly to the State Department, to the Foreign Office, to Sir Herbert Emerson, head of the Intergovernmental Committee for Refugees (established in July 1938 and continued in much the same form as a result of the Bermuda Conference in April 1943), and to his deputy, Gustav G. Kullmann. A long correspondence ensued between officials in London and Washington about financing the upkeep of the children and guarantees for their departure after the war.

By October 1943 the plan was no longer feasible. That month, most of the Danish Jews (about 7,500 people) were transferred to Sweden through a swift operation organized mainly by the Danish underground. Another 900 Norwegian Jews (half the Jewish population of Norway) infiltrated into Sweden by land. As a result, Swedish-German relations deteriorated; an appeal to the Germans concerning the release of any children seemed hopeless. [17]

Adler-Rudel blamed the failure of the plan on an "indifferent bureaucracy," ignoring the predominant role of the Germans in dooming the Jewish children and in rejecting Swedish overtures to save them. It is questionable whether a firm Allied declaration of immediate willingness to provide the guarantees requested by Sweden would have changed the German position at that stage of the war. It is also questionable whether the Jewish Agency acted wisely in letting Adler-

Rudel leave Stockholm, given his extensive contacts and achievements in the short time he was there, and in not replacing him with another emissary to Stockholm to take advantage of Sweden's willingness to help, its neutral status, and its proximity to the Baltic states and Poland.

SWITZERLAND

At the beginning of the war three Jewish organizations, including the Jewish Agency, already had offices in Geneva. More such organizations, both public and private, were established during 1940, thus endangering the efficiency and cohesiveness of operations. Indeed, the offices affiliated with the Yishuv suffered from duplication and lack of coordination, especially with regard to correspondence with Palestine and with Jewish and international organizations.[18]

When more rescue activity was initiated in Geneva, the JAE began to discuss, not enlarging its offices there but, rather, reducing them and cutting expenses. It appears that Geneva's potential as a center of information and contacts, though recognized in 1940 and 1941 by Yishuv and Jewish organizations gathering information, failed to impress the JAE.[19]

Several factors account for this mistaken evaluation. First, Italy had joined the war in mid-1940, blocking passage from Switzerland through Italy to Palestine via the Mediterranean; Switzerland was now surrounded by Axis states (with the exception of free France). Second, the Agency's Immigration Department in Geneva had with great difficulty got 2,000 families out of Europe to Palestine in the first half of 1940; with no further prospect of immigration permits, Barlas returned to Palestine. Third, the prevalent feeling in Palestine in 1940 was that the situation in Poland had more or less stabilized and that the war was nearing its end.

In the summer of 1940 the JAE appointed Kaplan, Shertok, and Emil Schmorak to streamline operations in Geneva, but no instructions from them ever reached Geneva, despite requests from Nathan Schwalb and Richard Lichtheim for guidelines. During 1941 and 1942 Geneva was seldom mentioned at JAE meetings, and at the end of 1942 Dobkin and Kaplan spoke mainly about Istanbul and Lisbon as the important centers of activity. Yet representatives in Geneva wrote to Palestine frequently: their correspondence now fills many volumes. They sent information, asked for money, and suggested aid and rescue activities.[20]

Lacking instructions from the JAE, the emissaries continued to exercise their own initiative. They established regular contacts with most of the occupied countries, found ways to transfer the little money they received from Palestine, sent parcels—mainly through the JDC—and tried to operate through the international Red Cross and the Vatican. From 1940 through 1942 they felt that there was little understanding in Palestine either of the situation in Europe as a whole or of their own situation in particular. It was, for example, extremely difficult to keep accurate books when quasi-legal and illegal operations were involved, or to adhere to the demands of the punctilious Swiss authorities.

At the beginning of 1943, contacts were established between Geneva and the Yishuv emissaries who began arriving in Istanbul. Most of the funds and correspondence from the Yishuv now went through Istanbul, and not necessarily because of postal difficulties. The representatives in Geneva assumed that their colleagues in Istanbul were better able to explain the needs and the possibilities of rescue operations from Geneva because of their frequent visits to Palestine. Indeed, in May the Agency discussed the situation in Geneva and assigned Barlas to organize a joint committee in Geneva parallel to the Rescue Committee in Jerusalem.[21]

In 1943 personal disputes broke out among the emissaries in Geneva; each accused the other of doing "whatever he likes, especially if the other dislikes it." Barlas tried unsuccessfully to reconcile them. Soon relations also deteriorated between Geneva and Istanbul, with the emissaries accusing each other of putting sectarian needs above the general good and of trying to dominate and to concentrate authority in too few hands. Jewish leaders in occupied Europe expressed both appreciation for the contacts developed by the center in Geneva and disapproval of the petty party intrigues.[22] The emissaries themselves deplored the situation but continued to operate separately, according to Gerhard Riegner; Chaim Posner later described it not as a rescue mission, but as "a collection of individuals" with flawed personal relationships despite the absence of major political disagreements among them. In Palestine Agudat Yisrael condemned the inability of the Jewish Agency and the Rescue Committee to maintain order in such a central place as Geneva: "It is already a topic of public discussion. How many of the People of Israel have been lost because of it—I had better not say."[23]

This state of affairs rendered the establishment of a joint committee impossible. Although Gruenbaum and Barlas kept trying, it did not materialize until the end of the war. The Histadrut emissaries in

Istanbul, on the other hand, did manage to set up a committee in Geneva, consisting of Schwalb, Abraham Silberschein, Shmuel Scheps, and Posner. They remained in close touch with the Histadrut's Committee for Alleviating the Distress of Our Comrades in the Diaspora, headed by Melech Neustadt in Tel Aviv. These four emissaries felt that they did most of the work in Geneva; they were young, energetic, willing to take risks. They considered some of the others, particularly Lichtheim, to be too old, too cautious, too despondent.[24]

In Shertok's view, Geneva's great distance from Palestine played a role: "We have a center there, with a rather decent delegation, but they are cut off. We cannot prod them, activate them, guide them."[25] Indeed, contact between Geneva and Palestine remained indirect, and no JAE members went there during the war.

TURKEY

Istanbul, on the other hand, was the main center of espionage and political intrigue and the bridge between Europe and Asia. It also served as the bridge between Palestine and occupied Europe. Istanbul became the center of the Yishuv's rescue operations during the second half of 1940, when it became impossible to reach Palestine from Italy. The new main route for refugees—especially for those from Poland who reached Lithuania—was through the Soviet Union, Turkey, and Syria. Barlas, who had just returned to Palestine from Geneva, was sent to Istanbul to deal with the refugees passing through Turkey. Joseph Goldin had been there as head of the Agency's Palestine office since before the war, and from the beginning of 1941 on, representatives from Palestine visited Istanbul from time to time. In July 1942 Gruenbaum dispatched his assistant, Eliezer Leder, who had been in charge of collecting information from occupied Europe's press for the Committee of Four, to continue this work in neutral Istanbul, where more news was available.

In August 1942 the JAE came under pressure from the pioneering youth movements, which maintained close contacts with their members in occupied Europe, to send a strong delegation of their own people to Istanbul. Barlas objected, saying that too many emissaries would do more harm than good. The JAE supported him, assuming that a person with his experience would be able to do the work for all the movements and parties and that operations in Istanbul would be limited to "writing letters and telegrams . . . to Geneva."[26] In November 1942, when the Agency finally addressed the need for rescue, its attitude toward an Istanbul mission had changed. By the beginning of 1943 five emissaries joined Barlas and Leder.

Barlas was granted quasi-official status by the Turkish government as the representative of the Jewish Agency, but the operations of the other emissaries were considered illegal. Only government-authorized public activity was permitted. The emissaries had to pass themselves off as merchants or journalists and operate out of rented apartments and cheap hotels. There were numerous difficulties to cope with: the general disorder prevailing in Turkey, the suspicions of the authorities, difficulties with mail delivery (especially in transfer-ring money), censorship, the hostility of British officials (especially those affiliated with the embassy, and not with the army or intelli-gence), and the ubiquity of agents and spies.[27]

Each of the first seven emissaries (not including Goldin, whose post-ing to Turkey was permanent) was affiliated with another group in the Yishuv: the Immigration and Political Departments of the Jewish Agency, the Rescue Committee, Aliya Bet, and the Histadrut youth movements. In March 1943 the JAE attempted to establish one gen-eral delegation of the Yishuv, to be headed by Barlas and Menachem Bader, the senior member among the new emissaries.

The presence of seven emissaries from the Yishuv did not, however, satisfy all the parties and organizations in Palestine. Each wanted to send its own representative to Istanbul "to look through the opening and greet his comrades," as Neustadt put it. He believed that each emissary could serve some purpose. Barlas and the other emissaries already in Istanbul continued to object on the grounds that greater numbers would make it difficult to coordinate operations and to maintain the necessary secrecy.[28]

Teddy Kollek, a representative of the Agency's Political Depart-ment, told the Histadrut Executive when he returned in October 1943 that some of the emissaries were unsuitable for their jobs; not all kept things confidential, not all had been equally educated to take risks or make sacrifices. He believed that four or five emissaries were enough to do the job and that the others should return to Palestine. At least fewer people, then, could get in the way. David Remez replied, reflect-ing the anger of some of his comrades. "Neither we [the Histadrut] nor they [the JAE] can redress this. We do not control the Revisionists; we cannot tell the bourgeois Zionists [the Religious and the General Zionists] that only we [the Labor movement] can do the job and that they are good for nothing. It is very hard to get any party to accept such a verdict."[29]

The Rescue Committee and the Immigration Department concluded that "in the present state of affairs, the dispatch of emissaries by various institutions in the Yishuv should not be prevented; however, a way must be found to define their respective areas of operation." By the end of 1943 there were sixteen emissaries in Istanbul. Still, not everyone was satisfied.[30]

In August 1943 Shertok visited Istanbul and, upon his return, told the JAE that there was "great confusion in terms of the personal composition, the institutions, and the constitutional character" of the delegation, and that this was detrimental to the operation and to relations between the emissaries; if the JAE wanted to remain in control, changes would have to be made. In addition to limiting the delegation to three or four emissaries, a senior representative would have to be appointed to direct political contacts with the Allies in Istanbul, since the end of the war seemed to be near. In his opinion, it was also of paramount importance to help organize and direct the survivors, whose attitude toward the Zionist enterprise could determine its fate after the war.

Most of the difficulties could apparently be traced to two major sources. The emissaries favored more energetic, illegal undertakings and considered Barlas (a General Zionist and the eldest) to be too cautious in his dealings with the Turkish authorities. And there were the usual frictions between members of the Labor parties and the others—including Revisionists and the Religious Zionists. Still, Shertok praised all the emissaries for investing "great stores of emotion" in their work.[31]

Shertok's recommendations were not accepted. Nor was another suggestion that JAE members take three-month tours of duty in Istanbul. Instead, in November the Agency established a council of eight members there despite fears that confidentiality might suffer. It also decided that all material sent to the occupied areas would bear the symbolic signature "My Homeland" rather than that of any one emissary from the various organizations, to help convey "the general, all-Yishuv character of the rescue operation."[32]

It seemed that a way had been found to strengthen the operation in Turkey and reduce conflicts. But at the end of 1943 a severe crisis erupted in Istanbul, with reverberations that reached not only Jerusalem and Tel Aviv but also occupied Europe. The "inner circle" of emissaries, who controlled clandestine operations, among their other tasks transmitted letters from Jews in occupied Europe to Palestine. An emissary not in this inner circle accused one of them of deleting, from letters describing uprising in the ghettos, the names of activists and fighters belonging to movements other than his own. The result was an uproar in Palestine. An immediate investigation of the scandal was demanded. Mutual recrimination was the order of the day. "We cannot yet act as one people," declared Ben-Gurion regretfully. Sprinzak was harsher: "If Frumka and Zivia [F. Plotnicka and Z. Lubetkin, two known ghetto fighters], who put their lives on the line every day without a thought, have to read about partisan intrigues, then this is a criminal incident."[33]

Shaul Meirov, head of the Mossad for Aliya Bet and considered a moral authority in the Yishuv, reluctantly agreed to look into the matter. In his final report he severely criticized all the emissaries, especially the older ones, for allowing relations to deteriorate to such an extent. He also criticized the JAE and the Histadrut for not sending someone with authority to Istanbul. Barlas, in his opinion, did not have either the necessary stature or the ideological authority. On the other hand, he rejected all accusations about deleting names from letters. Meirov's report ended the crisis.[34]

Toward the end of the year Aryeh Altman, the Revisionist leader, returned from Istanbul and proposed, as others had before, that one member of the JAE be present in Istanbul on a regular basis and that an authoritative delegation representative of the whole Jewish people be dispatched to Istanbul. Altman, like Shertok, thought that such a delegation should not limit its activities to rescue but should take advantage of the political contacts available in Istanbul for the benefit of the Yishuv after the war. The Rescue Committee felt that the main tasks of such a delegation should be to secure the lives of Jews in the Balkans and to obtain permission from the Turkish authorities to allow as many people as possible to pass through their country. In January 1944 the JAE decided not to send a delegation to Istanbul but instead to send someone who could stand up to Altman, should he return. The person chosen was Mordechai Eliash, a well-known jurist but not a member of the JAE.

It was left to Shertok to explain to Barlas, who kept objecting to new emissaries and short-term visitors, why Eliash was being sent. It was, he said,

> the result of a feeling that had been growing stronger and stronger among members of the Executive, and in the Yishuv in general, that we were not doing everything in our power to exploit all the possibilities for rescue. We received complaints from all sides over the absence of regular representation in Ankara that would keep its eyes open at all times . . . We could not see any reason not to agree to this demand and decided, for the time being, to make a onetime effort by sending someone [to Turkey] for a certain period.[35]

Thus the JAE's decision was the result of prolonged public pressure. But the JAE was also concerned to forestall the Revisionists from sending Altman again, who would then be the senior Yishuv personality in Istanbul.

Not only political controversies created conflicts regarding representation in Istanbul. Once a representative of Yugoslavian Jewry, Meir Tuval, reached Istanbul, Bulgarian, Rumanian, Dutch, Hungarian, and Greek immigrants in Palestine increased their pressure on the JAE, the Rescue Committee, and the Immigration Department. The Bulgarians claimed, for instance, that the emissaries in Istanbul were not sending information to Palestine regarding the situation of Bulgarian Jews; they declared that they were being discriminated against because they were Sephardim (Jews of Middle Eastern and Mediterranean origin) while Ashkenazim (Jews of European origin) were being given preferential treatment by those in charge. They demanded that the Agency "include Bulgaria in the list of countries whose Jews are its responsibility," implying that such was not the case at present.[36]

These claims, repeatedly aired during 1943, call for some comment. First, it is doubtful that the JAE discriminated against Sephardic Jews in Europe in matters of rescue. The Bulgarian immigrants' perceptions of discrimination probably had more to do with absorption difficulties they encountered in Palestine among the largely Ashkenazi Yishuv. Second, at that very time emissaries were sending a good deal of information about the situation in Bulgaria and the other countries in question. The Agency had long been convinced that the Balkans were the main gateway for rescue and immigration, and great efforts were being made to use it. The real problem was the lack of communication between the JAE and the new-immigrants' associations. The failure to share information with new immigrants may have stemmed from a certain disregard for their opinions and a sense of remoteness from them. The immigrants' complaints also undoubtedly reflected general frustration at the meager results of the rescue efforts.

Gruenbaum, to whom many of the demands of the new-immigrants' associations were addressed in his capacity as chairman of the Rescue Committee, admitted that the JAE knew that too many emissaries were being sent to Istanbul. However, because the associations were "restless and distrustful," they had to be mollified. After a prolonged discussion, Yitzhak Mitrani left in February 1944 as the representative of the Bulgarian Jews. In March, following Germany's occupation of Hungary, the JAE agreed to send representatives of the

Hungarian and the Rumanian immigrants. Apparently these representatives did not go, either because of the rapid changes in the Balkans and the advance of the Russians or because of political and personal disputes within the new-immigrants' associations. By 1944 more than twenty emissaries had operated in Istanbul at one time or another, besides numerous individuals sent by families in Palestine to get their relatives out.[37]

In the spring of 1944 Ira Hirschmann, the representative of the U.S. War Refugee Board who had been appointed by Roosevelt at the beginning of that year to conduct rescue operations, arrived in Istanbul. So did Eri Jabotinsky, a senior member of Etzel's New York–based Emergency Committee to Save the Jews of Europe. Joseph Klarman, the Revisionist on the Rescue Committee, grew tired of its impotence and also went to Istanbul. Together with Ya'acov Griffle of Agudat Yisrael, who acted in Istanbul on behalf of the Committee of Orthodox Rabbis in Switzerland, Klarman initiated independent activities to acquire a vessel with money from the United States.

In view of all these developments as well as the increase in the number of emissaries and representatives in Istanbul, Barlas, Kaplan, and Judah-Leib Magnes established a broad-based council supported by Laurence Steinhardt, the U.S. ambassador in Ankara, himself a Jew. The council elected eight committees and a steering committee headed by Hirschmann. Barlas was elected chairman of the council, Menachem Bader its secretary and deputy chairman. Kaplan described the council as a "promising tool" for coordinating operations sponsored by the U.S. embassy, the War Refugee Board, the JDC, and the Yishuv. A detailed, formally worded agreement specified work procedures and participation in committees, granted equal rights and responsibilities to all emissaries, and avoided duplication in matters of finance and immigration. The lessons of the past had apparently been learned. Another agreement specified the roles of Klarman and Griffle.[38]

Once again, as in the cases of the financial agreement signed by the JDC and the JAE in July 1944 and the rescue committee set up in Lisbon, the resolution of these problems came very late in the war and very late in the process of extermination.

Upon his return, Kaplan tried to convince the JAE that the situation in Istanbul was critical. A large office had been set up there, he said, and the fate of thousands of people was dependent on it. Hundreds of thousands of pounds were being spent, including considerable sums from the Yishuv. It was therefore unacceptable that the Agency should continue to refuse to send a responsible and authoritative person to assist Barlas, who was very tired after four years on the job. Such a person was needed more than ever before because of the possibility of saving thousands of Jews (mainly from Hungary). This was "an unprecedented situation, which may never come again. If we don't take advantage of it, it will be an unforgivable sin."[39]

Such a person was never sent. By the end of the summer Istanbul's role as a rescue center was nearing its end; the front was receding, and the Russians' advance into the Balkans had opened a new chapter in the war.

MEANS OF RESCUE

In most cases the Yishuv organizations dealt with rescue operations from Geneva and Istanbul when emissaries returned from Turkey to collect money and to consult leaders or when a leader visited Istanbul. During 1943 and 1944 the JAE, the Rescue Committee, the Histadrut Executive, and the Mapai Central Committee met with emissaries and returning visitors at least once a month, and usually two or three times a month, to discuss actual rescue operations in Geneva and Istanbul: the dispatch of food and money, the provision of documents, the crossing of borders, and specific rescue plans.

Food Parcels

After the first months of the war the Yishuv emissaries began sending food parcels from Geneva to Poland and western Europe. Ready-made parcels of food were ordered from non-Jewish companies that bought the products in Switzerland, Yugoslavia, and Portugal, packed them, and sent them to the addresses supplied to them. It was possible to send these packages through the regular mail as long as Jews still lived at their original addresses. By 1942, shipping methods had been improved. Yitzhak Weissman, together with Schwalb and Silber-schein, obtained a permit to send parcels through the Portuguese Red Cross and even to insure them. Soon parcels were also being sent to areas of the Reich, Italy, and Croatia. Zionist activists and members of the various youth movements were the first recipients of the several hundred parcels sent every year from 1940 through 1942.

Early in 1943 the emissaries tried to organize shipments on a larger scale. They were encouraged by the willingness of the International Red Cross to send aid to the ghettos once the Germans allowed that organization to resume operations in occupied Europe. Despite fears that this was merely a German plot, the emissaries requested large sums of money from the Yishuv for this purpose. Their feeling was that, even if only 30 to 40 percent of the parcels reached their destination, it was worth the effort. In January the Jewish Agency decided to express its "willingness, in advance, to give money for any practical proposal of aid to the Diaspora."[40]

Some emissaries asked the JAE about the "key" for the distribution of the parcels among the various groups and individuals. The party key was a central concept in the Yishuv and the Zionist movement. Immigration permits and all Zionist budgets for education and training abroad and settlement in Palestine were distributed according to the relative strength of the parties in the movement or as a result of interparty bargaining and negotiations.

Other emissaries, such as Barlas, Venia Pomerantz, and Lichtheim, objected to using the key at such a time: "We have to adhere now to a clear position of helping any Jew who can still be helped, regardless of partisan or other affiliation." The International Red Cross could not and should not be expected to check "who is a Zionist and who belongs to Poalei Zion." The key was a concept that belonged to "the days before the flood of decrees and extermination." Gruenbaum suggested that the JAE cancel the key immediately. His proposal was not put on the agenda although it dealt with a central question, perhaps second in importance only to the question of whom to get out of the occupied areas.[41]

It appears from the correspondence that any such formal discussion in the JAE was unnecessary. Dobkin and Neustadt, who agreed with Gruenbaum and felt sure that their other colleagues did too, instructed the emissaries in Istanbul and Geneva to disregard the key and to send the parcels to all organizations and local committees in the ghettos and other Jewish areas.[42] Still, canceling the key—even just as an official, symbolic gesture—might have been a turning point for the Zionist movement, especially in its relations with the Diaspora.

The shipments of parcels continued into the spring of 1943. Although hundreds were lost or fell into German hands, many hundreds more, mainly those sent from Lisbon, Geneva, and Istanbul, reached their destinations. From the responses they received, the emissaries felt that they were giving strength to tens of thousands of people. In the summer of 1943, 200 five-kilogram parcels were sent every month from Geneva to Poland. For half a year parcels were sent every month to the "exemplary ghetto" of Theresienstadt, established by the Germans in the Protectorate of Bohemia and Moravia, allegedly for the old, for war veterans, and for prominent Jews from the Reich and from western Europe. Confirmation of the arrival of these parcels, and of others sent to France, reached Geneva.[43]

During 1943 sending parcels became more difficult. The Allies objected to the dispatch of large shipments that might fall into the hands of the Germans or their allies; fewer and fewer Jews could be located at reliable addresses: the remnant of European Jewry was scattered in camps, forests, and hideaways. It was hardest to operate in those hunger-stricken areas most in need, such as the General Government area in Poland and in Transnistria, in the southern Ukraine. There were also financial difficulties. Until then, most of the funding for the parcels was supplied by the Yishuv; the cost of each parcel, including shipping and insurance, was about five pounds, at that time the equivalent of a week's salary in Palestine. The JDC was not yet involved in the rescue budget; the parcel project was supported by the World Jewish Congress and by refugee committees in various countries.

Only after August 1943, when the JDC began to help finance rescue operations, was the project really extended. In 1944 more parcels were sent from Lisbon to more places. After exasperating negotiations, the government of Turkey gave Barlas a onetime permit to send 250 tons of food to any country he wanted. He decided to send 50,000 five-kilogram parcels—valued at a total of $1 million to Poland and Transnistria. The International Red Cross got permission from the Germans to distribute the parcels in Poland, and Barlas made it a condition that a local Jewish representative or one appointed from Istanbul would participate in the distribution. The funding was supplied by the JDC, and all arrangements were made by the emissaries. Because of wartime conditions, the undertaking was an immense bureaucratic and organizational tangle, and the correspondence connected with it is voluminous.

The first shipment was made in January 1944; four freight cars of food and warm clothing left for Transnistria and one left for Theresienstadt. As the Russians moved closer, the ensuing chaos frustrated hopes of sending more food to Transnistria. As for Poland, at the end of 1943 the National Jewish Committee in Warsaw sent warnings that the permit given to the International Red Cross to distribute aid in Poland was a hoax and was being used to transfer money and goods from the Jews of the free world to the Germans; further shipments should be forwarded only through the Polish government-in-exile.[44]

The issue of the party key continued to resurface. Representatives of the Revisionists and Agudat Yisrael in the Rescue Committee claimed that, despite the unequivocal decision to discard the key, it was still very much alive and as a result their members in Europe were being shortchanged in the distribution of aid. The other parties considered these claims hypocritical; the Revisionists, they said, had collected money separately and sent it to Klarman in Istanbul, and Agudat Yisrael was continuing its own fundraising, both in Palestine and abroad. It was precisely because the two parties refused to cooperate with the others—and not as a result of discrimination—that aid was denied them in Europe. Klarman and Griffle ultimately settled these matters with the other emissaries, and in mid-1944 Klarman informed Kaplan that he had no more complaints concerning discrimination in the extension of aid or partisan use of funds. The Aguda activists, however, were not appeased, and conflicts erupted between them and the representatives of the other parties, especially in Rumania and Hungary, until the end of the war.[45]

In fact, given the circumstances, both the key and the lists of addresses were becoming utterly insignificant. When Barlas was asked, at the end of a heated debate in the Rescue Committee at the end of 1943, to whom the parcels were being sent, he answered simply, "We send them to anyone who has a definite address." Although an accurate evaluation is hard to make, the Yishuv seems to have been involved in the dispatch of at least 100,000 parcels, contributing some tens of thousands of pounds to their purchase.[46]

Money

The money that the emissaries transferred to occupied Europe came from three sources: Palestine, loans, and Jewish organizations. The money from Palestine was not always readily available when needed. The emissaries in Istanbul and Geneva therefore developed a system of loans, mainly from wealthy local Jews and, through them, from banks. The loans were returned, whenever possible, when funds arrived from Palestine. This method could be used in only a limited and discreet way, and the possibilities dwindled as the war went on. Among the various Jewish organizations, the first and foremost was the JDC, whose activists, unlike its executive in New York, made confidential arrangements with Yishuv emissaries in neutral countries.

British regulations forbade taking money out of Palestine, let alone transferring it to occupied Europe. Therefore, it was necessary to smuggle it out, and this was done, for the most part, by the emissaries, who took cash and precious stones with them each time they left the country. The next stage was getting the money into the neutral countries, all of which had strict currency regulations. Large sums could not, of course, be transferred without the authorities' knowledge, and complicated bank transactions had to be devised.

About 740,000 Palestinian pounds collected for rescue from the three sources were sent to occupied Europe and the satellites from or through Istanbul or Geneva. The money transferred was mostly in hard currencies—gold coins, and even diamonds—and was usually smuggled in by the same couriers who delivered written material from Palestine and from the emissaries in neutral countries.

The money was used in occupied Europe for purposes such as finding channels of communication, buying clothes or food, acquiring documents, crossing borders, obtaining arms, and bribing officials. Sometimes the money was spent solely at the discretion of the local community or at the discretion of the emissaries in Istanbul and in Geneva in consultation with the activists in occupied Europe. (See Table 3.)

As time went on and contacts with the occupied countries became more tenuous, the couriers found it increasingly difficult to find any more Jews. Still, the emissaries continued to forward money, whenever possible, to whoever was still organized and in contact with other Jews through youth movements, local committees, or similar organizations. Although the Yishuv was raising more and more money for rescue, the emissaries were not always able to get it to its destination. "How tragic it is, that when the Yishuv in Palestine musters all its financial strength to help, we do not have ways of transferring the aid," said emissary Ze'ev Shind.[47]

The bookkeeping and paperwork involved in the transfer of funds were of necessity minimal. For security reasons no receipts were kept. Barlas kept the books concerning immigration, and Bader kept a record of funds and parcels dispatched, illegal border crossings, and the like. But the system was necessarily based on mutual, personal trust among the emissaries and between them and the institutions in the Yishuv. According to a representative of the JDC who checked the bookkeeping, the operation was properly and honestly conducted.[48]

Documents

The provision of documents was another means of extending aid. The passport of a neutral country, a visa for a neutral country, an immigration permit to Palestine, or even a document confirming that such a permit existed might save a Jew from deportation or make him a candidate for exchange with Germans. The question was how to help without causing damage. The discovery of a forgery could have disastrous results for everyone involved. The Germans' behavior was unpredictable. Sometimes a forged passport worked; at other times, a legitimate one did not. More than once the valid passport of a neutral or Allied country was torn to pieces in front of the owner's eyes. It was, as Barlas said, "a tragic dilemma."[49]

At the beginning of 1943 the emissaries began collecting photographs and personal details in order to provide Jews in occupied Europe with forged documents. At the same time, Jews in Europe found out that documents of South and Central American countries with large German expatriate populations could be a preferable solution. Fearing reprisals after the war, many Germans were anxious to be returned home, and they could be offered in exchange for people held by the Germans in Europe. The passport or even the promise of one

Table 3. Aid from the Yishuv to Europe, 1943–1944

Destination	Value (Palestinian pounds)	Main purposes
Bulgaria	17,000	Public kitchens; releasing youth from forced labor
France, Holland, Belgium, and Theresienstadt	53,000	General aid
Greece (mainly Athens)	3,275	Smuggling people out through the Greek underground[a]
Hungary	135,000	Transfer and upkeep of refugees
Italy and Croatia	7,000	General aid
Poland	85,000	Food, arms[b]
Rumania	165,000	Releasing members of movements from prison; general aid
Slovakia	100,000	Bribes and maintenance of camps
Transnistria	30,000	Food and clothing

Sources: Eliyahu Dobkin, *Immigration and Rescue in the Years of the Holocaust* (Jerusalem, 1946) (in Hebrew), p. 103; Melech Neustadt, ed., *Destruction and Revolt of the Warsaw Jews* (Tel Aviv, 1947) (in Hebrew), pp. 128–145, 184; Rescue Committee, Oct. 3, 1944, file S26/1238a, Central Zionist Archive, Jerusalem; Menachem Bader, *Sad Missions,* rev. ed. (Tel Aviv, 1978) (in Hebrew), pp. 63, 85; letters from Athens, Sept. 9 and 21, 1943, file S26/1203, Central Zionist Archive; Bader in Histadrut Secretariat, May 13, 1943, and Aug. 2, 1944, file 15/40, Histradrut Archives, Tel Aviv; Benjamin Arditi, *Bulgarian Jews and the Nazi Regime, 1940–1944* (Holon, 1962), p. 313; Menachem Schelach, "The Murder of Jews in Croatia by the Germans and Their Assistants in World War II" (Ph.D. diss., Tel Aviv University, 1980), p. 312; Jewish Agency Executive, June 13 and Oct. 4, 1943, Central Zionist Archive; Adina Kochva, *In the Pioneering Underground in Occupied Holland* (Tel Aviv, 1969) (in Hebrew), p. 208.
a. For every Jew saved, one pound sterling in gold was paid in Istanbul.
b. About one-third of the aid sent reached Warsaw.

(once details reached the Central and South American consuls in neutral countries) was issued readily. The representatives of Agudat Yisrael in Switzerland may have been the first to discover the generosity of these consuls and acquired many passports for their members in Poland. Schwalb handed a written commitment to the South American ambassadors in Switzerland that the passports were requested only for the duration of the war and would not be used by their holders to remain permanently in South or Central America, if they ever got there.[50]

Tens of thousands of such passports were sent, mainly from Geneva, by Schwalb and Silberschein. Many saved lives, but others doomed their holders. Although the passports were issued by the consuls, sometimes their governments refused to confirm them. This happened to the people who arrived from Poland at the transit camp of Vittel, in France (among them the poet Yitzhak Katznelson), ostensibly for exchange. These people were eventually sent to Auschwitz. In late 1943, when word came that these passports were also causing harm, the emissaries decided—first in Geneva and then in Istanbul—to discontinue using them. Only at the end of May 1944 did the passports receive official retroactive validation.

In the spring of 1944 Jews in the Balkans and in Hungary began receiving confirmation of the existence of immigration permits for them. Their names were on lists that came from Palestine and from their own countries. Confirmation of being on such a list was issued by representatives of the Vatican, the Swiss government, the International Red Cross, and the British Consulate in Istanbul (which had approved of this action in May 1944). Seven thousand such confirmations were sent to Bulgaria, 18,500 to Hungary, and 9,000 to Rumania. Because each confirmation was for a family, a much larger number of people could be saved. Thousands of similar confirmations were also sent to France, Holland, and Belgium and to internees in concentration camps, notably Bergen-Belsen, which was considered a camp in which the Germans kept Jews intended to be exchanged.[51]

The permits did not actually assure immigration. On the contrary, the Immigration Department of the Jewish Agency promised Eric Mills, the director of the mandatory government's Immigration Department, that the confirmations would not serve as a basis for immigration requests—only as a means of protecting people from deportation and the death camps.[52] The permits became increasingly valuable to those who held them in 1944 when the satellites sought ways of making overtures to the victorious Allies.

At the end of 1944 emissaries in Geneva made great efforts to obtain documents of protection for Jews of Budapest who had received confirmations. This undertaking would not have succeeded without the initiative of the Swedish government representative, Raoul Wallenberg, and the Swiss consul, Charles Lutz, and, to a lesser extent, the help of the International Red Cross and the pope. Swiss and Swedish certificates of protection saved tens of thousands of Jews from the death marches to Austria and Germany. Following this success, requests for more confirmations reached Geneva from Hungary.[53]

It is hard to estimate just how many people were saved by the forged passports, the South American passports, and the confirmation-of-immigration permits, or how many of the tens of thousands who received these documents actually survived until the last stages of the war. Many individuals and groups did not wait for documents to arrive from the outside but attempted to buy or forge them themselves. In a few cases, Yishuv emissaries supplied the money to acquire the papers in occupied areas and satellite countries. Transfer of documents to occupied areas was done regardless of party key or any other partisan consideration, or even whether the recipients had any intention of immigrating to Palestine.

Illegal Crossing of Borders

Sometimes Jews in immediate danger escaped to neutral countries, sometimes to less dangerous areas where there was a temporary lull before extermination was started or resumed. The emissaries referred to this kind of escape as moving from the seventh circle of hell to the sixth.

Two main escape routes were used during the war. The first, in western Europe, was from Germany to Belgium and the Netherlands. After these countries were occupied, the route was extended to France and on to Switzerland or Spain. The second route, in eastern Europe, led from Poland to Slovakia (after the transports from there were stopped in October 1942), and from there to Hungary. There was an alternate route from Poland to Old Rumania—the Regat—in which there was also relative calm after the pogroms and deportations of 1940 and 1941. Some Jews escaped from Poland to the Reich areas, where, paradoxically, some Jews continued to live among the German population during 1941 and 1942. Jews also escaped from Yugoslavia and Greece to Italy or to areas under Italian control, since the Italians were known for their humane attitude.

Escape was usually by foot, wagon, or other primitive means of transportation. Because of the war, borders were strongly guarded. Refugees were considered a nuisance almost everywhere, and in many cases even the guides paid to smuggle refugees out took their fee and then robbed and deserted them. Crossing borders illegally was primarily for the young and strong. It was extremely dangerous, expensive, and risky for those who helped.

The emissaries decided to risk funds in bribing smugglers and border guards. Subsistence for the newly arrived was usually supplied by local Jews. Some of the bona fide couriers with relative freedom of movement who had carried money and written material to the occupied areas also helped in this type of work or found others to do it.

The emissaries also encouraged and then kept track of the creation of a network of Jewish smugglers; predominantly members of the pioneering movements, they risked their lives repeatedly to lead others to safety. Yishuv emissaries worked with local Jewish organizations to approach the satellite countries, especially through their secret services, which were often based in the neutral countries, and to persuade them to help by hiding Jews and allowing refugees without papers and a source of livelihood to remain in their countries.[54]

In the summer of 1943, after the liquidation of the ghettos, the number of Jews escaping from Poland to Hungary through Slovakia increased; in the fall, several dozen were arriving daily. The emissaries sent word to Palestine that "the extent of this operation depends on the amount of money available. If you send twice as much—we will bring out twice as many." Gruenbaum answered Barlas that these "trips," as they were referred to in correspondence with occupied Europe, would not be cut even though the costs were high. For example, smuggling out a Jew who had no specific address cost the 1989 equivalent of $1380. Smuggling a person specified by name and destination cost the 1989 equivalent of $6,900.[55]

Exactly how much money the Yishuv contributed for this activity is almost impossible to guess. The emissaries played a major role in organizing its operation and expedition. Their share, both financial and organizational, was especially large in eastern Europe, but smaller in western Europe, particularly Spain, where other Jewish organizations shouldered most of the burden.

EVALUATION

The emissaries in both Geneva and Istanbul, especially Meirov, continually stressed that if a group of bold young people was sent to operate in Spain and in Sweden, operations could be extended and improved. And indeed the facts seem to indicate that with sufficiently large groups in all the neutral countries, operations would have been more effective.

Istanbul was made the center of the Yishuv's rescue operations in the neutral countries. Was this because its location facilitated rescue operations and the extension of help, or because it could serve as an immigration route to Palestine? In other words, was the primary consideration rescue or Zionism? According to Shertok, Istanbul's physical proximity made it the only place that could function as a center directly operated from Palestine: "From our Jewish point of view, Istanbul cannot be compared to Geneva, Stockholm, or Lisbon. Geneva is besieged, Stockholm and Lisbon are far away; but to Istanbul we can send people, there is mail . . . there is distinct contact between us and them. We can provide them with instructions and inspire Jewish Europe through them." [56] Given the circumstances at the time, his explanation is apparently correct. However, it also seems that little effort was invested in attempts to activate the other centers.

As for the frequently strained relations among emissaries from the various movements and parties, most of them were very young and intensely partisan—as was the Yishuv as a whole. Lichtheim and Barlas, who held official positions and were older and more legalistic, were not totally accepted by the younger emissaries. The kibbutzim members and youth movement leaders tended to involve themselves in the more daring, unconventional, less legal activities with a conspiratorial flavor. Akiva Levinsky, the Youth Immigration emissary in Istanbul, later explained the feeling of exclusion felt by some emissaries as a result of "the secrecy that veiled Avigur and the people of Aliya Bet and their feeling that they were the avant-garde and that the illegal immigration and the revolt in Europe were their own private concern." Yet "each did a good job and was devoted heart and soul. Looking back, one can cite many instances of a good spirit of cooperation." [57]

There is no doubt that partisanship and age differences did complicate this devotion, but did it actually hurt the rescue work and reduce its chances of success? The answer appears to be no. A survey of the efforts made from Istanbul and Geneva reveals how complex the situation was and how limited the possibilities. Many attempts ended in failure. Relations among the emissaries themselves were a marginal problem, not a central one.

Why did the JAE decide against sending a member to work in Istanbul on a permanent basis, as both the emissaries and the public in

Palestine repeatedly suggested, even after it was clear that extensive activities were developing there? The prevalent feeling in the Agency Executive was that it lacked enough able members to handle all the urgent problems. Ben-Gurion handled the general problems of the "state-in-the-making," Shertok was mainly in charge of mobilization into the British army and the establishment of the Jewish Brigade within it, and Kaplan was in charge of finances. According to Yehiel Duvdvani, a member of the Mapai Central Committee, Ben-Gurion decided that Katznelson and Meirov would share responsibility for rescue efforts; Katznelson would be in charge of the spiritual and educational aspects of rescue (though there are very few signs of such activity on his part); and Meirov would supervise the practical work. Since no one else was as knowledgeable about the situation as Meirov, another person was unnecessary.[58]

Although it was never stated in so many words, it is possible that in 1943, when there seemed to be few rescue possibilities, the JAE thought that sending a member to work in Istanbul full-time would be a waste. In 1944, when possibilities increased, the expectation was that the emissaries could manage by themselves, with financial and political support from Palestine. The rescue work gave those involved much pain and very little satisfaction. Any member of the JAE who chose to devote himself to it for a long period would have had to cut himself off from the Yishuv and especially from the department he headed, entrusting it—at least temporarily—to someone else.

Today the former emissaries continue to believe, as they did at the time, that the Yishuv leaders should have made greater efforts. Yet they continue to respect those leaders; rarely do they express harsh criticism, as Schwalb did in a recent departure from his usual practice: "Their heads were reeling with Zionism."[59] They are also severe in evaluating their own work: "If you ask me today what we accomplished," Pomerantz said, "I will tell you very briefly—almost nothing." Their achievements were minute in proportion to the Holocaust. More important was the symbolic value of the existence of a contact for those in need of help. "The fact that we stayed in our places when the war broke out and didn't leave until the last day gave people tremendous encouragement," said Schwalb. Pomerantz agreed. "The one thing we did was we were there, we were an address."[60]

11

Political Negotiations

One basic assumption prevalent in the Yishuv at the end of 1942 was that the Allied countries, governments and people alike, who considered Nazism diametrically opposed to everything they stood for, would not only condemn the systematic extermination of the Jews but also take action to stop it. Some of the large-scale rescue plans made in Palestine at the time therefore centered on appeals to the Allies. For these appeals to succeed, the Yishuv thought it useful to keep the Allies constantly aware of the severity of the situation and the urgency of rescue operations.

Thus, in November 1942, as soon as it had confirmed the fact of systematic extermination, the JAE issued appeals to a wide variety of organizations and individuals: political leaders in the United States, the Soviet Union, and Great Britain; governments-in-exile, most of which sat in London; the International Red Cross; all members of the U.S. Congress, the Supreme Soviet, and the British Parliament; labor organizations and labor parties, notably the British Labour party; the pope, the royal families of Europe, Eleanor Roosevelt, the archbishop of Canterbury, and hundreds of writers, journalists, and other spiritual leaders and public figures. Various organizations in the Yishuv—teachers, writers, women, and so on—independently approached their counterparts in other countries.

Through 1943 the Agency presented the Allied governments with several proposals for action in an attempt to stop the extermination. First, it asked the Allies to threaten Germany directly through broadcasts and leaflets dropped by air, warning that those involved in the murder of Jews would not escape punishment. Lists of names and evidence of their crimes were being compiled. Although the Germans themselves might ignore the threats, the peoples in the satellite countries, especially in the Balkans, might not. Even if these threats proved futile, their existence would encourage Jews in the occupied areas.

Second, the Allies were asked to urge the neutral countries to approach the German government officially, through the International Red Cross, requesting that they allow Jews, and especially children, to depart from the occupied areas into their territories and from there to any haven possible. The Allies would guarantee their maintenance in Switzerland, Sweden, or Spain, as well as their transfer elsewhere either within a reasonable period or after the war. Most of the costs would be covered by Jewish institutions, including the Jewish Agency.[1]

Third, the governments-in-exile were asked to deliver instructions to the populations of their countries, through underground broadcasts or by messengers, to help the Jewish population and to resist the German measures against the Jews. This request was addressed particularly to Wladyslaw Sikorski, the prime minister of the Polish government-in-exile in London, and to his deputy, Stanislaw Kot, during his visit to Palestine at the end of 1942.

Fourth, public figures and organizations were asked to do what they could to arouse the press and public opinion in their countries to pressure governments to take action.[2]

After the Allies' declaration on December 17, 1942, condemning the extermination, Yishuv leaders felt that more ideas should be presented to their governments. The first suggestion was that an international body be established to handle the rescue of Jews, or that this task be entrusted to an existing body, such as the Intergovernmental Committee for Refugees, which had been established after the Evian Conference in July 1938. At the same time, Henrietta Szold, head of Youth Immigration to Palestine and founder of the American Hadassah, a Jewish women's welfare organization, suggested that the latter ask Eleanor Roosevelt to preside over an international body for the rescue of children. The emissaries in Geneva asked the International Organization for the Child in Geneva to become involved in rescue operations.[3]

Meanwhile, safe havens for Jewish refugees were sought. Cyprus and North Africa were mentioned; Gruenbaum suggested that the JAE ask South Africa to allow Jewish children from Poland to enter, and not just non-Jewish Polish children as had been the case till then. The Polish government-in-exile promised that after the war anyone who had escaped from Poland would be able to return, so that the children could return to Poland if they were not transferred to Palestine. Ben-Gurion, Dov Joseph, and Zionist leaders in South Africa firmly opposed Gruenbaum's proposal, perhaps because they were anxious not to antagonize General Jan Smuts, the South African prime minister, who had previously been sympathetic to the interests of Zionism and the Yishuv. Indeed, when Gruenbaum talked to Smuts in the summer of 1943, his attitude to Zionism was still positive. Nonetheless, he absolutely refused to let Jewish children into his country.[4]

The Yishuv did not call for acts of retaliation against Germany, such as the bombing of German cities or the arrest of German citizens living in Allied countries. The first debate on this issue took place when Kot visited Palestine and suggested that the JAE join his government in putting pressure on the Allies to bomb the civilian population of German cities or, for every murdered Jew, to evict five Germans to some remote territory. Gruenbaum added his own proposal that the 1,500 Germans living in Palestine in the religious Templar communities founded in the nineteenth century be expelled and their property confiscated, or at least that the threat be made. Most members of the Executive, however, thought such proposals were pointless: "No democratic government would agree to [them], for they cannot follow Hitler's example." Ben-Gurion added that the Allies would not agree to being told when and where to bomb. The Agency turned down Kot's request and reminded him that so far Britain had refused to declare its bombings of Germany in 1941 and 1942 a retaliatory action lest the Germans in turn kill more Jews and Poles or torture captured British air crews. Such a declaration would also undermine the British claim that they were conducting a just war against military targets only.[5]

When the JAE began its series of appeals, it was cautiously optimistic about the Allies' responsiveness. Its main concern in late 1942 was not that the Allies would refuse to help in rescue operations—provided that such operations would not interfere with the war effort— but that the Germans would not be impressed by the threats. The hope was inevitably mixed with feelings of helplessness and frustration at the Yishuv's inability to act independently: "We are in a pitiful situation," said Ben-Gurion, "because we have to appeal to Roosevelt to do our job, and it is impossible to know whether or not he will." Soon doubts about the Allied response increased. JAE members concluded that "we accomplished practically nothing on all fronts." Ben-Gurion agreed: "Something is wrong, though not as a result of inactivity on our part."[6] As time went on, it became apparent that neither a severe warning to the Germans concerning the extermination nor a demand to let the Jews out would be forthcoming. There was not even progress in getting children out. No international or intergovernmental body for rescue was established, the warnings on the radio were

few and far between, and numerous other plans were not implemented. In short, the Allied declaration in December 1942 was not
followed by any action.

In January 1943 the appeals and telegrams were temporarily
halted, apparently because of the mistaken belief that the extermination in Poland was being stopped. In February, however, news again
arrived about the transportation of Jews from western Europe to the
death camps in the east and their continued operation. Another wave
of telegrams, protests, and appeals issued from Palestine. The British
public continued to criticize Whitehall's inaction. Some major newspapers and a few prominent figures such as the archbishop of Canterbury, William Temple, and M. P. Eleanor Rathbone, deputy chairman
of the National Committee for Rescue from Nazi Terrorism, were particularly critical. The British undersecretary of state for foreign affairs, Richard Law, admitted to the staff of the American embassy that
public pressure was forcing his government to give "some sort of an
answer." [7]

THE BERMUDA CONFERENCE

In response to public pressure the British government held a conference with U.S. officials on the refugee problem. The conference
opened on April 19 in Bermuda, but its results were a foregone conclusion, agreed upon by the participants in March. Both the British
and U.S. governments were convinced they had already done enough
to absorb refugees and decided not to change either the British White
Paper policy on Palestine or U.S. immigration policy. Britain's ambassador to the United States, Lord Halifax, warned the State Department that Germany and its satellites might "change from a policy of
extermination to one of extrusion . . . [and] aim at embarrassing other
countries by flooding them with immigrants." Senior officials in the
State Department shared his apprehension. Eden warned President
Roosevelt—who had told Jewish members of Congress of his willingness to demand that Hitler let the children out—that if Jews were
helped in one area, they would soon insist on being helped in others.
Furthermore, he said, the Germans would use the opportunity to
plant their agents among the refugees. Finally, the shortage of ships
made it a practical impossibility to transfer large numbers of people. [8]

Although the JAE was not privy to either the correspondence or the
behind-the-scenes moves, there were a few indications that the con

ference was not going to have any practical results. First, only Britain and the United States were taking part; representatives of other countries or of refugee or Jewish organizations were barred from it. Second, the conference was called to discuss refugee problems in general, rather than any specific one. Third, the British and American officials could control flight priorities and present press coverage.

In April 1943 Nahum Goldmann informed Gruenbaum in a letter that Stephen Wise, the president of the American Jewish Congress, and Judge Joseph Proskauer, the president of the American Jewish Committee, had met Eden when he visited the United States in late March. In response to the request of the American Zionist Emergency Council to demand that Germany stop the extermination and let the Jews out of the occupied areas, Eden said that the idea of approaching Germany was "fantastically impossible."[9] With this answer he effectively ruled out the primary demand basic to all appeals made until then—namely, that the Allies approach the Germans regarding the situation of the Jews. From then on it was quite clear that the Bermuda Conference was going to be no more than empty rhetoric.

Moshe Shertok was in the United States at the time and, at a meeting with State Department officials, asked them point blank, "What do you need Bermuda for? If you want to do anything, the two governments have to make a decision . . . the conference is merely a cover-up." Their answer, as reported by Shertok, was frank. Hitler could not be approached because, as Eden had already said, it was "beneath our dignity," and "it will not help; Hitler will not release anyone." Furthermore, "if he does release hundreds of thousands or a million Jews—what shall we do with them, where shall we take them?"[10]

Apparently the JAE, neither realized nor discussed the full implications of these remarks: the Allied governments had no intention of making any effort on behalf of the Jews in the occupied countries. On the contrary, the Allies would have considered their release by the Germans exceedingly troublesome.

The JAE did conclude that there was no point either in Shertok's remaining in the United States after the conference opened or in anyone else's trying to get an exit visa and a flight to Bermuda. Instead, it decided to have Zionist leaders in London ask members of Parliament and non-Jews who were active in rescue matters to send an unofficial delegation of their own to the conference. It also resolved to "urge our comrades in America to take action" by sending memoranda to Bermuda about Palestine's capacity to absorb refugees and about the existence of other havens. All memoranda were to be sent to Shertok, who would coordinate efforts with the American Zionist Emergency Council. Shertok would also hold a press conference to publicize the demands of the Yishuv.[11]

The Histadrut Secretariat found these decisions unsatisfactory and demanded that Shertok drop everything else and "spend the month in Bermuda," and that the Yishuv issue another series of appeals to labor unions and other organizations abroad. Leading Zionists from London and New York should go to Bermuda in an unofficial Jewish delegation even though it was not certain that they would be given a hearing. Enschel Reiss, who devoted most of his time to rescue, protested that "we have not yet done anything concerning Bermuda." But the Agency stuck by its decisions,[12] including rejection of the idea of a protest demonstration before the Bermuda Conference opened.

The Rescue Committee appointed a forum to formulate a memorandum to be submitted to the Bermuda Conference, and a consensus was reached on the main points: stopping the extermination, getting the Jews out of occupied Europe, and sustaining them. There were differences of opinion, however, on whether the issue of Zionism should be kept separate from rescue matters. Joseph Klarman, the Revisionist representative, maintained that "the problem of the refugees is a Zionist problem; it is a political problem." Therefore, a demand to revoke the White Paper should be submitted with the demand to stop the extermination. Menachem Landau, a historian and public figure who was invited to participate in this forum, favored giving up "the attempt to use this conference for Zionist purposes" and limiting efforts "to matters of rescue only" for the present.

Landau tried to bring his colleagues to a balanced view of the situation. In his opinion, the Bermuda Conference was going to be neither a panacea nor a total loss. Instead of an outpouring of "help" cables to institutions and individuals all over the world, Landau recommended a thorough and meticulous check of all possibilities for transit, shipping provisions, absorption of refugees in various places, and cooperation with other nations persecuted by the Germans. Landau's proposals were based on the assumption that "the sympathy of the superpowers with our disaster is sincere, and their intentions are serious." The main problem was to overcome the practical obstacles to swift rescue operations.[13]

Compromise brought an agreement on seven proposals to be submitted to the Bermuda Conference. First, the Allies should ask the Axis to allow Jews to leave the territories under their control, either unilaterally or through exchange. Second, refuge for the duration should be assured for those leaving the occupied areas, either in Allied or neutral countries or in their colonies, and the governments of the occupied countries should guarantee that the refugees would be allowed to return after the war. Third, the Jewish people would pay the cost of transferring and maintaining the refugees. Fourth, the gates of Palestine "would be thrown open wide for the refugees." Fifth, Jewish organizations would be allowed to extend aid to Jews remaining in the occupied countries. Sixth, "strong retaliatory measures" would be taken to force the Axis to stop the extermination. And last, an international body would be established in which representatives of the Jewish people would be granted authority to act.

In the end, the sixth clause was omitted in deference to the JAE's decision not to request retaliatory measures. The proposals were sent to the Bermuda Conference on the day it opened, together with a memorandum from the Agency's Political Department specifying how Palestine could absorb 95,000 new immigrants a year.[14]

The conference opened on April 19 and lasted nine days. It was conducted behind closed doors. Three weeks after it ended, an announcement was released that the final report was being prepared but would not be made public for fear of helping the enemy and hurting the refugees. The conference had decided, apparently, that it would not approach Hitler, that letting Jewish refugees into the democratic countries would increase anti-Semitism there, that the White Paper could not be changed, and that transporting refugees would hurt the war effort. The JAE concluded that "the remnant of Jews in the Nazi-occupied countries were not going to be saved" and sent a letter of protest to that effect to the British Parliament. The Bermuda Conference had abandoned the Jews to the Nazis, sacrificing them to the interests of the Allies. "The Agency Executive repudiates these arguments, which are, in fact, only a ruse to cover their unwillingness to make any effort to save Jews." The letter urged Parliament to repair the damage done in Bermuda and "not take upon yourself this responsibility towards history and God, [and] abandon them to the butchers and murderers."[15]

Shertok summarized the situation for members of the Zionist Actions Committee: not only were the results of the conference "negative and futile," but the U.S. government's attitude to it had been "more than skeptical, almost negative, from the beginning." American Jews had assumed that Roosevelt, if not members of his administration, had a positive attitude toward rescue. But the results of the conference destroyed the hope that America's attitude would outbalance Britain's hostility to rescue.

Most of those present at the ZAC meeting on May 18 expressed deep disappointment at the results of the conference. Enschel Reiss, who had criticized the Agency's faulty preparations for it, now admitted that whatever the JAE had done, it would not have changed the situation and therefore could certainly not be blamed for Bermuda's failure. He agreed with Shertok that the only course left was to try to activate free world Jewry and public opinion.[16]

The events of the following day, however, frustrated these hopes too. Although several members of Parliament harshly attacked the government, Eden defended British policy. He maintained that the government was sensitive to the suffering of the Jews, promised to do anything that could be done, and accused the Germans and their allies of preventing the departure of the Jews; but he also expressed doubt that more than "very few" could be saved before the Allied victory.[17]

This debate in Parliament marked the end of one stage in the struggle for rescue. After May 1943 there was a perceptible decline in public interest in Britain in the rescue of Jews, and the government continued its previous policy without any challenge at home. In Palestine the expressions "the spirit of Bermuda" and "the atmosphere of Bermuda" became synonymous with impotence, deceit, and despair at the futility of hoping for any help from the Allied governments to save Jews. The general attitude was one of bitter disillusion, a perception that "the whole world is against us." This realization was reinforced by the irony of history. The day the conference opened, April 19, was the eve of Passover, the festival of freedom. It was also the day the revolt in the Warsaw ghetto began. The handful of rebels preserving the dignity of their suffering people with their own young lives contrasted sharply with the fears of the American and British governments' bureaucracies that their countries might be flooded with refugees.

THE EXCHANGE PLAN

About 1,200 people from the Yishuv, mostly women and children, were caught in Europe when the war broke out, and immediately, in October 1939, efforts were begun to effect an exchange between them and German residents of Palestine. Lists of names and whereabouts were compiled, the Jewish Agency office in Geneva alerted the International Red Cross to assist people holding Palestinian passports, and the Agency asked the U.S. State Department and the British Foreign Office to formulate agreements concerning exchanges of civilians.

It soon emerged that most of the 1,200 Yishuv members were in Poland, a fact that made it very difficult, first, to find them, and then to get them out: hundreds of thousands had fled their homes when the Germans started bombing Poland. After prolonged negotiations the mandatory government agreed to grant the whole group *laissez-passer* documents, which were forwarded to the British passport control officer in Istanbul. Not until the end of 1941 was a small group of Palestinian women in Europe exchanged for a group of German women. In mid-November 1942, 70 more Palestinians and 110 other British subjects were exchanged for Germans from various places in Allied territory. In February 1943 another 14 arrived in Palestine, bringing the total number of people exchanged to 220.[18]

As a result of such meager success, at the end of 1942 men whose wives and children were in Europe established a committee to get their families transferred to Palestine. Another committee was set up by a group of Zionist activists from Poland who had managed to reach Palestine when the war broke out but whose families had been left behind. They approached the Agency with lists, requesting that a special effort be made to assist people who had given "their best years to Zionism." They urged the Agency to impress upon the mandatory government that their families should be considered "the first in line to be exchanged."[19]

A third list, compiled toward the end of 1942, consisted of veteran Zionists who before the war had worked in Europe primarily for the Jewish National Fund and the Foundation Fund. Their colleagues in Palestine had maintained contact with them whenever possible, writing and sending them food packages since 1940. Names were continually added under pressure from the new-immigrants' associations, and by mid-1943, the list included 3,000 names. These constant additions prompted the two other committees to extend their lists, adding parents of people in Palestine, families of illegal immigrants, families of new immigrants not yet naturalized, and so on.[20]

When the second exchange group reached Palestine in November 1942 and brought news of the systematic extermination, there was a new spate of rescue plans. These included an extended exchange plan, calling—in the first stage—for the exchange of thousands of German women and children living in the various Allied countries for 200,000 Jews. Dobkin considered this the most reasonable plan because it entailed a profit for the Germans. Gruenbaum urged that the British be asked to undertake the exchange "at any cost" and that renewed appeals be made to Washington and London. Ben-Gurion likewise saw exchange as a realistic possibility. To some extent, his hopes were based on the fact that two Germans had been exchanged for each Jew in the second group—an indication, perhaps, that enough Germans could be found for exchange in the future.[21]

The JAE apparently did not know that the Germans had become interested in an exchange plan when several hundred Germans, mostly from the Templar colonies in Palestine, joined the German army and then asked that their families be transferred to Germany. Himmler, whose dream it was to settle all people of German descent in one contiguous German-dominated territory, for a while considered carrying out an exchange plan despite objections from the mufti (the leader of the Palestinian Arabs) and previous German declarations against Jewish immigration to Palestine, because he assumed that more Germans could in this way be harnessed to the war effort.[22]

Meanwhile pressure in Palestine mounted as people with relatives in Europe pleaded for more immigration permits, or at least transit visas. In spring of 1943 cables arrived from Holland reporting that the Jews there were about to be deported to Poland. The Agency's Political Department asked the mandatory government to include all degrees of kinship between Palestinians and Dutch Jews in the existing exchange schedules. Dutch Jews hoped to be exchanged in large numbers for the numerous Germans living in Dutch colonies.[23] Gruenbaum sought out possible German candidates for exchange in South Africa, Brazil, Australia, and eastern Africa. In his letters and cables to officials there he stressed the urgency of the situation. Shertok and the Agency's Immigration Department conducted "lengthy and elaborate negotiations" with the Immigration Department of the mandatory government and with British officials in London. And the Rescue Committee's first suggestion to the Bermuda Conference urged an immediate exchange program.[24]

By mid-1943 it became clear that there would be no large-scale exchange. First of all, the red tape was endless. Details about each candidate had to be sent from occupied Europe either to Geneva or to Istanbul and from there to Jerusalem, where each name had to be discussed with the mandatory government. Once agreed upon, the lists had to be sent first to London for final approval, then to Switzerland, which represented Britain in occupied Europe, then to Germany, and then back the same way. Second, many of the Jews in occupied Europe, particularly in Poland, with Palestinian passports or relatives in Palestine refused to register for exchange, suspecting a German plot to get them out of their hiding places and to send them to their deaths. More than once such lists had indeed served as snares, and stories about them abounded. Third, British officials in London, although they claimed that Britain was doing all it could to help, in fact opposed exchange for several reasons: sending able-bodied and skilled Germans back into the service of their homeland was contradictory to the Allied war effort; releasing Germans for Jews, most of whom were not British subjects, could reduce Britain's bargaining power in recovering its prisoners of war; and allowing still more Jews into Palestine would create problems in relation to the White Paper and the Arabs.[25]

As time went on, it became increasingly difficult to locate those who were entitled to be exchanged. It was generally assumed that mentioning their names again and again in the lists would only attract German attention to them, especially in western Europe, where they were hiding under assumed Christian names. The representatives in Geneva therefore suggested sending not names but only categories of people, such as veteran Zionists and orphans.

The only achievement of 1943 was that the mandatory government confirmed the eligibility of the people on the lists as candidates for exchange. This step enabled them to apply to Swiss consulates for protection until the negotiations were concluded. Confirmations were also sent from Geneva and Istanbul to people who were not on the exchange lists.[26] Another seemingly positive development was Germany's announcement to the Swiss that it would take no action against the exchange candidates until the end of negotiations. In October 1943, however, Eberhard von Thadden, head of the Department for Jewish Affairs in the German Foreign Ministry, declared in an internal memorandum that such a promise was "out of the question. If and to what extent Jews who have received entry permits to Palestine can be excluded from the evacuation so that eventually they can perhaps be included in the exchange is clearly an internal German affair—not open for negotiation with the Swiss."[27] Apparently either Himmler had abandoned his plan or the German Foreign Ministry was unaware of it. The rivalry between the Foreign Ministry and the S.S. was common knowledge in the Third Reich.

And indeed, in the summer of 1944, news reached the Agency that holders of South American passports and immigration permits to Palestine, especially from Holland and from Poland, had been concentrated in Bergen-Belsen and Vittel but that some had then been sent on to Drancy and from there "to an unknown destination." Dozens of these internees committed suicide on the day deportation began. A desperate call for help came from Vittel to the Agency to save those who were left, and a concerted effort followed: Shertok approached the British Colonial Office, the emissaries in Geneva approached the

Swiss government, and Goldmann appealed to the U.S. State Department. The threefold action succeeded: the deportations from Vittel stopped and negotiations began concerning the exchange of the certificate holders still there.[28]

The result of negotiations was the exchange of Germans from South Africa for one group of 283 people, who arrived in July through Istanbul, and another group of 200, who came through Spain. Although some of these had been on the lists, most had been chosen by the Germans because they were old or weak or because they seemed "unintelligent and rather wild," as Dobkin put it. Among the arrivals were Jews from Tripoli who had not been on any list. An inquiry revealed that the Germans had chosen the Tripoli Jews deliberately, transferred them to Bergen-Belsen, and included them in the exchange group. Thus, after drawing up lists for about five years, Dobkin and Barlas reached the conclusion that they were of very little value.[29]

More than 800 people were saved directly by exchange during the war. Others were undoubtedly saved by virtue of being candidates for exchange; activists in Holland claimed that the project "saved thousands" from deportation.[30]

The plan for exchanging hundreds of thousands of Jews for Germans was strongly opposed by the British. If Himmler was really interested in a large exchange, then the Allies must be blamed for not having implemented the plan. But conclusive evidence is lacking. From the German point of view, the addition of skilled manpower could have been of real help and was in accordance with Himmler's ideology and aspirations. On the other hand, Himmler was also in charge of the apparatus that was systematically carrying out the Final Solution all over Europe. To what extent he was willing to undertake a plan that was in direct contradiction to the Final Solution policy remains an open question.

A related question is why the Germans agreed, in the summer of 1944, to stop the transports from Vittel and to begin negotiating the exchange while transports from other places, such as Greece, Slovakia, and the Lodz ghetto, where there were also certificate holders, continued. Himmler must have been aware that the British rejected the exchange of Germans for Jews and would refuse to cooperate in any extensive program.

The Vittel case had perhaps a larger context. In the summer of 1944, Adolf Eichmann's "merchandise for blood" proposal, that is, exchanging Jews for various necessary goods, had already been delivered to the Agency Executive in Jerusalem. At the same time Eichmann was pressing Yisrael (Rezso-Rudolf) Kasztner, who maintained contacts with the Germans regarding rescue operations in Budapest, to give him a list of several hundred names. These individuals, according to Eichmann, would be released as a token of his willingness to negotiate the release of hundreds of thousands more. The stoppage of transports from Vittel and the S.S. willingness in Hungary to discuss an exchange may have been connected with Himmler's comprehensive plan to negotiate with the Allies on the eve of the Reich's potential downfall, to spare Germany a crushing defeat or surrender to the Soviet army. It remains an open question whether Himmler intended to facilitate such negotiations through the actual release of small numbers of Jews or whether he thought that mere contacts would be sufficient to bring about negotiations with the Allies. If the latter was the case, the Allies' rejection of proposals for large-scale exchange made no difference to the outcome.

THE AFFAIR OF THE 29,000 CHILDREN

According to information reaching Palestine, children were usually the first victims of the Nazis. Consequently, when the subject of rescue was first discussed in the Yishuv, one of the first suggestions made was to ask the mandatory government to allocate to children in the occupied areas the 29,000 unused immigration permits remaining from the 75,000 allowed by the White Paper. The British could not possibly claim that German spies would be planted among refugee children.

The JAE informed the mandatory government that it was ready to absorb as many children as could be saved and that the figure of 29,000 was only the beginning; plans for absorbing tens of thousands more would soon be submitted. Eliezer Kaplan gave the secretary of the mandatory government, John S. MacPherson, a commitment on behalf of the JAE to supply all the necessary means and told his colleagues that "this activity takes precedence over any other item in the budget." Ben-Gurion told the Mapai Secretariat: "There is only one matter that can brook no delay—bringing the children to Palestine."[31]

Even before an answer was received from Whitehall, the Mapai Secretariat devoted a long session to the practical problems involved. One issue was whether Youth Immigration, up until then responsible for the absorption of children, would remain in charge or whether the Histadrut or an all-Yishuv body would take over instead. Another issue was the kind of education the children would receive. The ultraorthodox Agudat Yisrael and the Mizrachi (Religious Zionists) would demand religious education, but the Histadrut wanted the children to be absorbed into the secular Labor settlements.

The main problem was considered to be financial. According to the findings of a committee appointed by the Histadrut, the upkeep of each child would be no less than four to five pounds a month, that is, between 1,200,000 and 1,750,000 pounds a year for the group as a whole. Since the entire budget of the Agency for 1943 was 1,150,000 pounds, this would be a heavy undertaking. In the preceding decade, only 7,200 children had been absorbed in Palestine, and most of them had been over the age of fourteen and could work part-time. Furthermore, children who had lived under Nazi occupation for three years might need a lot of care, both medical and emotional. The Yishuv, which numbered around 60,000 families altogether (half the population consisted of bachelors and only 12 percent were over age fifty), was facing an enterprise more extensive than any it had ever tackled.

Mapai leaders were divided on how to meet the problem. Some maintained that the absorption of the first several thousand children must be carefully planned and that the national institutions should cover the costs of the families and settlements absorbing them. Others protested that "this attitude is inappropriate for the proportions of the disaster . . . we cannot handle this matter according to financial calculations." Every family in the Yishuv, they said, should absorb a child at their own expense, and they should be reminded that "you are lucky to be in Palestine . . . You could have been in the Diaspora and your children would have been in the same situation." But scattering the children among the families of the Yishuv would have meant losing direct control over their education.

This session of the Mapai Secretariat was held at the beginning of December 1942, and the entire discussion was infused not only with hope but also with certainty that the children really would arrive soon. There was no intimation that the plan might meet obstacles. As Ben-Gurion (who supported the absorption of a few thousand first) said, "These five thousand are not the end but only the beginning. This number can grow tenfold." In his opinion, the problems of absorbing the first group should be settled as soon as possible and in such a way that "we would be able to fight to bring all the children of European Jewry immediately." He called for establishment of a central Zionist institution for this purpose and suggested that the project be presented as the main enterprise of Jews everywhere. Not only the Yishuv would adopt the children, but "the entire Jewish people."

Ben-Gurion's primary interest was to save the children, but he was not indifferent to the tremendous value that their immigration would have for the development of the Yishuv. "Each child is a Jew coming to settle in Palestine," he said, and it was therefore of utmost importance that the children receive an appropriate education. He did not favor handing the children over to just anyone or any educational institution.

> Not every Jew in Palestine is capable of receiving a child into his home . . . We do not want the children brought up in the spirit of Kibbutz Mishmar Haemek [the most notable educational center of Hashomer Hatzair, the left-wing section of the Labor movement, was located there] . . . the foundations have to be more general . . . we want to establish one nation . . . to see to it that these children are educated for any task we may want them to fulfill.

Their absorption, he believed, would set an example for immigration of Jews from England, the United States, and the rest of the world.

Eliyahu Golomb tried to bring the discussion back to firmer ground. He warned that many months would pass before the children arrived and that the financial problems were severe. Ben-Gurion concluded the meeting with the more sober remark: "as long as they are not here, decisions cannot be made" regarding their education and upkeep.[32]

Preparations were begun, however. The JAE appointed a committee consisting of Ben-Gurion, Kaplan, Gruenbaum, and the directors of the Immigration Department, Dobkin and Shapira, to discuss all the practical problems involved in the absorption of the children. The composition of the committee and the fact that the matter was not delegated to any other body or subcommittee attest to both the importance and the hopes the Executive attached to it.[33]

The British government, which was currently the target of harsh criticism at home for not adopting any practical measures to alleviate the plight of the Jews, was partially receptive to the Agency's requests. Early in January 1943, after lengthy negotiations with Shertok in London, it agreed to allow 4,500 children between the ages of ten and sixteen, accompanied by 500 adults from Bulgaria, into Palestine, within the framework of the White Paper. A month later, Secretary of State for the Colonies Oliver Stanley made the agreement public. He also announced that 500 more children from Rumania and Hungary would be permitted to immigrate to Palestine and that, if adequate means of transportation were available, the whole quota of 29,000 immigration permits would be allocated for children. Stanley reiterated, however, that the White Paper remained the British government's policy in Palestine, and thus checked hopes of exceeding the remaining 29,000 permits.[34]

Given the proportions of the catastrophe, such a figure offered a very limited solution. Nevertheless, the JAE decided to refrain from making any further demands on the government at that point and to use the available permits as soon as possible. To expedite matters, it allocated some of the permits to the satellite countries, which had indicated willingness to let Jews leave in spite of German objections. Using some of the permits would constitute proof that the rescue was indeed being carried out, after which a new quota could be demanded. Simultaneously, efforts would continue to extricate Jews from the occupied areas.

Shertok was still in England. When Stanley made his announcement, when he returned to Palestine he reported to the JAE that the announcement had made a favorable impression on public opinion, which in his view was totally unjustified. First, he said, the British government still adhered to White Paper policy. Second, his conversations with government officials indicated that the JAE had maneuvered itself into a situation that was both complicated for itself and convenient for the British. If all the permits were reserved for children, the Agency would not be able to rescue adults, since to do so would threaten the children's prospects. If saving children turned out to be impossible, then no rescue would take place. Moreover, transferring the children was bound to be slow and complex, which would prove convenient to the British. They wanted as many permits as possible left in their hands in April 1944, when the White Paper expired, in order to stave off a crisis and confrontation. Bringing many children to Palestine without their parents, Shertok continued, was going to constitute a heavy economic and organizational burden on the Yishuv without adding to its military strength. Furthermore, earmarking 29,000 immigration permits for the occupied areas and the satellites would preclude immigration from other places. And indeed, in August 1943 the mandatory government refused to renew the permits of Jews from free countries who had not managed to get to Palestine in time because of transportation difficulties. They claimed that all permits were now reserved for immigrants from enemy-controlled areas.[35]

Whitehall was now, according to Shertok, in a position to present itself as having accepted the just request of the Jewish Agency and of having made a noble human gesture in saving tens of thousands of children from mortal danger. The Agency, even after having discovered all the limitations of this arrangement, would not be able to back out. Shertok had insisted in London that the first 4,500 children should come from all occupied areas and not just from Bulgaria, but he had been told that the danger to Jews in that country was severe. This seemed questionable to Shertok, since it was common knowledge in Palestine that many Bulgarians, including the church and the royal family, were sympathetic to their Jewish neighbors. In any case, there were children in immediate danger in other places, such as the thousands of orphans left dying of cold, hunger, and disease in Transnistria.

Shertok's misgivings about the reasons for British acquiescence forced him to make one of the most difficult decisions of his life. He cabled Barlas in Istanbul to give preference to children at least thirteen years old so that the Yishuv would have fewer expenses for education and fewer years to wait until the children became self-supporting and able to bear arms.

There was, however, one ray of light in Shertok's summary. The British had insisted at first that the arrangements would apply only to children and their escorts, most of them women. Later, they agreed that veteran Zionists and "renowned persons" could also be included, comprising altogether up to 10 percent of the number of children. This was the first break in the British prohibition on the immigration of adults from enemy-controlled countries. Shertok informed his colleagues that Whitehall's promise was "only an understanding" or "an apparent commitment." The JAE would now have to muster public opinion in Britain and the United States in order to turn the understanding into an explicit commitment and have it implemented.[36]

In February 1943 Shertok went to the United States. He and Weizmann talked with the British ambassador, Lord Halifax, about the urgent necessity of bringing out not only children but also adults. Counting on Roosevelt's sympathy for the cause, the JAE decided that attempts should be made in the United States to acquire a ship to take the immigrants from a Turkish port to Palestine, assuming that a neutral ship would bring them from the Balkans to Turkey. Ben-Gurion wanted it explained very clearly to the leaders of the Zionist movement in the United States that there was indeed a possibility of saving 29,000 children, and that "it depends on them and on them alone, if they are willing . . . all the difficulties can be overcome if only our colleagues would realize the severity of the situation."[37]

At the time of this optimistic statement, neither British Foreign

Minister Eden nor U.S. State Department officials had yet answered Jewish delegates that an approach to Hitler was impossible and useless.

There was something else that neither Ben-Gurion nor his colleagues in Palestine knew until Bader arrived in Palestine from Istanbul in February. Even before the plan had reached the first stage, the British and the Turks were already taking steps to undermine it. Shortly before Stanley's announcement, the *New York Times* correspondent in Istanbul told the emissaries there that the British ambassador, Sir Hughe Montgomery Knatchbull-Hugessen, had told the Turkish authorities very clearly that "he would view it favorably if they broke their promise [achieved by Barlas at the beginning of 1941] to grant the refugees free passage through Turkey." [38] Despite the lack of written evidence, actual events showed that the British indeed exerted pressure to thwart the passage of the children and that the Turks were very accommodating, occasionally adding further obstacles of their own.

First, the Turks objected to a large group of refugees on Turkish soil at one time; only when the first fifty people crossed their southern border into Syria would the Turkish ambassador in the Balkans grant another fifty transit visas. "All attempts to increase the Turkish quota," according to Bader, "were to no avail." Second, Turkey required that every refugee have an entry visa to a specific country, to ensure that none would remain in Turkey. Switzerland represented Britain in Axis countries, but its consulates in Hungary, Rumania, and Bulgaria did not grant visas to Palestine. The passports were sent to Bern with a courier who went there once a month. If the passports were not stamped on the same day, before the courier left, a whole month would elapse until they could be returned to Istanbul. At this rate, complained Bader, "a whole generation would be required . . . to get the children out of that hell." [39] Shertok tried to get the British government to instruct the Swiss consuls to grant visas in the countries in which the applicants lived, rather than in Bern. He was given to understand that his request would be accepted. But Bader reported that the Swiss consuls in the Balkan states never received such instructions. Moreover, Barlas, who had good contacts with the Turkish authorities, found out that on January 5, 1943, the British had issued instructions to the contrary.

The backwardness of the Turkish railway system posed another difficulty. It barely managed to transport essential shipments for the Allied armies and for the Turkish army, despite pressure from foreign diplomats and from the Turkish authorities themselves. Adequate domestic service was out of the question. The Turks were reluctant to transport thousands of children by rail without a minimum payment of thirty to forty pounds per child, not to mention bribes, without which nothing ever moved. Kaplan instructed Barlas "to agree to any price and to get the operation going."[40]

In February 1943 Barlas reported that Turkey might not remain neutral much longer. If it joined the Axis, the only channel left between Palestine and European Jewry would be closed. It also seemed likely that the German retreat on the eastern front, following the defeat in Stalingrad that month, would result in the murder of those Jews encountered during the retreat. Rumania forbade its vessels to sail. Only Bulgaria was allowing Jews out of its territory. The 500 children from Rumania and Hungary whose departure had been promised by Stanley therefore had to be taken to Bulgaria first, a step that greatly complicated both paperwork and the travel arrangements. The time left for rescue was growing very short.

The emissaries in Istanbul were forced to conclude that transporting children by land was impossible and that the only way to get them to Palestine quickly was by sea. The problems of traveling by ship were not merely technical or organizational; the tragedy of the SS *Struma* was still fresh in everyone's mind, both in Europe and in Palestine. Parents were willing to send their children in unseaworthy vessels only when the alternative was sure deportation to the death camps. They were less willing when there was still hope, as was the case in Bulgaria, that deportation could be prevented.[41]

The Mapai Central Committee discussed the subject at length in February. Remez lamented that "there is no feeling of urgency" and that "it seems as if there is money for everything, but when we have to pay a few thousand pounds [in bribes], we do not have the money," and suggested ways of collecting the money required. Ben-Gurion, in response, addressed both the practical question of whether or not to use ships and the implicit criticism leveled at him and the rest of the Agency concerning their attitude to rescue: "By sea we can bring a thousand people at once. In two weeks, we can bring another thousand . . . Bringing five thousand would be a tremendous thing. It does not solve the problem of the millions, but not bringing the five thousand would not solve it either." He urged that 50,000 pounds be raised immediately to purchase ships because "this is a burning matter."

Kaplan, who had discussed the matter at length with Bader, suggested that it would be more realistic to lease ships from the Turks than to buy them. According to Bader, the owners of the ships were willing to try to transport children, albeit for a "huge price" and not without appropriate instructions from the influential British ambassador in Ankara. "We cannot possibly refuse to do this because of lack of funds," he said. "There is every reason to come to the Jewish Agency and demand that [its members] take responsibility for the matter." He revealed that the emissaries in Turkey had decided on their own initiative to try to send 300 people without immigration permits by sea from a port in the Balkans, adding that "the matter of the ships and boats is relevant not so much to the children as to this attempt." Kaplan ended by suggesting that Istanbul be instructed to lease ships and start operations for bringing the children immediately.

Neither Ben-Gurion's nor Kaplan's suggestions satisfied the Mapai Central Committee. These limited and cautious plans seemed completely out of proportion to the dimensions of the catastrophe. Golda Myerson demanded that Kaplan explain how he could talk about the Agency's appropriating huge sums for this project while he was haggling with the Mobilization Fund over 20,000 pounds. Golomb thought the tempo of the rescue should be increased: if the Turks were ready to provide ships, all 29,000 children should be evacuated and then more permits obtained. Avraham Haft, the Rescue Committee's financial secretary, said: "We do not have very deep feelings about saving the children. There is a fatalistic disbelief that anything can come out of it. This feeling is prevalent in the Agency too. There must be a major change." The committee's members urged that Ben-Gurion dedicate at least two or three months of his time solely to rescue; that hundreds of thousands, maybe even more than a million, pounds be allocated; and that the Jewish Agency assume charge of all rescue operations.

In response, Kaplan tried to defend Ben-Gurion and announced that he had already promised Bader 40,000 pounds to bring out 1,000 children and another 300 adults and another 10,000 pounds for leasing ships. Ben-Gurion reminded his critics that bringing the first 5,000 children, which was considered only a first stage, would require a great effort and enormous investments—from the Yishuv, the Zionist movement, and the Jewish people. "There are Jews living in Palestine too," he said, meaning that the Yishuv was also in need of efforts and resources. He ignored the criticism of his attitude to the rescue in general.[42]

The debate, which took place only a week after Stanley's announcement, revealed the gap between Kaplan and Ben-Gurion, on the one hand, and the other members of the Mapai Central Committee, a gap that Yehiel Duvdvani characterized as "the inability to communicate." Kaplan and Ben-Gurion were familiar with all the difficulties encountered since December, and their enthusiasm, especially Ben-Gurion's, had begun to wane. Apparently Kaplan had learned from Bader that the emissaries in Istanbul believed the British were already obstructing the whole project. He had conveyed this information to Ben-Gurion. The two had therefore decided to limit themselves, for the time being, to plans that seemed more feasible. The others were still hopeful and disappointed at what seemed to them fatalism and lack of imagination.

But "the inability to communicate" referred to more than the gap in information. The feeling was widespread that there was no real dialogue between the Central Committee and the JAE on such crucial issues as the Holocaust and rescue. The Mapai representatives in the JAE, especially Ben-Gurion, were not sharing their information and calculations with the top echelon of their party. Perhaps Ben-Gurion, who had previously been so enthusiastic about bringing the children, simply could not admit what a terrible disappointment it had turned out to be.

Indeed, at the beginning of March it was already clear to Ben-Gurion that "unfortunately, approval for the permits is, in fact, theoretical, and there is no assurance that we can actually use them to get such a number of Jews out." He therefore suggested that some of the permits be allocated to the Jews of Yemen, Syria, and Iraq, who might be in danger if Jewish-Arab conflict erupted after the war. Having lost hope of using the permits for the children, Ben-Gurion was already looking for other ways to use them. Perhaps it was not just the possible danger to Middle Eastern Jews that bothered him, but the conviction that without Jews "there is no Zionism and no Yishuv." If the Jews of Europe could not come because they were doomed, the Jews of the Arab countries still could.

Ben-Gurion's colleagues in the Agency were skeptical about the chances of bringing the Middle Eastern Jews over in a short time. But, more important, they feared, as Gruenbaum put it, that such an admission "will be used against us, since the government will say that the Jewish Agency itself admits that so many immigration permits are not needed." Ben-Gurion agreed to request additional permits for the Jews of the Middle East; only if the request was denied would some of the 29,000 permits be allocated to them.[43]

Events at that time in Europe would have reinforced the gloomiest predictions of the Yishuv leaders had they been aware of them. Even before the full plan had been discussed, the emissaries in Istanbul and the Jewish organizations in the satellites were doing their best to get whatever children they could out and to Palestine, even in small numbers. At the beginning of March the press in Palestine announced the arrival of seventy-two children from Hungary and the expected arrival of more. A group of sixty-five children had arrived in January but, as a result of pressure from the emissaries in Istanbul, received no publicity. Publicizing such transfers made it much easier for the Germans to try to obstruct them, although such information usually reached Eichmann or the German Foreign Ministry anyway within a few days, even without press coverage.

In fact, Germany immediately sent cables to its ambassador in Sofia instructing him to prevent the passage of more groups of children. The reasons given were, first, that it was contrary to German interests to allow Jews to leave any part of Europe while Germany was carrying out the Final Solution; second, that interference by the satellites in such an important issue as the Final Solution could not be tolerated, since if they acted on their own with regard to the Jews, they might aspire to act independently in other matters; third, that the adult escorts could be a source of information for the Allies about Germany's military situation; and, finally, that their departure for Palestine was contrary to Axis policy toward the Arab nations.

Eichmann summarized the position of the Reich Security Main Office much more clearly. He recommended a firm refusal to let 5,000 Jewish children leave the occupied countries unless they were exchanged for 20,000 able-bodied Germans of draft age. If negotiations for such exchange were to begin, they should be expedited, since "the time is approaching when our solution concerning the Jews would render the departure of five thousand Jewish children impossible."[44] Eichmann knew very well that the Allies would never agree to such a proposal, that attempts until then to find German candidates for exchange had been to little avail, and that the number of Jewish children in Europe was dwindling rapidly.

These specific German maneuvers were not known in Palestine, however, and the Yishuv continued to try to make use of the permits. In March 1943 Kaplan went to Turkey "to take all measures to expedite immigration and to save the maximum number . . . in the shortest possible time." He also wanted to check the best way of doing it under the prevailing circumstances—by railway through Turkey or by ship. While there he discovered even more obstacles unknown to the JAE, which made the situation "much more complex and tragic than I thought when I left." Not only was the railway system in Turkey in appalling condition, but the Turks were unwilling to allocate even three coaches a week for the transfer of children, insisted that no more than one hundred refugees could be on Turkish soil at one time—half of them coming and half of them leaving—and demanded proof that there was an actual possibility of leaving Turkey before any refugee would be let in. Ben-Gurion called these restrictions "idiotic, cruel, completely unnecessary."[45]

Kaplan first tried to acquire ships from neutral countries as the most desirable solution. The Swedes announced that they had given "a solemn commitment" to Germany to use their ships only to transport food. The International Red Cross did not see any way of trying to change or break this promise and agreed in principle to give its protection to the children only if another suitable ship were found. Rumanian ships were controlled by the Germans. Turkish vessels were either owned or controlled by the government, which rejected any combination Kaplan offered, including a willingness to use cargo ships.

Next Kaplan tried to influence the British authorities in Turkey to help him find means of transportation and to facilitate the transfer; presumably he tried to take advantage of the contacts of the emissaries and the representatives of the Agency's Political Department— Teddy Kollek and Ehud Avriel—with the army, with intelligence, and with officials who privately expressed sympathy with the suffering of the Jews. Kollek and Avriel had established good relations with Arthur Whittall, an intelligence operative whose cover was that of a passport control clerk in the British embassy in Ankara. Kollek referred to him as "a small crack in an impenetrable wall."[46]

Third, Kaplan tried political action. Together with the emissaries in Istanbul and the Political Department in Jerusalem, he sent memoranda to London insisting that the British embassy in Turkey be granted authority to solve the problems of transit through that country and to transmit the emissaries' proposals to the Turks. The British Foreign Office promised to deal with the memoranda without delay. In response to a parallel appeal, the American embassy in Ankara announced that the United States would support the Agency's claims only if Britain would, although their attitude, especially that of Ambassador Laurence Steinhardt, was very warm. Kaplan and Barlas also met with the staff of the Soviet embassy in Ankara, who promised them free passage through the Black Sea for refugee ships sailing under the auspices of the International Red Cross. Meetings were also held with the Polish legation and with the apostolic nuncio, Angelo Roncalli (later Pope John XXIII).

On the eve of the Bermuda Conference, in mid-April 1943, the long-awaited British instructions had not yet arrived. The JAE sent a delegation led by Myerson and Yitzhak Ben-Zvi to the high commissioner to protest the delay and to appeal to the British government to grant its ambassador in Turkey authority to issue entry visas and arrange for passage by land or sea or else send to Istanbul another person duly authorized. The deputy high commissioner, who received the delegation, said he would forward its demands to London. He also said that Britain was looking for ships, especially among those carrying supplies to Greece and coming back empty, and was discussing with Turkey the establishment of a refugee camp in its territory. He agreed to ask the director of railways in Palestine to send railway coaches and locomotives through Syria to Turkey to prove that the means of leaving Turkey were available. Finally, the deputy high commissioner asked the delegation not to suspect that his government saw its role as merely one of "granting immigration permits and of doing what it does only out of fear of Parliament."[47]

In May 1943, after five months of negotiations, Kaplan was informed by the British minister for Middle Eastern affairs, Richard C. Casey, that the British embassy in Ankara had received the authority to simplify administrative procedures and that he was "taking the responsibility for transferring the immigrants on himself." A similar communication reached the emissaries in Turkey. It seemed that a breakthrough had finally been achieved. Within a few days Barlas and Joseph Goldin sent messages to the Turkish government and to its ambassadors in the Balkans that any refugee who reached Turkish soil or waters would receive a visa to Palestine. On the basis of this commitment, the Turkish consul in Bulgaria issued transit visas through Turkey to Jews who came to him even on their own. When they reached Istanbul, they received visas to Palestine from Whittall, as members of the contingent of 500 adults who were supposed to accompany the children.

When some of these refugees reached Palestine, the mandatory government sent an envoy to Turkey to remind Whittall that adults were supposed to come only as escorts of children. Since the transfer of the children had not yet started, it was not legal to send adults. Whittall stopped issuing visas, but the refugees continued to arrive. So he found another way. He recalled the proposal of Lord Cranborne, who was secretary of state for the colonies when the SS *Struma* was sunk, that Jewish refugees who were not entitled to enter Palestine be sent "to Mauritius or somewhere else." He therefore granted visas to Cyprus to the Jews who came to him. The British legation in Turkey reprimanded Whittall for this interpretation of Cranborne's proposal and officially asked the Turkish Ministry of the Interior to instruct its consul in Sofia to stop giving Jews transit visas without consulting Ankara first. The Turks acquiesced.[48]

The Turkish foreign minister, with whom Barlas was on good terms, was sympathetic to the plight of the children and agreed that a Turkish vessel sailing under the flag of the International Red Cross would make several trips to Palestine carrying 300 to 400 children each time. This arrangement would enable the Yishuv to take advantage of a Bulgarian proposal to send the children by train. The British, however, announced that a special committee must examine each child and cable its opinion to London for approval; only after that could the British legation apply in writing to the Turkish Foreign Ministry.

"It is all in the hands of the British," Bader concluded. The British government wanted to appear generous—granting immigration permits, simplifying procedures—but "in fact, what they want is for us to choke on these permits so that they can use them after the war, when they are pressed . . . to give their share for the refugees." This was the same conclusion that Shertok had reached five months earlier. The Histadrut decided to send another representative to London immediately to take Shertok's place and "to prove to the members of Parliament that a reprehensible manipulation is taking place," that the British government was simply deceiving the Yishuv. The replacement was not sent, however, because Casey and MacPherson, the secretary of the mandatory government, convinced Kaplan that "matters are determined here, in the Middle East."[49]

In July Britain's Colonial Office informed Shertok that the government had decided that month that any Jew arriving in Istanbul would be transferred to Palestine and that the entrance of refugees to Palestine would continue until the quota of 75,000 permits had been used up, even after March 31, 1944, when the White Paper expired. Shertok was also promised that if it was still possible to get people out of Bulgaria, a ship would be sent to bring them.

This decision seemed to remove all obstacles to free passage to Palestine through Turkey. When he conveyed the news to Avriel and Kollek, Whittall called it "a new version of the Balfour Declaration." However, once refugees reached Palestine they would be considered illegal immigrants and kept in a detention camp until they could pass a security check and until it could be proved that they would be economically absorbed. The number of immigrants would be deducted from the immigration quota, as decided by Britain in May 1942.

Between the sinking of the SS *Struma* in February 1942 and July

1943, only 184 refugees had managed to reach Turkey. So in fact Britain was not taking any great risk. Furthermore, German pressure to forbid the exit of Jews in Rumania had increased, and in Bulgaria the Jews were expelled from Sofia to the countryside. This rendered communication with them almost impossible. Third, and most important, the decision was delivered to the Jewish Agency but was neither publicized nor officially delivered to the Turkish government. As a result, it had no practical value and could be denied if necessary.

In July information also reached Palestine from Istanbul that it might be possible to get 1,000 people out of Bulgaria. In August Shertok left for Istanbul to look into the matter. "All our efforts now center on these thousand people," Shertok said. "This is the only living issue in the plans to get Jews out of the Nazi domain." The Aliya Bet activists in Turkey had made a deal with a Bulgarian businessman who had promised, in return for a loan to buy a ship, to acquire the papers necessary for the departure of 1,000 people and to bring them to the Turkish port of Mersin. From there, Shertok was promised, they would be taken by a British ship to Palestine.[50]

The Aliya Bet activists were skeptical and warned Golomb and Shertok, who were depending on this help from the British navy, "not to rely on promises. A year of work in Istanbul has taught us that they are never kept." Shortly thereafter, the Bulgarian Ministry of the Interior announced its approval of the departure of 1,000 people as long as they were not of military age—that is, between eighteen and thirty. A list of 1,300 names, mostly children, their escorts, and veteran Zionists, was immediately submitted. But all those of working age, between fifteen and sixty, were soon struck off the list. Only 420 children and elderly people were left, and even then the list was further shortened to just 100 names.[51]

In August the situation deteriorated rapidly. The king of Bulgaria, Boris III, died suddenly after a visit to Hitler during which the issue of the Bulgarian Jews was raised. After the king's death German pressure increased, and Bulgaria's borders with Turkey and Rumania were sealed. "What is happening in Bulgaria reflects our total helplessness," said Venia Pomerantz toward the end of August. "The country is so close to Istanbul and still we cannot save its Jews."[52] Adding to the poignancy of the situation was the fact that Bulgaria was not even occupied. Its people had guarded the lives of its original Jewish citizens, and King Boris may even have paid with his life for standing up to the Final Solution.

In November 1943 Stanley announced in Parliament that the government had postponed the expiration of the White Paper until

30,000 more people entered Palestine. For a brief moment, there were tentative hopes of yet rescuing the children. The committee that had been elected a year earlier to prepare their absorption concluded its work. At the end of 1943 it submitted its conclusions on how much money would be needed to absorb the first 10,000 and where they would be absorbed. Ben-Gurion dismissed the unfinished debate concerning the children's education. "If a miracle occurs and we can get the children," the subject could be discussed then. In any case, the worst possible care that they could receive in Palestine would still be much better than "if the Nazis 'take care' of them."[53]

But the miracle did not occur. For a whole year the Agency and the emissaries tried to remove the obstacles to the rescue of the children: the chaos in Turkey and its dependence on the British, the military and political changes in southeastern Europe, the lack of ships at the disposal of the Yishuv, and Britain's refusal to fulfill its promises. This dream, as Pomerantz called it, born in enthusiasm and great hopes, shrank from 29,000, to 5,000, to 1,000, and ended in bitter disappointment with no more than a few dozen.

In October 1943 the emissaries concluded that the months of incessant negotiations had been futile. "In fact, we did not get anything" either from the British or from the Turks, who "smiled politely, passed the buck to each other, were 'sympathetic' and 'moved' in expressing their sorrow, and kept promising to help while behaving as cruelly as before."[54]

A few decades later, when the archives were opened, it became clear that the British, who had been accused of passivity in the face of the tragedy, had not been passive at all. This is perhaps the most heart-rending aspect of all the unsuccessful attempts to rescue the children. While Eichmann, his staff, and German Foreign Ministry officials exerted themselves lest a single Jewish child escape them, the British, self-righteous and seemingly passive, blocked all escape routes. In the middle were the handful of emissaries in Istanbul and officials in Palestine, who tried to break through the walls with their bare fists, and the children, who never came.

12

Ransom Plans

In addition to rescue plans initiated in Palestine and presented to the Allies, other plans reached the Agency from the outside: from the satellite government of Rumania, from leaders of the Slovakian Jewish community, and from German authorities in Hungary. All involved stopping the extermination or letting Jews out in large numbers in return for money or goods. The negotiations took place or were supposed to take place, between the Agency Executive and other Jewish bodies, and the respective German or satellite authorities. The main questions in these negotiations concerned the real intentions of the Germans and whether or not direct negotiation with them would be considered treason by the Allies.

THE TRANSNISTRIA AFFAIR

In late December 1942 a proposal reached the Agency from the Rumanian government, offering to let 70,000 Jews leave Transnistria in return for a payment of 200,000 Rumanian lei (about 100 Palestinian pounds) per capita. The proposal was submitted simultaneously by Radu Lecca, Rumania's general secretary for Jewish affairs and a confidant of the Rumanian ruler, Marshal Ion Antonescu, and by Dr. Wilhelm Fischer, a Rumanian Zionist leader. Lecca's proposal reached Chaim Barlas in Istanbul through a Swiss government official. Fischer conveyed it by telephone to Joseph Goldin, the representative of the Agency's Immigration Department in Turkey. A memorandum was immediately sent from Istanbul to Ben-Gurion and Yitzhak Gruenbaum with details of the proposal, accompanied by the request of Zionist leaders in Rumania "to treat it with all due seriousness." Barlas left for Palestine to submit the proposal in person to the Agency Executive.[1]

In determining its response the JAE had to clarify three issues. First, what was the situation of the Jews in Transnistria at that time, and how urgent was it to get them out? Second, did the Rumanian government really intend to release 70,000 people? What were its motives? Was it capable of carrying out an action diametrically opposed to German policy? Third, would the Allies permit a German ally and partner in the invasion of the Soviet Union to receive 7 million pounds? Regulations forbade any transfer of money and equipment that could help the enemy. Even if an arrangement agreeable to all sides could be found, how would the people be got out of Transnistria, and where would they be brought if Britain refused to let them into Palestine?

Transnistria, a remote area in the southern Ukraine between the Dniester and the Bug, had been annexed to Rumania in return for military help to Germany in its invasion of the Soviet Union. Rumanians oversaw the civil administration of the area, but the Germans had retained military control for a while. In October 1941 about 180,000 Rumanian Jews, mostly from Bessarabia and Bukovina, had been deported to the area at Antonescu's initiative. He was thus able in one move to manifest his adherence to German policy, to gain the property of the deportees, and to win popularity among the anti-Semites in his own country.

During the German invasion of the Soviet Union, most of the Jews in Transnistria—who might have been of some assistance to the new exiles—were murdered. Within a few months, more than half the deportees either died of hunger, cold, or disease or were murdered by Rumanians, Ukrainians, and local Germans. In May 1942 there were 70,000 Jews, including thousands of orphans, still alive in the area, and their condition was among the worst in Europe.[2]

Although contacts between Rumania and Transnistria were forbidden, information filtered through. At the end of 1941 Rumanian Jewish leaders sent memoranda and reports through Allied ambassadors in Bucharest to the International Red Cross, the British Foreign Office, the U.S. State Department, and Jewish organizations. This information and more also reached Palestine during 1942. Rumania's proposal at the end of that year was seen, on the one hand, as a surprising deviation from its previous policy, though on the other as compatible with the generally accepted assumption that it had always been after Jewish money.

The Agency had no way of knowing either Rumania's real intentions or Germany's attitude to the proposal. Despite the Rumanian Zionists' request to treat it "with all due seriousness," most Rumanian Jewish leaders believed that it was vague and "unrealistic" and that "the Rumanian intentions are to be doubted. It seems that this is a plan to acquire a large sum of money." Nevertheless, they asked the Agency to check details such as transit routes, transportation, destination, and guarantees of funds. They were particularly anxious to discover if similar proposals had been made in neighboring countries, and thus whether it was part of a broader German plan. Despite their doubts, the Rumanian Jews recommended starting and maintaining negotiations to create the impression that the proposal was being seriously considered. At least time could be gained, and the suffering of the deportees somewhat alleviated.[3]

Within a few days of delivering his government's offer to the representatives of Rumanian Jewry—alleging that the Germans had already agreed to it—Lecca informed the German ambassador in Bucharest, Baron Manfred von Killinger, that Marshal Antonescu had instructed him and the Jewish community to organize the emigration of 70,000 Jews to Palestine in return for 200,000 lei per capita. The German ambassador replied that such a proposal was contrary to promises given in Berlin to the mufti of Jerusalem and to Rashid el-Kailani, the pro-Nazi former prime minister of Iraq. Both firmly objected to any Jewish immigration to Palestine, let alone that of Jews of military age. Killinger reported the conversation to the Foreign Ministry in Berlin and received strict and unequivocal instructions to thwart the plan. The emigration of 70,000 Jews was only a partial solution, and Germany aspired to a comprehensive one; moreover, an agreement between a German ally and the enemy would compromise Germany politically. Therefore, Rumania should be warned that "it would not receive better treatment from the enemy in return for this." The Germans suspected, correctly, that Rumania was making the proposal in preparation for ultimately negotiating with the Allies.[4]

Unaware that the Germans had already decided to foil the plan, the JAE considered possible Allied reactions. Barlas reported that one of the emissaries in Istanbul had already told the British authorities there about the offer. The JAE did not consider this harmful: the British would have found out through their own sources anyway. Moreover, if the emissary had not reported to them, they would probably have suspected the Yishuv of establishing contacts with a German ally behind their backs. Second, a plan of such magnitude could not possibly be carried out without the knowledge of the Allies or their agreement to the transfer of millions of dollars to an enemy country, not to mention the transfer of tens of thousands of Jews to Palestine or anywhere else.

Concluding that Rumania had a reasonable motive for releasing Jews and that it would be very difficult to convince the Allies to accept and help implement the proposal, the JAE decided to open negotiations in order to clarify details and to investigate practical possibilities. It also intended to propose a more realistic plan, one that would not arouse Allied objections: either the Jews in Transnistria would be returned to Rumania, at least temporarily, until their emigration to Palestine or elsewhere became possible, or help would be given to enable them to survive where they were. The Yishuv would approach the Allied governments, the International Red Cross, other international bodies, and Jewish organizations regarding the Rumanian proposal. It would also send Gruenbaum to the United States immediately to handle contacts with all these bodies and would keep Moshe Shertok, who was in England, informed about developments. Barlas was empowered to start negotiations in Istanbul with the Rumanian envoys. Finally, the JAE agreed that the entire affair must be conducted in utmost secrecy.[5]

Nevertheless, the story got out. "In Tel Aviv, where they know everything, there are rumors that it is possible to get the Jews out of Rumania for money," complained Gruenbaum, denying that the Agency knew anything about such a proposal. David Remez demanded that the JAE use 50,000 pounds to check whether the rumors had any basis in fact: "We know these people and their officials." Meanwhile another Rumanian envoy arrived in Istanbul and met with the emissaries. As an army officer, he had witnessed the deportation to Transnistria and described the horror of it in detail. He expressed his opinion, or perhaps that of those who sent him, that "a hint from Washington or from London" could put an end to this suffering. He described the situation of deportees as much worse even than that of the Polish Jews. Pressured to look into the matter immediately and to decide on a course of action, the JAE assured Remez and other leaders that the emissaries in Istanbul were studying the details of the proposal and that, if it was feasible, the Agency would find the money.[6]

Toward the end of January 1943 the Aliya Bet emissaries in Istanbul received an offer from a Rumanian shipping company—with the knowledge of the Rumanian government—to transport up to 1,000 people a month from Odessa to Turkish territorial waters in small boats. At that point the vessels would have to turn around, because they were not allowed to leave Rumania's territorial waters. Other vessels would be needed to pick up the refugees and transport them to

Palestine. The emissaries forwarded this information to Palestine with the comment that Lecca showed "a definite inclination . . . to allow immigration instead of cruel extermination."[7]

Despite this seemingly positive development, the negotiations failed to produce results. Neither the JAE nor the emissaries in Istanbul could know that Lecca was still double-dealing. By the end of February, under pressure from the German Foreign Ministry, all marine travel out of Rumania was stopped, and the Jews in Transnistria were forbidden to reach the ports.

The Jews of Transnistria became one of the major preoccupations of the Yishuv leadership. In a meeting of the Mapai Secretariat in February 1943, Remez said: "There is no forum in which this issue has not been discussed. For the first time, we have to decide whether or not to spend money on a venture without any guarantee that it will succeed or that the money will not be lost." All speakers agreed that any publicity about negotiations on the Rumanian proposal would be harmful, but there was no unanimity about what should be done. Remez and Eliyahu Golomb believed that the risk had to be taken, at least once, to see if several hundred could actually be released. Time was running out; immediate action was vital regardless of the fact that neither the Jewish Agency nor the Yishuv had any control over the governments or factors involved or any access to relevant sources of information.

Ben-Gurion, on the other hand, asked his comrades to differentiate between "the Jews that we cannot bring . . . and those that we can bring over from Europe . . . if we do not bring over those that we can, we would never be forgiven." In his opinion, the Yishuv could bring only as many people as were allowed by the White Paper. Furthermore, they had to be brought by sea; travel by train through Turkey would take precious months (and, as the 29,000 children affair proved, was practically impossible).[8]

Menachem Bader, who had arrived from Istanbul, shared Ben-Gurion's view and expressed it frankly to the Histadrut Secretariat: "We do not have enough time to do it on a large scale. We cannot talk about saving 70,000 Jews. If we can get a ship . . . which can carry 1,200 people and if, in the course of the two months still left, it can make two or three trips, we will have done the maximum possible." Transporting 70,000 people, he said, could not be done without the knowledge and help of the British and without spending millions of pounds—which the Yishuv did not have. Even if the money could be raised from wealthy Jews left in Rumania and from other Jewish communities, fundraising would have to be kept secret, as would negotiations with the British. Both would take a long time, and success was not assured. Bader recommended that Aliya Bet try in the meanwhile to bring out a few thousand discreetly with the means that the Yishuv itself could muster. Apparently, his remarks prompted the Histadrut Secretariat to mobilize 60,000 pounds, which Aliya Bet wanted for buying small vessels and training Jewish crews.[9]

Negotiations between Jerusalem, Istanbul, and Bucharest dragged on while Aliya Bet waited for money to buy boats and while contradictory rumors about Rumanian intentions circulated in Palestine. A turning point came at the beginning of February 1943. The U.S. State Department, with British acquiescence, published a warning, accompanied by a threat of punishment, to anyone considering negotiations with the enemy in order to save Jews, because it was an attempt by the Germans to extort foreign currency. The notice was published in the press of the neutral countries, notably Switzerland. *Basler Nachrichten* and *Neue Züricher Zeitung* published the facts leading to the State Department's warning. The Rumanian government had made an offer to the United States and Britain to release the 70,000 Jews in Transnistria at $50 per person; the offer would become null and void if the Germans entered Rumania. The accuracy of these newspaper reports is open to question, especially since the amount mentioned was only one-eighth of the original. Another unanswered question is why the Rumanian government approached the Allies.[10]

Several days later, in mid-February, Cyrus L. Sulzberger of the *New York Times* published the details of the proposal. At the same time he told the American embassy in London that in his view it was nothing but a Nazi plot. Laurence Steinhardt, the American ambassador in Turkey, considered the offer to be a ploy by the satellite country to ingratiate itself with the Allies without actually releasing any Jews. He informed Barlas that Lecca's messengers had "tried to talk to him, too," and that he had rejected all their proposals as worthless: "They are dependent on their masters, who won't agree."[11]

Apparently the Agency, which had decided in late December 1942 to approach the Allies immediately concerning the Rumanian offer, had still not done so in mid-February, either because it doubted the seriousness of the proposal or because it feared an outright refusal— particularly since prolonged contact between the Yishuv emissaries and the emissaries of a German ally was bound to be discovered. Press coverage gave the Agency an opportunity to act.

The Zionist office in London told Shertok later in February that it was "out of the question" to approach the Allied governments after their threat. Nevertheless, Shertok insisted that the possibilities must be verified beyond doubt. He asked the British Foreign Office to clarify the issue both in Istanbul and in the United States. The Allies, apparently, were in no hurry, and in any case Shertok's carefully worded cable requesting immediate clarification was held up by the American censors.[12]

At the same time Chaim Weizmann asked the British ambassador in the United States, Lord Halifax, to ask his government to look into the Rumanian proposal on behalf of the Jewish Agency. He admitted that "we have no means of checking the authenticity of this," but it might prove an opportunity to save human lives, not merely an extortion plan. He hoped that the British would not regard the request as a stratagem to change the White Paper policy. Saving lives, he said, should be kept separate from relations between Britain and the Yishuv. Weizmann predicted that the Arabs would certainly object but added that their objections should not prevent "a great humanitarian act." To assuage Britain's fear that spies would infiltrate the refugees, he promised that the immigration would be closely supervised. He "urged and begged" that human beings who were otherwise doomed be saved.[13]

Halifax asked the Foreign Office for instructions, and it consulted the Colonial Office. The correspondence between them reveals that Halifax and the Foreign Office feared that an open rejection of the proposal would arouse harsh public criticism, particularly undesirable in an election year in the United States. On the other hand, they thought that there was not the slightest chance of agreeing to Rumanian extortion. The language used in this internal correspondence leaves no doubt about the British attitude to Jewish rescue or immigration, from Transnistria or anywhere else. One official confided to another that the immigration of 70,000 Jews was "a frightful prospect," while the other answered that there was no need firmly to object to the plan because years would pass before ships could be found. The British embassy in the United States sent Weizmann and Shertok a letter summarizing the British position as follows: first, the proposal was "clearly a piece of blackmail which, if successful, would open up the endless prospect on the part of Germany and its satellites . . . of unloading at a given price all their unwanted nationals on overseas countries"; second, with regard to the admission of refugees into Palestine, the British government had already "gone to the furthest practical limits"; third, no country could agree to the type of pressure being applied by the Rumanian proposal; fourth, Britain and the other Allies would carefully examine all practical means of alleviating the suffering of the refugees, as long as they were compatible with the war effort; and, finally, the humanitarian problems created by Germany in Europe, of which the Jewish problem "is an important but by no means the only" one, would be solved only with victory.[14]

By now it was clear that the Germans knew that the Allies had rejected the plan. The Agency, concluding that the prospects of success were even dimmer than before, tried to retrieve the situation by issuing a public denial that the proposal had ever been confirmed. The denial, made simultaneously by Stephen S. Wise in New York on behalf of the World Jewish Congress and by the office of the Jewish Agency in London, was also a reaction to a full-page advertisement in the New York papers: "For sale—70,000 Jews, at $50 apiece, guaranteed human beings." The ad, signed by Hillel Kook (known as Peter Bergson), Shmuel Merlin, and Ben Hecht, of Etzel's Emergency Committee for the Rescue of the Jews of Europe, was intended to generate public pressure on the U.S. government to take up the Rumanian proposal. The committee also denounced the Zionist leaders for not generating such public pressure before and for limiting themselves to clandestine negotiations. The official Zionist leadership in the United States regarded the Emergency Committee's action as rash and as jeopardizing the few possibilities that remained.[15]

Meanwhile the Yishuv leaders were trying to evaluate the situation as a whole. Toward the end of February the Mapai Central Committee met to hear Tzvi Yehieli, an important Aliya Bet activist. Although his contacts in Istanbul were still optimistic because the satellites wanted to prepare an alibi and because they were greedy, he warned against holding on to any illusions. The Transnistria plan, he said, had to be seen in the context of an ongoing debate in Germany and its satellites between those who favored eviction of the Jews and those who favored extermination. So far the advocates of extermination had always won. Even now, when the satellites were in doubt about continuing to support Germany, the Jews could still fall prey to "a horrible, awful murder." In Yehieli's opinion, the proposal to let Jews out of Transnistria was part of a general plan in Rumania to switch from deportation and extermination to emigration. The plan took different forms at different times, which explained the various versions of the Rumanian proposal.[16]

A few days later Kaplan went to Istanbul; when he returned at the end of March, he told the JAE and the Mapai Secretariat: "I do not see room for any sensational operations. The grandiose plan of bringing 70,000 people from Rumania turned out to have been neither serious nor realistic." The Germans were doing their best to obstruct attempts to get people out of Rumania, and passage through Turkey had been deliberately complicated. The only thing that could be done, in Kaplan's opinion—as in Ben-Gurion's and Bader's—was to try to act quietly, in coordination with Rumania and behind the backs of the Germans.[17]

Toward the end of April 1943, soon after the pitiful results of the Bermuda Conference became known, Apollinary Hartglas, the political secretary of the Rescue Committee, summarized the rescue efforts made until then and evaluated future prospects. In his opinion there was a built-in catch in the Transnistria plan: "The matter became widely known, and this was why the plan was canceled. On the other hand, a plan to rescue tens of thousands of people cannot be carried out in secret since it is impossible to receive the necessary means unless thousands of people know about it."[18]

The main catch was still the political one: even if Rumania had actually intended—for its own sake and in opposition to German policy—to release the Jews of Transnistria or of Rumania in general and even if the Jewish Agency was willing and able to pay the ransom and the costs of transportation, both would be restrained by stronger powers. The Germans were determined not to let the Jews leave. The Allies forbade negotiations with the Axis. The emigration of 70,000 Jews seemed to them, especially to the British, an unnecessary disruption of the war effort. Thus, after four months of discussing the plan, the Agency concluded that, under the circumstances, the idea was impractical.

There were, however, three other limited ways to take advantage of Rumania's willingness to moderate its policy toward its Jews: the dispossessed and starving Jews in Transnistria might be given material and medical assistance; they might even be allowed to return to Rumania proper, where they could be helped by the Jewish communities; and 5,000 children, referred to in Stanley's declaration of February 1943, might still be extricated.

Rumanian Jewish leaders initiated negotiations between the Rumanian government and Barlas and Eliezer Kaplan—when the latter was in Istanbul in March 1943—about transferring 5,000 orphans from Transnistria to Rumania proper. Once the Jewish Agency had assured the Rumanian government that there were immigration permits for the children, they would be allowed to leave Transnistria for transit camps in Rumania, where they would remain until their departure for Palestine. Rumanian Jews would finance the transportation to Rumania and the upkeep of the children in the transit camps, but Kaplan told them that they must not delay the transfer on account of insufficient funds; the Agency would make up any difference. Lecca sent the negotiators an official confirmation of the plan.[19]

In August Shertok received a letter in Istanbul from Michai Antonescu, chairman of the Rumanian Council of Ministers. The Rumanian government reiterated its agreement to the emigration of the 5,000 children and asked for practical suggestions regarding their departure. Once it had received these, the letter said, the government would approach neighboring countries for permission to bring the children through their territories.[20]

The practical suggestions were not sent. In mid-1943 German pressure on Rumania mounted, and an official committee that was supposed to go to Transnistria to arrange for the children's departure was canceled. German warships were ordered to sink vessels carrying refugees outside of Rumanian territorial waters. This measure was unnecessary. Throughout 1943 Aliya Bet was unsuccessful in acquiring vessels. At the end of the year Ze'ev Shind returned to Palestine from Istanbul and told the Mapai Secretariat: "Before, there was talk of 5,000 orphans. Now even that is not mentioned anymore . . . The whole thing is off."[21]

The next year brought some success. Altogether, 1,200 refugees arrived in Palestine from Transnistria on two ships in March and April. In the other two areas of activity, helping the deportees and getting them back to Rumania proper, there was greater success, especially after Rumania signed a truce with the Soviet Union in the summer of 1944. From 1945 to the end of 1946 about 40,000 Jews had been allowed to return to Rumania. The Jews of Rumania—who were well organized, resourceful, and willing—extended aid in the form of food, money, and medical supplies. The Jewish Agency provided 30,000 pounds. It was a modest sum compared with the aid extended by the Rumanian Jews, the JDC, the World Jewish Congress, and the War Refugee Board, but its value—according to letters received from Transnistria—should be measured in terms of the encouragement it gave the Jews there.[22]

Bader's comments to the Zionist Actions Committee in May 1943 summarize best the Yishuv's reaction to the Transnistria affair: "There are dreams, there are nightmares, there are hoaxes, and there are plans—some far-reaching, some big, and some small, but we are not free to ignore any lead although we cannot know how real it is or what will come of it."[23]

Rumania's motives for making the proposal remain unclear. It is possible that those who broached the Transnistria offer—even before

Lecca approached the Jewish Agency—named such a high price simply to find out just how much money Rumanian Jewry could raise from its own sources and from Jews in the free world. This attitude was compatible with the anti-Semitism prevalent in Rumania, according to which the Jews controlled both the local economy and the economic and political system in the Allied countries, especially in the United States, besides being a subversive Bolshevik element. According to these assumptions, the Jews could raise and transfer huge sums through their own channels without the knowledge of the Allies. The manner in which negotiations were conducted also indicates that this was not a comprehensive, official attempt at extortion. It was rather a diffuse effort, emanating from a variety of sources. None of the messengers was an official representative of the Rumanian government, which could thus extricate itself from the whole affair at any given moment. The government's real intentions have remained unexplained.

Several points, however, are clear: the Allies categorically objected to the proposal and undermined its chances by publishing their warning in the press, and the Germans vehemently opposed it. The Jewish Agency realized from the beginning that the prospects of success were meager and consequently invested most of its efforts in trying to improve the situation of the deportees and in getting at least some of the orphans out, at the time when the large plan of saving the 29,000 children was collapsing. As one British historian put it later, "It would seem incredible that the Agency would not have pressed the matter further if they had had reason to suppose that the offer was in fact genuine."[24]

THE EUROPA PLAN

While the Jewish Agency was discussing the Transnistria plan at the end of 1942 and during 1943, another large-scale ransom offer, which came to be known as the Europa Plan, originated in Slovakia.

In 1939, after the German occupation of Prague, Slovakia, a Catholic country with a long anti-Semitic tradition, had become nominally independent under German protection. In 1942, 58,000 Slovakian Jews, or two-thirds of the entire Jewish population, were sent to the extermination camps in Poland. The deportations took place in two waves: from March through July, and in September and October. A body of Slovakian Jewish leaders known as the Working Group tried to stop the deportations by bribing the Germans.

The Working Group was led by Rabbi Michael Dov-Beer Wiess-mandel, who was the son-in-law of the leader of orthodox Jewry in Slovakia; and by Gisi Fleischmann, Weissmandel's young relative and a recognized Zionist leader in Bratislava. She was the chairwoman of the Women's International Zionist Organization (WIZO) and the representative of both the JDC and World Jewish Congress. The Working Group paid Dieter Wisliceny, Himmler's adviser for Jewish affairs in Slovakia, $50,000 in two installments. The first was paid in June, and the deportations were stopped the next month but renewed in September. With the second installment, which was paid in October, the deportations were again stopped and an announcement made that they would not be renewed until April 1943. Another two trains left Slovakia for Poland at the end of October, but thereafter the deportations ceased until the Slovak rebellion against the Nazis in the fall of 1944.[25]

Convinced that the bribes paid to Wisliceny had stopped the transports from Slovakia, the Working Group started to negotiate with him for termination of the transports all over Europe—with the money to be paid in foreign currency·by free world Jewry. The group sent Wisliceny a letter ostensibly written by the Swiss representative of wealthy international Jewish relief organizations, requesting an end not only to the transports to the extermination camps in Poland, but also to the extermination of those already in the camps. It also asked for help and exit visas for the survivors. Priority was to be given to children and to those who had the appropriate papers. This was the framework of the Europa Plan.

According to his own testimony, Wisliceny received $20,000 as an advance payment, together with promises that his efforts would be remembered after the war. For his part, he promised to deliver the details of the negotiations to his superiors in Berlin. In November 1942 he reported that Himmler had agreed to transfer the advance to the S.S. Office of Economy and Administration and had authorized him to start negotiations with representatives of Slovakian Jewry. Wisliceny led the representatives of the Working Group to understand that for two or three million dollars the top echelon of the S.S. would be willing to consider their proposals seriously, and that the negotiations themselves could be construed as German agreement in principle.[26]

Following these talks the Working Group contacted the World Jewish Congress and the JDC in Switzerland and the JAE in Jerusalem through emissaries in Geneva and Istanbul. Rabbis Weissmandel and Armin Frieder appealed to the "People of Israel to consult among yourselves and inform us as soon as possible of your opinion on this matter . . . how much money the community is able and willing to contribute for this great cause." They insisted on absolute secrecy and asked that a Jewish citizen of a neutral country be appointed to conduct the negotiations with Wisliceny on behalf of the Jewish organizations.[27]

Rabbi Weissmandel's collected letters, published posthumously by his family and friends after the war, contain a notation that he received an answer from the Jewish institutions in less than six weeks. "And the answer, clearly and strongly put, was a definite 'no.' They had to observe the Allied regulations not to send a single penny to enemy territory . . . Only if the Germans begin to repent and stop the deportations and killings, should they be talked to." According to Weissmandel, the Jewish organizations further pointed out that the JDC's budget for 1942 allocated only a few thousand dollars to Slovakia, which was now asking for tens of thousands for advance money; that the Jews in eastern Europe usually exaggerated in order to get more money from the Jews of the West, while in fact the situation of people deported to Poland was really not so terrible; that Germany's end was in sight and, meanwhile, "you should be smart and pass the time in Talmudic disputations." For all these reasons, according to the book, the organizations refused to give money to finance the Europa Plan or to help the Jews of Slovakia and Poland.[28]

According to the editors of Weissmandel's book, the original and all copies of this answer had been lost, and he was quoting from memory. "It is a pity that the answers from Switzerland and from Turkey were lost, since they showed in what a ridiculous and frivolous manner they were going to make sure that the Germans would neither kill nor deport any more." The editors explain that such answers reflected the fact that secular Zionists "do not believe anyone who is pious."[29] This claim is questionable since, together with the rabbis' letters, Yishuv leaders received communications from Gisi Fleischmann and corresponded with other leading Zionists in Slovakia—such as Moshe Daks from the Hechalutz youth movement, Leo Rosenthal, the head of the Palestine office, and Oscar Neumann, the chairman of the Zionist Federation. All of them were active in the Working Group and forwarded the same details of the plan that the rabbis did. Moreover, Saly Mayer, the representative of the JDC in Geneva, can hardly be described as a devout Zionist.

The contents of the answer as reported in Weissmandel's book are even more questionable. First, at the end of 1942 the Jewish organizations already knew and publicized the fact that a systematic extermination was being carried out in Europe and could not claim that the Jews of eastern Europe were exaggerating.

Second, the money to bribe the S.S. was not the only money the Jewish community in Slovakia needed, nor was it the first to be paid. Bribes had also been paid to Anton Vašek, the official in charge of Jewish affairs in the Slovak Ministry of the Interior, and to several other Slovak officials to obtain their help in preventing further deportations or a worsening of conditions in Slovakia. Money was also needed for the upkeep of work camps, managed by the Jewish communities at their own expense, in which thousands of Jews worked for the Slovak and German armies; to provide food and clothing for the deportees to Poland; and to smuggle Jews from Poland to Slovakia and thence to Hungary. Most of the money was collected from the Jews of Slovakia. Until November 1942 Saly Mayer transferred about 35,000 pounds to Slovakia through Nathan Schwalb in order to bypass the Allies' regulations. Schwalb added the money he collected from Jews in Switzerland or received from Palestine. Although these sums were very small, they helped the Working Group to feel that "the People of Israel still lives."[30]

Third, although a few leaders in the Yishuv did maintain that the end of the war would bring deliverance, it was an argument that the Jewish public as a whole—both in Palestine and abroad—totally rejected: when the war ended, there would be no Jews left to deliver. Finally, it seems hardly possible that, in wartime conditions, the Jewish organizations in Jerusalem and New York could receive the appeal from Slovakia, consult with each other, coordinate their answer, and reply—via Geneva—in less than six weeks. Moreover, there was, lamentably, no unified Jewish policy regarding rescue, certainly not at this point.

According to the editors of Weissmandel's book, a similar letter from Schwalb, also lost, made it clear that Zionist goals outweighed rescue: "we must do all we can so that the Land of Israel becomes the State of Israel." All nations were shedding their blood in the war, "and if we don't make sacrifices, how can we earn the right to come to the [negotiating] table? And if that is so, it is foolish and even impudent on our part to ask the nations . . . to allow us to bring their money into their enemy's country in order to protect our blood: our land can be acquired only by our blood."[31]

Schwalb firmly denies ever having written such a letter. Furthermore, in other, surviving letters written by Weissmandel and Fleischmann, even after the Europa Plan fell through, expressions of affection and appreciation for Schwalb abound. Such a letter would undoubtedly have aroused the whole group against him. But more to the point, Schwalb favored the plan from the beginning and in his letters to Palestine he recommended that the money be sent. He could not possibly have referred to it as "foolish and impudent."

Letters from Slovakia reached Geneva and Istanbul at the end of 1942, and by mid-January 1943 the Yishuv leaders had received a detailed report from Schwalb, to which he added a recommendation to adopt the proposal. The Agency and the Rescue Committee were asked to look into the details immediately and be prepared to risk money if bribery could delay or terminate harsh measures. Three days later Eliyahu Dobkin cabled Abraham Silberschein in Geneva with news of "our acceptance of the proposal in principal . . . check how realistic it is and how much money would be required of us for the purpose." Silberschein was asked to inform the Working Group of this decision immediately.[32]

Contrary to Weissmandel's report of a negative answer from Palestine, a positive answer—positive in principle, that is—was dispatched about a week after the information was received. It is impossible to know, however, whether all those who discussed the proposal in Palestine were aware of the fact that it included two separate matters: bribes to prevent the resumption of the deportations from Slovakia, which were liable to be resumed in April 1943, and bribes to stop the deportations from the rest of Europe to Poland and the extermination. A few apparently treated both issues as one, referring to them as "the Slovakia issue," "the rabbis' issue," or "the proposal of the supplicant" (that is, Rabbi Weissmandel). To the extent that the distinction was made, it was generally agreed that the Yishuv should participate in protecting the 20,000 Jews left in Slovakia, whether by bribes or by maintaining a labor camp.

In February Bader came from Istanbul and reinforced the opinion that there was a chance to prevent additional deportations from Slovakia through bribery: "The issue of ransom concerns Slovakia . . . we can see from every letter that harsh measures can be stopped or delayed with money, and now, when . . . it seems that the war is only a matter of months, a break of one month in the deportations can mean rescuing an entire Jewish community."[33]

Although no one said so in so many words, this plan of allowing 20,000 Slovakian Jews to stay where they were appeared to be simpler than the Transnistria plan, which involved the immigration of tens of thousands of people. Bader's comments reinforced the opinion of Ben-Gurion, who reiterated at the end of February, "We must go on bribing . . . the Agency is willing to get involved in this matter." Other members of the Executive, such as Moshe Shapira and Gruenbaum, responded similarly.[34]

But the Agency had reservations, or at least doubts, about the Europa Plan. The details reached Palestine at the end of 1942, at the same time as news of Himmler's order to annihilate Polish Jewry, perhaps even all of European Jewry, by the beginning of 1943. The letters from Slovakia contradicted this information, claiming that Himmler had agreed in principle to negotiate the deportations. In light of the fact that news of continued deportations kept arriving in Palestine from all parts of Europe at the end of January and in February 1943, it is no wonder that the Agency was skeptical.

There is no evidence that the Agency took any practical steps with regard to the Europa Plan at the beginning of 1943. It could not accept the request of the rabbis that the Agency, the World Jewish Congress, and the JDC appoint a representative to conduct negotiations with the S.S. on their behalf. First of all, the Allies could have construed such an action as treason. Second, the transfer of any money to enemy territory was forbidden. Third, Saly Mayer, a Swiss citizen, could always act as mediator if necessary. But, in the main, the entire idea seemed to contradict the information they had.

Letters from Slovakia, especially from Fleischmann and Weissmandel, continued to reach the Jewish organizations in March 1943, urging them to support the Europa Plan. They claimed that the money would not go into the coffers of the Third Reich but would be used only for personal bribes and therefore would not involve violation of the currency regulations. As a rule, they pointed out, even the most fanatic Nazis could be bought. Finally, they argued that Wisliceny had so far "fulfilled his promises entirely—to the letter" and was not acting on his own but in agreement with his superiors.

Each letter was an urgent plea for help. Their hands were empty, and the date set for resumption of the deportations—April—was drawing closer and closer. The Slovakian Jewish leaders were convinced that this was an opportunity to save not only themselves but all the European Jews who were still alive and that all that was needed was a few million dollars. As time went on, the letters, especially Weissmandel's, became more supplicatory, both threatening and admonishing at the same time. He begged for "mercy fast," reminded them of

the hundreds and hundreds of thousands who still face deportation, and the hundreds and hundreds of thousands who are doomed to annihilation. In our humble opinion, there is a possibility of saving them. Apparently, such a thing has never happened in the history of Israel, that our people themselves would renounce the possibility of saving their brethren only because they wanted to cling to their money.

The deportations were inevitable if gold was not found to stanch the blood: the deportees would be "the casualties of money." Weissmandel's expressions were repeated frequently in letters from the emissaries to Palestine. Schwalb, who forwarded the letters to Kaplan, added arguments for accepting the Europa Plan and concluded: "We have to concentrate on this great issue and allocate the maximum resources possible for it because if it is implemented we will have saved . . . so many lives."[35]

In a March letter to Zionists in Slovakia Kaplan wrote:

> I read the shocking letters of the rabbis who are crying out for help. Unfortunately, we are not able to take responsibility for the whole task. But, as I have already said, we do not see ourselves free of this responsibility, and we will do all we can. We have forwarded this demand to the rest of the Jewish people. In the meantime, we are sending you a certain sum of money with the bearer of this letter for immediate action, and we will try to expand our help.[36]

With Kaplan's approval the emissaries immediately transferred most of the money then at their disposal—4,000 pounds; the JDC sent another 5,000 pounds. Receipt of the money, about $36,000 in all (equivalent to almost $250,000 in 1989), was acknowledged in April. Barlas and Kaplan also asked the apostolic nuncio in Istanbul, Monsignor Roncalli, who had more than once tried to help save Jews, to appeal to the government of Slovakia, which was predominantly Catholic.[37] It is not clear, however, whether they informed Roncalli about the Europa Plan.

In February 1943 Wisliceny was transferred from Bratislava to Greece, where he was put in charge of deportations from Salonika and the rest of Macedonia to Auschwitz. Nonetheless, he continued as Eichmann's representative in Slovakia, visiting often. When there, he continued his demands for money from the Working Group. Although he agreed to take the money in installments, he wanted it in cash and in foreign currency. The fact that discussions with him continued was not enough to convince the leadership in Palestine that the Europa Plan was feasible. The emissaries in Istanbul and in Geneva were in a double bind, caught between pressing demands from Slovakia and prevailing doubts in Palestine; in addition, each had his own opinion. For Venia Pomerantz there were "arguments for and arguments against." Richard Lichtheim considered the plan to be nothing but "deceit and exploitation. Who knows what the truth is and what should be done." Schwalb supported it.[38]

Kaplan himself doubted the chances of success of any "sensational" plan but assumed that the regular bribes paid to local officials, which had taken on the nature of a tax, did indeed help stop the deportations from Slovakia. He hoped that similar rescue possibilities might be found in other countries as well. At this point, in March and April 1943, the JAE still believed that the Europa Plan was a fraud and, even if it was not, could not be carried out without the Allies and without money from free world Jewry. It considered specific, small-scale plans more realistic, even if they carried no guarantees of success.

Two events apparently brought a change of mind about the Europa Plan. The deportations from Slovakia, which were supposed to have resumed in April, were indeed postponed. More important, on May 11 Wisliceny told Fleischmann that he had been authorized by his superiors to conduct concrete negotiations and that as soon as the Jewish representatives came up with concrete details, all deportations would stop except in Poland; there, in the heart of the Jewish world, Germany would not make any concessions. The relevant sum was two to three million dollars—$200,000 to be paid in advance, the rest to be paid in weekly installments until June 10, 1943.[39]

At that point the emissaries in Istanbul began to think that the Europa Plan might be authentic. This, they wrote to Palestine, might be an opportunity "to save everybody," and it was inconceivable that the Jewish people would open themselves to the accusation that they were responsible for the plan's failure. In response to continuing pressure from Schwalb, Saly Mayer agreed to allocate $100,000 for the advance money without consulting the JDC executives in either the United States or Europe. Bader urged the JAE not to allow the JDC exclusive responsibility for the rescue. The Yishuv must meet every proposal "because we will never be able to justify our refusal politically, strategically, or circumstantially, even if our money cannot be guaranteed."[40]

At the end of June Schwalb and Barlas informed the Working Group that the Jewish Agency, the JDC, and the World Jewish Congress had decided to adopt the plan. The JDC (supported by the World Jewish Congress) would send $200,000 for the advance, half of which would be repaid later by the Yishuv. Emissaries in Istanbul and in Geneva expressed doubts that the JDC would indeed transfer such large sums to enemy territory or be satisfied with promises to be paid after the war; they feared that the burden would fall on the Yishuv alone.[41]

Early in July, Stephen Wise and Nahum Goldmann persuaded President Roosevelt to agree in principle to the transfer of funds from Jewish organizations in the United States to a blocked bank account in Switzerland, from which it would be possible to withdraw money only after the war but against which Jews could in the meantime withdraw local currency. The British Foreign Office vehemently opposed the idea and corresponded with the State Department for months. Nevertheless, in December the State Department finally approved the transfer, mainly because of pressure from the secretary of the Treasury, Henry Morgenthau, Jr.[42]

In July, as soon as Roosevelt had agreed to the idea and without waiting for State Department approval, the JDC in coordination with the World Jewish Congress deposited the money in a Swiss bank. A courier from Geneva took papers to Fleischmann in Slovakia showing that $200,000 had been deposited. But this was not the kind of transaction that the emissaries, Fleischmann, or Wisliceny had in mind; what was needed was cash, in dollars, that could be handed from one person to another, on the spot. Meanwhile, Wisliceny's first deadline had passed. He agreed to another at the end of July and then to another at the end of August; at every extension he reiterated that the conditions remained basically the same. But the cash did not arrive. "Needless to say," Barlas later explained, "it was impossible to transfer millions of dollars illegally, through couriers, the way that regular transactions, in tens of thousands, were carried out." Yet the fact remains that only the advance payment of 50,000 pounds, or $200,000, had to be transferred at one time.[43]

In July and August Fleischmann sent desperate and angry letters to the emissaries in Istanbul and called Geneva every few days. The emissaries saw the leaders of Slovakian Jewry, themselves on the edge of the abyss, investing all their efforts in an attempt to rescue the Jewish people as a whole while they themselves were helpless. Pomerantz, Bader, and Shind wrote to Palestine:

> We are too poor, too weak to really help. We have spent the remainder of the budget you put at our disposal, and it does not amount to even a third of the advance payment. We want to remind you of what we said regarding this issue on different occasions and we feel miserable that we were not able to convince you in time . . . Leave all else for the moment, and help us save before the curtain falls on everything.

At the end of this emotional and desperate letter they demanded permission to do as they saw fit. At the beginning of August they sent to Slovakia another 15,000 pounds in cash, then equal to $60,000. Mayer sent the equivalent of $16,000 in Swiss francs, also in cash, a few days later.[44]

The JAE approved these measures after the fact. "We have decided to participate in the first stage of the rabbis' plan" with 12,000 pounds (to which the emissaries added 3,000), Dobkin wrote to Gruenbaum, who had gone to South Africa to raise money for the plan and for general rescue.[45] Joseph Schwartz, who met with Shertok in August in Palestine and Istanbul, agreed that the JDC and the Jewish Agency would continue to cooperate in trying to implement the Europa Plan. Schwartz committed himself without the knowledge of the JDC headquarters in New York, since the arrangement was clearly contrary to its official policy, "one cannot discuss this with the JDC," as Mayer put it. On August 10 Shertok cabled Mayer to send $150,000 in cash to Fleischmann immediately, assured him of the Agency's support in case Mayer got in trouble with the JDC directors in New York, and promised that the Agency would repay the rest of the money ($60,000 had already been sent from Istanbul) within a short time.

> After studying the material thoroughly, I have reached the conclusion that we would be taking a grave responsibility on ourselves and putting a heavy load on our conscience by not acting according to Gisi's offer. Under the present circumstances, this is a major issue, and we have to seize any small chance. All other considerations must be pushed aside. In spite of other heavy commitments, I am giving 50 for this special case and urge you to provide 150 immediately. I shall back you to the utmost in shouldering responsibility. This is an hour of extreme emergency.[46]

In August and September Mayer sent only about $53,000 to Slovakia. The sum of $100,000 was therefore sent from Istanbul with a double agent.

The records of the Rescue Committee on funds spent for rescue confirm the emissaries' letters and memoirs to the effect that in 1943 and 1944 the Yishuv sent 100,000 pounds to Slovakia, then the equivalent of $400,000. About half of this sum was sent, a few thousand pounds at a time, for bribing the Slovaks, aiding the Jews in the camps, supporting the deportees in Poland, and smuggling others across borders. The other $200,000 was earmarked for the Europa Plan to cover the advance payment demanded by Wisliceny. Receipts confirming the arrival of most of the money came in letters from Slovakia. The JDC apparently sent $42,000 in June 1943 for bribes and so on, and $53,000 for the Europa Plan in August and September; the rest was deposited in Swiss banks. The JDC sent a total of $122,600 in 1943 and 1944.[47] The Agency did not send the money in June, immediately after the decision was made, apparently because it mistakenly assumed that Mayer had large sums at his disposal and was going to send cash. It is possible that Mayer did not reveal his real financial situation and the discrepancy between his willingness to support the plan and the New York JDC's position toward such steps. Therefore, it is also possible that Schwalb pushed Mayer into a corner when he notified the Working Group of Mayer's willingness to pay at the end of June.

Meanwhile negotiations with Wisliceny failed. At the end of August he returned from Greece and told the Working Group that the situation had changed and that he had to discuss the matter again with his superiors. At the end of September he informed them that the Germans had reneged on their decision to stop the deportations in Europe and that they would reconsider it only at a later date. He received another $10,000 in cash from Fleischmann but said that this was only a deposit; he could not hold serious negotiations when the other side repeatedly failed to meet deadlines or to bring any real offers. Most of the money sent by Mayer as well as what came later from Istanbul arrived after the final deadline, that is, the end of August.

This marked the end of almost a year of negotiations between Wisliceny and the Working Group. In the letters that followed, Fleischmann expressed their bitter disappointment: had the money arrived on time, results would have been different. Now the end was approaching. "We do not hear anything from Willi any more." From October 1943 on, Slovakia was mentioned at meetings of the Agency and other bodies only in connection with the situation in Europe in general and not with regard to the Europa Plan. Issues that were discussed included the labor camps, steps for self-defense in case the Jews were brought together in preparation for deportation, and the need to continue the aid being sent from Istanbul, Geneva, and the JDC as well as the small sums from the Jews of Hungary. At the end of the year, Shind summarized the situation: "The issue of the famous lobbyist in Slovakia is off." The reference was, of course, to Rabbi Weissmandel and to the Europa Plan.[48]

Two questions remain to be asked about the Europa Plan. First, what were the intentions of the Germans when they agreed to negotiate with the Working Group—that is, did the money paid prevent more deportations, and could more money have prevented more? Second, if the Agency feared the plan was a German hoax, why did it invest such large sums in it?

A full answer to the first question is impossible, for no explicit references to the negotiations can be found in the internal German correspondence. There is circumstantial evidence, however, that the Europa Plan was just another item in the Final Solution and not a deviation from it.

To begin with, 58,000 Slovakian Jews, most of them young and strong, were sent to the extermination camps before the deportations were stopped. Documents of the Slovakian State Council reveal that in March 1942 the Slovaks initiated an agreement with Germany providing for an initial deportation of 60,000 Slovakian Jews. In May, however, the Slovakian parliament took measures that protected most of the remaining 22,000 Jews: they were provided with documents showing that they had been baptized before March 1939, were married to non-Jews, or worked in essential industries. These documents also extended protection to workers' families.[49] Thus, the deportations were stopped at that point not because of the bribes but because the Germans had carried out their policy regarding the Jews of Slovakia to the extent that they could. The deportations from Slovakia stopped in October 1942, and in December the Germans decided to deport the Jewish community of Salonika. These deportations began in mid-March 1943, and a few months later the deportations from France were resumed. Moreover, Eichmann and Himmler did not appoint another adviser in Slovakia when Wisliceny was transferred to Greece to begin deportations there; this fact seems to indicate that they considered his main job in Slovakia finished. The Germans seldom annihilated all the Jews of one country in one step. They usually deported the vast majority, leaving those they needed for the labor force and those who were hard to find, and moved on to another Jewish community. Thus their policy in Slovakia, where they deported about three-quarters of the Jews, was no different from their policy in any country where there was no ransom or talk of ransom.

It is also unlikely that Himmler had approved the Europa Plan, as Wisliceny claimed in October 1942. At that time the Germans had not yet met defeat on the Russian front or in North Africa, so S.S. leaders would have had no reason to seek safety by presenting themselves as rescuers of Jews or by negotiating with Jewish organizations in the free world. If that had indeed been the case, why did Himmler stop the negotiations with the Working Group in the second half of 1943, precisely when Germany was suffering severe setbacks?

According to Hans Ludin, the German ambassador in Bratislava at the time, domestic factors also played a role in halting the deportations from Slovakia.[50] The influence of the local church, interference by the Vatican as urged by Roncalli, breakdowns in the railway system, sympathy for the Jews in moderate and influential circles, the value of Jewish labor, and bribes to Slovakian officials delayed the Germans, at least temporarily, and not just in Slovakia.

The temporary halt in deportations may have also been the result of defects in the German extermination system. Most of the extermination camps started operating in the spring and summer of 1942, but various problems soon arose. The hastily built railway tracks to Sobibor went out of commission during August and September. In Belzec, Sobibor, and Treblinka gas chambers too small for the pace of the extermination were exchanged for larger ones and used for the Jews of eastern Poland. In Auschwitz only the small chamber was already in operation; the larger ones, which later operated in that part of Auschwitz called Birkenau, had not yet been built. Auschwitz was where most of the Jews deported from Slovakia were sent, since it was the camp closest to its border. At the end of the summer of 1942 the camps were probably not operating at full capacity; hence the halt in the deportations.

The sum of two to three million dollars requested by Wisliceny in exchange for about a million people seems amazingly small, given the Germans' view of the economic capability of free world Jewry. For the fanatics among the top Nazis, world Jewry was the invisible ruler of the West. On other occasions the Germans extorted much larger sums in return for much smaller numbers, as in the case of the Jews of Rome or those of the island of Jerba who were forced to collect dozens of kilograms of gold. Rumania demanded $400 for each of the Transnistria refugees, and this was the sum that Eichmann indirectly mentioned in 1944 in his "Merchandise for Blood" offer.

Furthermore, if the sum was intentionally small, to be used as a "personal bribe," as Fleischmann claimed, how could money that went, unreported, into somebody's pocket halt the extermination machine—even if the pocket was that of Himmler himself, and not of Wisliceny? There were certainly better and more efficient ways for Himmler to make a fortune. Such a large-scale plan to stop the extermination in various places and help a large number of Jews would have been very difficult to conceal and would have brought Himmler into a head-on collision with the extermination fanatics, most of whom were his own disciples. His adversaries could have used it to turn Hitler against him. To justify such a plan, which was diametrically opposed to basic Nazi ideology, not to mention Himmler's own record as commander of the S.S., he would have had to prove that it was to the Reich's interests and to demand really large sums in return.

The Working Group claimed in its letters that Wisliceny was not a strong believer in the Final Solution and that he was more amenable to negotiations than other S.S. officers. Even if this assessment was correct, the man was a small cog in a big wheel that imposed its will on him. Whether he wanted to or not, he fulfilled a major role in carrying out the Final Solution throughout the war. Those in charge frequently concealed their real intentions from their subordinates, and Wisliceny's superiors could only benefit from his misleading the Jewish leadership. This argument of the Working Group may have stemmed from its inability to see the German system in its entirety.

The JAE, without knowing all the details available today, correctly judged the Europa Plan to be a German hoax. Yet the amount of money sent to Slovakia, according to the records, was exceeded only by that sent to Rumania, Hungary, and Poland. Why?

There are several possible explanations for the Agency's decision. First of all, the Executive did not want to miss any opportunity, however slim its chances of success. Second, the very fact that Wisliceny reopened contacts in May 1943 reinforced the hope that the plan was genuine; hence the JAE's positive decision in June. Third, the JAE was reluctant to allow the JDC undue credit as the main supporter of the Europa Plan, the savior of European Jewry (if it worked), and the one body at least willing to take risks (if it did not). No one would have remembered that it was the Jewish Agency (Shertok and Schwalb) that had pushed the JDC (Mayer and Schwartz) to give the money and to transfer it as cash rather than as a bank deposit.

The Europa Plan affair underscores the deep gap that existed between the actual power of free world Jewry and Slovakian Jewry's perceptions, reflected in the letters from Slovakia. These were filled with anger and despair but were apologetic at the same time. "I did not wish to hurt you . . . What I have written," wrote Moshe Daks, the Hechalutz youth movement activist in Slovakia, to the emissaries in Istanbul, "I have written with tears" It also shows what esteem the Yishuv emissaries and leaders felt for the persistent struggle of the Working Group and its concern for the Jewish people as a whole. Rabbi Weissmandel was admired for his resourcefulness and for his pain, notwithstanding his harsh letters. And of Fleischmann, who repeatedly confronted, usually alone, Eichmann's representative, the emissaries in Istanbul wrote: "We find some comfort in the light emanating from Gisi's behavior, but this light only emphasizes the terrible darkness."[51]

The decisions made and the sums of money sent disprove the recent claim by the youth of Agudat Yisrael that the leaders of the Yishuv refused to send money that could have stopped the extermination and that the Zionist movement abandoned the Jews of Europe for the sake of establishing the state of Israel.[52] In fact the Yishuv was constantly worried that without Jews from Europe, the traditional source of immigration, no state would be possible.

"MERCHANDISE FOR BLOOD"

Adolf Eichmann's "Ware für Blut" proposal was perhaps the best-known ransom plan devised during the Holocaust. It was first presented to the Yishuv emissaries on May 19, 1944, by Joel Brand, a leading member of the Jewish Aid and Rescue Committee in Hungary whom Eichmann had dispatched Istanbul for that purpose. The plan was discussed in Jerusalem from May 25 until July 19, when press coverage made it public and marked its end. Although the proposal has prompted heated public controversy and both historical analysis and literary description, the Agency's attitude to it has received little study.

On May 24, 1944, Venia Pomerantz arrived in Jerusalem from Istanbul, bringing with him a summary of Eichmann's proposal concealed in a tube of shaving cream. Pomerantz spent the whole night with Ben-Gurion and Shertok; the next morning, at an emergency session of the JAE, he reported on developments in Hungary since the German occupation on March 19, 1944.

In Palestine the newspapers had already reported the harsh anti-Jewish regulations issued in Hungary with the Nazi takeover. They knew that the Nazis had begun to herd the Jewish population into ghettos in the small towns and that thousands had already been deported to the death camps in Poland. Large-scale deportations, though planned, had not yet been executed, but the press warned that the fate of Hungarian Jewry would be little different from that of the other doomed communities of Europe, and, since the German system appeared to be the same, the Jews of Hungary were terrified by the prospect of extermination.[53]

The newspaper reports had been confirmed by information sent to the Agency by the emissaries in Istanbul and in Geneva, but confirmation had not been made public. The public was, of course, unaware what Pomerantz's mission was—namely, to report on the prolonged negotiations between Eichmann and Wisliceny, among others, with

Joel Brand and Yisrael Kasztner of the Aid and Rescue Committee from the time the Germans had entered Hungary until May.

Eichmann announced that he had already killed 3,500,000 Jews but was nevertheless prepared to strike a deal with the Jewish Agency and the JDC. In Eichmann's conceptual world, the JDC was the epitome of the connection of Jews with money. The deal consisted in exchanging "merchandise for blood." The "merchandise" was to be 10,000 trucks, to be used only on the eastern front, 80 tons of coffee, 20 tons of tea, 20 tons of cocoa, and 2 million bars of soap. The exchange of Jews for German prisoners of war was also possible. The "blood" was 100 Jews in return for each truck, or its equivalent in money or kind, as agreed between the two sides—altogether, one million Jews. The Germans made it a condition that the Jews not emigrate to Palestine, but that they be brought to Spain and Portugal. Eichmann announced that he was willing to release 10,000 Jews as a token of his earnestness as soon as the agreement was confirmed in principle, even before he got his first payment. As a further sign of goodwill he was even ready to let 600 Jews go to Palestine and ordered a list of names for this purpose.

According to Pomerantz, the Germans had agreed that Brand could go not only to Istanbul but also, if necessary, to Portugal and Switzerland, and perhaps even to Palestine, but he had to return to Budapest within approximately two weeks. The Germans sent a double agent, a Hungarian Jew by the name of Andor (Bundy) Gross, or Andreas Georgi, to accompany Brand. They had conducted separate talks with the agent before the two left Budapest. The Germans indicated to Brand, through Gross, that money—about $400 per capita—might be acceptable instead of trucks and that the negotiations were being conducted with the knowledge of the top echelons in Germany. Gross had performed various errands before, transferring money and letters for the emissaries of the Yishuv and for the intelligence services of the Allies in Istanbul, and was well known as a dubious person who sold his services to the highest bidder. Joel Brand and his colleagues, mostly Mapai members, maintained regular contact with the emissaries in Istanbul and in Palestine. A refugee who was supported by the Aid and Rescue Committee described Brand as "devoted, risking his life, living with the rescue."[54]

In his report Pomerantz omitted to tell the Agency that the initial reaction of the emissaries in Istanbul, upon hearing from Brand, was a desire to get up and cry, "All lies! A deceptive, villainous proposal!" They had already been deceived too often, but they did not feel free to reject the proposal. Once again they hoped, as they had in the cases of Rumania and Slovakia, that maybe there was some chance of rescue. Neither Pomerantz nor the JAE knew that some members of the Budapest Aid and Rescue Committee had reacted the same way when Brand first reported to them the details of Eichmann's proposal: "We were stunned . . . We knew that the Allies would give neither trucks nor money since either would help the enemy . . . On the Jewish side, thousands of attempts at rescue through ransom had already been made although it was known that Eichmann's subordinates took money . . . and then sent their victims to their deaths." Nonetheless, the members of the committee in Budapest, like the emissaries, refused to reject the offer out of hand. As Kasztner later asked those who questioned his reaction, "Was there anything else left for us to do? Did anyone suggest other, better rescue possibilities?"[55]

Pomerantz also neglected to describe the difficult relations created between Brand and the emissaries in Istanbul from the moment he arrived. Brand was convinced that the emissaries were all-powerful. He thus construed even the slightest delay in obtaining the proper documents for him as a lack of willingness on their part, a refusal to cooperate to the extent that he had expected. "Our kind of thinking was as far from his as east is from west," was the way Ehud Avriel summarized the situation.[56]

After their discussions with Brand the emissaries raised several questions that Pomerantz in turn raised with the JAE. Had the discussions conducted in Budapest indeed been approved by the S.S. high command and by the Nazi regime? Was Brand going to be able to come to Palestine with the approval of the mandatory government and later be allowed to return to Budapest? Could one of the emissaries in Istanbul go to Hungary to conduct the negotiations? And, most crucial and urgent, could the opening of negotiations be used to stop the deportations immediately, and how? The deportations from Hungary to Poland—it was not yet known that their destination was Auschwitz—had started in the middle of May, three days before Brand's departure, and were going on at an unprecedented pace. Twelve thousand people were being sent by railway every day. Every hour that passed meant the death of another 500 Jews.

On the day of the meeting Barlas had sent a cable from Istanbul to the Agency:

> The emissary will give you the details, which speak—or rather cry out—for themselves. You have to weigh the situation and inform us immediately of your decision—whether we should start negotiating or whether, because of our helplessness, we should abstain. We are waiting for your

decision with trepidation. Tens of thousands of lives may depend on it
. . . Cable immediately. Do not wait—not even one day.[57]

The JAE meeting concerning Pomerantz's report centered on three
issues: Did the Germans really intend to stop the extermination?
What would the Allied reaction be? What should the Agency do?

In relation to the first question, most thought that the idea was "fantastic," "questionable," "a satanic provocation, devised to enable [the
Germans] to slaughter the Jews of Hungary." The JAE agreed, however, that full consideration should be given to the matter and that,
even if there were only one chance in a million, it should be seized.

As for the predictable reaction of the Allies, Gruenbaum and Dobkin suggested that the negotiations be concealed from the British, and
Gruenbaum recommended that they be concealed from the Americans too. Both men had been involved in rescue attempts for a year
and a half and apparently had very few illusions left regarding the
Allied attitude toward the rescue of Jews. Gruenbaum, who was the
more pessimistic of the two, was certain that the British would simply
obstruct the whole matter as they had other plans. Ben-Gurion and
Kaplan, however, were convinced that, without the Allies' cooperation, as Ben-Gurion said, "we will not be able to move." Most of the
others agreed.

The JAE decided by majority vote, with Gruenbaum dissenting, to
convey the details of the plan immediately to the high commissioner
and, through him, to the government in London and officials of the
Foreign Office there. In Washington they should first be conveyed to
Weizmann and Goldmann. It was further agreed that Shertok would
leave for Turkey immediately. These combined moves would create
the impression that the JAE's answer was positive. Contact with the
Germans would continue, and time might be gained during which
rescue might be possible.

The records indicate that the JAE was torn between distrust of the
Germans and skepticism toward the Allies, on the one hand, and
hope that the negotiations might produce some results, on the other.
Shertok best expressed these contradictory feelings. The Allies would
probably think as follows: "Let us assume that hundreds of thousands
arrive in Portugal, what shall be done with them? How will they be
fed?" But, as he went on, "we do not have a choice. We are compelled
to do everything in order to save the remnant in Europe. We have
nothing to lose. If the last million is not saved, it will be annihilated."[58]

The JAE was not yet aware that, in the meantime, Gross had revealed to Brand and Avriel in Istanbul that Brand's mission was in fact a cover for his own mission, which was to establish contacts between the S.S. officers in Budapest and the Allies in order to reach a separate peace agreement with the West. Nor were they aware that, immediately after Brand's arrival in Istanbul, the emissaries there had decided to disclose Eichmann's proposal to the British, since there was little chance anyway, in spy-ridden Istanbul, of concealing a matter of such importance from them. Moreover, it was reasonable to expect that Gross would shortly be in touch with his contacts in Allied intelligence, at which point the representatives of the Yishuv would be suspected of hiding their intentions of negotiating with the enemy.[59]

Brand later wrote in his memoirs that Kasztner had warned him before he left Budapest not to divulge the details of his mission to the British and that he (Brand) had conveyed this warning to the emissaries in Istanbul when he got there. No such warning, however, is mentioned either in the report Kasztner submitted to the Twenty-second Zionist Congress in Basel after the war or in the memoirs of any of the emissaries. On the day after their first meeting with Brand, Shind and Avriel approached the head of British intelligence in Turkey, Colonel Harold Gibson, and reported to him on Brand's mission. There was no need to elaborate on Gross's character; both sides knew what he was like. Gibson's reaction, according to Avriel, was "cold as ice." He was not willing to recommend to his superiors in London that they allow the emissaries in Istanbul to negotiate with the Germans or even to act as if they were. His main reason was that the Russians would find out about it and suspect the West of negotiating, not for the purpose of saving Jews, but for a separate peace. "We became entangled in a network of international intrigue and high diplomacy," Avriel wrote, "and from then on the British followed our every step."[60]

On May 26, the day after the Executive met, Shertok gave Sir Harold MacMichael, the high commissioner, the details of Eichmann's proposal, unaware that they had already reached British intelligence. MacMichael called the proposal "a Nazi intrigue" but added frankly that every possibility should nevertheless be checked so that Britain should not be accused later of ignoring opportunities for rescue. Finally, he promised to deliver the information to the governments of Britain and the United States and to Goldmann and Weizmann, which indeed he did. Shertok asked the high commissioner for a visa to Turkey. The visa, however, was repeatedly delayed.[61]

Meanwhile the emissaries in Istanbul sent a cable to Ira Hirschmann, who was then in Washington, and Barlas met with the American ambassador, Laurence Steinhardt, in Ankara. Steinhardt promised to report the matter to his government and to help the emissaries transmit information that was not meant for British knowledge. Most important, the emissaries also cabled Budapest, demanding a halt to the deportations and asking for an extension since the authorities to which the proposal was submitted were demonstrating a positive interest. They sent Kasztner another cable for Eichmann stating that the JAE was in consultation and that Shertok was coming to Istanbul to meet with Brand. The answer from Budapest was: "The deportations are continuing."[62]

The end of May was approaching, and Shertok had not yet arrived in Istanbul. The emissaries therefore decided to formulate a temporary agreement for Brand to take back to Eichmann. On May 29 Barlas, Avriel, and Bader, on the one hand, and Joel Brand, on the other, signed a protocol to the effect that representatives of the Jewish Agency were empowering Brand to inform those who sent him that they agreed in principle to practical negotiations and to the signing of an agreement.

The emissaries signed on behalf of "Homeland" and Brand as the authorized representative of the General Council of Hungarian Jews. Special envoys, the protocol went on, were on their way from Palestine to Istanbul, and the Jewish authorities were expecting the other party to send its representatives to meet them.

The terms of the interim agreement, to take effect immediately, were as follows:[63]

1. The deportations would stop immediately, since "the objects of rescue were dwindling and would eventually disappear." The other party would receive one million Swiss francs monthly.
2. Emigration to Palestine would be allowed according to a list compiled by the representatives of "Homeland"; $400,000 would be paid for every 1,000 people, that is, $400 per person.
3. Emigration to other countries overseas via neutral countries such as Spain would also be permitted; $1 million would be paid for every 10,000 people.
4. It would be permitted to send food, clothing, and medical supplies to the ghettos and camps, and for each van reaching its destination the other party would receive a van of goods of equal value. No trucks were mentioned.

On the following night, May 30, the agreement was sent with a Swiss courier who was instructed to give it to Kasztner in person. Since no authorized member of the Agency had signed it, the signers knew that it was worthless. Still, with the deportations going on at full speed, they had nothing to lose. Second, the Turks had already decided that

Brand and Gross would have to leave Turkey, either for Hungary or for Palestine, whichever they preferred. Shertok cabled the emissaries that Brand was not to come to Palestine because, as a citizen of an enemy country and potentially in possession of confidential information, the British could prevent him from returning to Hungary and thus thwart his mission. Shertok asked Brand to await him in Istanbul despite the Turkish order to leave.[64]

Under Turkish pressure, the emissaries were forced to convince Brand to return to Hungary before Shertok's arrival, and they provided him with the "miserable piece of paper" on which the interim agreement was signed. Brand himself decided, contrary to the emissaries' advice and contrary to what he wrote in later reports and in his memoirs, to go to Palestine. Returning to Hungary, he thought, would indicate to Eichmann that the Jewish Agency and its emissaries were not strong enough even to get him permission to stay in Turkey, much less to act as representative of "the Jews who control the whole world, and whom all the American senators obey," as Eichmann had told him before he left.[65]

At the beginning of June, Gibson promised Shind and Avriel that Brand would be allowed to return to Hungary via Turkey even after he went to Palestine to meet with Shertok, who was unable to reach Turkey without a visa. The emissaries suspected a trap and suggested that Brand meet Shertok on the Syrian-Turkish border. Gibson agreed. The secretary of the mandatory government in Jerusalem and the head of military intelligence there advised Shertok to arrange to meet Brand in the Syrian border city of Aleppo, from which Brand could then return to Hungary without delay. Shertok already knew of British intentions to allow Brand to come to Palestine and also feared a trap. Nonetheless, they all fell into it.[66]

Bader, Joseph Klarman, and Ya'acov Griffle warned Brand that it was "a dangerous step" to leave Turkey. Barlas was also against it, especially since Steinhardt had advised him not to trust the British. But the other emissaries were not. "Avriel and Shind did not understand that the British were deceiving them," Barlas said years later, "and Brand left Turkey without even saying goodby to me." Brand, however, claims in his memoirs that Barlas forced him to go.[67]

On June 7 Brand and Avriel boarded a train and headed south. On the way Avriel, according to his own testimony, began to suspect that the British were not going to honor their promises. That same day, Shertok left Jerusalem for the north to meet Brand, equipped with promises given him by the high commissioner and the head of the

British intelligence that he would be allowed to see Brand immediately, after which Brand would be allowed to return to Turkey.

Upon instructions from British intelligence in Cairo, Brand was arrested as soon as he arrived in Aleppo and was prevented from seeing Shertok. Shertok waited at a hotel for three days; on June 10 an order came from the Foreign Office to allow him to meet with Brand.[68]

In the meantime there had been other developments. At the end of May, with the information from Palestine in hand, the Governmental Committee for Refugees in London had called an urgent meeting attended by Foreign Secretary Eden, Secretary for the Colonies Stanley, and Secretary for Economic Warfare Lord Selborne to discuss the Eichmann proposal. The resolutions adopted were similar to those adopted with regard to the Transnistria affair. It was not possible to discuss the German proposal seriously; it was nothing but another German subterfuge to be used to fight the Allies. Transferring a million refugees to an Allied or neutral country would hurt the war effort. Furthermore, a British indication of willingness to negotiate with the Germans "might lead to an offer to unload an even greater number of Jews onto our hands."[69] The meeting took place exactly one week before the Allied invasion of Normandy and at the height of the great spring offensive by the Soviets, who were advancing toward Vitebsk. In terms of the military situation and the growing suspicion between East and West, this was bad timing.

The British ambassador in Moscow, Sir Clark A. Kerr, was instructed to convey the details of the proposals to the Soviets, stressing the need for cooperation among the three superpowers on the issue. The British ambassador to the United States, Lord Halifax, told the acting secretary of state, Edward Stettinius, Jr., that Britain would not enter into any negotiations on the basis of a proposal that was "a sheer case of blackmail or political warfare . . . a monstrous bargain." Halifax suggested that Shertok not be given any definite answer until the Allied position was clearer, but he should be warned against negotiating with the enemy. In the meantime, he said, Britain would discuss, in cooperation with the United States, any genuine rescue proposals and would not "close the door" on them, an expression that later became a key phrase in this affair.[70]

On June 7 Weizmann met with Eden and asked him to act immediately in a positive spirit and to enable Shertok to come to London at once. Eden promised Weizmann that "the door will stay open." Weizmann in turn promised that the Jewish Agency would do nothing without the knowledge and approval of the British government.[71] It appears that, acting alone, Britain would have rejected the German proposal outright on its own merits. But because its overall policy required cooperation with the United States to check Soviet expansion in eastern Europe, it had to show willingness to accommodate any American interest in saving Jews, especially on the eve of presidential elections in the United States.

The State Department had learned about Brand's mission from Steinhardt. The details had also been conveyed to Goldmann, who met immediately with Stettinius to convince him that the Germans must be led to believe that their proposal was being considered with utmost seriousness. The chairman of the War Refugee Board, John V. Pehle, gave Stettinius the minutes of his conversation with Roosevelt, in which the president agreed that the negotiations should be kept alive, if only to gain time. Hirschmann was asked to leave as soon as possible for Istanbul on behalf of the WRB and with Roosevelt's approval. There he was to meet Brand and hint to the Germans that negotiations were possible—although he was not authorized to conduct such negotiations himself.[72]

After his meeting with Shertok in Aleppo, Brand was transferred to Cairo, and Shertok returned to Palestine. On June 14 he reported to the JAE that "the matter is more complex and complicated than we thought, and it has become even more entangled by the interference of the British." He then expatiated on his six-hour conversation with Brand, which had been attended by a British officer and by Tzvi Yehieli of Aliya Bet.

Brand had given Shertok a detailed sequence of events. Immediately after the German invasion, Brand contacted Wisliceny, "nicknamed Willi, who helped the Slovakian Jews," through counterespionage agents who had previously transferred money and letters from Istanbul to Hungary and to the occupied areas. Wisliceny had letters with him from the Slovakian Working Group, notably from Weissmandel, recommending that the Jews in Hungary maintain contact with him. The idea was to try to reach a financial agreement with the S.S. that would delay the deportations from Hungary.

Soon afterward these agents were arrested; Wehrmacht officers who had been present at several of the meetings appeared no more. From then on, the negotiations were conducted by a group of S.S. officers: Wisliceny, Hermann Krumey, Otto Klages, and, in the last stages, Eichmann, who became the main figure in the negotiations. The Jewish side was usually represented by Brand and Kasztner. The latter offered the Germans money on condition that the concentration of Jews in ghettos and camps in Hungary be stopped, that there be an end to deportations and extermination, and that the Jews be allowed to leave for Palestine or elsewhere. In the first stages of the talks, Wisliceny agreed to some of the proposals, promising, first of all, that the exterminations would be stopped. "The present German method is not to kill Jews, but rather to take advantage of them as a labor force." He also promised that they would no longer be concentrated in ghettos and camps, although Jews living in villages and small towns would be transferred to larger cities. According to him, the Germans were interested in large-scale emigration of hundreds of thousands and asked for a plan to implement it. Kasztner and Brand answered that the Jewish Agency still had 30,000 immigration permits and that a ship anchored in Constantza could immediately take 750 people, 150 more than the group Eichmann offered to release as a token of goodwill, to Turkey. Eichmann gave them, as proof of such goodwill, money and unopened letters from Schwalb that had been intercepted by his staff.

Once Eichmann became fully involved in the negotiations, it became evident that, even if an agreement about massive emigration was reached, the Germans would not allow the destination to be Palestine. There were political reasons—they did not want to anger the Arabs by contributing to a strong Jewish Palestine—and ideological ones— "If you establish a strong power in Palestine, then, after a while, we will clash with you again," Eichmann predicted. He told Brand and Kasztner that because Nazis believed Judaism to be a malignant disease, they wanted the Jews spread through the Allied territories—including Spain, North Africa, and North America—in order to contaminate the enemy.

Shertok asked Brand a few questions, which he answered frankly, although the answers were not unambiguous. To the key question whether German intentions were serious, Brand replied that he believed that they were really interested in the goods although they had not specified them. Only once had Eichmann mentioned trucks for the S.S.; the tea, coffee, and other goods had been mentioned by a civilian whom Brand did not know. On another occasion Brand had been given a list of spare parts, and foreign currency had been mentioned as well. It was therefore Brand's opinion that German intentions were mainly political: they wanted the Allies to take their proposal into consideration once peace negotiations started. This opinion had been reinforced by Gross's revelation that his own special mission was really to prepare a meeting between the S.S. officers in Budapest and representatives of Britain and the United States.

Shertok told his colleagues that Brand's mission was "the thread" by which negotiations could eventually be led to include entirely different topics. Shertok was convinced that Gross had gone directly to the British with details of his mission as soon as he arrived in Istanbul. It was his opinion, therefore, that the British wanted to play the game from all angles: to bring Brand and Gross to Allied territory, in which case they would not be allowed to return to Hungary; "to acquit themselves of the charge of having caught them by deceit"; and to avoid having to enter into negotiations for rescuing Jews by claiming that the gist of Eichmann's proposal was "negotiations for a separate peace agreement with the Nazis. We cannot let them get away with this," he said. "We have to maintain that it is possible to save Jews and to postpone the deportations without making a commitment."

Shertok had asked Brand what he thought would happen if he returned with a positive answer, if he returned with a negative one, or if he failed to return altogether. Brand had replied that initially he had believed that a positive answer would result in rescue, but after he had left and had learned about Gross's mission, he was not so sure anymore. In fact even during the negotiations in Budapest, he had occasionally thought that the proposal "was a satanic plan that might be used to hide the rapid extermination of the remainder of European Jewry from the eyes of the world." Nevertheless, he was convinced he had to return to Hungary immediately to do what he could to prevent the total annihilation of Balkan Jewry.

Brand described in detail the cruel incarceration of the Jews in the rural towns. The Germans had answered the protest of the Aid and Rescue Committee members by claiming that the Hungarians were responsible. To Brand's protests Eichmann had responded that the deportations from Hungary to the death camps would continue at the rate of 12,000 a day in order to exercise pressure on the Jewish negotiators. Brand had believed (as it turned out, incorrectly) that the deportations had ceased while he was in Istanbul.

Brand also reported to Shertok on action taken by the committee in Budapest to aid the refugees from Poland and Slovakia and to purchase weapons for defense even before the German takeover. "The Jews of Hungary," he said, "know that 'deportation' means extermination." In Brand's opinion the Hungarian Jews who had served in various armies could serve as the nucleus of a larger defense force.

After his meeting with the JAE, Shertok summed up in writing the Agency's position. The fact that the Germans had sent Gross with Brand meant that they hoped to profit from the proposal. If they believed that serious negotiations were going to take place, they might stop the deportations, even if only for a short period, and thousands,

if not tens of thousands, of Jews would be saved. In other words, Shertok wrote, "We felt that we had to act in order to gain time." Thus the
Agency's attitude remained the same as in the cases of the Transnistria
and Europa plans: the ransom proposal was too fantastic to be accepted by the Allies, but some kind of rescue could be achieved by the
very fact that negotiations were in train.[73]

The JAE accepted Shertok's suggestions for action: to ask the British to announce that the chairman of the Intergovernmental Committee for Refugees, Sir Herbert Emerson, would be willing to meet with
a German representative in a neutral country regarding the rescue of
Jews; to do everything possible to make the British keep their promise
that Brand would be allowed to return to Hungary; to report their
decisions to the high commissioner; and to insist that Shertok be given
a flight permit to London, now difficult to obtain because of the invasion of Normandy.[74]

Shertok asked the emissaries in Istanbul to cable Brand's wife,
Hanzi, that his return was being delayed because the matter was
under serious consideration. He also asked the British to enable
Hirschmann, who was on his way from the United States to the
Middle East, to meet Brand in Cairo.

On June 15 Shertok and Ben-Gurion presented their requests to
the high commissioner. MacMichael objected to Brand's return, saying that the Germans would not return any citizen of an Allied country who got caught in Hungary. Shertok replied that preventing
Brand from returning meant closing the door to negotiations, which
was in contradiction to the "open door" policy promised by Eden to
Weizmann. He also mentioned the promises given to him in Jerusalem and to the emissaries in Istanbul that Brand would be allowed to
return from Aleppo to Turkey. MacMichael interrupted him, saying,
"My answer is very simple: this is war!" He did not even try to deny
that the British had deliberately broken their promises, and he
warned Shertok and Ben-Gurion firmly against contacting the enemy
on their own. In his written report on this conversation, MacMichael
stressed that Shertok had repeatedly pressed two points: the need to
allow Brand to return, since the Germans would construe failure to
do so as Allied permission to continue the murder; and the urgency
of pursuing the matter in any ways possible in London—and not
merely in the Middle East—first of all, by arranging a meeting with
authorized German representatives.[75]

Shertok and Ben-Gurion returned to a second meeting with their
colleagues with nothing to show for their efforts but MacMichael's
promise to forward their requests to London. Emil Schmorak consid-

ered the situation absurd. The Jewish Agency was necessarily loyal to the British and had immediately reported Eichmann's proposal to the high commissioner, while the British were deceitful. Moreover, the Agency, to whom Brand had been sent, would be considered responsible for Brand's failure to return, and the Germans would use this as a justification to continue the mass extermination. Thus, predicted Schmorak, "we would be considered guilty and they [the British] would be considered innocent."

Gruenbaum suggested that the negotiations be made conditional on stopping the deportations and that a representative of the British government, rather than Emerson, be in charge of the negotiations. He ended with the bitter observation that he had been right in objecting to disclosing the details of the proposal to the British; by the time the Allied governments were ready to negotiate, there would be no Jews left in Hungary to negotiate about.

At that point Ben-Gurion broke into the discussion. "The issue we are dealing with," he said, "is severe and bitter, and every member of the Executive must state his opinion clearly." It was the first time that he had made such a demand. In the case of the Transnistria proposal and the Europa Plan, he had made the decisions himself, expressing his opinions curtly. Gruenbaum's views, he said, were defeatist. Ben-Gurion could not accept the assumption that it was futile to hope for support from the Allies. Without them, it was impossible to act. Any person appointed as an Allied representative would be welcomed, and everything should be done to keep the negotiations alive. As for Brand who "sees himself as the ambassador of a million Jews who have been sentenced to death, if he wants to return, it is our duty to help him." [76]

On June 19 the Americans sent their reply to London. Large-scale transfer of refugees would indeed interfere with the war effort, but the proposal should not be rejected altogether. It might open the door to more reasonable offers. Meanwhile, they said, negotiations in themselves might delay the extermination. The United States was therefore willing to assure the Germans that the Allies would grant temporary shelter to any Jew whom they released. Steinhardt was instructed "not to close the door" on negotiations, and the ambassador in Moscow, Averell Harriman, was asked to convey the details of the proposal to the Soviet government, stressing America's "open door" policy and the need for cooperation among the three major Allies. [77]

On June 22 Shertok flew to Cairo to meet Hirschmann. Shertok considered Hirschmann's very presence in Cairo, supported as it was by President Roosevelt and Stettinius, as a positive indication of the

U.S. position. Hirschmann accepted Shertok's proposals and insisted that both he and the Agency take immediate and extraordinary steps. The wording of the cables sent to Washington and to London was a joint effort. In the report he wrote after meeting with Brand—a meeting that the British attempted to thwart—Hirschmann stressed Brand's honesty and his desire to act for rescue.[78]

Shertok returned from Cairo with the same suspicions that had been aroused in Aleppo, that the British were guilty of double-dealing and of generally hindering the Agency in its efforts. They had prevented him from seeing Brand in Cairo; they had delayed a cable to Barlas with the excuse that "its wording was somewhat far-reaching"; the high commissioner had delayed approval for Shertok's flight to London for five days. As for Brand, the head of the security service in Cairo told Shertok that, as far as he was concerned, there was no reason not to let Brand return to Hungary. On the other hand, Hirschmann was told by the office of the British minister for Middle Eastern affairs, Lord Walter Moyne, that Brand would be flown to London. Moyne himself told Shertok that the instructions to bring Brand from Aleppo to Cairo had not been issued by him and admitted that "there was confusion" when Brand arrived. In other words, different arms of the British administration had probably handled the mission simultaneously, without coordination or full exchange of information, and maybe even without instructions from London, either deliberately, or because they did not really know how to handle the issue.

These facts and others made Shertok warn the JAE before he left for London that "we have to take whatever we are told with a grain of salt." Ben-Gurion wanted Shertok to stay in London to deal with the Brand mission as long as required, postponing all Zionist political activities. The JAE organized itself to shift its center of operations to London. Meanwhile, cables from Kasztner in Budapest arrived in Istanbul saying that the Germans insisted that Brand and Gross return. The JAE informed Weizmann in London about these cables, Shertok's meetings with Brand, and Goldmann's suggestions to Stettinius, the gist of which was to keep the Jews of Hungary in camps, financed by the Jews and under the auspices of the International Red Cross or the Swiss government, if getting a million Jews out in wartime proved unfeasible.[79]

Upon receiving this information Weizmann asked Eden and other officials in the Foreign Office that everything be done in order to enable Brand to return to Hungary and that every possibility of rescue, on which the lives of hundreds of thousands might depend, be investigated. Weizmann stressed that each moment was precious because the deportations, especially of children, were continuing in full force, as the British government knew from information received regularly through the Polish government-in-exile. Weizmann was told by Alec W. G. Randall, head of the refugee department in the Foreign Office, that Brand would not be allowed to return before Shertok presented the proposal in London and that "it seems to us unthinkable that retaining Brand should be held to indicate that His Majesty's Government are not giving earnest attention to any practicable scheme for assisting Jews now suffering under German threats."[80]

The news Weizmann received from abroad reached him only after being processed by the British censorship and at British discretion. When Shertok arrived in England on June 27 and gave him firsthand information, the two were able to work faster. They composed a detailed report for the British government, surveying all the developments pertinent to Brand's mission up to that day. As soon as the report was finished, on June 29, they received a cable from Gruenbaum in Jerusalem that 430,000 Jews, mostly children and adolescents, had already been deported from Hungary, and the rest—more than 250,000—were to follow that week. Moshe Kraus, head of the Palestine office in Budapest, cabled Gruenbaum, holding the British responsible for the deportations because they had detained Brand and Gross. More cables arrived almost daily from Kraus, Kasztner, Barlas, and Lichtheim, all with news about the growing number of victims and calling for immediate action.[81]

With the alarming news came new suggestions. Kraus recommended issuing a great number of Palestine naturalization certificates attesting that the bearer had the right to naturalization in Palestine. Gruenbaum reiterated his suggestion of retaliatory measures against Germans detained by the Allies, although the JAE had rejected it at the end of 1942 and the high commissioner had warned the Jewish Agency not to bring it up in public. Dobkin suggested that the Allied governments and the Vatican issue a severe warning to the Hungarian administration, workers on the Hungarian railway, and anyone else who participated in the rounding up, deportations, and murder of Jews. Weizmann asked Eden to request Stalin to issue a similar warning.[82]

The JAE kept Weizmann and Shertok abreast of all developments initiated in Palestine. The Agency had appealed to the governments of Spain and Portugal to cooperate with Switzerland—Britain's representative in the occupied countries—to declare their willingness to give protection to the Jews of Hungary in possession of immigration permits or to issue citizenship certificates of their own. They asked Tito to let the Jews of Hungary and neighboring countries into the areas under his control in Yugoslavia and to allow the presence of a representative of the Jewish Agency. Requests were renewed to the U.S. government to establish the refugee camps in North Africa that had been mentioned several times since the Bermuda Conference. The Agency had also approached the king and the government of Sweden, requesting again that they let in 20,000 children, mainly from Hungary. Finally, the Rescue Committee and the emissaries in Istanbul and Geneva kept the foreign press regularly informed, urging them to give the news prominence.[83]

Shocked by the number of victims and feeling that time was running out, on June 30 Shertok and Weizmann urged the parliamentary undersecretary of the Foreign Office, George H. Hall, to send a message to the Germans immediately that the Allies were willing to discuss with their representatives the release of large numbers of Jews. They also insisted that the British let Brand return to Hungary and authorize him to inform those who had sent him that their proposals were being studied by the highest authorities. Hall replied that the war cabinet was studying the matter and would reach a decision as soon as possible, in conjunction with the U.S. government.[84]

On July 2 Ben-Gurion told the JAE that the emissaries in Istanbul had sent word that the Germans were offering to negotiate with them. They had invited Bader, through Kasztner, to come to Budapest and assured him of a safe return. The JAE unanimously decided to instruct Bader not to accept the invitation before the British finished their discussions, because the Jewish Agency was forbidden to negotiate independently with the enemy. This decision was strengthened by a cable from Shertok that the Foreign Office might allow Gross and Brand to return and might be willing to meet with a German representative if the Soviets agreed. Once again the JAE decided to pass on the information to the British and to refrain from direct contacts with the Germans.

Bader himself was willing to go to Budapest. A member of the German legation in Istanbul had informed him that the German Foreign Ministry had arranged the trip, and a plane would wait for him until the proper papers for a subject of an enemy power were prepared. But Kaplan, who had arrived from Jerusalem, refused to approve the trip before the Agency informed him of Whitehall's decision. The fact that this time it was the German Foreign Ministry and not the S.S. that initiated the proposal complicated the evaluation of the German position.[85]

At the beginning of July Dobkin, who was then in Spain, received cables from Kasztner that the Germans were pressing to renew the negotiations and that the S.S. was willing to send four emissaries to any place Dobkin chose, to meet with him and with Joseph Schwartz, the chief representative of the JDC in Europe. The Germans' request to meet with the JDC might mean that they would be willing to take money instead of trucks. Dobkin cabled Shertok asking him to find out whether the Foreign Office would be willing to discuss a deal involving money or goods of no military value. If the answer was positive, could Shertok meet the S.S. representatives and negotiate with them? While awaiting a reply Dobkin tried to avoid the Gestapo agents in Spain, but they followed him, discovered where he was, and informed him that their superiors were willing to meet him in Switzerland and to send a plane to take him there.[86]

By the beginning of July two things were clear to all the parties involved. The extermination machine at Auschwitz—the destination of deported Hungarian Jews—was working at full capacity, and the Germans, realizing that Gross and Brand were not coming back, invested considerable effort in establishing new, direct contacts with representatives of the Agency in Istanbul and in Spain. The question is whether this information expedited the Allies' discussions of the German proposals or changed the position of the Jewish Agency.

The Soviet reply, as expected, was negative. Had the Russians known that one of the German suggestions was to use the traded trucks only against them on the eastern front—information that the British withheld from them—their reply probably would have been even sharper. By June 20 Steinhardt and Hirschmann, who was now in Turkey, had received explicit instructions from the State Department to cease involvement in the Brand affair. The British Foreign Office immediately followed suit. In addition, British intelligence reports from Cairo conveyed negative impressions of Gross and Brand. Gross was an underworld character who maintained strong ties with Nazi agents and told the interrogators confused details about his current mission.

The interrogations in Cairo had also brought to light the facts that Brand had been a member of the Communist party for ten years and had participated in organizing Jewish self-defense in Hungary, which he referred to as "Haganah," also the name of the Jewish underground military organization in Palestine. This aroused the suspicions of the British that the Agency had more elaborate channels of communication in Europe, particularly in Hungary, than they had

thought. If this was the case, and if Brand returned, he would probably act on behalf of the Jewish Agency rather than on behalf of the
Allies.

Furthermore, Brand had stated in his interrogation that he had
brought the German proposals in writing and given them to Avriel
and Barlas, and Gross confirmed this. Shertok and the emissaries in
Istanbul denied having received any written proposal and, although
their denial was apparently true—Eichmann would not have incrimi-
nated himself—it deepened the suspicions of British intelligence.
They concluded that the German proposal was nothing but a con-
temptible attempt to trade Jewish lives for foreign currency to be used
after the German defeat. If they failed, they would at least have
achieved "a nice piece of psychological warfare," inserting a wedge
between East and West.[87] In contrast, Hirschmann and Shertok repeatedly underscored Brand's integrity and his known past as an active Zionist.

London's mounting suspicions of Brand and Gross and Moscow's
total refusal to consider the matter threatened to put an end to
Brand's mission. Nevertheless, Eden, replying to the American communication of June 19, expressed willingness to release Brand and to
inform the Germans that the Allies would be willing to negotiate,
through the Swiss, for the release of groups of Jews discussed previously, such as the 5,000 children from the Balkans. The Allies would
demand that the Germans release them immediately as a sign of
goodwill. Eden's reply was apparently designed to stave off charges of
British indifference to the fate of the Jews. At the end of June newspapers throughout the free world published detailed accounts of the
fate of Hungarian Jewry, based mainly on accounts by refugees who
had escaped from Auschwitz. The British public, whose attention had
turned elsewhere after the Bermuda Conference, now issued furious
calls for action. In response, on July 5 Eden delivered a statement in
Parliament condemning the deportations to Auschwitz and expressing the British government's sympathy.[88]

It is clear, however, that both Eden's announcement and his reply to
the U.S. government were nothing but lip service, for the Brand affair
had actually ended on June 20. Eden did not want to meet with Shertok and Weizmann any more and sent them to Hall, with whom they
had already met on June 30. Thus, ten days after Britain and the
United States had decided to end their involvement with Brand's mission, they had not yet conveyed the information to Shertok and Weizmann. This fact explains why Shertok cabled Ben-Gurion that the

Foreign Office might yet agree to meet the Germans—false information that, in addition to other factors, caused the Agency to disapprove of Bader's trip to Budapest.

Weizmann and Shertok continued to act without knowing the facts. They managed to meet with Eden on July 6, a whole month after Weizmann had first met with him concerning the Brand affair. The two thanked Eden for his expression of sympathy in Parliament and pressed him to allow Bader and Brand to go to Budapest together. They stressed that the invitation to Bader meant that the Germans were really interested in negotiations. Shertok urged that, if the Germans asked Bader for ransom, it be paid. They repeated their suggestions to Hall of a week before: issuing certificates of protection, arranging shelter in Allied territories, warning the Hungarians, and bombing Auschwitz and the railway tracks leading to it.

Eden reiterated his deep sympathy but stressed that the British government had to handle the matter with great care, in conjunction with the other Allies; Britain was waiting for approval from the Soviet Union (in fact the Soviets had sent their refusal more than two weeks earlier). He expressed doubts about the possibility of paying the Germans ransom, risking the life of Bader, an Allied subject, or agreeing to "anything which looked like negotiating with the enemy"; only the war cabinet could decide on that. He did promise to consider Shertok's suggestion that Churchill ask Stalin to warn the Hungarians and assured them that the bombing of the camps was already under discussion. Weizmann and Shertok left Eden a memorandum detailing their suggestions and stressing the urgency of the situation. That very week, the Germans were going to start deporting the hundreds of thousands of Jews still left in Hungary unless something was done about it.[89]

Eden presented Churchill with the two proposals from Weizmann and Shertok that still had relevance—bombing Auschwitz and requesting Stalin to warn the Hungarians. Churchill accepted the proposals and on July 11 sent Eden a memorandum summarizing his feelings about the entire Eichmann proposal and the extermination of European Jewry: "There is no doubt that this is probably the greatest and most horrible crime ever committed in the whole history of the world . . . and, there should, therefore, in my opinion, be no negotiations of any kind on this subject . . . I would not take it seriously."[90]

On July 12, after Shertok had discovered that the British were not about to accept any of the proposals connected with Brand, he had a trying conversation with Randall and other Foreign Office officials.

Randall told him that they were still waiting for a reply from Moscow and that it had been clear from the first moment that Bader would not be allowed to go (notwithstanding Eden's promise to Shertok to bring the matter before the war cabinet). Randall told Shertok that he was mistaken in attributing so much importance to Brand's return to Budapest, which, in his opinion, could not produce any results. He gave several reasons for rejecting the idea of equipping Jews in the occupied areas with certificates of protection: the enemy would treat such a British step with contempt; implementation would require finding Germans for exchange, and they were just not available; giving shelter to hundreds of thousands of people was practically impossible; and Allied acceptance of Shertok's proposals would prove that the Allies were willing to invest their efforts in the Jewish issue, and the Germans would increase their pressures even further.

These blunt arguments distorted the gist of Shertok's proposal, which had nothing to do with getting the Jews to another country or exchanging them for Germans. He remarked bitterly that it was incomprehensible to him how the Germans could exert even more pressure. In terms of Jewish lives, there was absolutely nothing to lose. It was now abundantly clear to him that "transferring the discussion" on this issue from one ministry to another was not a sign of hope, as he had thought until then, but rather an evasive form of refusal.[91]

A few days later the British government officially announced that it objected to Bader's trip and that Gustav G. Kullmann, a Swiss citizen and Emerson's deputy in the intergovernmental committee for refugees, would not be sent to Budapest instead of Bader as Shertok had suggested. Dobkin also received a totally negative answer: there would be no negotiations about goods or money, Shertok would not come to Spain, and Dobkin and Schwartz had better avoid any contact with the Germans. Schwartz received similar instructions from the State Department. When Dobkin came from Spain to Britain, he found out that his original cable to Shertok about the new German feelers had never been delivered.[92]

Despite their duplicity in dealing with Shertok, the British admired his tenacity. Randall wrote that Shertok and Weizmann were entitled to know the truth because Shertok "fought persistently for a decision on which, according to him, the lives of tens of thousands of people depended." Still, Shertok was told nothing explicitly, and only in mid-July, two months after Brand had first arrived, did the JAE realize that the German proposal would not be dealt with. As a last resort Ben-Gurion sent a cable to Roosevelt, entreating him to express his willingness to appoint a representative to rescue talks on condition that the deportations immediately stop. He begged him not to abandon "this unique and possibly last chance of saving the remains of European Jewry."[93]

It is unlikely that Ben-Gurion expected the cable to produce any concrete results, since the Americans had already forbidden Schwartz to meet the representatives of the S.S. in Spain. Moreover, whenever Gruenbaum had suggested making negotiations conditional on stopping the deportations, Ben-Gurion had often expressed his opinion that the Agency was dealing here with "wild animals" and that there was no point in making conditions. The cable was nothing but a desperate protest. The State Department replied that it had no objection to Brand's return, but that there did not seem to be any point in his returning empty-handed. In mid-July the JAE concluded that "everything we have heard indicates that the Brand affair will have no results whatsoever."[94]

When Britain decided not to pursue the Brand mission, the Foreign Office leaked the details to the press, which seized upon the story as a great sensation. It was published first in the United States on July 19 and on the following day all over the rest of the world and in Palestine. The surprised press in Palestine quoted American and British reporters who condemned the German proposal in toto. Once it was made public, no political body could handle Brand's mission, and it was clear that there was no point in his returning to Hungary. "What they did in publicizing these things is an unmatched villainy," said Gruenbaum. "They ignored the blood of our brethren altogether."[95]

On July 20 the Hungarian regent, Admiral Miklos Horthy, declared Hungary's willingness to stop the deportations of the Jews. His decision reflected fear of being overthrown by the civil guard units who were rounding up the Jews, his conviction that Jewish pressure brought about an American bombing of the Budapest railway on July 2, and joint international pressure: public opinion in the West was stunned by press reports about Auschwitz in June and July, and formal appeals were made to Horthy, most notably by Gustav V of Sweden, Pope Pius XII, and President Roosevelt. This was "a new ray of hope . . . exactly when the previous one had been extinguished," said Shertok,[96] and the JAE renewed its struggle to save the remnant.

Upon his return to Palestine, Shertok summarized the Brand mission for the JAE: "It was a heart-rending, discouraging affair . . . It consumed most of my time and energy and that of our other colleagues in London . . . for two months . . . We were determined to try to open every possible avenue," but the British rejected them all. They were afraid of becoming entangled politically and were careful to coordinate every step with Washington and Moscow. They were also afraid of "a flood of Jews in case something came of it." Low-ranking officials explicitly asked where and how the refugees would be taken and how so many of them would be fed. According to Brand, Lord Moyne had asked him, "What will I do with a million Jews? Where will I put them?" The British used this affair for political ends, putting the blame on the Russians for their own refusal to rescue Jews. Then, to "get rid of the whole business," they leaked it to the press. The Americans seemed less negative than the British, but they, too, finally rejected it. It was even more tragic than the massacre in Poland, Shertok said, because everyone knew exactly what was going to happen—and, still, it was allowed to happen.[97]

Shind saw the Brand affair from the point of view of the emissaries in Istanbul. In his opinion, if the emissaries had been able to conduct negotiations with the low-level officials with whom they had long been in touch rather than watch the affair become a matter of high-level politics in London and Washington, it would have been possible to get tens of thousands out to the neutral countries. When "300,000 are being deported a few thousand can possibly be spirited away." The German officials in Budapest would have been glad to collect the payment for their release.[98] Shind's comments implied not only criticism of the Allies but also criticism of the Agency and of the emissaries, including himself. It was he who went with Avriel to British intelligence in Istanbul.

Brand himself was finally released from prison in Cairo in October and brought to Palestine at the request of the Agency. Meeting with the Mapai Central Committee, he blamed it for the failure of his mission: it had been indifferent and had mismanaged rescue operations from the beginning of the war, largely because of loyalty to the Allies. The emissaries in Istanbul "handed me over to the British." He should have been freed by force, "even with dynamite," from the prison in Cairo so that he might return to Budapest. He stressed repeatedly that he had undertaken the mission as a member of the party and that "the party had to be considered responsible for the lives of the Jews who were murdered because of their mistakes."

Eliyahu Golomb rejected Brand's accusations. He described to him the overall situation, the Yishuv's limited power and its dependence on the Allies. Golomb contended that Brand's mission was one of the important factors in creating the international pressure that resulted in Horthy's declaration and the rescue of 250,000 Jews from deportation. "It was impossible to explain to him how helpless we were," Teddy Kollek wrote later.[99]

The committee may have felt that there was no common ground for an argument with Brand and that all its explanations were falling on deaf ears. Brand had been in prison for four months. He was overwhelmed by feelings of helplessness, of not being able to influence events and, perhaps, even of failing to understand them. Moreover, after his mission failed, he might have been viewed by others, even friends and relatives, as a traitor—having sought his own safety instead of returning.

Brand had left Budapest with Eichmann's words—"Jews control the whole world"—ringing in his ears and with Kasztner's confident assurance that "the Agency will find a way." He had thought that the cable from Chaim Barlas on the eve of his departure from Budapest—"Let Joel come, Chaim is waiting for him"—was from Chaim Weizmann and had therefore told Eichmann that the president of the World Zionist Organization was already waiting for him in Istanbul. Brand saw Weizmann, Shertok, Goldmann, and Ben-Gurion as high-ranking statesmen who had free access to governments and ministers and who could fly anywhere without delay.

It was difficult for Brand to understand the international context affecting this mission. In his memoirs Brand admitted that, before he left for Istanbul, it never occurred to him that the British, the symbol of freedom and courage in occupied Europe, would oppose saving Jews. "I firmly believed all the time that we and Britain had common interests . . . It was unbearable for me to see this element of my political outlook shattered."[100] From inside occupied Europe, the world seemed to him to be divided into black and white, the Nazis and the Allies. He was unfamiliar with the complexity of relations among the Allies: the suspiciousness of the Russians, Western fears of Russian expansion, Britain's worries about its deteriorating status in the Middle East and its increasing dependence upon the United States. And he certainly could not understand, at that point, either how low a place the saving of Jews occupied in the superpowers' priorities or how few were the Zionist movement's bargaining cards.

The JAE devoted more time to the Brand affair than to any other rescue issue. Its decisions were made collectively, responsibility for them shared, and confidentiality preserved for the two months during which it was considered a real possibility. Although the matter was discussed privately with other leaders who were not JAE members (such as Neustadt, Remez, Joseph Sprinzak, and Golomb), it was never raised in other forums, not even in the Mapai Central Committee or the Histadrut Executive. Those involved in rescue efforts at the time testify today that both the Agency and those consulted privately regarded the Eichmann proposal as perhaps the last opportunity to save large numbers of people. As such, it was accorded priority over all other issues. Ben-Gurion and Shertok, among others in the JAE, devoted time and energy to conducting an integrated political campaign in Jerusalem while Kaplan and the emissaries dealt with it in Istanbul, as did Goldmann in Washington and Shertok and Weizmann in London.

It appears that the JAE spent little time discussing German intentions and was unfamiliar with the tangle of German authorities and their internal conflicts, particularly those that had generated the Brand-Gross mission. After Shertok's meeting with Brand, however, it did realize that Gross's mission was the main issue, that certain German aides were trying to promote interests associated with the pending defeat: acquiring foreign currency for themselves, cooperating with the West to prevent the Russians from taking over Germany, acquiring a more humane image in relation to the Jews, and, perhaps, saving Germany from total destruction.

The JAE invested a lot of time and energy in the Brand affair: not only had previous efforts to save Jews in considerable numbers failed, but also the war was coming to an end and preparations for the international deliberations that would determine, among other matters, the future of the Yishuv had already begun. Every Jew who had been saved through the efforts of the Yishuv and who expressed a desire to immigrate to Palestine would constitute an argument for the achievement of political goals. The annihilation of the Jews of Hungary, Bulgaria, and Rumania could severely damage the very reason for the struggle to establish a Jewish state. How could there be a Jewish state without European Jewry? Who would inhabit it?

In fact the Executive was beating its head against an impenetrable wall. During 1944, nearly two years after the free world had learned the meaning of ghettos, deportations, and death camps, more than 400,000 Hungarian Jews were murdered. "It was as if [we] were convened to watch the performance of death," Gruenbaum said.[101]

13

Military Plans

THE APPEAL TO BOMB AUSCHWITZ

On May 25, 1944, Rabbi Benjamin of the Al Domi group came to the Jewish Agency offices in Jerusalem with a note for Moshe Shertok. It read, "You must insist that the Allied governments bomb the railway stations leading from Hungary to Poland, not for any strategic reasons but to stop the transport of those being taken there to die." The press in Palestine stressed the ominous meaning of the recently renewed concentration of Hungarian Jews in rural towns. The JAE had convened that day to hear Venia Pomerantz's report on Joel Brand's mission and on the deportation of Hungarian Jewry. It was the first time that the idea of bombing had been raised for consideration. Rabbi Benjamin later wrote that Shertok thanked him warmly for his idea and that Yitzhak Gruenbaum immediately started sending cables about it to the Allied governments.[1]

Rabbi Benjamin's recollections are not quite accurate. On June 2, that is, about a week after that urgent meeting, Gruenbaum approached Lowell C. Pinkerton, the American consul general in Jerusalem, on the subject. After telling him the recent news about the deportations from Hungary to Poland, he asked that a severe warning be issued to Hungary and that the U.S. air force bomb the death camps in Poland and the railroad tracks leading there from Budapest. Pinkerton agreed to send the first and third suggestions to Washington. As for bombing the camps, he expressed fear that it would cause the deaths of many Jews; German propaganda would then tell the world that the Americans were also exterminating Jews. Gruenbaum replied that those Jews were doomed anyway but that, in the chaos prevailing during the bombing, some of them might be able to escape. In any case, he said, destroying the installations would at least delay the extermination process, and the Germans might not be able to re-build them. Pinkerton, however, still refused to deliver this request unless it was submitted to him officially in writing.[2]

Gruenbaum, it appears, approached Pinkerton on his own initia-tive; not until the JAE met on June 11 did he tell his colleagues about this talk. To his surprise, the Executive objected to the bombing of the camps, for the following reasons: "We do not know the true situation in Poland" and "We cannot take responsibility for a bombing that might cause the death of a single Jew." Gruenbaum was reprimanded for meeting Pinkerton without prior approval. Ben-Gurion summa-rized, "It is the opinion of the Executive that it should not be sug-gested to the Allies that they bomb places in which there are Jews." Gruenbaum later reported to his colleagues in the Rescue Committee that the idea was "totally rejected by the members of the Agency."[3]

This sequence of events raises several questions. First if Gruen-baum was so convinced of the necessity and urgency of the bombings, why did he wait eight days before approaching Pinkerton, that is, eight days after Rabbi Benjamin's note and after learning from Pom-erantz that the deportations had already started? Why did he bring the issue before the JAE only nine days after his meeting with Pink-erton, even though they all knew by then that 12,000 Jews were being deported every day? The only possible explanation seems to be that the Agency was then deeply involved in Brand's proposal.

Second, what did the JAE actually know about Auschwitz? Ben-Gurion's reference to Auschwitz as a place "where there are Jews" and the minutes of the JAE up to mid-June make it clear that the Agency did not know that the camps in Treblinka, Belzec, Chelmno, and So-bibor had been out of operation for several months. Members of the JAE frequently mentioned "death camps," "Poland," and "deporta-tions to the east," but rarely Auschwitz, the main extermination camp for Jews from all over Europe that by then had replaced the camps in the east, and when they did, they gave it no special prominence. At the June 11 meeting, Emil Schmorak argued against the bombing be-cause "we are told that in Oświęcim [the Polish name of Auschwitz], there is a large labor camp." No one present corrected him. No one seemed to know that Auschwitz was the general name for a complex of camps, some of which were indeed labor camps, but one of which—Birkenau—included extermination installations, specially expanded for the annihilation of the Hungarian Jews. Birkenau was also the site where hundreds of thousands of prisoners were tortured and worked to death. Confirming this general ignorance is the fact that on the same day as the JAE meeting, Gruenbaum cabled the World Jewish

Congress in New York about transports of Jews from Hungary to "an unknown destination."[4]

How did it happen that in June 1944 the crucial role of Birkenau was not yet known? Members of the Executive received comments and letters from the emissaries in Istanbul and Geneva, who in turn received letters, testimonies, and newspapers from various parts of Europe. This material indicates that the Jews in Europe themselves did not know exactly what Auschwitz was all about. They mentioned other camps as being larger or as being the main sites of extermination. In November 1942, refugees who reached Palestine did mention Auschwitz as one of the camps in which extermination was taking place. In March 1943 Eliezer Kaplan quoted a Polish newspaper that gave details about "the large concentration camp in Oświęcim," where most of the prisoners had been Poles and "Bolsheviks" and where 15,000 people had been killed. According to the report, however, the camp had been closed down.[5] In April 1943 a letter from Bratislava mentioned the labor camps "Auschwitz, Birkenau, and Lublin" as places for able-bodied men and women. In July, leaders of the underground in Bendin wrote about the extermination in "Bonari" (Ponar, near Vilna, Lithuania), in "Chalemo" (Chełmno), in Belzec, in Sobibor, and especially in "Treblinky" (Treblinka), which "is a notorious place of annihilation, not just for the Jews of Poland but also for those of Holland, Belgium, etc." Oświęcim was mentioned as the place where 7,000 Jews from East Upper Silesia were being shot and burned. In November a Polish bulletin was quoted in Palestine describing Majdanek as "a place of horrible killing of Jews from Poland and abroad," in which more than half a million Jews had been poisoned by gas. Belzec was mentioned as "the place known as the main extermination site for Jews," and Auschwitz mainly as a detention camp from which people were sent to Germany. In January 1944, women arriving in Switzerland provided the emissaries with details about labor camps in the Upper Silesia and the extermination camps, including Auschwitz. However, other refugees gave even more minute details of the extermination in Treblinka, where, they thought, two million Jews had been liquidated. In early June 1944 the Swedish press quoted a Polish refugee's description of the "huge crematorium" in Belzec in which, he said, 10,000 people had been exterminated every day within one-half hour since mid-1942. Not until later in June, after the JAE meeting, did the newspaper of the Polish underground report for the first time that, up until the summer of 1943, 700,000 Jews from all over Europe had been exterminated in Auschwitz alone.[6]

Even in occupied Europe, Auschwitz was not always mentioned among the largest extermination centers. Belzec and Treblinka were considered the main centers of annihilation. Some of the details about Auschwitz were inaccurate, some imaginary. Neither figures nor places nor the procedures mentioned were always reliable. One reason for the misinformation was the fact that it was often relayed from one person to another before reaching Palestine. Even more important, all the information about Auschwitz that had reached the free world until then was inconclusive, because none of it came from someone who had actually been there.[7]

On the very day that the JAE scrutinized Gruenbaum's suggestion, however, a minutely detailed report about the extermination in Auschwitz was on its way to Palestine. In April 1944 two Jewish prisoners escaped from Auschwitz to Slovakia and were the first to reach a place where Jewish organizations and a Jewish leadership still operated and could convey their message further. Both had worked for two years in the registration office of the camp and thus could supply information about the structure of the camp, the names of its commanders, its procedures, and especially the course of the extermination.[8] Their testimony reached Geneva along with additional information from two more Jewish prisoners who had escaped from Auschwitz at the end of May, after the annihilation of Hungarian Jewry had already begun.

The turning point in the Auschwitz issue occurred, then, in early June 1944. All the Jewish organizations and representatives in Geneva did their best to publicize the information in the Swiss press and to relay it further. Nuncio Philipe Pernardini at first refused to believe them. "We also had not believed such information before," Abraham Silberschein and Nathan Schwalb told him. "We were also raised on Goethe, but for a long time now we have not needed any additional proof of what is happening." Only after two trying conversations did Pernardini agree to convey the testimony to the Vatican.

The testimony was transmitted in Yiddish to Orthodox Jews in Switzerland who passed it on to their organizations in the United States; in Hungarian to the leaders of Hungarian Jewry; and to the British foreign minister, Anthony Eden, by El Salvador's consul in Switzerland, George Mantello; to the U.S. State Department by Roswell MacClelland, of the War Refugee Board; and, of course, to Stephen Wise and Nahum Goldmann. It reached Palestine through Istanbul. The escapees attached to their testimony a proposal that the Allies warn Germany and Hungary that they would retaliate against nationals in their hands; that the Vatican issue a severe public condemnation; and—above all—that the Allies bomb the gas chambers and the crematoriums in Birkenau, which, they said, could be easily identified by their chimneys and by the watchtowers around them, and the railway tracks from Slovakia and Hungary to Poland.[9]

As early as May 16, one day after the great deportation from Hungary began, Rabbi Michael Dov-Beer Weissmandel, who was in hiding near the Slovakian-Hungarian border, sent a letter to Geneva addressed to free world Jewry in which he described—apparently after meeting the first two escapees—the route of the trains to Auschwitz, the terrible traveling conditions, the process of the killing and the burning of the bodies, and added a bitter outcry:

> And you, our brethren, the People of Israel, in all the free countries . . . how can you keep silent about this murder . . . You are cruel, you are murderers—for this cruel silence of yours, for your lack of action . . . We beg and plead and demand of you to take action immediately . . . Our brethren, People of Israel, have you gone mad? Don't you know what hell we are living in?

Weissmandel demanded that the Allies and the pope issue a severe warning to the Germans and Hungarians, get the International Red Cross to supervise the camps, and—written in large letters—"shatter from the air the houses of annihilation" in Auschwitz, as well as the railway tracks, the bridges, and the stations leading to it. In June Weissmandel added more letters of his own to the testimonies of the four escapees from Auschwitz and sent all this to Hungary, Switzerland, Turkey, the United States, and Palestine. The information thus reached the free world both through him and through the emissaries and representatives in Geneva.[10]

At the end of June, in the wake of this new information, the shocking effect of its dissemination throughout the free world, and additional confirmation that the deportations from Hungary were indeed to Auschwitz and were continuing in full force, the JAE reversed its decision. Gruenbaum bombarded Shertok, then in London handling the Brand affair, and Wise and Goldmann in the United States, with cables urging them to demand that the Allies bomb the camp installations immediately. He also suggested that the Polish underground be asked to break into the camps around the extermination area and release the prisoners held there.[11]

On June 30 Shertok and Weizmann met with the British parliamentary undersecretary of the Foreign Office, George H. Hall, and handed him two cables from Gruenbaum. A week later they met with Eden, repeated the suggestion to bomb the camp, and added a request to bomb the railway tracks. Eden told them that he had already contacted the Air Ministry about bombing the camps and would also discuss bombing the tracks. Shertok sent Eden a memorandum including a summary of the escapees' testimony as it had been published by Jewish Telegraphic Agency and delivered to the Allied governments, and stressed its overall credibility. He took exception to the figure of 60,000 given for the number of human beings being gassed or burned daily in Auschwitz—he thought that the correct number was 6,000. In fact 20,000 a day was the capacity at Auschwitz at that time.

In his memorandum Shertok admitted that bombing had certain disadvantages. It was doubtful whether it would bring about rescue on a large scale, and it could hasten the deaths of some of those already in Auschwitz. On the other hand, he said, the destruction of the installations would delay the deportation of the hundreds of thousands who were still in Hungary, at least until new installations were built. However, its main value would be its long-range influence. It would demonstrate that the Allies had declared direct war on the Nazi extermination; it would discredit German propaganda claiming that the Allies were actually satisfied with the killing of Jews; it would remove once and for all any doubts still lingering in Allied circles about the authenticity of the information about the mass murder; it would give weight to the threats of retaliation against the murderers and thus serve as a deterrent; and, finally, it might create domestic pressure in Germany against the continued extermination. The memorandum ended with the opinion that the first report announcing the bombing of the camps in Silesia by the British or U.S. air force would have great demonstrative value.[12]

Eden approached Secretary of State for Air Sir Archibald Sinclair with the plan, which had received Churchill's support, and expressed hope that "something could be done." But in mid-July Sinclair replied to Eden that the distance was too great, the operation too risky and costly, and the potential helpfulness to the prisoners doubtful. He suggested approaching the Americans. On the same day, Alec Randall told Shertok that the bombing issue is "receiving attention with the appropriate authorities."[13]

The Americans had already rejected the proposal two weeks earlier. While Shertok and Weizmann were trying to bring pressure on Whitehall, representatives of the World Jewish Congress and the War Refugee Board had approached the U.S. government and been told on July 4 by Undersecretary of War John McCloy that the bombing plan was not feasible because it required considerable forces that were needed elsewhere. Even if it were feasible, he pointed out later, "it might provoke more vindictive action by the Germans."[14]

Once Admiral Miklos Horthy announced that the deportations from Hungary would be stopped, the British Foreign Office suggested that the Zionist Office in London withdraw its request that Auschwitz be bombed. Joseph Linton, the secretary of the office, replied that the Germans still had many Jews in their hands who could be sent there, though not necessarily from Hungary, and that if the camps were destroyed, it would be hard for them, given their military situation in the summer of 1944, to build new ones. He enclosed a set of drawings and descriptions of Auschwitz obtained from the Polish government-in-exile (the Foreign Office had claimed it could not get them). Gruenbaum continued to send cables urging his colleagues not to give up, and the Agency continued to press the British on the issue throughout August.[15]

There was a moment near the end of August when Shertok thought that his efforts had borne fruit, and he cabled Gruenbaum: "Your idea was acted upon yesterday." But it was just an illusion. The rubber and synthetic oil plants in Monowitz, near Birkenau, had been bombed and a few bombs had accidentally fallen inside Birkenau. "This was not our target," Shertok glumly cabled to Gruenbaum.[16]

More activity was initiated in late August when information reached Palestine about the projected renewal of the deportations from Hungary. Gruenbaum again sent cables to Richard Lichtheim and Saly Mayer in Switzerland, to Wise and Goldmann in the United States, to Chaim Barlas in Istanbul, to Sweden, and to Shertok in London, urging them to apply pressure for bombing the installations and the tracks. The emissaries, supported by Laurence Steinhardt and Ira Hirschmann, also cabled from Istanbul to Sweden, to the United States, and to the International Red Cross, while Weissmandel continued to send appeals to every possible address.

Those who sent the cables did not know that the drawings supplied by Linton were filed away at the Foreign Office and never transferred to Sinclair, and that both British ministries discussed ways to avoid the bombings. At the beginning of September one of Eden's subordinates notified Weizmann of Britain's negative decision "in view of the very great technical difficulties involved."[17]

A few days later, Eliyahu Epstein (later Eilat) of the Agency's Political Department suggested to one of the advisers of the Soviet embassy in Cairo that the Russians bomb Auschwitz since their forces were closer to Auschwitz than those of the other Allies. As Epstein put it, the answer was that "there is no place for such a proposal from the political point of view"; no doubt the counselor was referring to the shaky relations between the Allies in the summer of 1944 and to Moscow's predictable refusal to implement a plan that had been rejected by the West. In September and October, both Gruenbaum and Goldmann continued to send cables to the same addresses, since they knew that other sites very close to the extermination installations were regularly being bombed at that time. Their appeals were to no avail. In January 1945 Gruenbaum again cabled Stalin, who apparently ignored the whole issue.[18]

The reasons given by the Allies for their refusal to bomb Auschwitz are greatly suspect. They claimed that the deportations from Hungary had stopped; but there were still Jews in the ghetto of Łodz, in Slovakia, and in other places who were murdered in the summer of 1944 in Auschwitz, and the camp continued to operate in full force until October of that year. They also claimed that the distance was too great; yet in August, during the Warsaw rebellion, Allied planes flew all the way from Italy to Warsaw and back. Another argument was the great expense involved; thousands of tons of bombs had been dropped on Germany and on military targets in the occupied countries since the spring. As for the claim that it was impossible to achieve accurate hits, industrial plants very close to Birkenau were hit with great accuracy, and Birkenau had tall, conspicuous, heavily smoking chimneys. Furthermore, aerial photographs of Birkenau taken at that time, which would have promoted accurate hits, have recently been discovered in the archives of the former Allies. Certainly the danger to the lives of the pilots on missions around Birkenau would not have been any greater if Birkenau had been added to their targets. Former Allied squadron commanders who flew from Italy northward in 1944 have recently acknowledged that bombing the crematoriums could have been carried out easily had accurate information been made available.[19]

Although Churchill and Eden agreed to the bombing—and it was one of the few plans, if not the only one, that Eden apparently agreed to—they did not exert any real pressure on their subordinates to carry it out. There is no way to avoid the conclusion that the Allies did not bomb Auschwitz because they were simply indifferent to the fate of the Jews.

Until June 1944 the real nature of Auschwitz—which since the war has become the most prominent symbol of Nazi atrocities—was not understood either in Palestine or anywhere else. At this point it seems unimportant to speculate whether this long period of ignorance stemmed more from German efficiency in camouflage and deception or from deficient collection and analysis of information by the Jews inside and outside occupied Europe and by the various European undergrounds and governments-in-exile.

It is an open question whether the JAE—once it found out what the real situation was—could have taken stronger steps than appeals, cables, and press publications and whether such steps could have brought about the desired bombing. That would have depended on one preliminary condition—that the reports of the escapees from Auschwitz gained general credence. Indeed, not everyone did, or could, believe them. What took place in Auschwitz was not easily grasped: alleged medical experiments performed on live men and women, on children, and on twins; living skeletons moving around in striped clothes with numbers tattooed on their arms; thousands of healthy people being turned into smoke and ash according to predetermined schedules. "Even if one allows for customary Jewish exaggeration, these stories are frightful," was the reaction of a British official to the escapees' report. But these stories could have been construed by anyone of normal mind and upbringing—whether they were government officials or new inmates entering the camp—as the ravings of wild imagination, born of disaster. An author who survived Auschwitz named it "the other planet"—and it was.[20]

THE PARACHUTISTS

Chaim Guri, the Israeli poet and fighter, asked Yitzhak (Antek) Zuckermann a few years ago whether fighters from the Yishuv could have been of any help had they flown to Poland. Zuckermann, one of the main leaders of the Warsaw ghetto rebellion, replied:

> If 500 fighters had taken off, antiaircraft fire would have brought 490 of them down on the way. And, if you had been among the remaining 10, we would have had a problem hiding you—because of your native Hebrew accent, your Mediterranean eyes, the fact that you don't speak Yiddish or Polish. You could not have saved us. You could not. Only a superpower could have saved us. A major power. But why didn't even one of you come? One! In the same way that Korniansky [and Unger] reached Palestine from there. It wouldn't have been a political or military question. It was only a question of ritual, of gesture, a sign, a hand extended as a token of sharing our fate. Why didn't a single person come to Poland?[21]

The question of sending Jews from Palestine to the occupied countries came up every now and then in the discussions by the national institutions. In August 1940 Dov Hoz demanded that something "bold and involving real sacrifices" be done to establish direct contact. At the end of 1941 a JAE member urged his colleagues to acquire firsthand information. Their proposals, however, were not accepted, and contacts between Geneva and Istanbul and the occupied countries were made through non-Jews. At the end of 1942, when the scale of the extermination became known, the subject was revived. Eliyahu Dobkin repeatedly asked Ben-Gurion to send a few men or women to Nazi-occupied areas, just as the Jewish underground had sent men and women from one ghetto or country to another, illegally and under the most difficult conditions, and as the governments-in-exile of Poland, Greece, Yugoslavia, and others had done. Ben-Gurion agreed that there was a need to send someone to Poland but warned that he or she "may not return."[22]

When Stanislaw Kot, the deputy prime minister of the Polish government-in-exile, visited Palestine at the end of 1942, Ben-Gurion suggested to him that people from the Yishuv be trained in London and leave for Poland from there, together with the emissaries of the Polish underground. Kot confirmed Ben-Gurion's apprehensions that people who went to the occupied countries on behalf of the Polish government-in-exile were not expected to return. Furthermore, however familiar people in the Yishuv might be with Poland and its language, he was very skeptical about their ability to survive there for long. But Ben-Gurion continued to press Kot until he agreed.

Both the JAE and the Mapai Central Committee approved his proposal to Kot. The goal of this mission was to establish contacts and not, as Gruenbaum suggested, to incite rebellion among the local Jews who "were waiting quietly for their death." "We cannot give the Jews instructions from here how to behave," Ben-Gurion replied. "We do not know what is going on there, and direct contact is necessary."[23]

Another idea proposed from time to time was the formation of Jewish commando units to fight the German army and Axis collaborators for the purpose of saving Jews. Such activity by Yishuv soldiers in the British army itself, whose targets were purely military, was impracticable. However, Yishuv volunteers in the army urged repeatedly during the last months of 1942 that "ghetto demolition squads" be sent to Europe immediately. The JAE rejected their requests, both because the British were unlikely to agree and because it would be almost impossible to transfer units to Europe independently for direct combat.

Several members also feared that the public might construe mobilization of that kind as a ploy to increase recruitment of Yishuv youngsters to the British army, advocated by the national institutions so that the Yishuv would be considered an active ally.[24]

Nevertheless, the idea tended to resurface whenever shocking new information reached Palestine. In December 1942, for example, the Rescue Committee invited members of Aliya Bet to one of its meetings with exchangees, among them a child. One of the activists, Zvi Hermann, reported years later:

> The horrors they spoke of stunned us, and Gruenbaum said, "This cannot be true. Let's hear what the child has to say." After the child's comments, which were more shocking than those of the adults, especially because of the weary, reserved tone in which they were spoken, a deep silence prevailed. The Aliya Bet activists left to hold their own meeting, in which the silence continued. Finally Enzo [Sereni, a promising young leader and thinker of the Labor movement] said, "We will reach them." "How?" asked Shaul [Meirov]. "From the air," answered Enzo. The wish, the desire to reach them was clear and self-evident.[25]

Dobkin suggested that the Yishuv put pressure on the Allies to establish a special Jewish squadron for retaliatory operations, including bombing German cities. Ben-Gurion expressed confidence that the United States would agree to the idea without delay, since it had already agreed to a similar demand from the Norwegians. The intention was to send the Palmach, the elite units of the Haganah, by sea or air. Because there had been cooperation between the Haganah and British intelligence in 1940 and 1941, Shertok submitted the proposal to British intelligence headquarters in Cairo in December 1942, noting that 150 to 200 suitable people had already registered as volunteers, and was promised that it would be looked into.[26]

And indeed, in January 1943 one of the British intelligence units that had worked with the Haganah and was, apparently, more flexible in its attitudes than other intelligence units suggested that fighters from the Yishuv be parachuted into Europe, especially into the Balkans. Shertok and Dov Joseph immediately elaborated on the suggestion: they would establish commando units of up to 1,000 altogether, to be parachuted primarily into Poland; in addition to tasks assigned them by the British, they would encourage the Jewish communities to defend themselves. In February, however, Shertok reported from London that the British considered it impossible to get into Poland. They were concerned that if the Germans found out about such units, they would react by accelerating the murders. The British did agree to handle the more restricted plan, which suited their own needs more closely, of parachuting soldiers into the Balkans.[27]

The British had their own reasons for rejecting the more extensive proposal. They did not want a large unit in the Yishuv trained by themselves that could later act against them. In addition, cooperation with local Jews and Jewish soldiers might result in military complications in anti-Semitic regions in occupied Europe. More important were the long-term political implications, bound to arise after the war, when the Yishuv demanded a reward for its military contribution to the war effort.

Shertok continued through 1943 to submit extensive proposals regarding Poland. All were rejected. At the end of the year, it was clear that operations in Poland were no longer practical: the rebellions in the ghettos had already taken place, most ghettos had been liquidated, and the Russians were advancing from the east.

The JAE had to be content with parachuting a small number of people into the Balkans. As a result of a meeting in March 1943 between Kaplan and Epstein and British intelligence in Turkey, a group of fourteen volunteers was sent for training in Cairo. Soon afterward the group was returned to Palestine. The volunteers had made it clear that they considered their duty to the Jewish people more important than their military obligations to the Allies. Some of them had refused to go to Germany, claiming that there were no more Jews there, and most of them had refused to pledge allegiance to the British army or wear its uniform even though their chances of survival were clearly much better if they were captured wearing British uniforms.[28]

In Palestine, mutual suspicion and conflicts continued between the future parachutists, with their informal attitudes, and the British army officers who were training them. Moshe Dayan, who had been acting as liaison, resigned. There were also internal problems in the Yishuv between the Defense Committee of the Histadrut, which was handling the parachutist issue, and the Agency's Political Department over the question of whether the British would actually let the parachutists do rescue work. Finally, in May 1943 a coordinating committee with representatives from Palmach headquarters, the Histadrut, and the Political Department assumed charge of mobilizing and training the volunteers.

Meanwhile, time was passing, and the group had not yet been called into service. A combination of factors seems to have promoted the delay. For one thing, relations between the mandatory government and the Yishuv deteriorated in the second half of 1943. Second, after El Alamein and Stalingrad the Allies were less in need of the Yishuv volunteers. Third, the British were encountering technical, military, and political problems in the Balkans. Finally, in the British view the political implications of the plan were far greater than its military benefits. Meirov later wrote, "More than once we were openly told that the Zionist movement was using the project more for its own ends than for the general military need."[29]

Debate in the Yishuv about the limited independence of the operation also contributed to the delay. Enzo Sereni, who succeeded Dayan as liaison with the British, argued that because it was possible to get to occupied Europe only with the help of the Allies, "there must be some concessions made." He did not elaborate, but presumably he meant that the trainees had to accommodate themselves to the military demands of the British—uniform, oath, accepting all assignments, and going wherever sent—as long as they finally succeeded in reaching the Jews in Europe. Not everyone accepted this position. The trainees in particular had "doubts—Zionist, ideological, and moral considerations." Some were unwilling to accept "the double role—the general and the Jewish." Some resigned.[30]

Repeated investigations made it abundantly clear that without the help of the British, who were in charge of the Mediterranean theater of operations, it was impossible to reach the occupied areas. At that point, Yishuv leaders decided to work on the project only with the British and to increase efforts to get things moving.

By the end of 1943, 240 Yishuv volunteers in the British army or in the Palmach had started intensive training, and 3 had been parachuted into Europe. The rest waited. Progress was very slow. Fearing that the Balkans would be occupied by the Germans because the Allied invasion had not been carried out, the JAE increased pressure on the British. Eliyahu Golomb and Yitzhak Sadeh, the leader of the Palmach, pushed for drafting entirely new military plans. News reached Palestine that the Jews in the Balkans were making preparations for self-defense and wanted advice and help from the Yishuv. The Agency resolved to help as much as possible, financially and otherwise, and gathered information for that purpose, especially from refugees, about the situation there.[31]

In January 1944, Shertok went to Cairo with a plan to organize the Jewish communities (which still numbered more than a million) in Bulgaria, Rumania, Hungary, and Slovakia to resist the Germans. Two fighters were to be sent immediately to each country to establish small cells of Jewish youth, after which training instructors would arrive. Eventually at least fifty properly equipped fighters would be sent to each country and would constitute the local command. Reuven Zaslany (later Shiloach) of the Agency's Political Department stressed the importance of well-organized resistance in saving the lives of Jews or inflicting harm on the enemy. Shertok and Zaslany proposed that the operation be subject to British supervision and to the needs of the war but also maintained that "guidance from Palestine is necessary." [32]

British government officials considered the proposals politically unacceptable. They argued that the uprising in Warsaw had been motivated by despair and had occurred without guidance from Palestine. They also expressed fears about the increased military strength of the Yishuv. Despite support from several high officers, the plan was rejected. Shertok was informed on May 1 that the plan would neither help the Jews resist nor contribute anything to the war effort.

The Agency did not give up yet. In June 1944, when Shertok was in London in connection with Brand's mission, he suggested to Churchill through his son, Randolph, that parachute units be transferred to Tito's Yugoslavia. Tito's representatives were inclined to agree on condition that their wounded be given medical treatment in Palestine. Churchill agreed, and at the end of July Zaslany arrived in Italy to organize the operation. But by now the British had reduced the suggested scope to only twenty or thirty people. Detailed practical preparations began in Palestine, but in August the British again cancelled the plan. The same fate befell another plan, initiated after Brand's mission, that proposed parachuting dozens of soldiers into Hungary and establishing a Jewish military base there in coordination with the Yugoslav partisans.

Nevertheless, apparently in response to growing Western public pressure over the annihilation of Hungarian Jewry, the departure of few parachutists was approved at the end of August. In the view of Lord Moyne, Britain would even gain in "removing from Palestine a number of active and resourceful Jews," especially since "the chances of many of them returning in the future to give trouble in Palestine seem slight." [33]

Most of the 32 parachutists, of the 240 candidates, who were allowed to go to Europe left between March and September 1944. They operated in Rumania, Yugoslavia, Slovakia, Bulgaria, Italy, and Austria. Twelve of them were captured; seven of these were executed. Their missions and operations have been chronicled elsewhere. The crucial issue here is the purpose of the Yishuv in sending the parachutists.

At the end of 1942 the role of all emissaries from Palestine was to establish contact with the Jewish communities in the occupied areas and, first and foremost, with those in Poland. In the spring of 1943 their chief objectives were to increase contacts with the Jewish population and to encourage Jewish self-defense in Poland. From the beginning of 1944, the main role was to urge the Balkan Jews to rebel and inflict losses on the enemy.

Being useful to the Jews of Europe was clearly paramount for the volunteers themselves. The military tasks assigned them by the British—such as radio communication, transmitting information to and from Allied prisoners of war, and establishing contacts with partisans—were inevitable concomitants. "The British can send their own agents without us," said the parachutist Joel Palgi, "But we cannot act without them." [34]

Although the parachutists' goals were clearly defined in terms of Zionist Jewish and military-political interests, they were not uniform. In their memoirs, parachutists Palgi and Chaim Chermesh describe how they questioned the leaders of the Yishuv, "people who have been for us a symbol of our way," before leaving on their missions.

> What is our main task? "To teach Jews how to fight," said Eliyahu [Golomb]. "To let the Jews know that Palestine is their land and their stronghold," said Ben-Gurion, "and that immediately after the victory, they should come in masses and knock on the locked gates of Palestine to open them." "Save Jews," said Berl, "all the rest, later. If there are no Jews left, Palestine and the Zionist enterprise will also be annihilated." [35]

To another parachutist, Golomb said, "The great purpose is to reach our tortured brothers, to bring them our ideas. Our future depends on the success of your mission. Be a proud Jew, know where you are going, and remember who sent you." Dobkin simply told two other parachutists, "If you deliver greetings from Palestine to the Diaspora, you will have fulfilled your mission." [36] The parachutists did not receive specific operational guidelines. The situation in Europe was volatile, and at that late stage it was not known what practical goals could be achieved. And, indeed, the parachutists continued to debate among themselves after they reached Europe.

One of the major subjects they discussed concerned the risks they had to undertake. "Did we come here only so the Yishuv in Palestine can consider itself as having discharged its obligation, by sending people to die here? Our goal is to help and not to sacrifice ourselves . . . we are not interested in becoming symbols without actually doing anything," argued Reuven Dafni when it turned out that the Yugoslav partisans were wary of helping them cross the border to Hungary. Hanna Senesh, however, firmly insisted that the parachutists cross the border on their own:

we did not come here "on condition," that we would cross the border only if everything was assured beforehand . . . we have to act without calculations or unnecessary deliberations. We must not be late. If Hitler succeeds in annihilating all the Jews of Europe, there is no future for us in Palestine, either. The Yishuv will degenerate without the momentum of immigration and building the country. I do not know why I was chosen for this noble task, but I do know clearly that, once having started, there is no turning back. To save myself—for what? For whom? We will not be blamed even if we don't succeed, but there is the judgment of conscience. Will it be possible to go on living? I have to go. And if I fail, my death will not be in vain. Maybe the rumor will reach the Jews that an emissary from Palestine arrived and was caught and hearts will throb in the ghettos and in the woods: We have to hold on, we have not been deserted, we have not been forgotten, and maybe salvation is near. Faith can work miracles.[37]

On the eve of their departure to Hungary, which was already occupied by the Germans, Palgi told Senesh that he felt "we are not going there to save Jews any more, but rather to pay our last respects to those still left to be annihilated." And when he arrived in Hungary and found that there was indeed no time for organizing and training, he asked himself:

What is my task now? Is it not my duty to join those being transported in the death wagons and, at the door of the gas chambers, tell them about Palestine? . . . Or maybe this is the task today: to go and stand among the diggers, to turn the shovels into swords and give a signal and an example to the Jews to follow me? And maybe the task is, if there are no more Jews, to fight the Germans, to expedite the end of the war for those who are still living in the death camps, for those who are still living in Rumania, in Sweden, in France, in Switzerland, in England, in America, and in Palestine, those whose turn will come, too, if we do not defeat the Nazis.[38]

It seems, then, that both in their discussions and in their encounters with reality in occupied Europe, the parachutists reached the same definitions of goals that their leaders in Palestine had reached before their departure.

Some of the parachutists managed to complete only the military assignments given them by the British. Some fought alongside the Yugoslav and Slovak partisans. Others did reach and help save Jews. Their main activities, however, turned out to be neither rescue nor organizing Jews for defense but rather assisting the Jews during the interim stages of the war until the Russians or the Western Allies arrived. They provided leadership; they helped care for thousands of refugees, Palestinian prisoners of war, members of youth movements; they prepared people for immigration to Palestine, and at the end of the war they played a crucial role in organizing it.

The 32 who left for their mission so late were a tiny fraction of the 1,000 whom the Agency planned to send. The parachutists were from the same mold as the youth who fought in the ghettos, who crossed borders, who took care of orphans and forged documents. They happened to have immigrated to Palestine earlier than their European counterparts, but they came from the same background, received the same youth movement education. Yet to many Jews in Europe they represented the spirit of the Yishuv, and as such they helped renew faith in Palestine and in Zionism during the Holocaust.

But Zuckermann's question to the leaders in Palestine is still pertinent. Why did the Yishuv send no emissaries in the way that the movements in Europe sent their own emissaries—from one ghetto to the next, independently, without the support of outside bodies, Jewish or non-Jewish? Were such emissaries not sent because it was too painful to sacrifice young boys and girls for a mission that might fail? Why did no one leave Geneva, Istanbul, or Sweden on foot to serve as "a gesture, a sign, a hand extended as a token of sharing our fate"? There is no simple or easy answer to this question.

14

The End of the Rescue Effort

During 1943, while the various rescue plans were being discussed and negotiated, most emissaries and activists agreed that "nothing can be done for the time being, except bringing out small groups of people."[1] And, indeed, beginning in January 1943 small groups of children and adults made their way to Palestine through Turkey. They left on their own initiative, aided by the emissaries, with or without transit visas and immigration permits. In January 56 children arrived from Rumania; in March, 72 children from Hungary; in March and April, a few dozen Jews from Bulgaria; in July, 15 children and 5 adults from Zagreb. In the summer, when sailing conditions were better, people arrived at Izmir from Greece, 5 or 6 to a tiny boat; 200 came from Rumania after acquiring the right to pass through Bulgaria and crossed Turkey in groups of 10 a week; and there were others. According to Chaim Barlas' calculations in 1943, 857 people passed through Turkey, with or without permits, on their way to Palestine.[2]

At the end of 1943, after failure of the plan to use the 29,000 remaining permits for children, the Yishuv undertook two separate courses of action. On the one hand, the JAE continued to try to obtain from the British as many immigration permits as possible before the end of the White Paper term in March 1944. The British maintained that the permits were available and that any Jew who reached Turkey would be allowed to enter Palestine, as had been promised in July 1943.[3]

Hence the second course of action. The emissaries in Istanbul, and especially the activists of Aliya Bet, continued to look for ways of getting Jews out of Europe even without the necessary transit visas or other legal papers, which seemed almost impossible to acquire. They hoped that if departure from the Balkans continued "drop by drop, the Gestapo would not interfere" and that vessels might still be found, although in this matter "failures are enormous . . . we have lost a great deal of money."[4] From September 1943 and during 1944 the Greek underground cooperated steadily with the emissaries to get about 1,000 Jews out of Greece by boat. Another avenue of rescue also opened at the end of 1943: the Turkish government, having been approached by the emissaries "for the hundredth or thousandth time," instructed its consuls in Rumania, Hungary, Slovakia, and Bulgaria to issue each of the nine transit visas permitted each week, to families rather than to individuals. They would not, however, allow all thirty-six visas to be used in any one of the four countries. In addition, the paperwork that the travelers had to cope with remained "a horrible procedure," both on the British side and on the side of the pro-German government that was established in Bulgaria in the summer of 1944: no fewer than twelve different permits were required per person.[5]

Nevertheless, at the beginning of 1944 there was a discernible improvement. Largely because of the approaching end of the war, the governments of the Balkan states were more willing to close their eyes and let the emissaries operate "legally or illegally." In February Ira Hirschmann, Roosevelt's special representative on the War Refugee Board, arrived in Istanbul and, having failed in his first attempts to acquire ships independently, cooperated with emissaries. The JDC also increased its presence in Istanbul, and Laurence Steinhardt was more willing to cooperate than he had been before the WRB had been established.

Encouraged by these changes, the emissaries increased their efforts to acquire vessels. Their first attempt to lease a Turkish ship, in cooperation with Hirschmann, failed. The Turks had insisted on compensation in case the ship sank and on a guarantee of safe conduct through their waters from the Germans. The German ambassador in Turkey, Franz von Papen, received the guarantee from Berlin, but soon afterward the approval was suddenly revoked. The emissaries blamed the failure not only on foreign governments but also on Hirschmann's vociferous methods. Additional attempts to acquire a Rumanian, Bulgarian, Portuguese, or Swedish ship failed for the same reasons.[6]

The Aliya Bet emissaries became convinced that only illegal action, without the proper permits, could succeed. And indeed, in the spring of 1944 they persuaded the owners of two Bulgarian ships to take the risk for a high fee. From March through May the SS *Milka* and the SS *Maritza* made two trips each between Constantza and Istanbul, bringing out 1,300 people. With Steinhardt's help the passengers acquired

Turkish transit visas upon their arrival. In Istanbul the JDC provided them with clothing and with food for the train trip from Turkey to Palestine.

Shaul Meirov, Venia Pomerantz, and Ze'ev Shind notified the Histadrut Secretariat in person a few months later: "We succeeded in breaking through this wall." After legal attempts and many promises failed, "the only things left were the ships of the 'Jewish navy' . . . in the Black Sea. Obstacles here, German mines there, but the ships got through."[7]

In March 1944, when the ships started sailing, the British announced to the Turkish government that every Jew arriving in Istanbul would receive permission to enter Palestine. Eight months had passed since the British had first made this promise to the Jewish Agency and to its emissaries in Istanbul. Why did they make a formal announcement in March 1944? Perhaps because, with the White Paper expiration deadline imminent, 21,000 permits still had not been used. Perhaps because Hirschmann and Steinhardt had created a precedent by acquiring visas for the passengers on the *Milka* and *Maritza* from the Turks, and "the British had no alternative but to follow suit" as Aliya Bet emissaries put it. And perhaps because the Nazis had taken over Hungary that month and were about to take over Rumania and Bulgaria too; with the exit from the Balkans blocked, there would be no danger of large-scale Jewish immigration to Palestine.[8]

In any case, after the British announcement the Turks agreed to apply the nine transit visas a week not to individuals or families, but to groups, and to raise the number of children allowed to pass through Turkey from 50 per week to 150. In July the U.S. and British governments made a joint announcement that any Jews who showed the Turkish consul in their country a letter from a representative of the Jewish Agency attesting that immigration permits were waiting for them would immediately receive entry visas to Turkey. The JAE made a commitment to the Turkish government to take responsibility for the conduct and maintenance of any Jew who arrived and to transfer them to Palestine.[9]

In the summer of 1944, with Hungary under German occupation and the Bulgarian and the Rumanian fleets both under German control, Greek and Turkish boat owners were willing to sail from Rumania and Bulgaria in return for substantial profits. Thus, after a year and a half of fighting obstacles, all necessary measures for getting the Jews from the Balkans to Palestine had been secured: exit from the Balkan states, ships, British and Turkish permission for passage through Turkey and entry into Palestine, money—the agreement with the JDC was signed in July—and cooperation among the various representatives and emissaries in Istanbul. And indeed, during July and August Aliya Bet got nearly 2,000 more people from Rumania to Istanbul and from there to Palestine, though with casualties on the way. The *Kazebek* (with 735 passengers), the *Maritza* (308—third sailing), and the *Bulbul* (410) arrived safely; the *Mafkura*, with 344, went down in the Black Sea.[10]

This period of successful rescue work was short. At the end of the summer the Arab League was founded in Cairo, and the British feared its reaction to another increase in the rate of Jewish immigration to Palestine. In November the British learned that tens of thousands of Jews in Rumania—which had been liberated by the Russians—were registering to immigrate and that another ship, the SS *Saladin*, had left for Istanbul with 547 passengers. "It is an absolute hydra," wrote an official of the British Foreign Office, referring to Jewish exit from the Balkans. In December the British government therefore revoked its previous assurance that any Jews who arrived in Turkey would receive an immigration permit and be allowed to continue to Palestine; instead, 10,000 people would be allowed to enter Palestine by April 1945, at the rate of 1,500 a month. The Yishuv responded by demanding permission to bring 100,000 survivors to Palestine within a short period. These developments mark the beginning of another period, one involving primarily immigration from the liberated areas rather than the rescue of survivors from areas under German control.[11]

Altogether, more than 5,000 refugees passed through Istanbul in the summer and fall of 1944. About 3,350 of these were brought by Aliya Bet, and about 1,550 came through what Meirov described as "the conventional channels"—that is, by land and equipped with appropriate papers. Together with those who came in 1943, they numbered about 6,000. The difference in the results achieved by the Aliya Bet and by the Jewish Agency's Immigration Department "teaches us something," he added, implying, of course, that unconventional methods were the correct solution.[12]

It appears that, had the Aliya Bet emissaries waited until all the permits and approvals had been received, the ships would not have sailed. Nevertheless, Meirov's distinction between legal and illegal immigration in 1944 seems unwarranted. The immigrants did board ships without the necessary papers, but they received them upon their arrival in Turkey from the Turks and from the British. As for the vessels that sailed without papers or assurance of safe conduct, both the Turkish and the British authorities knew about their coming and going. This wave of immigration should therefore be considered both legal and illegal at the same time—as Barlas said, "joined together and inseparable." He did not delude himself that the movement of thousands of people could be hidden from the authorities.[13]

In the two years when the greater part of the extermination was taking place, from February 1942 to March 1944, Aliya Bet did not succeed in buying or leasing any vessels. The course of events shows clearly that lack of vessels in those years prevented rescue from the Balkans on a larger scale. But for all the activists' perseverance and resourcefulness, the acquisition and use of ships became possible only when an appropriate political and military situation existed in Europe. Nor could Aliya Bet have succeeded without the help of the Agency's Immigration and Political Departments and their contacts with the Americans and the Turks.

Six thousand people were saved through the joint efforts of Aliya Bet and the emissaries. There was some comfort for them in the belief that "by getting thousands out, we kept the spark of hope alive for the Jews, we gave meaning to life, we raised the prestige of the Zionist movement."[14]

While the search for ships was going on, the JAE was discussing use of the remaining immigration permits with the mandatory government. In January 1944 Shertok asked Eric Mills, the director of the government's Immigration Department, for the first quota of permits for the year. Mills replied that he would not issue more than 900 for the first quarter, because, according to his calculations, the overall quota of 75,000 permits for five years had already been exceeded by 14,000. (This overrun reflected the numerous confirmations of entitlement to permits that had been sent to the occupied countries.) Therefore, permits would be released a few at a time. As for Oliver Stanley's announcement that the time for using all remaining permits would be extended after the White Paper deadline, Mills claimed that it would best suit him if "the date came and it was all over."

Shertok told Mills that thousands of Jews were waiting in Aden, Teheran, Portugal, Spain, Italy, and North Africa and that 900 permits "simply means suffocating us." Given the British government's intention to extend the White Paper deadline and prevent a crisis at the end of March, it was Mills's obligation, Shertok said, to continue to issue permits. Mills answered that if "you will not make our lives miserable over every man and woman," it might be possible to distribute the permits.

Gruenbaum and Dobkin were afraid that Shertok's argument

would be construed as concerning immigration in general, whereas for them the crucial question was how many permits would be issued for the occupied countries. Mills had claimed that if the tens of thousands of people who had received confirmations arrived, he would not have permits for them; but Mills knew very well that the permits were for rescue and not for immigration. The Agency had committed itself to him on that point. Furthermore, the prospects for immigration at the beginning of 1944 were still very slim. Despite their objection the JAE accepted the proposed distribution and decided to renew the struggle to obtain immigration permits once the White Paper deadline had passed.[15]

At the beginning of April, Shertok cabled Palestine from London that the British had officially announced to the Turks that anyone reaching their territory would receive permission to enter Palestine. At the same time, Stanley had informed him sub rosa, reflecting Mills' suspicions, that the government would be prepared not to consider the confirmations as actual permits. However, only 1,000 permits would be reserved for wives and children of residents of Palestine; all the rest of the 21,000, not including the confirmations, would be available for Jews in enemy countries. Having been disappointed before by apparently noble British gestures that proved spurious in practice, Shertok reacted immediately. He pointed out that although refugees from enemy territory had first claim to the permits, the prospects of any of them getting out were, for the time being, limited. In the meantime the permits should be used for those who had already escaped and were now suffering in various places. Stanley agreed to give special cases "a liberal interpretation." Policy as a whole would be reassessed if escape from the occupied countries became possible.[16]

Shertok's cable produced a storm in Palestine. Ben-Gurion met with High Commissioner Sir Harold MacMichael and told him in so many words that the JAE did not trust the British. According to Ben-Gurion, MacMichael flushed with anger and accused the Yishuv of never being satisfied with whatever was done for them concerning immigration. Britain, he said, was the only nation helping the Jews, and all it got in return was insults. He also took exception to the way Whitehall kept sending him new regulations and interpretations concerning immigration policy every other day.[17]

A few days later the situation deteriorated further. Mills announced that he would accept no more lists of names for confirmations of entitlement permits, since the Yishuv had already exceeded the quota. His announcement came the very time that Switzerland expressed willingness to deliver official notices to everyone on the lists. Demands came from Hungary and Rumania to continue sending confirmations, which were saving lives; and word came from Nazi-occupied western Europe, especially from Holland, that the names appearing in the approved lists served as a basis for exchange with the Germans.

Dobkin said that "this typical behavior again shows how much the White Paper is preventing us from saving Jews." The JAE condemned British hypocrisy. During the first three years of the war, when it was possible to leave Europe, Britain had claimed that it could not allow refugees from enemy territories into Palestine because there might be spies among them. Now, in the spring of 1944, when it was impossible to get out of Europe, it wanted to assign all the permits left to the occupied countries while those who had already been saved from the Nazis and were now in Allied or neutral countries were forbidden to enter Palestine.[18]

"We have reached a crisis," Shertok announced in May. "I have a serious suggestion. We have to start an open fight. We have to conduct it publicly, here, in England and in America . . . When the certificates that are still available run out, we will have reached an impossible situation . . . This is why they are dragging it out. This is our struggle. We have to condemn this game and create a furor."[19]

At the end of May, news arrived about the fate of Hungarian Jewry, and in June, information about Auschwitz. Then, on July 20, Horthy notified the International Red Cross that he was stopping the deportations and was willing to allow aid to the prisoners in the hard-labor camps in Hungary, to release all those who had certificates of protection or immigration permits, and to release children under the age of ten, who could receive visas to any country. The Hungarian minister in Istanbul met on his own initiative with Barlas and Kaplan and gave them official notice of this proposal. He added that those holding confirmation of entitlement to permits—there were now 8,000—would be allowed to start leaving Hungary within two weeks, either by sea, via Rumania, or by train, via Bulgaria. The Hungarian government asked the Agency to handle all travel arrangements from the Hungarian border and promised to halt all deportations while the emigration was taking place. "This is both a tremendous task and a tremendous privilege which has fallen to us," said Kaplan upon his return from Turkey; "there is now a unique constellation" for rescue.[20] These developments were an incentive for a new stage in the struggle against the White Paper.

The delegation in Istanbul started arranging transportation by train; the emissaries in Geneva tried to distribute more immigration permits in Hungary. The Agency appealed to all countries, especially the United States, to receive the tens of thousands of children still alive in Hungary. On the day that Horthy's declaration was issued, Shertok asked Switzerland and Sweden if they were still willing to receive the children. Switzerland replied that it was willing to receive "a certain number," and Sweden agreed to receive any Jew from Hungary for whom a Swedish citizen would guarantee maintenance. Dobkin acquired permission for 3,000 children to go directly to Spain in case there were difficulties with the passage through Turkey. Gruenbaum approached the Jewish community in Australia to acquire Australian visas for children from Hungary and a list of candidates for exchange; even these lists might ensure the safety of some. He also delivered the names of Polish refugees in Hungary to the Polish government-in-exile so that it would help get them out.

The JDC had helped support International Red Cross operations since the beginning of 1943. Now the War Refugee Board also offered financial support. The Agency asked the Red Cross to enlarge its staff in Hungary, to visit the prisoners in the camps there and in Germany, and to report at least once a week to the Agency and to the JDC. The Yishuv emissaries offered their services to the Red Cross in supervising the relief work in general.[21]

Shertok reported all these developments to the Colonial Office and asked that Britain change its policy and at least allow the children and veteran Zionists from the Balkans into Palestine. The two weeks from July 20 to August 7 were a time of "tremendous, exhausting work," according to Shertok. Hope was high in the Yishuv that, with so many affirmative responses, a large-scale rescue operation would finally become possible. Britain and the United States, however, had not yet officially reacted to Horthy's declaration. Moreover, Eden had told Parliament that he was not completely sure that the declaration had indeed been given to the International Red Cross, as Shertok and Weizmann had claimed.[22]

At meetings of the Foreign Office, the Colonial Office, and an intergovernmental committee, officials expressed fears concerning Horthy's declaration. "We are afraid that we may be on the verge of a flood of refugees" immigrating to Palestine from Hungary. Stanley suggested urgent action "to stop this movement," to make it clear to the International Red Cross that it had no right to send refugees to Palestine, which was a British mandate, and to reach an understanding with the U.S. government to refrain from making any actual commitment.[23]

A whole month passed before Britain and the United States accepted Horthy's proposal, on July 17. They assumed responsibility for providing temporary shelter to Jews who reached either an Allied or a neutral country, and they appealed to neutral countries to open their gates to Jews. However, the announcement concluded, the two governments "in accepting the offer . . . do not in any way condone the action of the Hungarian Government in forcing the emigration of Jews as an alternative to persecution and death."[24]

At the beginning of September news reached Palestine that Eichmann was pressing Horthy to renew the deportations to Auschwitz and that preparations were fully under way. In the meantime, thousands were being sent to forced-labor camps in Germany. Gruenbaum sent another series of cables to governments and organizations, urging them to put pressure on Hungary.[25] The deportations were delayed, but for reasons not connected with external pressure.

On October 15 the Germans moved into Budapest, and the Jews there fell into their hands. Now cables were sent to Churchill and Stalin, who were conferring in Moscow, and to Roosevelt.[26] The Agency again concentrated on acquiring certificates of protection from neutral countries and from South America and on transferring more lists of names. Current information confirmed that people holding the various certificates were not being deported. Thousands of others between the ages of ten and eighty were sent to labor camps around Budapest where they were forced to work under extremely difficult conditions. Tens of thousands of others, including women and children, were sent on foot that winter, their belongings on their backs, toward the Austrian border, in the operation orchestrated by Eichmann that came to be known as the death marches. According to reports at the end of 1944, only 220,000 Jews were left in Budapest. The 8,000 who held certificates of protection and permits recognized by the Hungarian government were gathered into protective custody by the Red Cross and by representatives of Sweden and Switzerland, among them Raoul Wallenberg and Charles Lutz. However, even those in protective custody were at the mercy of anyone who wore a uniform in the Budapest of those chaotic days.

From mid-October to December 1944 the JAE was at a loss as to what to do. Gruenbaum finally gave up. The means at the disposal of the JAE did not permit any practical action, either in Hungary or in those parts of Poland and Holland that were still occupied, and certainly not in Germany. The high hopes aroused by the Horthy declaration were dashed in the bitterest disappointment of all. This had clearly been the last chance.

From December 1944 until the end of the war, the Agency's rescue attempts were limited to sending appeals for help, dispatching parcels to the camps in Germany and Theresienstadt, and attempting to release the Jews there or at least prevent their murder until the Allies arrived. In the last months of the war, communication and transportation were cut off. Hundreds of thousands, if not millions, of people of all nationalities were on the move. As the front advanced into the heart of Europe and the end of the war brought even greater chaos, it became impossible for the Yishuv to reach the survivors. The Executive gave up on rescue efforts and turned its attention to assisting the Jews still left in the liberated areas and to postwar plans.

Conclusion:
Rescue and Zionist Policy

Analysis of the Yishuv's attitude toward the rescue of European Jewry centers on the crucial question: How, and to what extent, did the Holocaust affect Zionist policy and ideology while it was happening? Did it change, or at least influence, Zionist policymaking on major issues such as the attitude of the Zionist center in Palestine to the Jews of the Diaspora, immigration priorities, structures and relations within the Zionist movement, attitudes toward the Western world, and the establishment of a Jewish state? In other words, did the Yishuv leaders revise their views enough to face the catastrophe? And did they review their priorities to make the rescue of European Jewry paramount?

Regarding the attitude of the Zionist center in Palestine to the Jews of the Diaspora, the assumption prevailing in Israel since the end of the war has been that the Yishuv respected only those who took up arms; that the rest were considered inferior human beings who went "like lambs to the slaughter".[1] Only the Zionist undertaking in Palestine had succeeded in raising a courageous and resourceful new generation of Jewish youth, the very antithesis of Diaspora Jews. The source material, however, particularly minutes of meetings of leaders, reveals a more complex attitude.

During 1942, when the deportations to the death camps started, the reports that reached Palestine, mainly from the members of the exchange groups, described passive, almost apathetic Jewish communities, mesmerized by fear, especially during roundups and executions; Jewish leaders, members of the Jewish councils in the ghettos, and the Jewish police allowed themselves to be used by the Germans against their brothers. Most leaders in the Yishuv, such as Eliyahu Dobkin and Joseph Sprinzak, refused to comment; they needed time to grasp what had really happened. Others, such as Shneur-Zalman Rubashov and Israel Galili, a central figure in the Labor movement and in all defense problems, repudiated the public tendency to belittle the Jews of Europe: "We are all from there," received the same education, and "Jewish fate is the same everywhere." Ben-Gurion tried to be realistic: "There are quislings and rascals among every people." Only a few expressed "shame of their weakness" (Yitzhak Tabenkin) and considered Jewish defenselessness "a burning disgrace" (Yitzhak Gruenbaum).[2] There was, then, a mixture of programmatic Zionist declarations against the Diaspora as a concept and as a destructive reality, and deep feeling for the Jews of Europe and their suffering.

The news that reached Palestine at the beginning of the war and especially during 1943 enhanced the prestige of the pioneering youth movements in Europe—and not simply because they had decided to take up arms. They had decided to ignore all ideological and political differences. At the end of April 1943 Ze'ev Shind reported that the youth movements had joined to become one united underground. Similarly, in August Venia Pomerantz reported that the terrible situation in Europe had reconciled all the formerly fanatically partisan movements on the basis of an unprecedented equality "incomprehensible in Palestine." This did not mean that the movements had given up their respective beliefs; in light of the catastrophe, they had simply "discovered more important values." The emissaries now had difficulty even discerning who was writing the letters they received.[3]

The youth movements in Poland also established a common treasury, pooling all their resources, selling clothes and goods in order to send money to their starving comrades in the concentration camps and ghettos. There were heated discussions among the leaders about whether or not they should use the food packages they received from Istanbul and Geneva to keep themselves alive instead of running underground community activities. Antek Zuckermann, one of the foremost youth movement leaders, wrote: "We didn't eat the food; we used the packages to enable us to hold seminars and keep the movement going." It was also well known in Palestine that young movement leaders in Europe endangered their lives over and over again, moving in and out of the ghettos to succor their comrades and their younger charges; they were active in the communities regarding education, public welfare, care for the elderly and the weak, encouraged and inspired—often paying for their zeal with their lives.[4]

The revolt of the Warsaw ghetto in April 1943 stirred the Yishuv profoundly. People were proud but also conscience-stricken. The revolt had taken place with almost no help from the Yishuv and at a tremendous cost in human life. Indeed, it soon became apparent that the youth movement leadership in occupied Europe might be entirely destroyed, not only as a result of the extermination programs but also because, in the wake of the general destruction of the House of Israel, they would have been ashamed to have remained alive. "A psychosis is taking over . . . to die, down to the last person," warned Melech Neustadt. After the revolt he repeatedly implored the youth movement leaders in Palestine to save those still alive—even against their will— by issuing a directive that they were to leave immediately by whatever ways possible. Neustadt's appeal was discussed in a number of meetings. The issue was whether or not the Yishuv was morally justified in instructing these comrades to abandon their communities, save themselves, and thereby stop the armed uprisings. The question also involved the future of the Yishuv: the numerous revolts in the summer of 1943 would ultimately deprive the Yishuv of the cream of Europe's potential pioneering force. Sprinzak opposed Neustadt: "Who is more significant in this chapter of Jewish history—we or Frumka [Plonicka, a leader of the revolt in Będzin]? Frumka is more significant, and it is questionable if we have the right to drag her away." Shind reminded the disputants that the discussion was largely academic; at that point, toward the end of 1943, there was hardly any permanent address to which they could get any message to the youth movements in Europe.[5] The ghetto uprisings were already fact, and most of the ghettos had already been destroyed.

A formal decision was not reached, apparently. But among the major youth movements in Palestine, Neustadt's view prevailed, and attempts to extricate the activists failed: they refused to leave. When an emissary arrived in Będzin in July 1943 to convince Frumka Plotnicka to leave, she replied, "I have a responsibility for my brethren . . . I have lived with them, and I will die with them." Antek Zuckermann gave a similar answer. Zivia Lubetkin "rejected the outstretched hand" from Palestine; "On principle," she refused to consider leaving. She and Tossia Altman, another famous leader, refused to be included in any of the exchange lists and asked that younger charges be saved in their stead. They did agree to accept South American passports as protection against deportation. As Moshe Daks wrote from Bratislava, "There was an atmosphere of heroism in the movement . . . and that is why our comrades stayed behind and died defending the honor of the Jewish people."[6]

Years later Ruzka Korczak, a leader in the Vilna underground, recalled that the first question that Meir Ya'ari asked me when I reached Palestine and visited him in Kibbutz Merchavia, in December 1944, was if I had received the telegram he had sent together with Tabenkin ordering us to try and save ourselves. I told him that Vilna [in Lithuania] was too far away, and we never received it. But even if we had, we wouldn't have obeyed, just as we refused to obey the order we received from Zivia and Tossia not to carry out the revolt because the casualties in Warsaw had been too heavy.[7]

The telegram apparently did reach Będzin, in southwestern Poland. When Chaika Klinger of the local underground arrived in Palestine in March 1944, she told the Histadrut Executive that

> we received an order not to organize any more defense—since those who were still alive were important to the Yishuv as witnesses of what had happened to the movement. It was hard for us to accept that kind of thinking. We felt that it was not permissible for us to remain alive because of what the comrades in Warsaw had done . . . nothing could justify us saving ourselves. We decided to prepare to defend ourselves.

Klinger said her comrades in occupied Europe felt that "in Palestine they didn't properly understand us." The Yishuv should not have construed their joining the partisans or defending themselves to the last person as in any way "renouncing Palestine." The Zionists in Europe had not given up one iota of their ideals. "The pioneering vanguard of a people without the people is of no value. If rescue is the order of the day, then the entire people has to be rescued. If destruction is—then the pioneers will be destroyed, too." Turning to David Remez, who apparently was in tears, she said, "Now is not the time or place to lament the fate of the movement. Our people in the movement went the right way—the only way they could have gone—though tragic and terrible." Remez replied, "I am weeping because we were too late, really late."[8]

The youth movement members were correct in their feeling that the uprisings were not properly understood in Palestine. Dobkin acknowledged, "I am not sure that we can really understand the depth of their tragedy." And Pomerantz asked, "Can we possibly comprehend what a ghetto is, or what an uprising against the Nazis is?" Indeed, leaders in the Yishuv argued that thousands of years of Jewish martyrdom obliged the current generation not to revolt, but to preserve the Jewish people; therefore, "the idea of Masada cannot be tolerated." According to this view, the ghetto fighters were not committing suicide, going to their deaths in desperation, or seeking a beautiful death and a high price for their lives, which were lost to begin with; on the contrary, they believed in life and in their ultimate victory.[9]

Those leaders living outside Europe in 1943 had no way of understanding that there were no possibilities open for Jews of fighting for military gains or for sheer physical safety, which did not exist anymore, without also fighting to the death to the last man, as at Masada. When they could no longer join the partisans and when they decided to remain in the ghettos and be with the inhabitants to the very end even if those inhabitants refused to join them or accept their idea, and even if this meant fighting alone for the dignity of the Jewish people, those young men and women did in fact choose almost certain death.

Leaders in the Yishuv consistently held to their view of survival: at the beginning of 1944 the Jews left in Slovakia believed that the final stage of the extermination was imminent; it appeared that the Germans were about to invade Hungary and Rumania. Members of the pioneering movements and other Zionists wanted to organize for self-defense and requested directives from Palestine. Yishuv leaders feared that, if events in the satellites followed the pattern of events in Poland the year before, no young leaders would be left from European Jewry. According to Shaul Meirov, "we told them that our national duty was to preserve our existence. Only in the most extreme case was self-defense permissible."[10]

As time passed and more information arrived on conditions in Europe, respect for the Jews in Europe grew—and not only for members of the youth movements. Older Zionist leaders had refused offers from Palestine or from the various undergrounds to help them escape—Gisi Fleischmann in Slovakia, Wilhelm Filderman in Rumania, Rabbi Leo Baeck and Jacob Edelstein in Theresienstadt, Mark Jarblum in France, Chaim Hilfstein and Joseph Salpeter in Poland. Many refused because they knew that dozens of people would be tortured and executed in the wake of their escape.[11]

The emissaries reported to Palestine on the organization of mutual aid among the Jewish communities. The Jews of Rumania were sharing their meager rations with the people in Transnistria and endangering themselves to arrange for the delivery of food, clothing, and medical supplies to them. The Jews of Slovakia helped make life in the forced-labor camps bearable. Furthermore, although they themselves did not have enough, they sent packages to the Slovak Jews deported to Poland and helped organize escape routes from there. Jews in Hungary helped maintain thousands of refugees and extended aid to the Jews of Slovakia, Zagreb, and Poland. The Armæe Juif smuggled thousands out of France, found hiding places for orphans, and forged documents. Neustadt reflected later, "The Diaspora did not lose the age-old tradition of mutual aid in times of trouble . . . this created moral and spiritual forces in the Jewish communities of Europe."[12]

Stories of individual heroism also spread, of ordinary people with no particular ideological or organizational affiliations. Legends sprang up among the Jews of Europe, and different versions of the same legend reached Palestine and were passed along. But there were also true stories of people who escaped from the sealed camps, despite machine guns and bloodhounds, who swam or crawled through heavily guarded borders, who jumped from speeding trains or hid for months in bunkers; of mothers who committed suicide because they heard orphans would have safe passage to Switzerland; of rabbis such as the brother of the rabbi of Gur and teachers such as Janusz Korczak, who refused to abandon their pupils.

In the emissaries' opinion, people in Palestine knew far too little of "deeds that could serve as educational material for generations to come." As Neustadt wrote later, the "meaning of this heroism wasn't properly understood . . . It didn't get the admiration it deserved. We were unable to comprehend their spirit and their way of thinking."[13] Only now, decades later, is the full significance of their behavior really grasped, of the spiritual courage required, day by day and hour by hour, to face the routine horror and continue the joint struggle for existence—of the family, the movement, the community—while attempting to preserve the values of the Jewish people and of humanity. The Yishuv had always regarded itself as contributing to the spiritual well-being of the Diaspora. Dobkin was the first to claim, as early as May 1942, that in Palestine "we can learn a great deal from them [the Jews of the Diaspora], of the many values they have created." And, if this was the case, asked Dobkin, "What right do we have to lay claim to being the leaders of the Jewish people? Just because we have enjoyed wartime prosperity and were miraculously saved from the great catastrophe? Aren't they our public and spiritual superiors?" The behavior of the Diaspora placed an obligation on the Yishuv to maintain just as high a moral standard and evince just as great a willingness for sacrifice; otherwise, it would cease to be a beacon of light and would not attract people after the war. Avraham Haft, the financial secretary of the Rescue Committee, put it bluntly: "After the war, we will face a supreme court, represented by Frumka and Zivia . . . every one of us must prepare himself, heart and soul, for their verdict and emerge pure and innocent; ready to sacrifice ourselves for the cause and for the people."[14]

During 1943, then, the Yishuv's attitude changed, from disdain for the Diaspora's passivity—and for the emergence of corruption and deterioration in the ghettos' public life, to a steadily growing admiration for demonstrations of human and moral heroism, not necessarily for armed resistance. Even so, few in Palestine properly understood the impossibility of the situation of the Jews in Europe until the middle of 1943; by the time its meaning was clear, it was too late to save the youthful lives lost in the ghetto uprisings.

One notion remained unchanged in the Yishuv: that the Jewish resistance was organized and sustained primarily by Zionist leaders and youth movements. Such a view failed to acknowledge that the Bund and the Communist party also played an important role, and that the Coordination—as the umbrella organization of the Jewish parties and movements was called—spanned the whole spectrum of Jewish political life, although not every one was involved in every place. The Jews in Palestine believed that the education provided by the Zionist movement between the wars had imbued youngsters with the moral values and Jewish self-respect that enabled them to display exceptional personal valor in crushing situations. Zionist education explained the willingness of youth movements and Zionist leaders to reject offers of personal safety and to endanger themselves for the sake of their young charges and for the dignity of the Jewish people.

Did the Yishuv's newfound respect for European Jewry affect immigration priorities? Between the wars, the concept of "selective immigration" prevailed—a preference for young pioneers who were trained for life in Palestine over "just any Jew." From the outbreak of war to the end of 1942, selective immigration remained Yishuv policy: certificates continued to be sent primarily to veteran Zionists and their families and to members of the youth movements.

At the end of April 1943, after the Bermuda Conference, Apollinary Hartglas, the political secretary of the Rescue Committee, wrote a memorandum titled "Notes on Aid and Rescue." Intended for the eyes of "Zionist bodies only," Hartglas analyzed rescue possibilities and concluded that millions of European Jews were doomed. The Yishuv did not have the means to embark on a comprehensive rescue mission, and the Allies were neither capable of nor interested in large-scale rescue. By investing enormous sums and effort, however, the Rescue Committee might be able to save some tens of thousand of Jews. The question was, who should be saved? Hartglas concluded:

> Isn't it reasonable to turn the rescue into a national-Zionist effort and try primarily to save people who can be of benefit to Palestine and the Jewish

people? It is clear to me that even putting it in such words sounds cruel but, unfortunately, we must . . . save children first because they comprise the best material for the Yishuv. We must save the pioneering youth but only those who have already undergone training and are fit for Zionist work. We must save the veterans who worked for the Zionist organizations since they deserve some consideration from us for their work. They will be able to forgive the Yishuv a good deal, to understand us, and perhaps even to contribute a little more.

Indiscriminate rescue, in Hartglas' view, might even prove harmful. There were already people who had arrived from Teheran and in exchange groups from other places who had no feelings for Palestine or Zionism. They were hostile to Zionist values, shirked work, and tried to lead an easy life at public expense. Who knows—they might return to the Diaspora after the war and slander the Zionist enterprise even though it had saved their lives.[15] Some of the emissaries in Geneva and Istanbul and youth movement leaders in the occupied countries, who refused to save themselves but struggled to rescue the younger members, agreed with Hartglas in unequivocal terms.[16]

Even after Hartglas' memorandum, there appears to have been no discussion of the subject. As news continued to arrive from occupied Europe, it became clear that the complex reality did not permit selective rescue. In mid-1943 the Rescue Committee decided to extend help to any Jew who could be helped. Smugglers and couriers were instructed to "take any Jew . . . any Jewish child" who could still be found.[17] On the other hand, immigration permits continued to be distributed along party lines in the satellite countries, with which communication was better. The Rescue Committee reached an agreement to divide the nine transit visas per country issued weekly by the Turkish government for Jews from Slovakia, Hungary, Rumania, and Bulgaria; one went to Agudat Yisrael, one to the Revisionists, and seven to members of movements affiliated with the World Zionist Organization. And efforts continued to find comrades and Zionist supporters in occupied Europe. Eliezer Kaplan instructed Meirov that no pioneers should be prevented from immigrating because of lack of funds.[18]

Toward the end of 1943, however, it emerged that, of the 857 refugees who had made their way to Istanbul through the Balkans, the majority were members of Agudat Yisrael and wealthy Jews, few of whom had ever given a thought to Palestine. No one from the pioneering movements was among them.

The composition of the immigration—after a year of intense efforts—generated heated arguments in Palestine and resulted in the first extensive discussions of the subject in the various forums. Most of the leaders supported the decision to save "any Jew who could be found" as the right decision: "If the first seven families saved happened to be from Agudat Yisrael, that is no reason to go into mourning," said Sprinzak. But others, including Neustadt, differed. "There are Jews and there are Jews . . . The first Jew you meet in the street is not necessarily the kind of Jew we are seeking."[19] Zionist activists in occupied Europe were bitter; "I feel as if I had been spat on," wrote one. An investigation revealed three reasons for these results. First, the representative of Aguda Yisrael in Istanbul, Ya'acov Griffle, had submitted a list of party members to the British embassy in Ankara long before the Zionists submitted their lists; as a result, their people were given priority. Second, new immigrants in Palestine, not all of them Zionists, had changed certain lists of Zionists that had been drawn up according to a party key, removing names of members of the youth movements. Finally, and most significant, the decisions about who would be saved were in fact being made in Bucharest, Sofia, and Bratislava contrary to the Rescue Committee's policy. People struggled so furiously that even the few children who succeeded in leaving during 1943 left according to a party key—depending on their parents' affiliation. In this respect, the main fight was between the religious Jews, including the Mizrachi, and the youth movements, a fight "for life and death."[20]

After the investigation the Rescue Committee formulated a new agreement: 60 percent for pioneers (divided according to the relative size of their movements); 25 percent for refugees from occupied countries who reached Hungary; 6 for Agudat Yisrael; and the rest for veteran Zionists, according to the party key. And indeed, in the spring of 1944, after the German invasion of Hungary, Aliya Bet vessels began to arrive from Rumania, and the proportion of pioneering youth among the immigrants grew: on the first there were 35 out of 161 adults (21 percent); on the third, 94 out of 274 (34 percent). But these figures were still not in accordance with the agreement. "It is true that not only Zionists should be saved, but we cannot allow . . . such a high proportion of anti-Zionists." The Histadrut insisted on another investigation and sanctions against the guilty. Meirov admitted that the emissaries in Istanbul had no control over the choice of immigrants in Rumania; telephones and mail delivery were often cut for weeks at a time. The activists on the spot operated according to their own lights. Certainly the Immigration Department and the Rescue Committee had no influence.[21]

In May and July more ships arrived, and the controversy continued.

Forty-five youth movement members had been left in Rumania and their places taken by wealthy people. Judah-Leib Magnes, returning from Istanbul in July, reported: "I don't envy anyone who has to choose the immigrants. One hundred hands are stretched out to you and you can take only ten. If I had seen my father among them, I would have taken him or other members of the family or friends or associates. It is so terribly natural." Two weeks later Kaplan likewise asked all the members of the Rescue Committee to try to understand the "terrible situation" in Rumania, where fear of both the Germans and the Soviets caused people to fight viciously to save themselves and their families.[22]

New quotas were again dispatched from Palestine to Istanbul and then to Rumania: at least 30 percent of the permits were to go to orphans, especially to those from Transnistria; another 30 percent were for pioneers and refugees, especially those from Poland; and the rest were for various organizations and veteran Zionists, with 8 percent going to Agudat Yisrael.[23]

At the end of July, three days after the Horthy declaration, the JAE discussed the composition of possible immigration from Hungary. Ben-Gurion said:

> We are not in a position to bring all the Jews over from there . . . Perhaps we can bring out thousands, perhaps tens of thousands. The question of whom we chose to bring is very serious—to the extent that the choice is ours . . . of course, we will bring over Jews in danger of being killed even if we know for sure that they will leave Palestine within three months. But, if we have a choice between bringing over people who will return to Rumania the minute the war ends and who will be alienated while they are here or people who will remain—then we have to bring those Jews who will remain here.

There would be a "political catastrophe" after the war if a large number of Jews left Palestine just as the Yishuv began to fight for mass immigration. Consequently, priority should be given to immigrants of whom "we can be absolutely sure—children and youth. We will bring them over and educate them and make Hebrew citizens of them." They were also the easiest to care for; they didn't need jobs or housing as adults did, and the American Jews would be ready to provide money for them. Besides the children and youth from Rumania and Hungary, Ben-Gurion declared, "Polish refugees come first."

Gruenbaum opposed a "Zionist criterion" for determining rescue priorities, just as he had previously opposed the party key; world Jewry would simply not understand it and would become critical of the Zionist leadership. Emil Schmorak agreed with him: "As long as people are threatened with death, it is impossible to choose among them." Ben-Gurion answered them both tersely: "Everyone is threatened. We can only take a certain number of people. If that is the case, we have to take those that will remain. Polish refugees have to be taken first. Veteran Zionists—no. For the future of Palestine, youth and children are more important."[24] Ben-Gurion's position was more extreme than that of Hartglas, who had proposed saving Zionist functionaries out of a sense of obligation.

The argument was not resolved. Predictably, a committee—composed of Ben-Gurion, Gruenbaum, Moshe Shapira, Kaplan, and Rabbi Yehuda-Leib Fishman—was elected to look into the question. What it decided is not known, but on the ships that arrived in August, November, and December very little changed in the composition of the immigrants. There was no change in the management of the immigration in Rumania. The infighting continued.

Thus it seems that the Yishuv's immigration policy did change during the war. Children and youth everywhere, particularly orphans, must be saved first. After that came refugees from the Nazi-occupied areas, particularly Poland: they had suffered the most, and the Yishuv's closest ties were to Polish Jewry and Polish Zionism. These two categories were exempt from the party key. Following them came pioneers and Zionist functionaries from Slovakia, Hungary, Rumania, and Bulgaria, according to a Zionist party key and an allocation for Agudat Yisrael. Then came the rest, as far as possible.

The leaders in Palestine knew that because of British policy and German objections, large-scale rescue would not be followed by immigration to Palestine. There was unanimous agreement, however, that all Jews who could be rescued should be, whatever their eventual destination. On the other hand, there were more limited possibilities of bringing thousands, perhaps even tens of thousands, to Palestine.

The Holocaust did not significantly change Ben-Gurion's views on immigration. During 1943 he harbored hopes for large-scale rescue, but after several failures of these plans he reverted to his original prewar preference for those who would be able to fight to establish a Jewish state.

Ben-Gurion's position was not accepted. Aliya Bet activists continued to bring anti-Zionists or Zionists with a different orientation from their own; Gruenbaum worked honestly with the non-Zionists on the Rescue Committee; Kaplan consistently fought a "Zionist-only" rescue policy, particularly in cases of children and orphans; the emissaries and the Immigration Department in Istanbul brought over whoever managed to reach Turkey; and there were many others who were convinced that the advantage to the Yishuv could not be the only standard and that humane standards—to the ultimate benefit of the Yishuv's image—had to be applied. Schmorak later maintained that "with regard to rescue, we were not selective." Gruenbaum agreed: when death threatened, "we saved even the blind, the paralyzed, and the insane."[25]

Ultimately the composition of Jewish immigration to Palestine was determined not by theoretical considerations or by decisions made in Jerusalem, but primarily by the struggles conducted on the spot in Europe, particularly between Zionists and the religious non-Zionists. The latter insisted, even in Jerusalem, that the principle of indiscriminate rescue be applied, knowing full well that the Zionists owed them nothing and yet could not, as the self-proclaimed leaders of the Jewish people, abandon them. Ironically, it was probably the non-Zionists' obstinate struggle to be saved through immigration to Palestine that forced the Yishuv to act upon fine nonpartisan ideals.[26]

The dispute over immigration priorities was only one of many inside the Zionist movement, or between Zionism and the Jewish people. There was no attempt to overcome them, to change existing patterns, or to convince leaders to modify their personal styles and occupations in order to face the Holocaust more united. On the contrary: some of the dividing issues even sharpened.

Such was the case of the constant contention between Weizmann and Ben-Gurion. Weizmann was undeniably the leader most admired by the majority of Zionists before the war, yet from the end of 1939 until the fall of 1944 he stayed mostly in England and the United States; he did not visit Palestine once during that period. As a result, none of the committees handling rescue work in the Yishuv had any regular contact with him. Moshe Shertok was in contact with him in London and in the United States, especially in the winter of 1943 and the summer of 1944. Shertok and Weizmann then jointly conducted negotiations with both governments with regard to the Transnistria Plan, the extrication of children from the occupied countries, the rescue of Hungarian Jewry, the bombing of Auschwitz, and related issues. None of these negotiations, however, was undertaken at Weizmann's initiative, and there is little evidence that he launched any others. He made no direct appeals on behalf of European Jewry to either Churchill or Roosevelt, although he met with both more than once during the war. He later acknowledged that while he was in the United States, from April 1942 to July 1943, he "did very little outside [his] scientific work," and the same pattern prevailed when he was in England. By then he was in his seventies, no longer in his prime. Yet

Rabbi Benjamin apparently expressed the feelings of many when he appealed to Weizmann, "Mr. President, get out of the laboratory . . ."[27]

Relations between Weizmann and Ben-Gurion were very strained throughout the war, and in 1943 the rift between them threatened the unit of the Zionist movement. Ben-Gurion had no confidence in Weizmann's pro-British policies or in his ability to lead during the crucial times to come. The situation diverted energy that could have been devoted to the rescue of European Jewry. As Berl Katznelson rebuked Ben-Gurion, "There are far more important problems at the moment than Weizmann. There is the loss of European Jewry."[28]

Some of Ben-Gurion's colleagues also criticized him for his apparent detachment from rescue work. Gruenbaum reproached him for being "barricaded within his own thoughts," for refusing to listen to others. The fact that he made fewer statements about the Holocaust and rescue operations than about other issues, especially those connected with the political future of the Yishuv, led many of his friends to conclude that he "was not involved in the Holocaust."[29] Yet Ben-Gurion was far more involved in rescue work than has generally been assumed—in fundraising meetings in Palestine, in attempts to obtain immigration permits for children, and in Brand's mission. Like others, he put his hopes in exchange programs and the establishment of an international rescue body. He kept abreast of developments; Pomerantz, among others, later recalled that upon returning from Istanbul he would sit with Ben-Gurion "for hours on end, on numerous occasions," to bring him up to date and to evaluate the information with him.[30]

Ben-Gurion's lack of extensive commentary on the subject did not reflect lack of interest: "I'm at a loss for words. I cannot talk about the catastrophe. I do not think the right language has yet been invented."[31] His reticence can be explained by two factors. One was his leadership style, which was to go his own way on all issues: he refused to act under public pressure, did not discuss matters with those closest to him, and paid little heed to the entreaties of his colleagues or his public. The other factor was his evaluation of rescue possibilities; once he concluded, like Hartglas after Bermuda, that there was no possibility of saving the millions and that the Yishuv was unable to force the Allies, much less the Germans, to listen to its claims, he ceased to view the matter as central from the practical point of view and concentrated on the political future of Palestine. With the almost cruel clarity that characterized him, he realized that the Yishuv could save only a limited number of people, and he kept the full significance of these conclusions to himself.

Ben-Gurion turned his attention to postwar goals. Shertok handled the negotiations for several rescue plans, but much of his time was occupied with enlistment in the British army and the establishment of a Jewish brigade. Gruenbaum became more and more involved in rescue work but did not add authority or means to the Rescue Committee. The question remains: Who in the Yishuv did head rescue operations? Among all the people living in the Yishuv, working in the settlements, at the university, on newspaper editorial boards, or in the many organizations and committees, it seems that no one could be found who was willing to give up all other commitments to deal solely with the rescue of European Jewry. The matter was not referred to Chaim Barlas or Menachem Bader or the other emissaries, all of whom devoted themselves entirely to rescue operations in the neutral countries; nor to Meirov, who was the central figure in all practical activities abroad. What was needed was someone who would have put the subject constantly on the agenda of the Yishuv and whose personal influence would have made the issue a central one. Both Katznelson and Weizmann wielded great personal and moral influence and enjoyed immense popularity—Weizmann among Jews and politicians in the western world, Katznelson in the Yishuv. As Ben-Gurion's closest and most admired friend, Katznelson would have had the best chances of working closely with him.

The lively, even stormy arguments between the Jewish Agency and the Histadrut took place "in the family," among close friends and comrades. And as the Yishuv's executive body, the Jewish Agency was naturally subject to criticism by the other Yishuv institutions. But the criticism leveled at the Agency's rescue policy by the opposition parties—Agudat Yisrael and the Revisionists, especially Etzel—was of a different nature. It stemmed, of course, from intense pain over the great destruction, but it also served as a means to challenge Mapai and the Agency and to question their ability to lead the Yishuv in general. The opposition could allow itself to recommend extreme solutions, such as an open breach with the British, because they were not responsible for the welfare and safety of the Yishuv as the Agency was.[32]

From 1942 through the end of the war, the institutions of the Yishuv had long and detailed ideological and political debates about relations with the Arabs and the Soviet Union, the political future of the Yishuv, and interparty problems. Few discussions dealt with the plight of European Jewry. There were indeed discussions about the practical aspects of rescue (the dispatch of emissaries, the allocation of funds, and so on); but there were few theoretical deliberations on the significance of the destruction of European Jewry and its full implications for the future of Zionism. Perhaps the catastrophe was too great, too overwhelming to be grasped while it was taking place and before its full extent was known. Such deliberations were liable to raise questions not only about the future of Zionism and the Yishuv but also about the continuing existence of the Jewish people in a hostile world and the weight of human values in the systems, Jewish and non-Jewish, that would be set up after the war. Only recently, in the 1970s and 1980s, did these deliberations begin. Their absence during the Holocaust strengthens the conclusion that the response of Yishuv officials at the time was largely a personal matter.

On the other hand, much energy was channeled within the Labor movement to cope with the challenge of Communism and the Soviet Union. Attitudes toward the Soviet Union lay at the root of much of the discord in the Labor movement during the 1940s, and in some circles they caused an ideological and emotional alienation from the problems of the Jewish people.

Communism had always posed a challenge to Zionism, especially when the Soviet Union, after being attacked by Germany in June 1941, led the struggle against fascism and became to many the symbol of this struggle. To a Europe under arms, the USSR also presented a human ideal diametrically opposed to that of Germany; the Soviet soldier was warm, rough, and very human. It was with admiration that the left in Palestine and the rest of the world followed the military fortunes of the Soviet people and the Red Army against the Nazis, and it hoped, despite its many reservations and disappointments, that Soviet society would provide an ideological and human response to the right-wing ideas and all they stood for.

The challenge of Communism forced Zionism to justify its ideology because Zionism pointed to a local and national solution, whereas Communism aimed at a world of equality, without classes and national frictions. The climax of this confrontation occurred just when reports on the extermination were reaching Palestine, at the end of October 1942. The internal discussions of this issue at the Mapai conference in Kfar Vitkin at that very time split the party. Its members quarrelled with a fervor that is incomprehensible today and seems detached from the burning issues of the period.

Eliezer Livne, a Labor movement intellectual, tried to explain this phenomenon some years later:

> The tendency to entertain leftist views of varying degrees is connected with a relative shallowness toward the Jewish people and their fate in the Diaspora, joined to an enthusiasm for religious socialist experiences. That is to say—the energy, the thought, the intuition, and the dedication that should have been applied to Jewish issues were, in part, unknow-

ingly and unintentionally but nevertheless with enormous force, applied to socialist issues. For Jewish youth at that time, these issues served as a kind of substitute; they exchanged their Jewish beliefs for socialism, which made claims similar to those of religion.[33]

The prominence of leftist tendencies may have accounted in part for the lack of discussion in the Yishuv of Nazi ideology, the centrality of the Jewish issue in it, or the difference between Nazism and the profound anti-Semitism of other peoples. This was so despite the fact that since the time of Theodore Herzl, the father of political Zionism, Zionists had foreseen the catastrophe that anti-Semitism would bring upon the Jews. Ironically, the Jewish left devoted its best minds to questions concerning Soviet Communism, which took almost no notice of Zionism, while ignoring those concerning Nazism, which devoted time and energy to Jewish questions in a way that proved disastrous for the Jews.

The Jews of the free world did not view the Zionist movement or the Yishuv as a source of leadership for rescue operations, and no other source was created. The Jewish Agency Executive did not, and could not, claim to represent even the Yishuv, with all its political, religious, and ethnic factions, let alone the entire Jewish people. The history of the Zionist movement and of the Jewish people in the free world during the Holocaust is one of endless contentions over personal, partisan, institutional, political, ideological, and general issues. The lack of a unified Jewish front under a strong leadership at such a time is in the long run a national problem no less acute than that of the actual rescue possibilities: "Try to juxtapose the news about the annihilation of thousands of Jewish communities and the facts about the dissension and splits within the parties and factions day by day," said the historian Ben-Zion Dinaburg in 1943. "Future generations will examine and recount and record everything we say and do today . . . and I am very much afraid that the verdict of the next generation, the generation of our children, will be extremely severe."[34]

Did this state of affairs interfere with rescue activities and diminish their chances of success? To what extent were they dependent upon factors outside the Yishuv, first and foremost the Allies?

Hopes for rescue operations supported by the Allies were based on a belief in the humanity, stature, and goodwill of Roosevelt and Churchill and the usefulness of direct contacts with them. Although there can be little doubt that the nature of the catastrophe shocked the two leaders, it soon became apparent that their responses were largely declarative. Their government bureaucracies did nothing to translate their words into action, nor did either head of state try to see that they did: the murder of Jews was only one aspect of a long and bloody world war.

During 1943 it became clear not only that such hopes were unrealistic but also that the Allies were in fact rejecting or hindering every rescue plan laid before them. Some Yishuv leaders, such as Ben-Gurion and Gruenbaum, were pessimistic even before the Bermuda Conference. Others, especially in the Histadrut, still hoped to influence the British by rousing public opinion in Britain or the United States. The chances of influencing the Soviet Union were far slighter, being as they were contingent upon success with the Western powers.

In the 1940s the Yishuv, unlike the Arab countries, had no bargaining card of any importance to the Allies—no oil or other natural resources, no strategic territories. Its manpower, which was considered loyal and skilled, was not particularly necessary after El Alamein. The mostly European Yishuv did not even possess the oriental charm that had enchanted many British officers and officials. Britain continued its prewar policy of rapprochement with the Arab countries even when it was apparent that their loyalties were dubious and their contribution to the war effort practically nil. The governments-in-exile in London had the status of poor relations, with virtually no influence on the three superpowers; and the Yishuv—a minority in a mandated territory—could not hope for more. As far as the Allies were concerned, Weizmann, Ben-Gurion, and Shertok were a tolerated annoyance, ceaselessly pressing, appealing, and demanding despite the war and all the difficulties it involved. In short, the Yishuv's position was even weaker than it had been before the war.

The Yishuv did what it could to exploit the conflicts and differences between the various British and U.S. government bodies and agencies, such as Congress and the administration, or the intelligence, political, and military echelons. The emissaries in Istanbul, for instance, were well aware of the differences between what they called the "good Englishmen"—British intelligence—and the "bad Englishmen"—the Foreign Office, as embodied in the British embassy in Turkey, and especially the Colonial Office, as embodied in the high commissioner and his officials in Palestine. But the possibilities available for influencing Allied policy through such channels were few and far between.

By the second half of 1944 Ben-Gurion appears to have had no illusions left about the Allies' attitude to the suffering of the Jews. On July 10, on the fortieth anniversary of Herzl's death, when it was evident that no negotiations or bargaining would stop the deportation of the Jews of Hungary and other communities to Auschwitz, he uttered "a long and bitter outcry" against the Allies:

> Why have you mistreated us so—you lovers of freedom and justice, fight-
> ers for democracy, liberty, equality, and socialism? Why have you so mis-
> treated the Jewish people, standing by while our blood flows unceasingly
> . . . without raising a finger, without coming to our aid, without saying to
> the slaughterer, Enough! . . . Why don't you send arms to our rebels or
> let us come to them . . .
>
> Would you behave thus if thousands of American, English, or Russian
> women and old people were burned alive every day? Would you be so
> silent if Allied babes and sucklings were smashed daily against the paving
> stones? Why do you discriminate between the Jewish people and every
> other people on your side? Isn't our blood as red as yours and our honor
> as precious as yours?[35]

Yet only a few days earlier, Ben-Gurion attacked Gruenbaum for say-ing, in connection with the immigration of refugees, that "the English will use nice words . . . and then hinder us on all sides just as they are doing over the rescue work." Ben-Gurion answered sharply: "Mr. Gruenbaum's words reek of despair as far as England and the United States are concerned. To whom does he propose that we turn? Left entirely on our own, we will be unable to determine the political re-gime in Palestine immediately after the war. Does Mr. Gruenbaum have any other suggestions for international political action?"[36]

Before the war, Ben-Gurion had envisaged the future of the Jewish people and of Zionism as a single entity. The events of the Holocaust led him to distinguish between the two. Even if he despaired of Allied support for rescue operations on any scale, he could not risk leaving the Yishuv isolated in the international political arena. Nobody had any illusions about Britain's attitude toward the eventual establish-ment of a Jewish state. But Ben-Gurion hoped that after the war Brit-ain would be forced by either circumstances, a change of government, or American and world public opinion, to change its policy.

Shertok, as director of the Agency's Political Department, negoti-ated with the British on immigration and rescue, enlistment and the Jewish brigade, and other issues more than any other member of the Agency. Although his experience with the British was far from en-couraging, he too, like Ben-Gurion and Weizmann—who clung to his prewar British-oriented policies—knew that there was nowhere else to turn. "We should, on no account, despair of England. We should in fact, increase our efforts there and not lay all our burdens at Ameri-ca's door."[37] This remained the JAE's policy until the end of 1944.

Perhaps the most incisive analysis of the complex relations between the Yishuv and the Allies at that time came from Eliyahu Golomb when he tried to explain to Joel Brand why the Yishuv acted as it did regarding his mission. "We were not all that much 'Allies' of the English . . . but, without governments, nothing is possible. It was for that very same reason that you turned to the Germans."[38] In other words, seeking the assistance of those in power did not necessarily make one either an accomplice or an ally of that power. With regard to Brand's mission, the negotiations were not between "allies" but between an empire and a frail public dependent on its goodwill.

All these political calculations were, apparently, correct, and the Agency was understandably unwilling to take risks that might have jeopardized the continued existence of the Yishuv, the only remaining shelter for the Jews. On an emotional level, however, it is difficult to accept the fact that logical calculations and common sense arguments prevailed in the face of the continuing annihilation. Nearly all the steps taken by the JAE and the emissaries were within the bounds of "the rules of the game"; Germans living in Palestine were never taken hostage; the Agency did not support the Polish demand for reprisal bombings; there were no attempts to broadcast to Jews under the occupation; there was no persistent attempt to harass the British and Americans through massive strikes, hunger strikes, demonstrations, or hard-hitting exposés of their indifference; no one was dispatched independently to the areas under occupation, and there were no contacts with German authorities to discuss ransom offers. There was no uncontrollable impulse to make an extraordinary response in an extraordinary situation.

Possibly such actions would have changed nothing. The strong public pressure applied in Britain before the Bermuda Conference produced no concrete results. On the other hand, public outrage over the destruction of Hungarian Jewry in Auschwitz did play a role in stopping the transports from Hungary in July 1944 (although Horthy had other good reasons for responding); but it failed to move the Allies to bomb the gas chamber and the crematoria or to extricate the remnant of Hungarian Jewry. Such actions could at least have encouraged the Jewish people to believe that every possibility was being tried.

In retrospect, the Yishuv's faith in the Allies appears somewhat naive. The Allied nations and their leaders were seen as peoples guided by democratic values, their central tenet as the sanctity of human life. Faith in the moral progress of human civilization was a cornerstone of Zionism, and the idea that the Jewish people would find an honorable place in the family of nations pervades Herzl's *Altneu-*

land. Certainly it was logical to hope that such a place would be found after such terrible suffering. Without deeply rooted belief, it would probably have been impossible to continue the Zionist enterprise or go on living as a Jew.

Did the Holocaust affect the Yishuv's major Zionist goal? This goal was defined at the Biltmore Conference in New York in May 1942: the establishment of a Jewish commonwealth in western Palestine. To Ben-Gurion, this implied the speedy immigration to Palestine of millions of Jews left homeless at the end of the war, creating a Jewish majority that would constitute the basis for the state. The Biltmore Program was approved by the Zionist Actions Committee in Jerusalem in October of that year. At that time the Yishuv numbered half a million people, and its absorptive capacity was at the core of every discussion of immigration. Ben-Gurion believed that Palestine could absorb many times that number—a revolutionary approach—whereas Weizmann was prepared to settle for the gradual immigration of 100,000 a year after the war; Shertok spoke of the immediate absorption of tens of thousands.[39] It is therefore likely that many of the supporters of the Biltmore Program, both in the United States and Palestine, regarded it as a basis for bargaining while believing, as Weizmann did, that immigration would be much more modest.

From the beginning of 1942 on, the American Jewish press reported frequently on the invading Germans' mass murder of Jews in the Soviet Union; there can be no question that the delegates to the Biltmore Conference had this information. In October reliable reports reached Palestine on the Final Solution, and in November the first exchange group brought news to Palestine from Europe. The Zionist Actions Committee mentioned these reports in its discussions in Jerusalem, but they had no effect on its subsequent approval of the Biltmore Program. The reports referred to the deaths so far of two million Jews, but there were nearly ten million Jews in Europe. Furthermore, there were millions of Jews living on other continents. Thus the general belief prevailed that after the war there would be millions of Jews to bring to Palestine. At the same time Ben-Gurion warned about the precarious position of the Jews in the Muslim countries: "There exists the danger of a terrible slaughter there that would make the slaughter in Europe seem less terrible by comparison." He also foresaw dangers to the Jews in postwar Europe (and his fears proved correct for the Jews of Poland, dozens of whom were murdered when they returned from the camps and forests hoping to find their families and homes). The Zionist enterprise was in danger:

"There has never yet been a time like today when we have all been threatened with destruction . . . the destruction of the Jews of Europe is ruinous for Zionism for there will be no one left to build the state of Israel."[40]

One must differentiate, then, between Ben-Gurion's public allegiance to the Biltmore Program and the fears for the future he expressed in less public forums; and between the public presentation of Biltmore as a solution to the plight of the Jews in Europe in a way that would gain the support of the Allies and the Jews of the free world, and the deliberations within the Agency Executive and Mapai that dealt not only with the Jews of Europe but also with the plight of the Jews in Muslim countries.

Had the Zionist Actions Committee voted against the Biltmore Program on the grounds that the millions it intended to save would not be alive at the end of the war, it would have been a declaration of bankruptcy—a position that could not be countenanced. Biltmore was intended for all the "surviving remnant," and in 1943 this term was already being used in Palestine to refer to the more than a million Jews in Hungary and the Balkans, the 800,000 Jews of the Muslim countries, the half million who already lived in Palestine, and, of course, those remaining in the areas under Nazi occupation.

A subsequent issue concerned Zionist priorities. Gruenbaum's declaration that Zionism, or "the war of redemption" for building the Yishuv and establishing a state, conflicted with the rescue of European Jewry roused a storm of controversy. Most Mapai members, let alone the opposition parties, claimed that this was an artificial distinction: the Yishuv did not have the moral right to concentrate only on its own problems and existence just because it despaired of rescue operations; nor did it have the right to desist from making intensive rescue efforts out of fear that they would jeopardize the Yishuv's usefulness as a future haven.[41] In their view, the rescue operation should be considered as at least one of the central tasks of Zionism and a responsibility of the Jewish Agency. Ben-Gurion, however, made it clear in August 1943 in a Mapai Center meeting that he favored a clear distinction between rescue operations and the tasks of the Agency: "a confusion of terms [would be] a mistake both for the Agency and for the assistance given to the Jews of Nazi Europe." The Jewish world had not given the Agency

authority over the Jewish pocketbook for all Jewish affairs. Unfortunately, there is no such multipurpose organization. There is the World Jewish Congress and the American Jewish Congress; there is the JDC and there are others, but the institution known as the Jewish Agency is a comprehensive Jewish organization for building Palestine. I do not want to say which is more important—building Palestine or saving one Jew from Zagreb. Perhaps it may sometimes be more important to save one child from Zagreb, but these are two different things . . . The Jewish Agency must concern itself with rescue—and it seems to me that it has indeed taken upon itself everything concerning the rescue of Jews by bringing them to Palestine. That is its task . . . the other thing—assistance, saving one more Jew, trying to prevent their eviction . . . it's extremely important. But this requires a different organization and different funds.[42]

A month later, during Diaspora Month, Ben-Gurion spoke at a conference of industrialists and businessmen about a "threefold rescue. First and foremost is the rescue of Jewish men, women, and children. This is enough to make any one of us unrestful until our conscience agrees that every one of us did at least a bit for this rescue." The second was "the rescue of the Yishuv's honor. We were greatly privileged. We were saved . . . not for ourselves alone, just as we did not come here for ourselves alone . . . This imposes a sacred duty upon us," not only to enjoy the economic prosperity of the Yishuv but also to use it to help, in some way, "to save the Jewish people." The third was the rescue of the Yishuv and Zionism. "No change of policy, no reiteration, even in the greatest faith, of the Balfour Declaration will be of any use if, God forbid, the remaining Jews of Europe are destroyed. What hope can there be then for the Jewish people? What will be the fate of the Yishuv in Palestine? I do not want to think about this; the idea is too terrible."[43]

The contradiction between these two statements made only a month apart—that the Jewish Agency's task was the building of Palestine and that rescue was the duty of every person living in Palestine—can perhaps be explained by Ben-Gurion's belief that, although the Jewish Agency did not have the authority to devote time and energy to rescue work, other organizations, such as the Histadrut and the Yishuv in general, should undertake rescue work and that funds from outside the Agency budget could and should be devoted to it. On this distinction, and on another one, he remained consistent throughout. On Herzl's anniversary and during Diaspora Month, both public occasions, Ben-Gurion expressed his emotions vehemently. Yet as a politician he suppressed them; he would not let his rage against Britain or his pain over European Jewry isolate or endanger the Yishuv. This seems to be the core of the endless public and historical debate about Ben-Gurion during the Holocaust.

In any case, any conflict of interest, if one ever really existed, between rescue and developing the Yishuv ceased to be relevant. Once the JAE despaired of large-scale rescue, small-scale operations could go on being carried out alongside the development of the Yishuv and not at its expense while Zionist activity proper continued: new settlements were created, the Palmach and the Haganah were strengthened by arms and more training, and new industrial enterprises were established. There was no practical change in the Yishuv's priorities. Rescue work became one more task among many, but not the most important.

Possibly the Yishuv could have invested more effort, personnel, and money in small rescue operations without damaging either its own development or its relations with the Allies. Perhaps more money, packages, and permits could have been sent; more people could have been smuggled across borders, especially in western Europe to Spain and Portugal; a mission could have been set up in Sweden; more could have been done to supervise activities in Istanbul, and more resourceful people could have been sent there. Maybe a way could have been found to transmit more encouragement, warnings, and information from Palestine or some other location to the areas under occupation, especially to the Nazi satellites. It might have been possible to save a few thousand—perhaps as many as 10,000 or 20,000—more.

But the Agency could not save the millions entrapped between their killers and those who were indifferent to or even interested in their deaths. The Jewish Agency Executive was a leadership caught in a double bind. On the one hand, it had to maintain and nurture the Yishuv so that it would survive and be able to absorb the refugees and fight for its own political future. To this end, it had to maintain its political contacts. On the other hand, a substantial number of the people for whom the Yishuv was being nurtured as a haven were being annihilated.

Today, there are two lapses in particular that disturb Jews: the time gap between events in Europe and the response to them, and the attitude gap between the nature of the Holocaust and the response of the Yishuv.

When the Yishuv finally grasped what was happening, the death camps were already working at full capacity, and trains were speeding toward them from all parts of the continent. The majority of emissaries did not leave for Istanbul until Himmler's deadline for the destruction of Polish Jewry had already passed. When the agreement between the Mobilization Fund and the Rescue Committee was signed, the revolt in the Warsaw ghetto had already broken out. Himmler's order to stop the slaughter at Auschwitz was issued only months after the stark facts about that death factory had become known. The Jewish Agency and the JDC did not sign an agreement until shortly after the Allied invasion of Normandy and the Balkans. However great the difficulties in communications that delayed transmission of the facts to Palestine and the time required to absorb them, the gap between event and response cannot be fully explained.

The attitude of the Yishuv as a body politic is also disturbing. While the Holocaust was taking place there were, of course, individual leaders and private citizens who felt impelled to respond to the disaster; they volunteered for various tasks, donated large sums of money, pressed for radical action, housed the refugees. About 30,000 men and women joined the British army in order to fight the Nazis, and 5,000 others formed the Jewish brigade in the summer of 1944, fought on the fronts in Europe, and met the survivors with open arms. But the Yishuv continued its daily life as before; there was no mass display of outrage over the Holocaust, and attention was devoted chiefly to domestic problems, political factionalism, accelerated building, settlement, and industrial progress. Jews who have grown up in Israel find it extremely difficult to understand why the Yishuv never launched any unconditional, extraordinary action—outside the rules of the game—some preemptive operation commensurate with the pain and the rage. They are astounded by the Yishuv's failure to understand that, in the long run, the significance of Zionism's political achievements would be undermined if later generations were not sure that the plight of the Jewish people was the chief concern of the Zionist leadership.

However, Israelis today have long since forgotten or are unaware of the difficulties facing the Yishuv at the time. It was a minority in a country ruled by foreigners. It was a social-national experiment in its early stages. Its resources—in manpower, money, and arms—were small. Nor do they realize that, for all its limitations—and in the face of the efficiency of the German death machine and the interference of the Allies—the Yishuv in fact did more than it was ever given credit for—either then or now.

CHRONOLOGY
NOTES
BIBLIOGRAPHY
BIOGRAPHICAL GLOSSARY
INDEX

CHRONOLOGY

THE FINAL SOLUTION

September 21, 1939	Germany orders ghettos headed by Jewish councils to be established in occupied Poland.
October 1939	First expulsions from the Reich to Poland.
October 1939 through 1940	Concentration of Polish Jewry in ghettos; Star of David as obligatory identification; severe food rationing; hard labor; denial of free movement.
May 1940	Establishment of a concentration camp at Auschwitz.
July 1940	Pogroms in Rumania.
August 1940	Anti-Jewish legislation in Rumania.
October 1940	Anti-Jewish legislation in France and Belgium.
November 1940	Warsaw ghetto is sealed.

THE WAR FRONTS

September 1, 1939	German army invades Poland: World War II begins.
End of September 1939	Polish army surrenders in Warsaw.
October 1939	Poland is divided between Germany and the Soviet Union, according to the Ribbentrop-Molotov Pact of August 1939: annexation of western Poland to Germany. Central Poland is an occupied area, called the General Government.
April 1940	German army occupies Denmark and southern Norway.
May 1940	Germany invades Holland, Belgium, and France. Evacuation of British army from Dunkirk.
June 1940	Norway and France surrender. Two-thirds of France occupied by Germany; government of the southern third, based in Vichy, collaborates. Italy joins the war, siding with Germany. Mediterranean closed to civilian traffic. Vichy France invades Syria. The Soviet Union annexes the Baltic states and northern Rumania.
July 1940	The Battle of Britain begins.
September 1940	The Berlin-Rome-Tokyo Axis is established.
October 1940	German army enters Rumania. Italy invades Greece.
November 1940	Hungary, Slovakia, and Rumania join the Axis.

January 1941	More pogroms in Rumania. Anti-Jewish legislation in Bulgaria.
June 1941	Vichy France enacts anti-Jewish laws in French North Africa. Rumanian army massacres the Jews of Jassi.
End of June 1941	Special German killing units (*Einsatzgruppen*), assisted by local population, start mass murder of Jews in areas taken by the Wehrmacht, by shooting them into pits. By mid-1942 1,500,000 Jews are thus killed.
July 1941	Pogroms by Ukrainians against local Jews. The Star of David requirement enforced in the Baltic states. Mass murder in Ponar, near Vilna (by July 1944, 100,000 Jews killed there). Goering charges Reinhard Heydrich, head of the Reich's Security Main Office and Eichmann's superior, with implementation of the Final Solution in all of Europe.
September 1941	34,000 Jews killed in Babi-Yar, near Kiev. Racial laws in Slovakia.
October 1941	The Jews of Odessa and Belgrade are killed. Expulsions of Jews from Germany and Austria to the ghettos of Łodz, Minsk, Riga, and Kovno. Destruction of synagogues in Paris. A death camp in Jasenovac, a ghetto in Theresienstadt, and Auschwitz II (Birkenau) are established.
December 1941	Chelmno death camp, near Łodz, starts operating. By April 1943, 360,000 murdered there.
January 20, 1942	The Wannsee conference in Berlin discusses means to annihilate eleven million European Jews.
January 1942	Resistance organizations in the ghettos of Vilna and Kovno and in the forests of western Byelorussia.

March 1941	Bulgaria joins the Axis.
April–May 1941	British forces withdraw from Greece and Crete and retreat in North Africa. A German-inspired revolt against British forces in Iraq. Germany takes over Greece and Yugoslavia.
End of May 1941	German armies reach Egypt's borders. The British conquer Baghdad and invade Syria.
June 22, 1941	Germany and its allies invade the Soviet Union and swiftly take over the Baltic states, western Ukraine, and Byelorussia. Britain and the Soviet Union sign a military treaty.
August 1941	Smolensk falls to the Germans.
September 1941	Kiev falls to the Germans.
October 1941	The Germans take Odessa and reach the outskirts of Moscow; the city is partially evacuated.
December 7, 1941	Japan attacks the American fleet in Pearl Harbor.
December 11, 1941	Germany and Italy declare war on the United States.
January–February 1942	British withdrawal in North Africa.

March 1942	Mass killing begins at Sobibor (250,000 Jews killed by October 1943) and Belzec (600,000 by the end of 1942). Extermination installations are introduced in Auschwitz (1,500,000 killed by the end of the war) and in Majdanek (200,000 killed). Deportation of Slovakian, French, and Polish Jews to death camps begins.
June–July 1942	Jewish resistance in ghettos of western Byelorussia. Jewish fighting organization established in the Warsaw ghetto.
July 1942	Treblinka death camp starts operation. Between July 22 and September 13, 270,000 Jews of the Warsaw ghetto killed there; 850,000 by August 1943. Himmler orders the annihilation of Polish Jewry by the end of 1942. Jews from Holland and Paris are sent to death camps.
August 1942	Jews from southern France, Belgium, and Croatia are sent to death camps.
August–September 1942	More resistance in ghettos and forests of western Byelorussia and western Ukraine. Star of David required in Bulgaria.
October 1942	A fighting organization formed in France. First deportations from Theresienstadt.
November 1942	A fighting organization formed in Theresienstadt. First deportations from Norway to Auschwitz.
December 1942	First deportations of German Jews to Auschwitz.
December 1942– January 1943	Resistance in ghettos and by Jewish partisans in Poland.
1943	Gradual liquidation of ghettos and camps from eastern Europe westward.
March 1943	Deportations from Salonika to Auschwitz. Organization for Resistance in Lithuania.
April 19–May 10, 1943	The Warsaw ghetto revolt.
May 1943	The Jews of Amsterdam are sent to Auschwitz.
June 1943	Himmler orders accelerated liquidation of ghettos in Poland and the Soviet Union.

June 1942	German and Italian armies reach El Alamein, 100 kilometers from Alexandria.
November 1942	British victory over German and Italian forces at El Alamein. American forces land in North Africa. Red Army begins counterattack near Stalingrad. The turning point in the war.
February 1943	Sixth German army surrenders near Stalingrad.
May 1943	German army surrenders in Tunisia.

June–July 1943	Resistance in Polish ghettos. Vilna ghetto underground leaves for the forests.
August 1943	Revolts in Treblinka, Będzin, and Bialystok.
September 1943	The ghettos of Minsk and Vilna are liquidated. Jews leave ghettos for the forests in Poland, Lithuania, and western Byelorussia.
October 1943	7,000 Danish Jews transferred by underground to Sweden. Revolt in Sobibor.
February–March 1944	Deportations from Amsterdam and Athens to Auschwitz.
May 15, 1944	Deportations from Hungary to Auschwitz start; 430,000 deported by mid-July.
July–August 1944	Liquidation of ghettos in Łodz and Lithuania. Jewish resistance in France, Slovakia, and Polish Warsaw.
October 1944	Uprising and end of extermination in Auschwitz.
November 1944–April 1945	Death marches into and in Germany.

July 1943	Revolution in Italy: Mussolini deposed. The Allies land in Sicily.
September 1943	The Allies invade southern Italy; the Germans occupy most of the country.
End of 1943–beginning of 1944	Gradual liberation of the Soviet Union. The Red Army advances westward. The Allies intensify bombardment of the Reich.
March 1944	German army invades Hungary.
June 1944	Rome is liberated. The Allies invade Normandy and advance eastward.
July 1944	Vilna and Minsk are liberated.
August 1944	Uprising in Polish Warsaw and Slovakia (suppressed in October). France is liberated. Rumania sides with the Allies.
September 1944	Liberation of Sofia.
October 1944	The Germans take Budapest; it is liberated in February.
November 1944	Liberation of Salonika.
January 1945	Liberation of Warsaw.
March 1945	Allied forces cross the Rhine into Germany.
April 30, 1945	Hitler commits suicide.
May 8, 1945	Germany surrenders.

NOTES

ABBREVIATIONS

CZA   Central Zionist Archive (Jerusalem)

DBG   David Ben-Gurion

HA   Histadrut Archives (Tel Aviv)

HE   Histadrut Executive

HS   Histadrut Secretariat

JAE   Jewish Agency Executive

JDCA   Joint Distribution Committee Archive (New York)

LA   Labor Archives (Tel Aviv)

LPA   Labor Party Archives (Beit Berl, Kfar-Saba)

MA   Moreshet Archive (Givat Haviva)

MCC   Mapai Central Committee

MC   Mapai Center

MPC   Mapai Political Committee

MS   Mapai Secretariat

NC   National Council

RC   Rescue Committee

WA   Weizmann Archives (Rechovot)

YVA   Yad Vashem Archives (Jerusalem)

ZAC   Zionist Actions Committee

Sources are cited by author's last name and short title only. Full documentation is provided in the Bibliography.

INTRODUCTION

1. MC, 7.12.1938, 23/38, LPA.

1. FIRST WARNINGS

1. JAE, 17.9.1939, 8,22.10.1939, CZA; DBG, MPC, 2.11.1939, LPA.
2. Cana'an, *War of the Press,* pp. 97–105, 140–155.

3. Schwarzbart files, M2, YVA.
4. Gruenbaum office and archive, S46, S127, CZA.
5. Azriel Begun, interview with author, 30.4.1982.
6. Moshe Kol, 17.3.1940, S6/1870, CZA.
7. Weizmann, 18.10.1939, Z5/3092, CZA.
8. Lichtheim, 12.10.1939, S46/275; 5.12.1939, Z5/3072, 3092; 21.3.1940, S6/4559; and S46/272, L22/10; all in CZA; Schwalb and Silberschein, 3, 101/40, vol. a, LPA; and P12/22/, M20/78, 79, YVA.
9. Gurevitch et al., *Statistical Handbook of Jewish Palestine*, p. 102.
10. JAE, 11.2.1940, CZA; Committe for Polish Jewry, *Holocaust of the Jews of Poland,* esp. pp. 3–4.
11. Gruenbaum, ZAC, 29.2.1940, S25/1828, CZA.
12. Hoz, ZAC, 6.8.1940, S25/1830; JAE, 17.3.1940, CZA.
13. Cana'an, *War of the Press,* pp. 144–152.
14. Debate, Mapai World Union, 22.1.1940, 3, 101/40, vol. a, LPA.
15. Ofer, *Illegal Immigration,* chap. 1.
16. Avneri, *First Decade,* chap. 1.
17. Gurevitch et al., *Statistical Handbook of Jewish Palestine,* pp. 104–105; Gelber, "Zionist Policy and the Ha'avara Agreement."
18. Wasserstein, *Britain and the Jews of Europe,* pp. 11–17.
19. Daily Hebrew newspapers, 19.5.1939.
20. Avneri, *First Decade,* chaps. 2, 3, and 5.
21. DBG, MC, 12.9.1939, 23/39, LPA.
22. Gurevitch et al., *Statistical Handbook of Jewish Palestine,* p. 76.
23. Ofer, *Illegal Immigration,* p. 471.
24. Ibid.

2. A SEMBLANCE OF STABILIZATION

1. DBG, MC, 19.2.1941, 23/41, LPA; JAE, 23.2.1941, ZAC; 24.2.1941, S25/1838, and 7.5.1941, S25/1856, CZA.
2. DBG, JAE, 9.3.1941, CZA.
3. JAE, 6.4.194, 16,28.5.1941, 15.6.1941, CZA.
4. Prager, *In the New Deep Mire,* p. 192. See Gruenbaum's preface, pp. 6–7.
5. Chaim Barlas (19.3.1978) and Yitzhak Berman (25.8.1982), interviews with author; Weissman, *In the Face of Evil,* pp. 44–46.
6. Prager, *In the Deep Mire,* p. 189, in a chapter written after the German invasion of the USSR.
7. MS, 25.6.1941, 24/41; MC, 9,27.7.1941, 23/41, LPA; ZAC, 26.8.1941, S25/1857, CZA.
8. MC, 9.7.1941, 23/41, LPA.
9. Lewis, *Semites and Anti-Semites,* p. 158.
10. Cana'an, *War of the Press,* p. 152. Researchers today assume that British intelligence had the information but did not disclose it to government authorities (e.g., Laqueur, *The Terrible Secret,* pp. 86–88; see esp. Hinsley et al., *British Intelligence,* vol. 2, app. 5, pp. 669–670). MacPherson might

have had private information from British intelligence in Jerusalem or in Cairo.

11. Lichtheim, 16.9.1941, S46/275, CZA; Brand and Brand, *The Devil and the Soul*, p. 33; Barlas, in *Rescue Activities from Istanbul*, pp. 20–21; *Hatzofe*, 1.9.1941, 21,26.10.1941; *Ha'aretz*, 24.8.1941, 30.10.1941; *Ha'olam*, 20.11.1941; Schwalb, 10.12.1941, 3, 101/41, vol. b, LPA; Dobkin, JAE, 19.11.1941; Shertok, ZAC, 26.8.1941, S25/1837, CZA.

12. JAE, 9.11.1941, 23.11.1941, CZA.

13. Chazan, ZAC, 10.9.1941, S25/1840; JAE, 4.9.1941, 31.10.1941, 5.1.1942, CZA.

3. THE BEGINNINGS OF CHANGE

1. Daily Jewish press, London, New York, and Palestine, 9,10.1.1942; MC, 28.1.1942, 23/42, LPA.

2. JAE, 1.2.1942, CZA. Reuters published the news only on 3.4.1942, and PALCOR in July 1942; see Cana'an, *War of the Press*, p. 151.

3. NC, *Book of Documents*, pp. 321–323.

4. MS and MC, 16.3.1942, 23,24/42, LPA.

5. Letters, 16.1.1942, 20.3.1942, S6/501, CZA; Reiss, "Chapters of Aid and Rescue Activities," p. 23.

6. *Hatzofe*, 18.3.1942; Information Bulletin of the Baltic Countries Immigrants, no. 5, Spring 1942, S6/4639, CZA.

7. MCC, 20.5.1942, 23/42, LPA; JAE, 29.6.1941, 16.11.1941, CZA; Mapai World Union, *In the Bondage of War*, p. 97.

8. JAE, 24.5.1942, 29.6.1941, 4,16.8.1941, CZA; MC, 17.6.1942, 23/42, LPA.

9. Closed meeting, 46th Histadrut Convention, 26.5.1942, vol. 41M, HA; Moshe Kol, interview with author, 29.11.1981.

10. *Zygielbojm-Book*, pp. 341–351; Ringelblum, *Notes from the Warsaw Ghetto*, p. 239; Bauer, "When Did They Know?" pp. 57–58; daily press, 30.6.1942.

11. JAE, 30.6.1942, CZA.

12. Brenner, ed., *Facing the German Invasion*, pp. 71–76; Cana'an, *200 Days of Anxiety*, p. 215.

13. Brenner, ed., *Facing the German Invasion*, p. 72.

14. Ibid., p. 73.

15. JAE, 30.6.1942 and 5.7.1942, CZA.

16. *Zygielbojm-Book*, esp. pp. 341–343; Lichtheim, 3,5.7.1942, S46/2722, and 15.9.1942, Z4/354, CZA; Silberschein, 20.7.1942, 3.8.1942, 3, vol. A, 102/42, LPA; see also Wise, *Challenging Years*, p. 277; Morse, *While Six Million Died*, pp. 26–28; daily press, Palestine.

4. THE TURNING POINT

1. The two versions, one by Gerhard Riegner and one by Chaim Posner, and the exposure of E. Schulte as the German source have already been ex-

tensively discussed; see esp. Laqueur and Breitman, *Breaking the Silence.* Both Riegner and Posner claim to have been the first to get the information. Most researchers believe that Riegner was the first.

2. Morse, *While Six Million Died,* p. 14.
3. Wise, *Challenging Years,* pp. 274–276; Goldmann, 5.4.1943, S6/1234, CZA.
4. Lichtheim, 6.10.1942, 10.10.1942; Gruenbaum's answer, 6.10.1942, S6/1255, and 8.10.1942, L22/3, CZA.
5. Reiss, "Chapters of the Aid and Rescue," p. 24; information gathered in Sweden, 10.9.1942 (reached Jerusalem 25.11.1942), S6/4639, CZA.
6. JAE, 11,25.10.1942, CZA.
7. Ibid.; JAC, 15.10.1942, S25/293, CZA.
8. RC report to Zionist Congress in Basel, S6/4526, S26/1159, p. 6; JAE, 22.11.1942, CZA.
9. Kurtz, *Book of Witness,* pp. 6–7.
10. Shertok, 20.11.1942, S25/5183, CZA; Hannah Schneerson, interview with author, March 1978; DBG, 8.12.1942, 3/6, LPA.
11. According to *Rescue Activities from Istanbul,* pp. 13, 38, reporting was unlimited.
12. Rubashov in *Davar,* 4.12.1942.
13. ZAC, 18.1.1943, S25/295, CZA.
14. Dobkin, HE, 31.12.1942, vol. 66, HA; JAE, 6.12.1942, CZA; DBG, 8.12.1942, box 3/6, LPA.

5. THE EBB OF THE TIDE

1. Cana'an, *War of the Press,* p. 150.
2. Neustadt, ZAC, 18.5.1943, S25/297; DBG, JAE, 11.6.1944, CZA.
3. ZAC, 18.1.1943, S25/295, CZA.
4. On the office of information, see Porat, "Al Domi." In JAE's Story of the Holocaust series, five books were published, in 1945, 1947, and 1948.
5. For example, Zur, *The Day Approaches,* p. 129.
6. Barlas, in *Rescue Activities from Istanbul,* p. 58; Hartglas, 18.4.1944, A127/543, CZA.
7. HE, 27.1.1944, vol. 70M, HA.
8. Meir, *My Life,* p. 107.
9. Kovner, *On the Narrow Bridge,* p. 203.
10. Palgi, *A Great Wind Came,* p. 243.

6. PUBLIC RESPONSE

1. JAE, 22.11.1942, CZA.
2. NC, 23.11.1942, J1/7255, CZA.
3. Gil, *Aliyah Pages,* pp. 12–13; Gurevitch et al., *Statistical Handbook of Jewish Palestine,* pp. 104–105.
4. See NC, *Book of Documents,* p. 332; letters in daily press.

5. *Ha'aretz*, 4.12.1942; Bar-Yehezkel, *In the Incomprehensible Circle*, p. 49.

6. 8.12.1942, box 3/6, and MC, 30.11.1942, 4/3a, LPA; JAE, 6.12.1942, CZA.

7. JAE, 4.1.1943; NC, 27.4.1943, J1/7255; Shertok, ZAC, 18.5.1943, S25/297; Goldmann, 11.1.1943, S25/1504; Rabbi Berlin's report, NC, J1/7256; all CZA.

8. JAE, 6.12.1942, CZA.

9. Anthony Eden, *The Reckoning*, p. 415. Jews are mentioned once more, in connection with Kristallnacht (pp. 45–46) and the consequent "Jewish migration to Palestine" (p. 48).

10. NC, *Book of Documents*, pp. 334–335. For local reaction see daily press, 5–19.12.1942.

11. NC, *Book of Documents*, p. 335; daily press, 17–18.12.1942; for Himmler's order see Arad, Gutman, and Margeliot, *The Holocaust in Documentation*, pp. 219–220.

12. *Davar*, 10,12,13,19.12.1942; RC, 14.3.1943, S26/1237; ZAC, 18.5.1943, S25/297, CZA; see Feingold, *Politics of Rescue*, p. 177; Wasserstein, *Britain and the Jews of Europe*, pp. 172–178.

13. DBG, JAE, 6.12.1942; others, ZAC, 18.5.1943, S25/297; NC 15.2.1943, J1/7255; all CZA; *Hashomer Hatzair*, 9.12.1942; *Hapo'el Hatzair*, 10.12.1942; editorial, *Ha'aretz* 5.6.1944.

14. Tabenkin in *Zror Michtavim*, 22.1.1943; Katznelson, *Writings*, vol. 12, p. 222.

15. Ben-Zvi, NC, 14.12.1942, J1/7255; NC, 12.7.1943, J1/7256; RC, 31.1.1943, S26/1239; all CZA.

16. On Al Domi see Porat, "Al Domi"; letter to the press, *Ha'aretz*, 8.1.1943.

17. Ben-Zvi, NC, 17,31.1.1943, J1/7255, CZA; Bar-Yehezkel, *In the Incomprehensible Circle*, pp. 88–106; Dinur, *Zachor*, pp. 14–34; RC, weekly meetings, 10.1–15.3.1943, S26/1237,1239, CZA.

18. HE, 27–28.1.1943, vol. 67M, HA; Gruenbaum, RC, 15.1.1943, S26/1239; Goldmann, 5.4.1943, S26/1234, CZA.

19. NC, *Book of Documents*, pp. 339–340. For a summary of news see daily press and S26/1240, CZA.

20. NC, *Book of Documents*, pp. 341–342.

21. According to Feingold, *Politics of Rescue*, p. 175.

22. Ben-Zvi, NC, 27.4.1943, J1/7256. Left Poalei Zion: *Kol Hapoel*, March 1943. Immigrants: RC, 8.3.1943, S26/1237, CZA; HE, 31.3.1943, vol. 67M, HA.

23. NC, 12,15,27.4.1943, J1/7256, CZA; Remez and Myerson, HE, 4.4.1943, 14/43, HA.

24. JAE, 11.4.1943; NC, 12.4.1943, J1/7256, CZA; NC, *Book of Documents*, p. 342; Myerson, HS, 29.4.1943, 14/39, HA.

25. Histadrut conference: 5–7.5.1943, vol. 68M, HA. Petition: RC, 11.6.1943, S26/1235; NC, 21.6.1943, J1/7256, CZA.

26. ZAC, 18.5.1943, S25/297, CZA.

27. Petition: NC, *Book of Documents*, pp. 343–344. The high commissioner:

NC, 21.6.1943, J1/7256; also see NC, 28.6.1943 and 2.7.1943, J1/7256; all CZA.

28. DBG, JAE, 4.4.1943; Shertok, ZAC, 18.5.1943, A25/297; Gruenbaum, RC, 23.3.1943, S26/1239; all CZA.
29. Kaplan and others, JAE, 20.12.1943; NC, 31.5.1943, 1,3.6.1943, J1/7256, CZA.
30. Wyman, *The Abandonment of the Jews,* pp. 143–156.
31. DBG, JAE, 4.6.1944, CZA.
32. Gruenbaum, ZAC, 18.5.1943, S25/297, and 3.1.1944, S25/18. RC on Altman's proposal, 16.12.1943, A25/1235; JAE, 19,20.12.1943; all CZA.
33. ZAC, 18.1.1943, CZA; Al Domi to Gruenbaum, open letter in daily press, 6.12.1944; Yaffe, *Writings,* p. 201.
34. Gruenbaum, JAE, 21.5.1944, CZA.
35. HS, 25.4.1944, 2/66, HA.
36. NC, *Book of Documents,* pp. 355–356; and daily press.
37. Ibid., p. 366.

7. THE JOINT RESCUE COMMITTEE

1. JAE, 29.11.1942; see also JAE, 22.11.1942, 6,20,23.12.1942; NC, 4,23.12.1942, J1/7255. The Action Committee: 23.11.1942, 10.12.1942, S26/1237, and 15.12.1942, S26/1236; Minz and Rabbi Levin to Gruenbaum, in retrospect, 23.9.1943, S46/280, and 15.9.1944, S6/4588; all CZA.
2. NC, 15.12.1942, J1/7255; undated report, S26/1235; Klarman to Gruenbaum, in retrospect, 27.8.1943, S46/280; all CZA; Joseph Klarman, interview with author, 22.9.1980.
3. RC, 14,15.1.1943, S26/1239, CZA; Morgenstern, "Joint Rescue Committee, 1939–1945"; and daily press.
4. JAE, 20.27.12.1942, CZA.
5. NC, 17.1.1943, J1/7255; ZAC, 18.1.1943, S25/295, CZA.
6. The Agency's commitment: HE, 27–28.1.1943, vol. 67M, HA;
7. ZAC, 2.2.1943,S25/296,CZA. RC, 31.1.1943, S26/1239, CZA.
8. RC, 28.1.1943, S26/1237; and 31.1.1943, 1,7.2.1943, S26/1239, CZA.
9. JAE, 29.12.1942, 14.2.1943; NC, 15.2.1943, J1/7255; letters cited in note 1 above; all CZA.
10. JAE, 20.12.1942, 10.1.1943, 4,11.4.1943; RC, 20.9.1943, S26/1237, CZA.
11. Avraham Silberberg (18.6.1980), Eliezer Shostak (20.8.1982), Chaim Barlas (19.3.1978), and Joseph Klarman (22.9.1980), interviews with author.
12. Landau files; RC, 10,26.2.1943, 16.6.1943, S26/1240; 28.2.1943, 4.3.1943, 17.9.1943, 18.10.1943, S26/1237; 23.3.1943, 11.6.1943, S26/1239; all CZA.
13. Rabbi Benjamin, review of Gruenbaum's *In Days of Destruction and Holocaust, Ha'aretz,* 20.9.1946.

8. RESCUE FUND ALLOCATIONS FROM THE YISHUV

1. Unemployment: Pines, *1943 Yearbook of Journalists Association,* p. 77; Bank deposits: Gurevitch et al., *Statistical Handbook of Jewish Palestine,* pp. 353–376 (finance and banking) and 312–326 (standard of living and prices).
2. Bein, *History of Zionist Settlement,* pp. 381–384; Horowitz, *Palestinian Economy,* pp. 180–240; NC, *Book of the Yishuv Economy,* pp. 79–98. Salaries: see esp. *Ha'aretz Almanac, 1942–1943,* p. 209. The value of the pound courtesy of Nahum Gross, Hebrew University, based on *Statistical Abstract of the U.S., 1989.*
3. Zieman, *Jubilee for Jewish National Fund,* pp. 117–142.
4. See esp. Harussi, *Book of the Mobilization and Rescue Fund,* pp. 42–49; Berger, *Mobilization and Rescue Fund,* 1970.
5. Harussi, *Book of the Mobilization and Rescue Fund,* pp. 53, 62; Berger, *Mobilization and Rescue Fund,* pp. 38–44, 104; NC, *Book of the Yishuv Economy,* p. 104; Niv, *Struggles of the Etzel,* pp. 134, 256.
6. JAE, 13,27.12.1942, CZA; HE, 31.12.1942, vol. 66M, HA.
7. ZAC budget committee, 10.1.1943, S26/1235, and 17.1.1943, S46/48b; JAE, 17,24.1.1943; HE decision reported in ZAC, 18.1.1943, S25/295; all CZA.
8. Dobkin, ZAC budget committee, 10.1.1943, S26/1235, CZA.
9. HE, 31.12.1942, vol. 66M, HA; NC, 17.1.1943, J1/7256, CZA.
10. ZAC, 18.1.1943, S25/295, CZA.
11. The Agency's promises: HE, 27–28.1.1943, vol. 67M, HA; RC, 31.1.1943, S26/1239, CZA; MS, 10.2.1943, 24/43, LPA.
12. HS, 21.1.1943, 3/28; 11.2.1943, 5/30; 5.8.1943, 25/50; all HA.
13. JAE, 24.1.1943, CZA.
14. HE, 27–28.1.1943, vol. 67M, HA.
15. Ibid.; HS, 11.2.1943, 5/30, HA; JAE, 14.2.1943, CZA.
16. ZAC, 2.2.1943, S25/296; Gruenbaum to Michael Gruber, same day, S46/340; Gruenbaum to A. Fieschler, 20.5.1956, A127/582; all CZA.
17. RC, five meetings, January 1943, S26/1237,1239, CZA.
18. Bader, *Sad Missions,* p. 56; HS, 11.2.1943, 5/30, HA.
19. JAE and RC, 14.2.1943, S26/1241, CZA.
20. Histadrut to Kaplan, 28.3.1943, S53/1612; Kaplan, RC, 23.3.1943, S26/1237, CZA.
21. The agreement: 13.4.1943, S26/1240; confirmed by JAE, 18.4.1943, CZA.
22. NC, *Book of Documents,* p. 343.
23. HS, 15.3.1943, 10.35, HA; see Chabas, ed., *Letters from the Ghettoes,* p. 49.
24. HS, 29.4.1943, 14/39, HA.
25. The HE decided on 5.5.1943 to have the conference on 6.5.1943; see results in HE, 26.5.1943, vol. 68M, HA; on Myerson's tactics see Z. Or-Hof, letter, *Ha'aretz,* 13.12.1978.
26. Debates: ZAC, 24.6.1943, S25/298, CZA; and HS, 5.8.1943, 25/50, HA. According to 1943 balance sheets, interviews with activists, Gruenbaum

(JAE, 16.1.1944, CZA), and Dobkin (HS, 18.11.1943, 33/58, HA), most of the funds were included in the budget of the Mobilization and Rescue Fund and only 7,000 pounds was allocated specifically for rescue; see also Bart to HS, 2–3.12.1943, 36/41, HA.

27. HE, 5–7.5.1943, vol. 68M, HA; RC, 17.5.1943, S26/1237, CZA.
28. HS, 22.7.1943, 23/48, and 5.8.1943, 25/50, HA.
29. RC, 25.8.1943, S26/1239, CZA; HS, same day, 28/53, HA. For details of the month's program, see plans, 7.9.1943, S53/1617, and 12.9.1943, S53/612, CZA.
30. JAE, 5.9.1943, CZA.
31. JAE, 5,12.9.1943, CZA.
32. NC, *Book of Documents,* p. 346; Berger, *Mobilization and Rescue Fund,* p. 65; Harussi, *Book of the Mobilization and Rescue Fund,* p. 97; Frieling, "Ben-Gurion's Involvement in Rescue of Children," pp. 18–21.
33. HS, 18.11.1943, 33/58, HA. Detailed calculation of results: Bart to Gruenbaum, 14.11.1943, S26/1266, CZA. Bart's thanks to Remez, 28.11.1943, in Berger, *Mobilization and Rescue Fund,* p. 64.
34. Emissaries: HS, 5.8.1943, 25/50, HA. People's complaints: JAE, 5.9.1943, CZA.
35. RC, 1,23.11.1943, S26/1237; JAE, 20.12.1943, CZA; HS, 12.10.1943, 30/55, HA.
36. HE, 30.12.1943, vol. 69M, HA.
37. MRF balance sheet: 30.4.1944, 26/1140; RC balance sheet: 31.12.1943, S26/1089; Foundation Fund and Agency's budget: Kaplan, ZAC, 2.2.1943, S25/296; all CZA. See also Bart to HS, 3.12.1943, 36/61, HA. His calculations are the same as those in Gruenbaum's report to RC, 23.11.1943, S26/1237, CZA; and those in Dobkin's report to HS, 29.12.1943, 40/65, HA.
38. Sprinzak, NC, 31.1.1944 and 7.2.1944, J1/7256, CZA.
39. Golomb and Remez, ZAC minutes, 7.2.1944, J1/7256; Bart to NC, 12.2.1944, S26/1140; Gruenbaum, JAE, 13.2.1944; RC, 1.2.1944, S26/1239, and 10.2.1944, S26/1237; all CZA.
40. HE, 23–24.2.1944, vol. 70M, HA.
41. MRF report, beginning of 1944, S26/1140, CZA.
42. HS, 29.3.1944, 7/72, HA. Private funds in banks: Horowitz, *The Palestinian Economy,* p. 239; *Ha'aretz Almanac, 1942–1943,* p. 191; Gurevitch et al., *Statistical Handbook of Jewish Palestine,* p. 375.
43. Kaplan, JAE, 9.4.1944, CZA. The cable was taken on 22.2.1944 by an emissary of the Polish government-in-exile from Poland to Schwarzbart in London, reached Palestine 18.4.1944, and was read in HS, 19.4.1944, 8/73, HA.
44. Berger, *Mobilization and Rescue Fund,* p. 65; HS, 14.6.1944, 4/79, HA; JAE, 11,18.6,1944, CZA.
45. See *Hamashkif,* 20.3.1944, 13.4.1944; *Davar,* 27.1.1944, 2.3.1944; JAE, 20,27.2.1944, 12.3.1944, 23.4.1944, CZA; Berger, *Mobilization and Rescue Fund,* pp. 38–44.

46. Gruenbaum, RC, 20.3.1944, S26/1237; JAE, 12.3.1944, 2.4.1944, CZA.
47. DBG, JAE, 30.4.1944, 14.5.1944, 4.6.1944; Gruenbaum to Shostak, 5.5.1944, S26/1241, CZA; Joseph Klarman, interview with author, 5.4.1982; Niv, *Struggles of the Etzel,* p. 263; MS, 17.10.1944, 23/44, LPA.
48. JAE, 31.7.1944, 10,14,15,21,28.9.1944, 13,27.10.1944, CZA.
49. Berger, *Mobilization and Rescue Fund,* p. 67; Barlas, *Rescue in Days of Holocaust,* pp. 108, 299–300; balance sheet of income from JDC, February 1945, S26/1266, CZA; MS, 17.10.1944, 24/44, LPA.
50. RC balance sheets, 1.6.1945, S26/1268, CZA.
51. Ofer, *Illegal Immigration,* p. 473; and esp. "JDC payments for rescue and immigration of refugees," S26/1266, CZA.
52. HS, 18.11.1943, 33/58, HA.

9. RESCUE FUND ALLOCATIONS FROM FREE WORLD JEWRY

1. Remez, NC, 24.1.1944, J1/7256, CZA.
2. JAE, 13.12.1942, 24.2.1943, CZA.
3. M. A. Leavitt, 21.8.1942, S6/4639; JDC report, 5.9.1943, S6/902, CZA; Barlas, *Rescue in Days of Holocaust,* pp. 82–88; Bauer, *American Jewry and the Holocaust,* p. 352.
4. ZAC, 2.2.1943, S25/296, and 24.6.1943, S25/298, CZA.
5. HE, 26.5.1943, vol. 68, HA; Bader, *Sad Missions,* pp. 69–70.
6. Magnes to Baerwald, 14.5.1943, 258, JDCA; Neustadt, HE, 26.5.1943, vol. 63, HA; Barlas, in *Rescue Activities from Istanbul,* p. 28.
7. ZAC, 24.6.1943, S25/298, CZA.
8. NC, 9.8.1943, J1/7256, CZA.
9. RC, 9.8.1943, S26/1239, CZA; HS, 12.8.1943, 26/51, HA.
10. Schwartz to Leavitt, 23.8.1943, 258, JDCA.
11. JAE, 12.9.1943 and 19,20.12.1943, CZA; Ofer, "Activities of 'The Palestinian Delegation,'" p. 369.
12. JAE, 30.1.1944 and 18.6.1944, CZA; HS, 29.12.1943, 40/65, HA.
13. ZAC, 3.1.1944, S25/118; Dobkin, JAE, 9.1.1944, CZA; Dobkin, HS, 29.12.1943, 40/65, and 14.6.1944, 4/79, HA.
14. Leavitt to Schwartz, 26.2.1944, 258, JDCA; Bauer, *American Jewry and the Holocaust,* p. 215.
15. Schwartz to Leavitt, 18.2.1944; report by Leavitt, 11.2.1944; JDC to Shertok, 15.9.1944; all in 258, JDCA.
16. Barlas, cable to RC, 6.6.1944, S56/1232, CZA; Meirov and Sprinzak, HS, 14.6.1944, 4/79, HA.
17. JAE, 18.6.1944, CZA; Harussi, *Book of the Mobilization and Rescue Fund,* pp. 103–104.
18. Kaplan, JAE, 23.7.1944; RC, 14.7.1944 and 28.7.1944, S26/1238a, CZA; Avriel, *Open the Gates,* p. 135; Hirschmann, *Life Line to a Promised Land,* p. 62.
19. Baerwald to Schwarz, 7.9.1944, 258, JDCA. Praise for Schwartz: Kollek, *One Jerusalem,* p. 61; Bauer, *American Jewry and the Holocaust,* p. 185.

20. Schwartz to Leavitt, 18.9.1944; Leavitt to JAE, 11.11.1944, 258, JDCA.
21. MS, 17.10.1944, 24/44, LPA. Cables to the Jewish world: 6.11.1944, S26/1236; 3.12.1944, S26/1237; 7.12.1944, S26/1251, CZA.
22. ZAC, 24.6.1943, S25/208, CZA; Shimoni, *Jews and Zionism.*
23. Reports on Gruenbaum's trip: 25.8.1943, Landau files; RC, 27.8.1943, S26/1255, CZA.
24. JAE, 26.9.1943; RC, 20.9.1943, S26/1237; see correspondence, August–September 1943, S40/1255, CZA.
25. RC, 1.11.1943, S26/1237, CZA.
26. Gruenbaum: 11.5.1944, S6/4587, and 6.6.1944, S26/1232. South Africa: 5,26.6.1944, S44/679; RC, 18.6.1944, S26/1238a; all CZA.
27. See balance sheet, 25.4.1945, including RC incomes until October 1944, S6/4588; reports, JAE, 23.4.1945, CZA.
28. Klieger, S53/2118, CZA.
29. Kaplan and Myerson, HS, 17.8.1943, 27/52, HA.
30. RC, 9.11.1943, S26/1239, and 23.11.1943, 19.1.1944, S26/1237; NC, 7.2.1944, J1/7256; all CZA; Barlas, *Rescue in Days of Holocaust,* p. 300.
31. JAE, 21.5.1944, 11.6.1944, CZA.
32. Report on London meeting, HS, 19.4.1944, 8/73, HA.
33. Gruenbaum to Marks, 8.6.1944, S26/1089, CZA.
34. Kaplan to Jewish National Fund, 4.7.1944; Jewish National Fund, 25.8.1944, S26/1266; all CZA; Barlas, *Rescue in Days of Holocaust,* p. 300.
35. Barlas, *Rescue in Days of Holocaust,* pp. 83, 85; JDC, *So They May Live Again,* p. 30; NC, *Book of the Yishuv Economy,* p. 80; Dobkin, *Immigration and Rescue,* pp. 78, 102.
36. Shertok, ZAC, 1.9.1943, 25/301; JAE, 4.10.1943; Gruenbaum, 22.5.1944, S26/1086; all CZA.

10. RESCUE OPERATIONS IN NEUTRAL COUNTRIES

1. Goldmann, 28,30.8.1940, with reference to his 1940 and 1941 proposals, S46/363; Gruenbaum, 5.11.1942, S26/1253; Shmuelevich, 27.12.1942, S6/1165; all CZA; Shmuelevich in *Haboker,* 27.6.1945; Weissman, *In the Face of Evil,* pp. 89–90.
2. London office to Shertok, 21.11.1942, A127/543, and JAE, 25.4.1943, CZA; HS, 29.5.1943, 14/39, HA; Avni, *Spain and the Jews,* pp. 108, 136–137.
3. Avni, *Spain and the Jews,* p. 211; JAE, 1,22.11.1942; RC, 31.1.1943, S26/1239, CZA; MC, 30.11.1942, 23/42; MS, 10.2.1943, 23/43, LPA.
4. Cable, Israel to Jerusalem, 25.4.1943, S6/1678, CZA; Avni, *Spain and the Jews,* p. 213; Bader, HS, 13.5.1943, 15/40, HA.
5. Barlas to Immigration Department, 9.5.1943, S6/1678; Immigration Department to Barlas, 8.8.1943, S6/1166, CZA; Weissman, *In the Face of Evil,* pp. 88–112; Avni, *Spain and the Jews,* pp. 210–222; Bauer, *American Jewry and the Holocaust,* pp. 197–217; see Israel's reports in Adler-Rudel, "A Chronicle of Rescue Efforts," pp. 219–221.

6. Leshem, "Agency's Mission in Iberian Peninsula," pp. 309–313; Peretz Leshem, interview with author, February 1985.

7. Lichtenstein, 24.5.1943, S6/836; Immigration Department, 20.5.1943, S6/1165, and 8.8.1943, S6/1166, CZA.

8. Lichtenstein, 25.12.1943, S6/3874, and 5.2.1944, L32/27, CZA; MS, 24.9.1944, 24/44, LPA; Kochva, *Pioneering Underground in Occupied Holland,* pp. 268–269, 277.

9. Reports: 16.2.1944, S6/1452, CZA; Sh/300/3359, Wolyn House, YVA; Kapel, *Jewish Struggle in Occupied France,* pp. 172, 175.

10. Dobkin's reports: JAE, 21.9.1944; RC, 3.10.1944, S26/1238b, CZA; HS, 11.10.1944, 24/44, HA; MS, 24.9.1944, 24/44, LPA.

11. Immigration Department to emissaries in Istanbul, 2.9.1944, S6/1678, CZA.

12. The agreement: 13.7.1944, S26/1240, CZA; Avni, *Spain and the Jews,* pp. 210, 222. Dobkin: HS, 11.10.1944, 23/44, HA.

13. Dobkin, HS, 11.10.1944, 23/44, HA.

14. Adler-Rudel, "Chronicle of Rescue Efforts," pp. 213–241, is a very modest account; see also Yahil, *Rescue of Jews of Denmark,* which includes material from Rudel's archive.

15. Adler-Rudel, "Chronicle of Rescue Efforts," pp. 217–225.

16. Ibid., pp. 232–233.

17. Ibid., pp. 228–235, includes intergovernmental correspondence.

18. Lichtheim: 12.9.1939, S46/275; 9.8.1940, S46/363; 27.9.1939, S26/1232; 4.6.1940, S6/1162; all CZA.

19. JAE, 24.11.1940; Immigration Department, 11.2.1940, S6/112, and 28.8.1940, S46/363, CZA.

20. Chaim Pazner (5.3.1978), Gerhard Riegner (3.9.1982), and Nathan Schwalb (Dror) (5.3.1985), interviews with author.

21. Ibid.; Barlas to Schwalb, 26.5.1943, S6/1166, CZA.

22. Barlas: 24.4.1943, S6/1165; 26.5.1943, S6/1166; 25.6.1943, S46/536; 22.12.1943, S6/4648; Levinsky, 20.10.1943, S6/832; Schwalb: 21.10.1943, S6/832; all CZA; HS, 15.3.1944, 6/71, HA.

23. Riegner (3.9.1982) and Pazner (5.3.1978), interviews with author; Minz and Levin to Gruenbaum, 23.9.1943, S26/1240, and 5.9.1944, S6/4588; RC, 7,27.3.1944, S26/1237, and 28.11.1944, S26/1238, CZA.

24. As in note 20.

25. Shertok, MC, 24.8.1943, 23/43, LPA.

26. JAE, 16.8.1942, CZA; NC, 11.6.1942, vol. 65M, HA.

27. Nathan Schwalb (3.9.1982), Chaim Barlas (19.3.1978), and Joseph Klarman (22.9.1980), interviews with author.

28. Bader, *Sad Missions,* p. 42; HS, 5.8.1943, 25/50, HA; RC, 20.9.1943, S26/1237; ZAC, 3.1.1944, S25/118; Barlas, 12.11.1942, S6/1956, CZA.

29. Remez, HE, 12.10.1943, 30/55; HS, 2.8.1944, 22/87, HA; Barlas, 2.6.1943, S6/4587, CZA; MC, 24.11.1942, 23/42, LPA.

30. Immigration Department, 24.12.1942, S6/1142, and S6/1232,4587, CZA.

31. Shertok, JAE, 22.8.1943, and esp. his letter, 16.8.1943, S26/1132, CZA; Bader, *Sad Missions,* pp. 46–47, 60, 62, 68.

32. JAE, 12,19.9.1943, 10.10.1943. The council of eight members: 5.11.1943, S26/1239, CZA; Kollek, *One Jerusalem*, p. 54.
33. DBG, JAE, 5.3.1944, CZA; Sprinzak, MS, 15.12.1943, 24/43, LPA. Letters: from Levinsky: 20,23.10.1943, and 2.11.1943, S6/832; from Europe: 14.9.1943, 17.10.1943, S6/4587, and 5.10.1943, S6/1956; from Dobkin: 23,24.12.1943, S6/832; all CZA.
34. Meirov's report, 15.3.1944, S6/1956, CZA.
35. Shertok to Barlas, 25.1.1944, 56/4587; JAE, 19.12.1943, and 9,23,30.1.1944; all CZA.
36. Immigrants' organizations to Immigration Department, S6/1422, esp. 29.11.1943, CZA.
37. Gruenbaum, JAE, 26.3.1944; immigrants' organizations to Immigration Department, March–August 1944, 56/4587, S6/1251, CZA.
38. JAE, 20.2.1944, 5,26.3.1944, 9.4.1944, 14.5.1944; Barlas' report: 6.7.144, S6/1166; the agreements: 5,15.7.1944; S26/1238a; all CZA.
39. Kaplan's report: JAE, 23.7.1944, and RC, 28.7.1944, S26/1238a; Magnes' report: RC, 14.7.1944, CZA; Steinhardt to his minister, 1.6.1944, P12/25, YVA.
40. RC, 31.1.1943, S26/1239, CZA; Nathan Schwalb, interview with author, 20.5.1984.
41. Barlas and Lichtheim, 3.1.1943, S6/1165; Pomerantz, 2.3.1943, S6/1850; Gruenbaum, JAE, 24.1.1943; all CZA.
42. Neustadt, 31.12.1942, S6/1998; Dobkin, 25.1.1943, S6/832, CZA.
43. MS, 29.4.1943, 24/43, LPA; RC, 3.10.1944, S26/1238a; emissaries in Istanbul to Dobkin, 21.6.1943, S6/1850, CZA.
44. Barlas, JAE, 4.10.1943, CZA; HS, 12.10.1943, 30/55, and HE, 27.1.1944 and 23–24.2.1944, HA; Gutman, *The Jews of Warsaw*, pp. 60–61.
45. Barlas' report: S6/4588, p. 9; letter from Melbourne, Australia, warning Gruenbaum that Revisionists and Agudat Yisrael were collecting money there, 23.8.1944, S6/1232; JAE, 16.1.1944; the Aguda's fundraising: RC, 28.7.1944; S26/1238a; all CZA.
46. Barlas, RC, 15.10.1943, S26/1237, and 18.6.1944, S26/1235a; number of parcels: RC, 3.10.1944, S26/1238a, CZA; HE, 27.1.1944, vol. 70, HA; their value: Gutman, *The Jews of Warsaw*, p. 141.
47. Shind in *Beit-Hashita*, 2.9.1944; Stern, "Contacts between Istanbul and Polish Jewry," p. 147.
48. JAE, 23.7.1944, CZA.
49. Barlas, RC, 3.10.1944, S26/1238a, CZA; HS, 13.5.1943, 15/40, HA.
50. Schwalb's testimony, Histadrut oral documentation project, 9.8.1982, HA.
51. Lichtheim, 9.5.1944, S6/4587; Barlas' report, S6/4588, CZA; Eck, "Rescue by Latin American Passports," pp. 93–111; Stern, "Contacts between Istanbul and Polish Jewry," pp. 141–144.
52. JAE, 23.4.1944, 7.5.1944, 4.10.1943, S26/1234, A127/543,544, CZA.
53. Correspondence between Hungary and RC, S26/1234,1251, and A127/543,544, CZA.

54. HE, 27.1.1944, vol. 70M, HA; MS, 24.2.1943, 30.3.1943, 24/43, LPA.
55. Schwalb's letters, S26/1235; Gruenbaum, RC, 4.11.1943, S26/1237, CZA; HE, 16,29–30.12.1943, vol. 69M, and 27.1.1944, vol. 70M; Kollek, HS, 12.10.1943, 30/55, HA.
56. JAE, 22.8.1943, CZA; Shertok, MC, 24.8.1943, 23/43, LPA.
57. Levinsky, interview with author, August 1984.
58. Yehiel Duvdvani, interview with author, 25.6.1981; for Katznelson see Shapira, *Berl,* pp. 663–673.
59. Venia Pomerantz (3.11.1984), Nathan Schwalb (13.11.1984, 5.3.1985, 20.5.1984), and Chaim Barlas (19.3.1978, 2.4.1978), interviews with author.
60. Pomerantz (3.11.84) and Schwalb (5.3.1985), interviews with author; RC, 3.10.1944, S26/1238a, CZA; HE, 23–24.2.1944, 6.9.1944, vol. 70, HA.

11. POLITICAL NEGOTIATIONS

1. JAE, 22,29.11.1942, S26/1144, and 6,20,27.12.1942, A127/543, CZA; HE, 3.12.1942, vol. 66M, HA; MC, 24,30.11.1942, 23/42, LPA.
2. JAE, 22.11.1942; Gruenbaum and Schmorak to Zionist office in London, 5.1.1943, A127/543, CZA.
3. See note 1.
4. MC, 24.11.1942, 23/42, LPA; see esp. Frieling, "Ben-Gurion's Involvement in Rescue of Children," pp. 12–16.
5. JAE, 29.11.1942, 6.12.1942, 10.1.1943, CZA; Wasserstein, *Britain and the Jews of Europe,* pp. 249–251.
6. HE, 31.12.1942, vol. 66M, HA; DBG, JAE, 6.12.1942 and 4.1.1943, CZA.
7. Wasserstein, *Britain and the Jews of Europe,* pp. 158, 183–188, 241–248; Feingold, *Politics of Rescue,* pp. 190–197; HS, 29.4.1943, 14/39, HA.
8. Halifax: Wasserstein, *Britain and the Jews of Europe,* p. 184, Eden: Feingold, *Politics of Rescue,* p. 195.
9. Goldmann to Gruenbaum, 5.4.1943, S26/1234, CZA.
10. Shertok, JAE, 27.4.1943, and ZAC, 18.5.1943, S25/297, CZA.
11. JAE, 4,11,18.4.1943; RC, 8.3.1943 and 16.4.1943, S26/1237, CZA.
12. HS, 13.4.1943, 13/48, HA.
13. Landau files.
14. Hebrew version: NC, *Book of Documents,* p. 343; English: 19.4.1943, S26/1144; memorandum: JAE, 18.4.1943, CZA.
15. JAE to Parliament, 17.5.1943; Hebrew: S26/1144; English: S26/1232, CZA.
16. ZAC, 18.5.1943, S25/297, CZA.
17. See daily press on May 20, quoting Eden.
18. The exchange plan: S46/273; and S6/4526, and letters from Immigration Department to Barlas, 14.2.1943 and 4.6.1943, S6/1165, including lists, CZA.
19. Zionist activists to DBG, 11.11.1942, 544/442, CZA.
20. Gruenbaum on lists, RC, 23.3.1943, 526/1239, CZA.

21. Dobkin, HS, 31.12.1942 and 11.2.1943, 5/30, HA; Gruenbaum, 16.3.1943, S26/1255, and 6,14.6.1943, A127/543; DBG, JAE, 29.11.1942, 6.12.1942, 28.2.1943, CZA; Frieling, "Ben-Gurion's Involvement in Rescue of Children," pp. 7–8.
22. See esp. Kolb, *Bergen-Belsen*, pp. 83–105.
23. Zariz, "Rescue from Holland," pp. 135–162.
24. Gruenbaum, A127/543; letters of relatives, 16.7.1943, S6/1404; Shertok, JAE, 25.4.1943; all CZA.
25. Report on meeting with British officials, Immigration Department, 29.7.1943, S6/1166; JAE, 27.4.1943, CZA.
26. Correspondence, summer 1943, S26/1225,1251, and S6/1404,1165, CZA.
27. On von Thadden see Eck, "Jews for Germans," pp. 44–46.
28. 3.1.1944, 28.3.1944, 29.6.1944, S26/1232, and esp. 7.8.1944, S26/1251; JAE, 12.9.1943 and 4.10.1943; all CZA.
29. Barlas, in *Rescue Activities from Istanbul*, p. 25; Dobkin, RC, 14.7.1944 and 3.10.1944, S26/1238a, CZA.
30. Dobkin's report, 17.8.1944, A127/544, CZA; Eck, "Jews for Germans," p. 34.
31. Kaplan, JAE, 20.12.1942, CZA; DBG, MS, 9.12.1942, 24/42, LPA; see also JAE, 13,27.12.1942, CZA.
32. MS, 9.12.1942, 24/42, and 20.1.1943, 23/43, LPA.
33. JAE, 7.2.1943 and 28.3.1943, CZA.
34. Wasserstein, *Britain and the Jews of Europe*, pp. 179–180; JAE, 21.2.1943, CZA.
35. JAE, 29.8.1943 and 19.9.1943, CZA.
36. Shertok, JAE, 25.4.1943, CZA; and HS, 29.4.1943, 14/39, HA.
37. DBG, JAE, 28.2.1943; see also JAE, 25.4.1943, 2.5.1943, CZA.
38. Bader, *Sad Missions*, p. 54.
39. Bader, HE, 31.12.1942, vol. 66M, HA; Barlas, in *Rescue Activities from Istanbul*, pp. 12, 25.
40. Kaplan, MS, 30.3.1943, 24/43, LPA; JAE, 14.2.1943, CZA; Bader, *Sad Missions*, p. 51.
41. DBG, MCC, 24.2.1943, 23/43; and MS, 10.2.1943, 42/43, LPA; Shertok, JAE, 14.2.1943 and 22.8.1943, CZA.
42. MCC, 24.2.1943, 23/43, LPA.
43. DBG on permits, JAE, 7.3.1943; Gruenbaum, JAE, 4.4.1943, CZA; Frieling, "Ben-Gurion's Involvement in Rescue of Children," p. 20 (DBG on Zionism and the Yishuv).
44. See German Foreign Office documents in *United Restitution Organizatin* (Frankfurt am Main, 1959), vol. 3, pp. 370–376 (Eichmann, p. 384); and Browning, *Final Solution and German Foreign Office*, pp. 172–173.
45. Kaplan, JAE, 28.3.1943, CZA; MS, 10.3.1943, 24/43; DBG, MS, 24.2.1943, 24/43, LPA.
46. See Kollek in Avriel, *Open the Gates*, pp. 102–104.

47. Myerson, HS, 13.4.1943, 13/38, HA; Kaplan, JAE, 28.3.1943, CZA.
48. Kaplan, JAE, 4.4.1943, 16.5.1943, 6.6.1943, CZA. Cranborne: Wasserstein, *Britain and the Jews of Europe*, pp. 134–135. Bader on Whittall, HS, 13.5.1943, 15/40, HA.
49. HE,. 31.3–2.4.1943, vol. 69, HA.
50. Shertok, HS, 22.7.1943, 23/48, and 5.8.1943, 25/50, HA; JAE, 25.7.1943, 22.8.1943, CZA.
51. MC, 24.8.1943, 23/43, LPA.
52. Ibid.
53. Ibid.
54. Ibid.; HS, 12.10.1943, 30/55, HA; Bader, *Sad Missions,* p. 51.

12. RANSOM PLANS

1. I could not locate this memorandum in CZA; however, see Barlas, JAE, 23.12.1942; Goldin, 6.12.1942, S26/1466, CZA.
2. For the situation in Transnistria see Shechtman, "The Transnistria Reservation"; *Les Juifs en Europe;* Reiffer, *The Death Journey;* and Shachan, "The Ghettos in Transnistria."
3. Rumanian Jewish leaders to Silberschein, Geneva, 4.12.1942, M20/903, YVA.
4. See Chapter 11, note 44. Shertok and Gruenbaum, 5.1.1943, S26/1251; Dobkin, ZAC, 18.1.1943, S25/295, CZA. Kaplan, interview, *Palestine,* 14.4.1943.
5. JAE, 23.12.1942, CZA.
6. NC, 17.1.1943, J1/7255; ZAC, 18.1.1943, S25/295, and 2.2.1943, S25/296; RC to immigrants from Rumania, 10.2.1943, S26/1240; all CZA.
7. Tzvi Yehieli, HS, 21.1.1943, 3/28, and 1.2.1943, 5/30, HA; MS, 10.2.1943, 24/43, LPA.
8. MS, 10.2.1943, 24/43, LPA.
9. HS, 11.2.1943, 5/30. HA.
10. Wasserstein, *Britain and the Jews of Europe,* p. 224; Feingold, *Politics of Rescue,* p. 182.; Morse, *While Six Million Died,* p. 62.
11. Sulzberger: Morse, *While Six Million Died,* p. 62; Barlas, 15.1.1943, S6/1165, CZA.
12. Shertok, JAE, 27.4.1943, CZA.
13. 16.2.1943 and 4.3.1943, WA; Kedem, "Chaim Weizmann's Political Activity," pp. 239–241.
14. Wasserstein, *Britain and the Jews of Europe,* pp. 179, 245–249; Feingold, *Politics of Rescue,* pp. 182–183; Sykes, *Cross Roads to Israel,* p. 228; based on very accurate private information; R. I. Campbell, answering Weizmann at Halifax's request, 4.3.1943, A127/543, CZA.
15. Hecht, *Perfidy,* pp. 224–225; *New York Times,* 16.2.1943; *Personal Letters of Stephen S. Wise,* p. 265.
16. MCC, 24.2.1943, LPA.

17. Kaplan, JAE, 28.3.1943, CZA, and MS, 30.3.1943, 24/43, LPA.
18. Hartglas, 24.4.1943, S26/1232, CZA.
19. See note 17 and MC, 24.2.1943, 23/43, LPA. Commitment to pay: Barlas, 4.3.1943, A127/543, CZA.
20. JAE, 22.8.1943 and 4.10.1943, CZA. Antonescu's letter: Barlas, *Rescue in Days of Holocaust*, p. 268.
21. MS, 15.12.1943, 24/43, LPA; correspondence between Agency and Colonial Office, S25/1675, CZA.
22. Money and aid: HE, 25.8.1943, 28/53, and 12.10.1943, 30/55, HA; RC, 20.9.1943, 2.11.1943, 6.12.1943, S26/1237; JAE, 22.8.1943, 4.10.1943, CZA. According to Bader, *Sad Missions*, p. 88, 50,000 pounds were sent to Transnistria.
23. ZAC, 18.5.1943, S25/297, CZA.
24. Sykes, *Cross Roads to Israel*, p. 228.
25. The Europa Plan: both Weissmandel, *In Distress* (pp. 67–74), and Rotkirchen, *The Destruction of Slovakian Jewry* (pp. 30–31, 145, 224), claim that Weissmandel initiated the negotiations; Neumann, *In the Shadow of Death* (pp. 160–161), claims that Gisi Fleischmann did. According to Barlas, *Rescue in Days of Holocaust* (pp. 109, 112), and Brand and Brand, *The Devil and the Soul* (p. 34), Wisliceny did.
26. Neumann, *In the Shadow of Death*, esp. pp. 112–123; Rotkirchen, *The Destruction of Slovakian Jewry*, esp. pp. 22–33; Bauer, *American Jewry and the Holocaust*, pp. 336–369; idem in *Ha'aretz*, 24.5.1954; Kaplan, JAE, 28.3.1943, CZA, and MS, summing up developments, 30.3.1943, 24/43, LPA.
27. Letters from rabbis to "the People of Israel," 5.11.1942, S26/1419, and January 1943, S26/1232, CZA.
28. Weissmandel, *In Distress*, pp. 66, 70, 77 n. 34, 80 n. 49.
29. Ibid., pp. 68, 77 n. 38, 161.
30. Neumann, *In the Shadow of Death*, pp. 112–113, 128, 149–151; Bauer, *American Jewry and the Holocaust*, pp. 359, 368; Nathan Schwalb (Dror), interview with author, 3.9.1982; see also note 26.
31. Weissmandel, *In Distress*, p. 92.
32. Dobkin's cable, 25.1.1943, S6/823; Schwalb's report, 4.12.1942, S26/1444; NC, 17.1.1943, J1/7255; ZAC, 18.1.1943, S25/295; all CZA; MS, 10.2.1943, 24/43, LPA.
33. Bader, HE, 11.2.1943, 5/30, HA.
34. DBG, MC, 24.2.1943, 23/43, LPA.
35. Letters: Weissmandel, *In Distress*, p. 76 and appendixes; Fleischmann to Schwalb, Landau files, K6/114, S6/1850; all CZA; and file LXVI, LA; Schwalb to Kaplan: Terek-Yablonka, "The Europa Plan," p. 45.
36. Kaplan's letter, 10.3.1943, S25/5183, and JAE, 28.3.1943, CZA.
37. Bader, *Sad Missions*, pp. 51–53, 59, 61; Pomerantz, NC, 25.4.1943, S6/4582; Barlas to Kaplan, 15.4.1943, L15/278; confirmation from Bratislava, 6.4.1943, 86/1850; all CZA.

38. Pomerantz, 2.3.1943, S6/1850; Kaplan, quoting Lichtheim, JAE, 28.3.1943; Schwalb to Barlas, 17.4.1943, S6/4887; all CZA.

39. Fleischmann to Mayer, 11.5.1943, K16/114; CZA.

40. Pomerantz and Bader, 25.4.1943, L15/278, CZA; Pomerantz to HE, 25.4.1943, S6/4582, HA; Bader, RC, 17.5.1943, S26/1237, CZA; and HS, 13.5.1943, 15/40, HA.

41. Barlas (speaking for Schwalb) and Dobkin, ZAC, 24.6.1943, S26/298; Pomerantz and Bader, 21.6.1943, S6/1850, CZA.

42. Wise, *Challenging Years*, pp. 274–279; Goldmann, *Memoirs*, pp. 186–187.

43. Barlas, *Rescue in Days of Holocaust*, p. 110; Bader, *Sad Missions*, pp. 78–80; Neumann, *In the Shadow of Death*, pp. 162–164; Fleischmann to Mayer, 17.7.1943, S6/1850, and 19.7.1943, K6/114, CZA.

44. Letters from Istanbul, 25.6.1943, S6/1850, and 21.7.1943, S26/1240, CZA.

45. Dobkin to Gruenbaum, 27.8.1943, S26/1255, CZA.

46. Ibid.; Shertok to Mayer: Terek-Yablonka, "The Europa Plan," p. 52; Mayer: Bauer, *American Jewry and the Holocaust*, p. 376; see esp. Schwalb to Barlas, 11.8.1943 S6/4587, CZA.

47. Bauer, *American Jewry and the Holocaust*, p. 377; Kollek, *One Jerusalem*, pp. 59–60, writes, mistakenly, about 1944; confirmations from Bratislava, 17,18.10.1943, S6/1850; Barlas, JAE, 5.10.1943, CZA.

48. Fleischmann, 25.10.1943, Landau files; Shind, MS, 15.12.1943, 24/43, LPA; Neumann, *In the Shadow of Death*, p. 165. Aid: Shertok, JAE, 22.8.1943, CZA; Barlas, HS, 12.10.1943, 30/55, HA.

49. Hilberg, *The Destruction of European Jewry*, pp. 466–468; 22/45, TNL-UD, Slovak State Central Archive, courtesy of Prof. Y. Yelinek.

50. Rotkirchen, *The Destructon of Slovakian Jewry*, p. 23.

51. 9.4.1943, and 19.11.1943, Landau files.

52. Rabbi Moshe Schoenfeld, *Those Burnt in the Crematoriums Accuse* (Bnei Brak: Bnei Tora, 1978).

53. Ze'ev Hadari, interview with author, 3.11.1984; *Haboker*, 16.5.1944; *Davar*, 11,23.5.1944.

54. MC, 2.2.1944, 23/44, LPA.

55. Bader, *Sad Missions*, p. 100; Andre Biss, interview with Daniel Carpi and author, summer 1982; Kasztner, *Kasztner's Truth*, pp. 18–19.

56. Avriel, *Open the Gates*, pp. 141–144; Barlas, *Rescue in Days of Holocaust*, pp. 113–115; Klarman in *Allgemeiner Journal* (Yiddish), 21.9.1979; Bader, *Sad Missions*, pp. 100–102; Brand, *An Emissary of the Condemned*, pp. 109–113; see esp. Brand's report, Joel/a, 23.1.1945, S26/1190ab, CZA.

57. Barlas' cable, 20.5.1944, no. 785/44, J26/1251, CZA.

58. JAE, 25.5.1944, CZA.

59. Gross's mission: Bader, *Sad Missions*, p. 103; Brand, *An Emissary of the Condemned*, pp. 119–121; Avriel, *Open the Gates*, p. 141; Rosenfeld, *Criminal File 124/53*, pp. 78–80 and esp. p. 88; Brand-Shertok conversation, 11.6.1944, S26/1251, CZA.

60. Avriel, *Open the Gates,* pp. 102–103; Bader, *Sad Missions,* p. 103; Brand, *An Emissary of the Condemned,* pp. 119–121.

61. MacMichael to Steinhardt, 26.5.1944, P12/25, YVA; Randall and Hall to Weizmann, 5.6.1944, WA; Shertok's report, written 27.6.1944 in the Dorchester Hotel, Z4/14870, CZA (hereafter cited as Dorchester report).

62. Bader to Pomerantz: 10.6.1944, D1.1720, MA; Bauer, "Joel Brand's Mission," p. 38.

63. See agreement, 29.5.1944, S26/1251, CZA.

64. Cable, Dorchester report, p. 3.

65. Eichmann, quoted in Brand-Shertok conversation, 11.6.1944, S26/1251, CZA. On Brand's return see Rosenfeld, *Criminal File 124/53,* pp. 55 (Bader's testimony), 63 (Avriel's testimony); Bader to Pomerantz, 27.5.1944 and 10.6.1944; quoted in Bauer, "Joel Brand's Mission," pp. 38–39.

66. Rosenfeld, *Criminal File, 124/53,* pp. 62–64 (Avriel's testimony); Avriel, *Open the Gates,* p. 145; Dorchester report, p. 3. On British intelligence see Vago, "Intelligence Activites and Brand Mission," p. 81.

67. Bader, *Sad Missions,* p. 105; Joseph Klarman (21.9.1979) and Chaim Barlas (19.3.1978), interviews with author; Brand, *An Emissary of the Condemned,* pp. 129–131, admits being warned; Rosenfeld, *Criminal File 124/53,* esp. p. 55.

68. Dorchester report, p. 37.

69. Wasserstein, *Britain and the Jews of Europe,* p. 251; see ibid., pp. 250–253.

70. Halifax to Foreign Office, 5.6.1944, P12/25, YVA; JAE, 24.6.1944, CZA; Hirschmann, *Life Line,* p. 185.

71. Eden, quoted in Kedem, "Chaim Weizmann's Political Activity," p. 256; Hall to Weizmann, 5.6.1944, and Weizmann to Eden, 6.6.1944, WA. See also Hadar, "The Allies' Attitude to Brand's Mission," p. 117.

72. Steinhardt's report: Morse, *While Six Million Died,* p. 284; Hirschmann, *Life Line,* pp. 84–85; report by Reuben Reznik of the JDC in Istanbul, written at Steinhardt's request for the State Department, 4.6.1944, P12/25, YVA. Goldmann-Stettinius meeting: RC, 16.10.1944, S26/1238a, CZA; Hausner, *Justice in Jerusalem,* p. 249.

73. JAE, 14.6.1944; Brand-Shertok conversation, 11.6.1944, S26/1251, CZA; Dorchester report, p. 7.

74. Shertok's proposals: Hall to Weizmann, 22.6.1944, Z4/15202, CZA.

75. Dorchester report, pp. 7–8; Shertok's epilogue in Brand, *An Emissary of the Condemned,* p. 237; MacMichael to Colonial Office, 15.6.1944, quoted in Wasserstein, *Britian and the Jews of Europe,* p. 255.

76. JAE, 18.6.1944, CZA; Brand and Brand, *The Devil and the Soul,* p. 57. In his memoirs Brand accuses the JAE several times of having prevented him from returning to Hungary; see *An Emissary of the Condemned,* esp. p. 163.

77. The American answer, 19.6.1944, P12/25, YVA. Instructions to ambassadors: Hadar, "The Allies' Attitude to Brand's Mission," pp. 119–121, Bauer, "Joel Brand's Mission," p. 44.

78. Hirschmann, *Life Line*, pp. 90–92; Morse, *While Six Million Died*, p. 287; Feingold, *Roosevelt Administration*, pp. 211–253.

79. Shertok, JAE, 24.6.1944, CZA.

80. Shertok and Randall to Weizmann, and Weizmann to Hall, 23.6.1944, Z4/15202; DBG, JAE, 2.7.1944, CZA; Shertok to Goldman, 19.6.1944, quoted in Feingold, *Roosevelt Administration*, p. 247.

81. Randall to Weizmann, 24.6.1944, Z4/14870; Goldmann to Weizmann, 1.7.1944, Z6/1/16, CZA; British Foreign Office memorandum, 26.6.1944, quoted in Bauer, "Joel Brand's Mission," p. 46; cables and appeals, Z4/14890, CZA.

82. MacMichael's warning, 12.7.1944, S26/1190aa.

83. Cables S26/1251, A122/544, CZA.

84. Shertok to DBG, 30.6.1944, Z4/14870, CZA; Wasserstein, *Britain and the Jews of Europe*, p. 255.

85. DBG, JAE, and cable to Shertok, 2.7.1944, Z4/14870, CZA; cable from Budapest, 23.6.1944, quoted in Bader, *Sad Missions*, pp. 110–111; Bader to Pomerantz, 24.6.1944, quoted in Bauer, "Joel Brand's Mission," p. 54.

86. Dobkin's reports: JAE, 21.9.1944, CZA; MS, 24.9.1944, 23/44, LPA; HS, 11.10.1944, 29/44, HA.

87. Hadar, "The Allies' Attitude to Brand's Mission," p. 121; Feingold, *Roosevelt Administration*, p. 237. Brand's interrogation: Brand, *An Emissary of the Condemned*, pp. 140–148; Vago, "Intelligence Activities and the Brand Mission"; Gelber, "Zionist Policy, 1943–1944," p. 159; and Wasserstein, *Britain and the Jews of Europe*, pp. 256–258.

88. Wasserstein, *Britain and the Jews of Europe*, p. 256; Eden's statement in Parliament, 5.7.1944, and editorials in the British press were widely quoted in Hebrew press.

89. Minutes of meeting and memorandum, 6.7.1944, Z4/14870; cable, Shertok to DBG and Goldmann and DBG, JAE, 9.7.1944, CZA.

90. Churchill to Eden, 11.7.1944, FO 371/42809/115, Public Record Office, London.

91. Minutes of meeting, 12.7.1944, and cable, Shertok to DBG, 14.7.1944, Z4/14780, CZA.

92. Shertok to Randall, 14.7.1944; Randall to Shertok, 15.7.1944, Z4/14840; Dobkin's reports, as in note 86; all CZA; U.S. embassy in Lisbon, 28.7.1944, P12/25, YVA.

93. Randall on Shertok, 18.7.1944, quoted in Kedem "Chaim Weizmann's Political Activity," p. 263; cable, DBG to Roosevelt, 11.7.1944, P12/83, YVA.

94. JAE, 16.7.1944, CZA.

95. Gruenbaum, JAE, 23.7.1944. Hall admitted the leak; see Sompolinsky, "Jewish Leadership in Britain," p. 208.

96. Shertok, JAE, 20.10.1944, and ZAC, 19.11.1944, S25/1804, CZA; Wyman, *The Abandonment of the Jews*, pp. 235–240.

97. Shertok, as in note 96; Brand, *An Emissary of the Condemned*, pp. 155–156.

98. Shind, HS, 6.9.1944, 26/91, HA.

99. Brand, *An Emissary of the Condemend,* pp. 168–169; Kollek, *One Jerusalem,* p. 63; MCC, 17.10.1944, 23/44, LPA.

100. Brand, *An Emissary of the Condemned,* pp. 94, 101, 130, 140–141.

101. Gruenbaum, JAE, 23.7.1944 and 3.9.1944, CZA.

13. MILITARY PLANS

1. Rabbi Benjamin to Shertok, 25.5.1944, S26/1251, CZA; Rabbi Benjamin in *Ha'aretz,* 9.6.1944, and *Bamishor,* 29.6.1944.

2. Report on Gruenbaum-Pinkerton meeting, 7.6.1944, and Pinkerton's answer, 23.6.1944, S26/1232, CZA.

3. JAE, 11.6.1944, and RC, 18.6.1944, S26/1238a, CZA.

4. Cable, Gruenbaum to World Jewish Congress, 11.6.1944, A127/544, CZA.

5. RC Press Committee on Kaplan's report, 5.3.1943, S26/1240, CZA.

6. RC bulletins, October–November 1943, January and June 1944, Landau files; Chabas, ed., *Letters from the Ghettos,* pp. 56–58; Hakibutz Hameuchad bulletin, T11/198, p. 4, Beth-Hatefutsoth Archive, Tel Aviv.

7. Gilbert, *Auschwitz and the Allies,* esp. pp. 233–235.

8. Ibid., pp. 202–205; Rotkirchen, *The Destruction of Slovakian Jewry,* p. 36.

9. Nathan Schwalb (Dror), interview with author, 5.3.1985; Wyman, "Why Auschwitz Was Never Bombed," pp. 37–46.

10. See Weissmandel's letter in Rotkirchen, *The Destruction of Slovakian Jewry,* pp. 237–242; and Fuchs, *I Called and No One Answered,* pp. 126–127.

11. Gruenbaum sent the first of the cables on 27.6.1944; see Z4/14870 and A127/544, CZA.

12. Shertok to DBG, 30.6.1944; meeting with Eden, report memorandum, and witness from Auschwitz, 6.7.1944; Shertok's memorandum, 11.7.1944; all Z4/14870, CZA. Shertok's memorandum is reprinted in Barlas, *Rescue in Days of Holocaust,* pp. 293–295.

13. Wassserstein, *Britain and the Jews of Europe,* p. 254; Randall to Shertok, 15.7.1944, Z4/14870. CZA.

14. McCloy to Phele, 4.7.1944 and 14.8.1944, quoted in Barlas, *Rescue in Days of Holocaust,* p. 293. See also World Jewish Congress, *Unity in Dispersion,* p. 167; Wyman, "Why Auschwitz Was Never Bombed"; Penkower, *The Jews Were Expendable,* p. 193.

15. Linton, 16.8.1944, Z4/15202; Shertok, 29.7.1944, S26/1232, CZA.

16. Cables, Shertok to Gruenbaum, 21.8.1944, S26/1232, and 13.9.1944, S26/1251, CZA.

17. Law to Weizmann, 1.9.1944, Z4/15202, CZA.

18. Epstein, 3.9.1944, S25/286; Gruenbaum to Stalin, 18.1.1945, S26/1232, CZA.

19. Wyman, *The Abandonment of the Jews,* chap. 15; Gilbert, *Auschwitz and the Allies,* chap. 31.

20. Gilbert, *Auschwitz and the Allies*. Dinur, *Attorney General against Eichmann*, pp. 1122–23.
21. *Koteret Rashit*, 15.2.1984, pp. 14, 33.
22. Hoz, ZAC, 6.8.1940, S25/1830; JAE, 23.11.1941, CZA; DBG, MC, 24,30.11.1942, 23/42, LPA.
23. JAE, 29.11.1942 and 6.12.1942, CZA; MPC, 26.1.1943, LPA.
24. JAE, 6.12.1942, CZA.
25. Z. Hermann, oral statement during conference in memory of paratrooper Abba Berditchev, Alonei Abba, 23.2.1985 (text in author's possession).
26. JAE, 6,13.12.1942 and 10.1.1943, CZA; MCC, 24.11.1942, 23/42, LPA.
27. JAE, 14.2.1943, CZA; Bauer, "The Paratroopers," p. 88.
28. Bondi, *The Emissary*, p. 371.
29. Avigur, *With the Generation of the Haganah*, pp. 52–53; Gelber, *Jewish Palestinian Volunteering*, p. 159.
30. Sereni in HS, 5.8.1943, 25/50, HA; Avigur, *With the Generation of the Haganah*, p. 56; Bondi, *The Emissary*, p. 384.
31. HE, 29–30.12.1944, vol. 66, HA; Gelber, *Jewish Palestinian Volunteering*, p. 157.
32. JAE, 13.2.1944, CZA; Bauer, "The Paratroopers," pp. 91–92; see esp. MPC, 26.1.1944, LPA.
33. Bauer, "The Paratroopers," pp. 92–94; Gelber, *Jewish Palestinian Volunteering*, pp. 160–169; Lord Moyne in Wasserstein, *Britain and the Jews of Europe*, pp. 293.
34. Palgi, *A Great Wind Came*, p. 15.
35. Chermesh, *Operation Amsterdam*, pp. 55–56; Palgi, *A Great Wind Came*, p. 17.
36. Golomb in Palgi, *A Great Wind Came*, p. 249; Dobkin, quoted by paratrooper Elie Zohar, speaking at Tel Aviv University, 3.12.1981.
37. Dafni, *Book of the Haganah*, vol. 3a, p. 630; Palgi, *A Great Wind Came*, pp. 54, 60–61.
38. Palgi, *A Great Wind Came*, p. 91.

14. THE END OF THE RESCUE EFFORT

1. JAE, 28.3.1943, CZA.
2. Bader, in *Rescue Activities from Istanbul*, p. 12; HE, 21.1.1943, and HS, 29.4.1943, 14/93, HA; Barlas, JAE, 4.10.1943; Barlas' report, S6/4588, CZA.
3. MS, 15.12.1943, 24/43, LPA.
4. Dobkin, RC, 6.12.1943, S26/1237, CZA; Shind, HS, 16.12.1943, 38/63, HA.
5. Meirov, JAE, 30.1.1944; see also JAE, 20.2.1944, 2.4.1944, CZA; HE, 23–24.2.1944, vol. 70M, HA.
6. JAE, 13,20,27.2.1944 and 5.3.1944, CZA; see esp. Bader, *Sad Missions*, pp. 93–94.

7. Emissaries, HS, 14.6.1944, 4/79, and 6.9.1944, 26/91, HA; Bader, *Sad Missions,* pp. 94–99; Avriel, *Open the Gates,* pp. 114–116.

8. Shind, quoted, JAE, 26.3.1944 and 7.5.1944, CZA; MC, 8.5.1944, 23/44, LPA.

9. JAE, 5.3.1944, 23.7.1944, 10.9.1944; the Agency's commitment; 8.6.1944, S26/1251, CZA.

10. Bader, *Sad Missions,* p. 103–110, 114–117; Barlas, *Rescue in Days of Holocaust,* p. 196; Ofer, *Illegal Immigration,* p. 476.

11. Wasserstein, *Britain and the Jews of Europe,* p. 341; JAE, 20.10.1944, and RC, 3.10.1944, S26/1238a, CZA.

12. Meirov, HE, 11.10.1944, 29/44, HA.

13. Chaim Barlas, interview with author, 19.3.1978.

14. Shind, HS, 6.9.1944, 26/91, HA.

15. JAE, 30.1.1944, CZA.

16. MC, 8.5.1944, 23/44, LPA; JAE, 3.4.1944, CZA.

17. DBG, JAE, 30.1.1944, CZA.

18. Dobkin, JAE, 23.4.1944 and 7.5.1944, CZA.

19. Shertok, JAE, 21.5.1944 and 18.6.1944, CZA.

20. Kaplan, JAE, 23.7.1944; Kaplan to Shertok, 28.7.1944, Z4/14870, CZA.

21. Correspondence, July–August 1944, 26/1251, CZA.

22. Shertok, JAE, 20.10.1944; Shertok in London to JAE, 20.7.1944, S26/1251, CZA.

23. Gilbert, *Auschwitz and the Allies,* p. 312.

24. *New York Times,* 18.8.1944.

25. JAE, 20.10.1944, CZA.

26. Cables, A127/544, CZA.

CONCLUSION

1. See Kovner, *On the Narrow Bridge,* p. 17, for the origins of "like lambs to the slaughter."

2. 47th Histadrut Convention, 5–7.5.1943, vol. 68M, HA. Galili at youth convention, 15.1.1943, quoted in *The Youth Facing the Holocaust of the Diaspora* (n.p., n.d.), p. 37; Rubashov, HS, 15.3.1944, 6/71, HA; Tabenkin in *Zror Michtavim,* 134 (199), 30.3.1943; Gruenbaum in *Moznaim,* 15 (Winter 1943): 258, and 16 (Spring 1943): 250; DBG, JAE, 27.12.1942, CZA; HS, 11.2.1943, 5/30, HA.

3. Shind, HS, 29.4.1943, 14/39, HA; Pomerantz, MS, 24.8.1943, 24/43, LPA.

4. Zuckermann in *Koteret Roshit,* 15.2.1984, p. 33; see esp. Neustadt, *A Year of Extermination,* pp. 8–11; Dobkin, 26.5.1942, vol. 41M, HA; DBG, MS, 24.2.1943, LPA.

5. Sprinzak and Neustadt, MS, 15.12.1943, 24/43, LPA; Bader, HS, 29–30.12.1943, vol. 70M, HA; Shind, HS, 16.12.1943, HA.

6. Chabas, *Letters from the Ghettoes,* p. 45; on refusals to be rescued see also

JAE, 22.8.1943; Daks, 18.10.1943, S6/1850, CZA; MC, 24.8.1943, 23/43, LPA.

7. Ruzka Korczak, interview with author, 23.3.1983. Meir Ya'ari and Yitzhak Tabenkin, who lived in Palestine, were the spiritual leaders of the two youth movements most involved in the revolts in Poland.

8. HS, 15.3.1944, 6/71, HA; see also Klinger, *From a Diary in the Ghetto*, p. 95; Stern, "Contacts between Istanbul and Polish Jewry," p. 150.

9. Dobkin, 46th Histadrut Convention, 26.5.1942, vol. 41M, HA; Pomerantz, MC, 24.8.1943, 23/43, LPA; Ya'ari, 47th Histadrut Convention, vol. 68M; Zerubavel, HS, 29.4.1943, 14/39, HA.

10. Meirov, JAE, 20.2.1944, CZA; HE, 23–24.2.1944, vol. 70M, HA.

11. RC, 20.9.1943, S26/1237, CZA; see also MS, 30.3.1943, 24/43, LPA; Neustadt, *A Year of Extermination*, p. 13.

12. Neustadt, *A Year of Extermination*, p. 7; JAE, 21.9.1944 and 4,11.10.1944, CZA.

13. Pomerantz, MC, 24.8.1943, 23/43, LPA; Neustadt, *A Year of Extermination*, pp. 9–11; JAE, 28.3.1943, CZA; HE, 29–30.12.1943, vol. 69M, HA.

14. Dobkin, 46th Histadrut Convention, 26.5.1942, vol. 41M; Haft, 47th Histadrut Convention, 5–7.5.1943, vol. 68M, HA.

15. Hartglas, "Notes on Aid and Rescue," 24.4.1943, S26/1232, CZA.

16. HE, 11.2.1943 and 29.4.1943, 5/30, HA; Tenenbaum-Tamaroff, *Pages from Fire*, pp. 39, 41.

17. Daks to Histadrut, 13.7.1943, Landau files; Pomerantz, MC, 24.8.1943, 24/43, LPA.

18. See lists in RC file S6/1956, CZA; Kaplan, JAE, 30.4.1944, CZA; Meirov, HS, 19.4.1944, 8/73, HA.

19. MS, 15.12.1943, 24/43, LPA.

20. Daks to Histadrut, 21.10.1943, Landau files. On the struggles see MS, 15.12.1943, 24/43, and MC, 2.2.1944, 23/44, LPA.

21. Kolodni and Meirov, HS, 19.4.1944, 8/73, HA. Numbers of newcomers: 19.5.1944, S26/1251; letters to Gruenbaum, 15.9.1944, S6/4588, and 10.10.1944, S53/1612, CZA; Avriel, *Open the Gates*, pp. 106–107.

22. Magnes, RC, 14.7.1944, S26/1238a; Kaplan, 28.7.1944, S26/1238a; JAE, 16.7.1944; all CZA.

23. Barlas to Gruenbaum, 12.8.1944, S26/1232, CZA.

24. JAE, 23.7.1944, CZA.

25. Schmorak, JAE, 31.12.1944; Gruenbaum, JAE, 14.9.1944, CZA.

26. Shind, HE, 6.9.1944, HA; Avriel, *Open the Gates*, p. 107.

27. Weizmann, *Trial and Error*, pp. 409, 415 (quote); Rabbi Benjamin in *Be'ayot*, January–February 1945, p. 92; Weizmann-Roosevelt meetings: February 1940, July 1942, June 1943; on Weizmann-Churchill see Kedem, "Chaim Weizmann's Political Activity," p. 248.

28. Katznelson, MPC, 16.6.1943, LPA.

29. Gruenbaum, JAE, 23.7.1944, CZA; Yehiel Duvdvani (25.6.1981), Moshe Kol (29.11.1981), Avraham Silberberg (18.6.1980), and Azriel Begun (30.4.1982), interviews with author.

30. Venia Pomerantz, interview with author, 3.11.1984; survey by Tuvia Frieling, chief archivist of the Ben-Gurion Archives, Sde Boker.
31. Frieling, "Ben-Gurion's Involvement in Rescue of Children," p. 19.
32. For the most thorough discussion of that theme, see HS, 15.8.1943, 25/50, HA.
33. Eliezer Livne, interview with Ayala Dan-Caspi, 11.5.1972, p. 7, 191/72, LPA.
34. Dinur, *Zachor,* p. 63.
35. Undated draft corrected in DBG's handwriting, S44/201, CZA, published in daily press 11.7.1944.
36. Gruenbaum, JAE, 20.6.1944; DBG, JAE, 2.7.1944, CZA.
37. Shertok, MS, 27.4.1943, 24/43, LPA; JAE, 7.5.1944, CZA.
38. Golomb, MS, 17.10.1944, 24/44, LPA.
39. DBG, JAE, 6.12.1942; Shertok, JAE, 25.4.1943; Weizmann, quoted in JAE, 27.4.1943; all CZA.
40. DBG, MC, 24.2.1943, 23/42, LPA; and JAE, 6.12.1942, CZA.
41. Gruenbaum, ZAC, 18.1.1943, S25/295, and JAE, 16.1.1944, CZA; HS, 11.2.1943, 5/30; HE, 30.11.1942, 26.5.1943, and 18.11.1943, vol. 68M, HA.
42. DBG, MC, 24.8.1943, 23/43, LPA.
43. DBG, quoted in Frieling, "Ben-Gurion's Involvement in Rescue of Children," pp. 20–21.

BIBLIOGRAPHY

Citations followed by (H) indicate that a work is written in Hebrew, although the title is translated here.

ARCHIVAL SOURCES

Bulletins and collections of letters and information on the situation in Europe, issued by Jewish Agency departments and centers of the pioneering youth movements, are to be found in the Central Zionist Archive, the Labor Party Archives, and the Beth-Hatefutsoth Archive (Tel Aviv).

Central Zionist Archive (Jerusalem)

Barlas, Chaim. "Report on Aid and Rescue Activities in Turkey, October 1943–September 1944." Undated photocopy (H).

David Ben-Gurion's office	File S44
Delegation in Istanbul	L15
Yitzhak Gruenbaum's archive	S127
Yitzhak Gruenbaum's office	S46
Immigration Department	S6
Immigration Department in Portugal and Spain	L31, L32
Jewish Agency Executive minutes	
Eliezer Kaplan's office	S53
National Council (Vaad Leumi) minutes	J1
Palestine Office in Geneva	L17
Political Department	S25
Rescue and Mobilization Fund	J8
Rescue Committee minutes and files	S26
Zionist Actions Committee minutes	S25
Zionist Federation in Geneva	L22
Zionist Federation in London	Z4

Labor Party Archives (Kfar-Saba)

Correspondence with emissaries	Unit 3
Mapai Center minutes	23
Mapai Central Committee and Mapai Political Committee minutes	24

Mapai Secretariat minutes   Unit 24
Mapai World Union minutes   3

Yad Vashem Archives (Jerusalem)

Chaim Posner's office   File P12
Ignacy Schwarzbart's office   M2
Abraham Silberschein's office   M20

Private Collections

Landau files: Minutes of Rescue Committee plenum meetings and letters
    from occupied Europe (courtesy of Mrs. Miriam Dolan [Landau], Tel
    Aviv)
Minutes of Histadrut Committee for Alleviating the Distress of Our Com-
    rades in the Diaspora (courtesy of Moshe Kol, Jerusalem)

Interviews Conducted by the Author and in Her Possession

Aryeh Altman, chairman of Revisionist party in Palestine

Chaim Barlas, head of Immigration Department in Geneva and Istanbul

Azriel Begun, secretary of Mapai World Union

Yitzhak Bermann, British intelligence officer

Nathan Dror (Schwalb), representative of Hechalutz in Geneva

Yehiel Duvdvani, member of Mapai Center

Yehonathan Gruenbaum, youngest son of Yitzhak Gruenbaum

Ze'ev Hadari (Venia Pomerantz), emissary in Istanbul

Zvi Hermann, member of Mossad for Aliya Bet

Joseph Klarman, Revisionist party representative on Rescue Committee

Moshe Kol, member of Histadrut Committee for Alleviating the Distress of
    Our Comrades in the Diaspora

Hillel Kook (alias Peter Bergson), member of Emergency Committee for the
    Rescue of the European Jewry in the United States

Ruzka Korczak, member of underground in Vilna Ghetto

Peretz Leshem (Fritz Lichtenstein), Jewish Agency representative in Iberian
    peninsula

Akiva Levinsky, emissary in Istanbul

Amir (Francis) Offner, liaison officer with Balkan countries, U.S. Information
    Office, Istanbul

Chaim Pazner (Posner), member of Palestine Office in Geneva

Enschel Reiss, member of Rescue Committee

Gerhard Riegner, representative of World Jewish Congress in Geneva

Eliezer Shostak, member of Rescue Committee

Shlomo-Zalman Shragai, member of Rescue Committee

Avraham Silberberg, secretary of Immigration Department

PRESS

Daily newspapers: *Davar, Ha'aretz, Haboker, Hamashkif, Hatzofe, Haz'man*
Periodicals: *Bamishor, Be'ayot, Hado'ar, Ha'olam, Hapo'el Hatzair, Hashomer Hatzair, Koteret Rashit, Kol Hapoel, Kuntress, Moznaim, Zror Michtavim*

COLLECTIONS OF DOCUMENTS, REPORTS, AND OFFICIAL PUBLICATIONS

Arad, Yisrael, Yisrael Gutman, and Abraham Margaliot, eds. *The Holocaust in Documentation.* Jerusalem: Yad Vashem, 1978 (H).

Atias, Moshe. *Knesset Israel in Eretz-Israel.* Jerusalem: National Council (Vaad Leumi), 1944 (H).

Braham, Randolph L., ed. *The Destruction of Hungarian Jewry.* New York, 1963.

Brenner, Uri, ed. *Facing the German Invasion to Eretz-Israel, 1940–1942.* Research brochure D. Yad-Tabenkin, 1981 (H).

Carp, Matatais. *Black Book, 1941–1944.* Vol. 3: *Transnistria.* Bucharest, 1947 (in Rumanian).

Committee for Polish Jewry. *The Holocaust of the Jews of Poland.* Jerusalem, 1940 (H).

Dinur (Kazetnik), Yechiel. *The Attorney General against Eichmann.* Vol. 2: *Testimonies.* Jerusalem: Information Center, 1974 (H).

Gil, Binyamin. *Aliyah Pages: Thirty Years of Immigration to Eretz-Israel, 1919–1949.* Jerusalem: Jewish Agency Aliyah Department, 1950 (H).

Gurevitch, David, et al. *Statistical Handbook of Jewish Palestine.* Jerusalem: Jewish Agency Statistics Department, 1947.

Ha'aretz Almanac, 1942–1943. Tel Aviv, 1943 (H).

Jewish Agency. *The Israeli Economy in Transition.* Tel Aviv, 1946 (H).

———. *Report on the Activities in the Years 1940–1946.* Presented to the 46th Zionist Congress in Basel in 1947. Jerusalem, 1947 (H).

Joint Distribution Committee. *Aiding Jews Overseas.* New York, 1939–40, 1940–41, 1942.

———. *Joint Distribution Committee.* New York, 1944.

———. *The Rescue of Stricken Jews in a World at War.* New York, 1944.

———. *So They May Live Again.* 1945 Annual Report, New York, 1946.

Mintz, Benjamin, and Joseph Klausner, eds. *Book of Horror.* Jerusalem: Jewish Agency Rescue Committee, 1945 (H).

National Council. *Book of Documents, 1878–1948.* Edited by Moshe Atias. Jerusalem, 1963 (H).

———. *Book of the Yishuv Economy.* Tel Aviv, 1947 (H).

Neustadt, Melech, ed. *Destruction and Revolt of the Warsaw Jews.* Tel Aviv: Histadrut Committee for Alleviating the Distress of Our Comrades in the Diaspora, 1947 (H).

Pines, Dan. *The 1943 Yearbook of the Journalists Association.* Tel Aviv, 1943 (H).

Prager, Moshe, with Joint Committee for Help to the Jews in Poland. *The New Deep Mire.* Tel Aviv, 1941 (H).

World Jewish Congress. *Unity in Dispersion: The History of the World Jewish Congress.* New York, 1948.

Zieman, Yehoshua. *Jubilee for the Jewish National Fund.* Jerusalem: Jewish National Fund Publications, 1951 (H).

MEMOIRS, TESTIMONIES, AND COLLECTIONS OF SPEECHES, ESSAYS, AND LETTERS

Adler-Rudel, Shlomo. "A Chronicle of Rescue Efforts." *Leo Baeck Institute Yearbook* 2 (1966): 213–241.

Avigur, Shaul. *With the Generation of the Haganah.* Tel Aviv, 1962 (H).

Avriel, Ehud. *Open the Gates.* Tel Aviv, 1976 (H).

Bader, Menachem. *Sad Missions.* Rev. ed. Tel Aviv, 1978 (H).

Barlas, Chaim. "Meetings in Istanbul." *Masua* 4 (April 1976): 125–133 (H).

Bar-Yehezkel, M. *In the Incomprehensible Circle.* Tel Aviv, 1973 (H).

Ben-Gurion, David. *In the Struggle.* Tel Aviv, 1950 (H).

———. *Mission and Path.* Tel-Aviv, 1942 (H).

Biss, Andre. *Der Storr der Endlösung.* Stuttgart, 1966.

Brand, Joel. *An Emissary of the Condemned.* Tel Aviv, 1957 (H).

Brand, Joel, and Hanzi Brand. *The Devil and the Soul.* Tel Aviv, 1960 (H).

Chabas, Bracha, ed. *Letters from the Ghettos.* Tel Aviv, 1943 (H).

Chermesh, Chaim. *Operation Amsterdam.* Tel Aviv, 1971 (H).

Dinur, Ben-Zion. *Zachor: On the Holocaust and Its Significance.* Jerusalem, 1957 (H).

Dobkin, Eliyahu. *Immigration and Rescue in the Years of the Holocaust.* Jerusalem, 1946 (H).

Eden, Anthony. *The Reckoning: The Memoirs of Anthony Eden.* Cambridge, 1965.

Eivschitz, Yehoshua. *The Influence of Eretz-Israel in the Ghettoes and Concentration Camps.* Kiriat-Ata, 1973 (photocopied edition) (H).

The Flames of Poland. Merchavia, 1940 (H).

Frieder, Emanuel. *To Deliver Their Souls.* Jerusalem, 1986 (H).

Gelber, Yoav. "Reactions in the Zionist Movement and the Yishuv to the Nazi Seizure of Power." *Kovetz Yad-Vashem* 17–18 (1987): 97–138 (H).

———. "Zionist Policy and the Ha'avara Agreement, 1933–1935." *Yalkut Moreshet* 17 (February 1974): 97–152 and 18 (November 1974): 23–100 (H).

Goldmann, Nahum. *A Generation of Destruction and Redemption.* Jerusalem, 1967 (H).

———. *Memoirs.* Jerusalem, 1972 (H).

Gruenbaum, Yitzhak. *In Days of Destruction and Holocaust.* Jerusalem, 1946 (H).

Hacohen, David. *Time to Tell.* Tel Aviv, 1974 (H).

Hecht, Ben. *Perfidy.* New York, 1961.

Hirschmann, A. Ira. *Caution to the Wind.* New York, 1962.

——. *Life Line to a Promised Land.* New York, 1946.

In Days of Holocaust. Hechalutz emissaries' report. Tel Aviv, 1940.

Les Juifs en Europe, 1939–1945. Paris: Centre de Documentation Juive Contemporaine, 1949.

Kapel, Schmuel-Rene. *Jewish Struggle in Occupied France.* Jerusalem, 1981 (H).

Kasztner, Yisrael. "Report of the Jewish Rescue Committee in Budapest, 1942–1945." In *Kasztner's Truth.* Haifa, 1983, pp. 43–206 (H).

Katznelson, Berl. *Writings.* 12 vols. Tel Aviv, 1950 (H).

Klinger, Chaika. *From a Diary in the Ghetto.* Tel Aviv, 1959 (H).

Kochva, Adina. *In the Pioneering Underground in Occupied Holland.* Tel Aviv, 1969 (H).

Kol, Moshe. "Aid and Rescue Efforts." *Masua* 2 (September 1974): 30–42 (H).

Kollek, Teddy. *One Jerusalem.* Tel Aviv, 1979 (H).

Korniansky, Joseph. *An Emissary of the Pioneers.* Haifa, 1979 (H).

Kovner, Abba. *On the Narrow Bridge.* Edited by Shalom Lurie. Tel Aviv, 1981 (H).

Kurtz, Ya'acov. *Book of Witness.* Tel Aviv, 1944 (H).

Landau, Michael. "The Yishuv in Times of Storm." *Masua* 5 (April 1977): 179–198 (H).

Leshem, Peretz. "On the Agency's Mission in the Iberian Peninsula." *Dapim Lecheker Hasho'a Ve'hamered* 2/a (1970): 309–313 (H).

Locker, Berl. *In the Struggle for Existence and Rebirth.* Jerusalem, 1963 (H).

Mapai World Union. *In the Bondage of War.* Minutes of MWU conference, Ayanot, 1940. Tel Aviv, 1941 (H).

Mastbojm, Joel. *Sixty Days in Hitler's Poland.* Tel Aviv, 1940 (H).

Meinerzhagen, Richard. *Middle Eastern Diary, 1917–1956.* Haifa, 1973 (H).

Meir, Golda. *My Life.* Tel Aviv, 1975 (H).

Neumann, Yirmiahu (Oscar). *In the Shadow of Death.* Tel Aviv, 1958 (H).

Neustadt, Melech. *A Year of Extermination.* Tel Aviv, 1944 (H).

Palgi, Joel. *A Great Wind Came.* Tel Aviv, 1977 (H).

Reiffer, Manfred. *The Death Journey.* Tel Aviv, 1946 (H).

Reiss, Enschel. "Chapters of the Aid and Rescue Activities." *Dapim Lecheker Hasho'a Ve'hamered* 2 (1952): 19–37 (H).

——. *In the Storms of Our Time.* Tel Aviv, 1983 (H).

Remba, Isaac, ed. *Shimshon Unitzmann.* Tel Aviv, 1962 (H).

Repetur, Berl. *Incessantly.* Tel Aviv, 1973 (H).

Rescue Activities from Istanbul, 1940–1945. Minutes of an emissaries' conference, 1968. Jerusalem, 1969 (H).

Ringelblum, Emanuel. *Notes from the Warsaw Ghetto.* Warsaw, 1952 (Yiddish).

Rosenfeld, Shalom. *Criminal File 124/53.* Tel Aviv, 1956 (H).

Schneerson, Fischel. *Historical Psychology of Holocaust and Revival.* Tel Aviv, 1965 (H).

Schwarzbaum, Alf. "Help from Switzerland, 1940–1945." *Masua* 2 (September 1974): 138–145 (H).

Tenenbaum-Tamaroff, Mordechai. *Pages from Fire.* Tel Aviv, 1948 (H).

Tevet, Shabtai. *The Zeal of David.* Vol. 3. Tel Aviv, 1987 (H).

Weichert, Michael. *Jewish Mutual Aid.* Tel Aviv, 1962 (Yiddish).

Weissman, Yitzhak. *In the Face of Evil.* Tel Aviv, 1968 (H).

Weissmandel, Michael Dov-Beer. *In Distress.* Jerusalem, 1960 (H).

Weizmann, Chaim. *Trial and Error.* Jerusalem and Tel Aviv, 1953 (H).

Wise, Stephen S. *Challenging Years.* New York, 1949.

———. *Personal Letters of Stephen S. Wise.* Edited by Y. W. Polier and Y. W. Wise. Boston, 1956.

Yaffe, Leib. *Writings, Letters, and Diaries.* Jerusalem, 1964 (H).

Yishai, Moshe. *Delegate without a Title.* Tel Aviv, 1950 (H).

Zerubavel, Ya'acov, ed. *Chantze and Frumka.* Tel Aviv, 1945 (H).

Ziemand, David. "Rescue Mission." *Masua* 4 (April 1976): 89–124 (H).

Zur, Ya'acov. *The Day Approaches.* Jerusalem, 1979 (H).

Zweig, Ronald W. *Britain and Palestine during the Second World War.* London, 1986.

Zygielbojm-Book. New York, 1947 (Yiddish).

RESEARCH

Adler, Zelig. "The U.S., Palestine, and the Holocaust." *Gesher* 1 (April 1975): 12–19 (H).

Arad, Yitzchak. "Jewish Refugees in Vilna on the Eve of World War II." *Kovetz Yad-Vashem* 9 (1973): 165–176 (H).

Avneri, Aryie L. *The First Decade of Jewish "Illegal" Immigration to Mandatory Palestine, 1934–1944.* Tel Aviv, 1985 (H).

Avni, Chaim. *Spain and the Jews in the Days of the Holocaust and the Emancipation.* Tel Aviv, 1975 (H).

Barlas, Chaim. "Operation Lithuania-Immigration." *Dapim Lecheker Hasho'a Vehamered,* 2/a (1970): 246–255 (H).

———. *Rescue in Days of Holocaust.* Tel Aviv, 1975 (H).

Bar-Zohar, Michael. *David Ben-Gurion.* Tel Aviv, 1975 (H).

Bauer, Yehuda. *American Jewry and the Holocaust: The American Jewish Joint Distribution Committee, 1939–1945.* Detroit, 1981.

———. *Diplomacy and Underground in Zionist Policy 1939–1945.* Merchavia, 1963 (H).

———. "From Biltmore to Paris—The Influence of the Holocaust on Zionist Policy 1942–1946." *Sixth World Congress of Jewish Studies.* Vol. 2. Jerusalem, 1976, pp. 471–475 (H).

———. *The Holocaust in Historical Perspective.* Tel Aviv, 1982 (H).

———. "Jewish Paratroopers in Europe in World War II." *Skira Hodshit* (October 1979): 30–36 (H).

———. "Joel Brand's Mission." *Yalkut Moreshet* 26 (November 1978): 23–60 (H).

———. "The Paratroopers and the Defense Plan." *Yalkut Moreshet* 1 (November 1963): 86–94 (H).

———. "When Did They Know?" *Midstream* 14 (April 1968): 51–58.

Bein, Alex. *The History of Zionist Settlement*. Tel Aviv, 1954 (H).

Beit-Zvi, B. Shabtai. *Post-Ugandan Zionism in the Holocaust Crisis*. Tel Aviv, 1977 (H).

Ben, Joseph. "The Holocaust of the Jews in Greece." M.A. thesis, Tel Aviv University, 1977 (H).

Berger, Mordechai. *Mobilization and Rescue Fund*. Jerusalem: Taxation Museum, 1970 (H).

———. *Ransom Fund*. Jerusalem: Taxation Museum, 1964 (H).

Bondi, Ruth. *The Emissary: The Life and Death of Enzo Sereni*. Tel Aviv, 1974 (H).

Braham, L. Randolph. *Politics of Genocide: The Holocaust in Hungary*. 2 vols. New York, 1981.

Browning, Christopher. *The Final Solution and the German Foreign Office*. New York and London, 1978.

Cana'an, Chaviv. "The Jewish Community in Palestine during World War II." *Masua* 4 (April 1976): 134–162 (H).

———. *200 Days of Anxiety: Palestine Facing Rommel's Army*. Tel Aviv, n.d. (H).

———. *War of the Press: The Struggle of the Hebrew Press against the British Mandate*. Jerusalem, 1969 (H).

Carpi, Daniel. "The Jews of Greece in the Holocaust, 1941–1943." *Yalkut Moreshet* 31 (April 1981): 7–39 (H).

———. "The Mufti of Jerusalem, Haj Amin el-Huseini, and His Political Activity during the Second World War," *Hazionut* 9 (1984): 286–316 (H).

Eck, Nathan. "Jews for Germans." *Dapim Lecheker Hasho'a Ve'hamered* 2/b (1973): 23–49 (H).

———. "Rescue Attempts by Means of Latin American Passports." *Kovetz Yad-Vashem* 1 (1957): 93–111 (H).

Feingold, Henry L. *Politics of Rescue: The Roosevelt Administration and the Holocaust, 1938–1945*. New York, 1970.

———. *The Roosevelt Administration and the Effort to Save the Jews of Hungary*. Hungarian Jewish Studies, no. 2, edited by Randolph L. Braham. New York, 1969, pp. 211–253.

Friedman, S. Mordechai. "Political-Public Reaction of American Jewry to the Holocaust, 1939–1945." Ph.D. diss., Tel Aviv University, 1985 (H).

Frieling, Tuviah. "Ben-Gurion's Involvement in the Rescue of Children and in the Debate on Absorption, November 1942–May 1945." M.A. thesis, Hebrew University of Jerusalem, 1984 (H).

Fuchs, Avraham. *I Called and No One Answered*. New York, privately published, 1983 (H).

Gelber, Yoav. "Hebrew Press in Palestine on the Destruction of European Jewry 1941–1942." *Dapim Lecheker Hasho'a Ve'hamered* 2/a (1970): 30–58 (H).

———. *Jewish Palestinian Volunteering in the British Army during the Second World War*. Vol. 3. Jerusalem, 1983 (H).

————. "Zionist Policy and the Fate of European Jewry, 1939–1942." *Kovetz Yad-Vashem* 13 (1980): 129–158 (H).

————. "Zionist Policy and the Fate of European Jewry, 1943–1944." *Studies in Zionism* 17 (Spring 1983): 153–162.

Gilbert, Martin. *Auschwitz and the Allies.* New York, 1981.

Gorni, Yosef. "Strength in Weakness—The Personality of Chaim Weizmann." In *The Dream and Its Fulfillment: Thinking and Practice in Zionism.* Tel Aviv, 1979 (H).

Gutman, Yisrael. *The Jews of Warsaw, 1939–1943, Ghetto-Underground Revolt.* Tel Aviv, 1977 (H).

Hadar, David. "The Allies' Attitude to Brand's Mission." *Molad* 19–20 (June–July 1971): 112–125 (H).

Harussi, Emanuel. *Book of the Mobilization and Rescue Fund.* Tel Aviv, 1950 (H).

Hausner, Gideon. *Justice in Jerusalem.* New York, 1966.

Hilberg, Raul. *The Destruction of European Jewry.* New York, 1973.

Hinsley, F. H., et al. *British Intelligence in the Second World War.* 2 vols. London, 1979.

Horowitz, Dan, and Moshe Lissak. *The Origins of the Israeli Polity.* Tel Aviv, 1977.

Horowitz, David. *The Palestinian Economy in the Making.* Tel Aviv, 1944 (H).

Horwitz, Ariel. "Menachem Bader's Mission in Istanbul and the Contacts of Hashomer-Hatzair with European Jewry." *Yalkut Moreshet* 35 (April 1983): 152–202 (H).

Kedem, Menachem, "Chaim Weizmann's Political Activity during World War II." Ph.D. diss., Hebrew University of Jerusalem, 1973 (H).

Kolatt, Yisrael. "Ben-Gurion, Image and Greatness." *Molad* 22 (December 1971): 340–351 (H).

Kolb, Eberhard. *Bergen-Belsen.* Hannover, 1962.

Kulka, Erich. "Five Escapes from Auschwitz." *Yalkut Moreshet* 3 (December 1964): 23–38 (H).

Landau, Michael. "The Yishuv in Times of Storm." *Masua* 5 (April 1977): 179–198 (H).

Laqueur, Ze'ev (Walter). *The Terrible Secret.* London, 1980.

Laqueur, Ze'ev (Walter), and Richard Breitman. *Breaking the Silence.* New York, 1986.

Lavi, Theodor. *Rumanian Jewry Struggling for Rescue.* Jerusalem, 1965 (H).

Lewis, Bernard. *Semites and Anti-Semites.* New York, 1986.

Lorberbaum, Abraham. "The Hebrew Press in Eretz-Israel in the Year 1942—An Intensive Silencing?" *Yalkut Moreshet* 39 (May 1985): 152–180 (H).

Morgenstern, Aryeh. "The Agency's Joint Rescue Committee, 1943–1945." *Yalkut Moreshet* 13 (June 1971): 60–103 (H).

Morse, D. Arthur. *While Six Million Died.* New York, 1967.

Muskat, Aryeh. "Spain and Its Attitude toward Jews during the Second World War." *Masua* 5 (April 1977): 146–151 (H).

Niv, David. *The Struggles of the Etzel.* Tel Aviv, 1976 (H).

Ofer, Daliah. "Activities of 'the Palestinian Delegation' in Istanbul 1943." In

Rescue Attempts and Efforts during the Holocaust. Jerusalem, 1976, pp. 360–370 (H).

——. "Aid and Rescue Activities of the Palestinian Delegation in Istanbul, 1943." *Yalkut Moreshet* 15 (November 1972): 33–58 (H).

——. "Illegal Immigration to Palestine during World War II, 1939–1942." Ph.D. diss., Hebrew University of Jerusalem, 1981 (H).

Ophir, Ephraim. "Was It Possible to Save 70,000 Jews from Transnistria?" *Yalkut Moreshet* 33 (June 1982): 103–128 (H).

Penkower, Monti N. *The Jews Were Expendable: Free World Diplomacy and the Holocaust.* Urbana, Ill., 1984.

Porat, Dina. "Al Domi: Palestinian Intellectuals and the Holocaust, 1943–1945." *Studies in Zionism* 5 (Spring 1984): 97–124 (H).

Preiss, Aryeh. "Reactions of the Underground Movements in Palestine to the Extermination of European Jewry." *Masua* 8 (April 1980): 51–82 (H).

Reitlinger, Gerald. *The Final Solution.* London, 1968.

Rotkirchen, Livia. *The Destruction of Slovakian Jewry.* Jerusalem, 1961 (H).

——. "Routes of Escape during World War II." In *Jewish Resistance in the Holocaust Period.* Jerusalem, 1970, pp. 322–327 (H).

Shacham, Avigdor. "The Ghettos in Transnistria, 1941–1944." Ph.D. diss., Hebrew University of Jerusalem, 1980 (H).

Shapira, Anita. *Berl.* Tel Aviv, 1980 (H). English trans. Cambridge, 1985.

Shapira, David. "The Zionist Emergency Committee in the United States, 1938–1943." Ph.D. diss., Hebrew University of Jerusalem, 1982 (H).

Shechtman, Yehiel B. "The Transnistria Reservation." *Yivo Annual of Jewish Social Science* 8 (1953): 178–198.

Shelach, Menachem. "The Murder of Jews in Croatia by the Germans and Their Assistants in World War II." Ph.D. diss., Tel Aviv University, 1980 (H).

Shepherd, Naomi. *Wilfrid Israel, German Jewry's Secret Ambassador.* London, 1984.

Shimoni, Gideon. *Jews and Zionism: The South-African Experience, 1910–1967.* Cape Town, 1980.

Sluzky, Yehuda. "The Yishuv in Palestine and Help to European Jewry in the Holocaust Years." In *Jewish Resistance in the Holocaust Period.* Jerusalem, 1970, pp. 327–336 (H).

Sompolinsky, Meir. "Jewish Leadership in Britain, the British Government, and the Holocaust." Ph.D. diss., Bar-Ilan University, 1977 (H).

Stern, Eliyahu. "Contacts between the Delegation in Istanbul and Polish Jewry." *Yalkut Moreshet* 39 (May 1985): 135–152 (H).

——. "Tabenkin's Cable to the Pioneering Underground in Bendin." *Mibifnim* 41 (Autumn 1980): 323–325 (H).

Sykes, Christopher. *Cross Roads to Israel.* London, 1965.

Tal, Uriel. "On the Research of the Holocaust and Genocide." *Kovetz Yad-Vashem* 13 (1980): 7–43 (H).

Tartakower, Aryeh. "Political Activity for Polish Jews on German Soil in World War II." *Gal-Ed* 6 (1982): 167–184 (H).

Tenenbaum, Joseph. *The Kingdom of Race and Evil.* Jerusalem, 1961 (H).

Terek-Yablonka, Hanna. "The Europa Plan." M.A. thesis, Hebrew University of Jerusalem, 1984.

Tevet, Shabtai. *The Zeal of David.* Vol. 3. Tel Aviv, 1987 (H).

Vagman-Eshkoli, Chava. "The Attitude of the Jewish Leadership in Palestine toward the Rescue of European Jewry." *Yalkut Moreshet* 24 (October 1977): 87–116 (H).

———. "The Debate on Mobilizing Funds for Rescue Activities in 1943." *Dapim Lecheker Hasho'a Ve'hamered* 3 (1984): 123–138 (H).

———. "The Transnistria Plan—A Chance for Rescue or a Fraud?" *Yalkut Moreshet* 27 (April 1979): 155–171 (H).

Vago, Bella. "The British Government and the Fate of Hungarian Jewry in 1944." In *Rescue Attempts and Efforts during the Holocaust.* Jerusalem, 1976, pp. 168–172 (H).

———. "Intelligence Activities and the Brand Mission." *Kovetz Yad-Vashem* 10 (1975): 84–93 (H).

Wasserstein, Bernard. *Britain and the Jews of Europe 1939–1945.* London, 1979.

Wyman, S. David. *The Abandonment of the Jews.* New York, 1984.

———. "Why Auschwitz Was Never Bombed." *Commentary,* May 1978, pp. 37–46.

Yahil, Leny. *The Rescue of the Jews in Denmark.* Jerusalem, 1967 (H).

Zariz, Ruth. "Rescue from Holland by Means of Confirming Certificates." *Yalkut Moreshet* 23 (April 1977): 135–162 (H).

Zeinfeld, Chava. "The Awareness of the Jewish Community and Its Leadership of the Approaching Holocaust, as Reflected in the Hebrew Press in Palestine, 1939–1942." M.A. thesis, Tel Aviv University, 1987.

Zweig, Ronald W. *Britain and Palestine during the Second World War,* London, 1986.

BIOGRAPHICAL GLOSSARY

Adler-Rudel, Shlomo. Rumania, 1894–Jerusalem, 1967. A social worker. Director of Jewish welfare organizations in Berlin, 1919–1934. Secretary general of the German Jews' Organization, 1934–1936. Vice-president of the Zionist Federation in Great Britain, 1936–1945. Director of the Jewish Agency's International Relations Department, Jerusalem, 1949–1955.

Agronsky (later Agron), Gershon. Russia, 1893–Jerusalem, 1959. Joined the Jewish Battalion in World War I. Emigrated in 1924. Founder and first editor of the *Palestine Post,* later the *Jerusalem Post,* the only English-language daily in Israel, 1932–1955. Mayor of Jerusalem, 1955–1959.

Aharonovich (later Aranne), Zalman. Russia, 1899–Israel, 1970. First secretary of Mapai, 1930 and again from 1948 to 1951. Held central positions in the Histadrut and the Zionist Actions Committee. Member of the Knesset, 1949–1969. Minister without portfolio, 1953–1955; minister of culture and education, 1955–1960, 1963–1969.

Altman, Aryeh. Russia, 1902–Jerusalem, 1982. Emigrated in 1925. Joined the Revisionist party while living in the U.S.A., 1926–1937. Official leader of the Revisionist party in Palestine (1937), head of its political world office after Z. Jabotinsky's death, in 1940, and chairman of its world presidium, 1945–1947. Member of the Knesset, 1951–1965.

Altman, Tossia. Poland, 1918–1943. A leader of the Hashomer Hatzair youth movement in Poland. Left for Lithuania at the beginning of the war; returned to Nazi-occupied Poland in December 1939 to rebuild the movement. Infiltrated ghettos to maintain contacts and smuggle arms. Fought in the Warsaw ghetto revolt and was killed shortly afterward.

Avriel, Ehud. Vienna, 1917–Israel, 1980. Emigrated in 1938. Member of the kibbutz Neot Mordechai. An emissary of the Jewish Agency's Political Department in Istanbul for rescue matters (1942–1946) and in Europe for arms acquisition (1946–1948). Director general of the Prime Minister's Office, 1951–52. A Mapai member of the Knesset, 1955–1957. Consul and ambassador to many countries, 1957–1961, 1965–1968, 1974–1976. Deputy director general of the Foreign Ministry, 1961–1965. Chairman of the Zionist Actions Committee, 1968–1971.

Bader, Menachem. Galicia, 1895–Israel, 1985. Emigrated in 1920. A founder of the kibbutz Mizra. A leader of Hashomer Hatzair. Held central positions in the Histadrut and the Zionist Actions Committee in the 1920s and 1930s. An emissary in Istanbul during World War II. Director general of the Ministry of Labor and Construction, 1948–49. A Mapai member of the Knesset, 1949–1951. Director general of the Ministry of Development, 1955–1961.

Barlas, Chaim. Lithuania, 1898–Jerusalem, 1984. Director of the Palestine Office in Warsaw, 1919–1925. Director of the Jewish Agency's Immigration Department (1926–1948) and its emissary to Geneva (1939–1940) and to Istanbul (1940–1945). Director general of the Ministry of Immigration, 1948–49.

Bart, Aharon. Berlin, 1890–Israel, 1957. A leader of the Jewish community and of the Mizrachi movement in Berlin. Emigrated in 1933. Deputy chairman (from 1938) and director general (from 1947) of the Anglo-Palestine Bank. Chairman of fund-raising committees in the Yishuv in the 1930s, including the Mobilization and Rescue Fund, 1942–1945.

Ben-Gurion, David. Russia, 1886–Israel, 1973. Emigrated in 1906. Secretary general of the Histadrut, 1921–1935. Chairman of the Jewish Agency, 1935–1948. Prime minister of Israel, 1948–1953 and 1955–1963.

Benjamin, Rabbi. *See* Rabbi Benjamin.

Ben-Zvi, Yitzhak. Russia, 1884–Israel, 1963. Emigrated in 1907. An initiator of Jewish self-defense, first in Russia, then in Palestine. Promoted recruitment in the Jewish Battalion in World War I. A Labor leader; chairman and president of the National Council, 1931–1948. Second president of Israel, 1952–1963. A scholar and historian.

Berlin, Meir. Russia, 1880–Jerusalem, 1949. A writer and rabbi. Lived in the U.S.A., 1914–1924. A leader (1911) and president (1937–1949) of the World Mizrachi Organization. Founder (1936) and editor of the Religious Zionists' daily, *Hatzofe*. Member of the National Council (1944–1949) and the Zionist Actions Committee, 1929–1931. Member of the Jewish National Fund board, 1925–1949. Initiated publication of the *Talmudic Encyclopedia*. Bar-Ilan University is named after him.

Braginsky, Yehuda. Russia, 1897–Israel, 1979. Member of Hechalutz in Poland. Emigrated in 1929. An Aliya Bet activist, 1934–1948. Member of the kibbutz Yagur (1930–1979), the Zionist Actions Committee, and the Histadrut Executive in the 1930s. Head of the Jewish Agency Executive's Absorption Department, 1948–1960.

Chazan, Ya'acov. Lithuania, 1899. A founder and leader of the Hashomer Hatzair youth movement in Poland, the Mapam party in Israel, and the kibbutz Mishmar Ha'emek. Member of the Histadrut central bodies, the Zionist Actions Committee, and the Knesset (1949–1977). Received the Israel Prize in 1989 for his lifelong spiritual leadership.

Dafni, Reuven. Yugoslavia, 1913. Emigrated in 1936. Joined the British army in 1940 and parachuted into occupied Europe in 1944. A Haganah emissary in the U.S.A., 1946–47. Consul and ambassador in many countries, 1965–1973, 1975–1979. Head of the North American desk in the Foreign Ministry, 1973–1975. Since 1982 vice-chairman of Yad Vashem, the Holocaust Remembrance Authority.

Dayan, Moshe. Palestine, 1915–Israel, 1981. Born in Degania, the first kibbutz like settlement in Palestine, and raised in Nahallal, the first Mosh collective village. Member of the Haganah, 1933–1948. Lost an eye in action in Syria, 1941. Commander of the Jerusalem regiment in the war of independence. Chief of the Southern and Northern commands, 1950–1957. Chief of staff, 1954–1957. Member of the Knesset, 1959–1981. Minister of agriculture (1959–1964) and defense (1967–1974); foreign minister, 1977–1979.

Dinaburg (later Dinur), Ben-Zion. Russia, 1884–Israel, 1973. Emigrated in 1921. Professor of Jewish history at the Hebrew University in Jerusalem, 1936. Minister of culture and education, 1951–1955. A founder of Yad Vashem (the Holocaust Remembrance Authority) and chairman of its council, 1953–1959. Member of the Israeli Academy of Sciences.

Dobkin, Eliyahu. Russia, 1898–Israel, 1976. An activist in the Hechalutz youth movement in Russia and Poland. Emigrated in 1932. Member of the Zionist Actions Committee, 1923–1932, and of Mapai central bodies in the 1930s. Head of the Histadrut Immigration Department, 1933–1945. Cohead (with M. Shapira) of the Jewish Agency Executive's Immigration Department, 1935–1945; head of its Youth and Pioneer Department, 1945–46. Chairman of the Foundation Fund Board, 1956–1961.

Duvdvani, Yehiel. Russia, 1896–Israel, 1987. Emigrated in 1923. A founder of the kibbutzim Givat-Hashlosha (1925) and Einat (1952). Member of Mapai Center for decades. An emissary of the Yishuv to survivors in Italy, 1944–1947. Secretary of Mapai (1948–49) and member of the Knesset, 1949–1951. Chairman of Mekorot, the Israeli water sources company, 1950–1962.

Eliash, Mordechai. Russia, 1892–London, 1950. Emigrated in 1919. Legal adviser of the National Council, 1921–1947. Represented the Yishuv on several mandatory and international commissions (1921, 1929, 1930, 1936, 1946, and 1947). First president of the Jewish Lawyers' Association in Palestine. A special diplomatic emissary in Britain from 1949 until his sudden death.

Epstein (later Eilat), Eliyahu. Russia, 1903. Emigrated in 1924. Head of the Middle East desk in the Jewish Agency's Political Department, 1934–1945. A representative of the Jewish Agency in Washington, 1945–1948. Ambassador to the U.S.A. (1949–50) and to Britain (1950–1959). President of the Hebrew University in Jerusalem, 1962–1968, and of the Red Star of David (parallel to the Red Cross) and the Israeli-Asian Friendship Association in the 1970s.

Fleischmann, Gisi. Bratislava, 1894–Auschwitz, 1944. A Zionist leader in Slovakia. Chairwoman of the Women's International Zionist Organization (WIZO). A representative of the Joint Distribution Committee and the World Jewish Congress in Slovakia. A leader of the Working Group in Slovakia, 1941–1944. Caught by the Germans in October 1944 and sent to Auschwitz.

Galili, Israel. Russia, 1911–Israel, 1986. Emigrated in 1914. A founder of the kibbutz Na'an, 1930. Joined the Haganah in 1927, becoming commander in 1935, commander in chief in 1947. A member of the Knesset, 1949–1977; active in central Knesset committees. Minister without portfolio and minister of information, 1965–1977. An unofficial adviser to the prime ministers on defense and security affairs.

Goldmann, Nahum. Lithuania, 1895–Switzerland, 1982. Initiated and published *Encyclopedia Judaica*, 1923–1933. Representative of the Jewish Agency at the League of Nations, 1935. Cofounder (with S. Wise) of the World Jewish Congress (1936) and of the American Emergency Committee for Zionist Affairs (1940). President of the World Zionist Organization (1956–1968), the World Jewish Congress (1949–1977), and the Claims Conference (1951–1965), which became (in 1965) the Memorial Foundation for Jewish Culture (1965–1977).

Golomb, Eliyahu. Russia, 1893–Tel Aviv, 1945. A founder of the Jewish Battalion in World War I. From 1921 until his death, a central leader of the Haganah (was an unofficial defense minister in the prestate decades), Mapai, the Histadrut, and the National Council.

Griffle, Ya'acov. Poland, 1900–New York, 1962. Emigrated in 1939. An emissary of Agudat Yisrael to Istanbul (1943–44) and Rumania (1944) for rescue activities. After the war helped find Jewish orphans; in the 1950s continued this work from New York in the Children's Salvation Association.

Gruenbaum, Yitzhak. Poland, 1879–Israel, 1970. A member of the Polish Sejm, 1919–1932. Emigrated in 1933. Head of the Jewish Agency Executive's

Labor Department, 1935–1948. Head of the Rescue Committee, 1943–1947. Minister of the interior, 1948.

Guri, Chaim. Tel Aviv, 1922. A poet, translator, and publicist. Volunteered for the Palmach, the Haganah elite units, in 1942. A Haganah emissary to Europe for illegal immigration, 1947. A Palmach fighter in the war of independence, 1948–49. *The* poet of "the Palmach Generation."

Haft, Avraham. Russia, 1892–Israel, 1965. Emigrated in 1913. A member of Mapai Center, the Histadrut Executive, and central fund-raising committees of the Yishuv. A founder of Degania B (1920), near Degania, the first collective settlement in Palestine.

Hartglas, Apollinary M. Poland, 1883–Israel, 1953. A member of the Polish Sejm, 1919–1930, and last president of the Zionist Organization in Poland before World War II. A member of the first Jewish council in the Warsaw ghetto; escaped and reached Palestine in 1940. Political secretary of the Rescue Committee, 1943–1947.

Hecht, Ben. New York, 1893–1964. An author, playwright, and journalist. During World War II worked with H. Kook on the Emergency Committee for the Rescue of European Jews and in organizing illegal immigration. In 1947 the Etzel named an illegal immigration ship after him.

Herzl, Theodor (Benjamin-Ze'ev). Budapest, 1860–Austria, 1904. The father of political Zionism, founder of the World Zionist Organization. A law student, publicist, journalist, author, and playwright. In 1896 published *The Jewish State,* a plan for the establishment of a Jewish state, which led to the first Zionist Congress in Basel, 1897, under his presidency.

Hirschmann, Ira. U.S.A., 1901. A banker, businessman, author, and financial supporter of musical and educational enterprises. A special assistant to the National War Labor Board (1942–1944), President Roosevelt's special representative of the War Refugee Board in Turkey (1944), and a special inspector-general of the United Nations Relief and Rehabilitation Agency (1946).

Hoz, Dov. Russia, 1894–Palestine, 1940. Emigrated in 1906. An officer in the Turkish army and a sergeant in the Jewish Battalion in World War I. Between the wars was one of the main leaders of the Haganah and of the Labor movement in Palestine, and its representative in the British Labour Party. An initiator of Jewish aviation. Deputy mayor of Tel Aviv, 1935–1940. D. Hoz, E. Golomb, S. Meirov (Avigur), and M. Shertok (Sharett) were brothers-in-law.

el-Husseini, Haj Amin. Palestine, 1895–Lebanon, 1974. A political and religious leader of the Palestinian Arabs. Mufti (religious leader) of Muslim Jerusalem, 1921. President of the Supreme Muslim Council (1922) and the

Higher Arab Committee (1936). In 1937, when the British outlawed the latter, he fled to Syria, and in 1939 to Iraq and Iran. Tried to further the Arab cause by meetings with Hitler and Mussolini, 1941–1943. From 1951 was active in pan-Arab conferences and organizations, but with lessening influence.

Jabotinsky, Eri (Theodor). Russia, 1910–Israel, 1969. Son of Z. Jabotinsky. Emigrated in 1935. Leader of Betar, the Revisionists' youth movement, in Palestine, 1935–1940. Worked with H. Kook in the U.S.A. on the Committee for a Jewish Army and the Emergency Committee for the Rescue of European Jews, 1940–1944. Accompanied I. Hirschmann to Turkey in connection with the War Refugee Board, 1944. After the war, a professor of mathematics.

Jabotinsky, Ze'ev (Vladimir). Russia, 1880–New York, 1940. A founder of the Jewish Battalion in World War I and of the Haganah in 1920. Founder and leader of the Revisionist movement and party, 1925–1940; head of its youth movement, Betar, 1931–1940. Member of central Zionist committees, 1921. Established the New Zionist Organization, 1935, which later became the Herut (Freedom) party, and the core of Likud. A gifted writer, speaker, and linguist.

Joseph, Dov (Bernard). Canada, 1899–Jerusalem, 1980. Joined the Jewish Battalion in World War I. Emigrated in 1921. Legal adviser of the Jewish Agency's Political Department and replaced its head, M. Shertok, when needed, 1936–1945. Governor of Jerusalem in the war of independence. A Mapai member of the Knesset, 1949–1966. Minister of supply and rationing (1949–50), trade and industry (1951–52), and development (1952–1955). Treasurer of the Jewish Agency, 1956–1961. Minister of justice, 1961–1966.

Kaplan, Eliezer. Russia, 1891–Israel, 1952. Emigrated in 1923. A central leader of Mapai. Treasurer and member of the Jewish Agency Executive, 1933–1948. First minister of finance, 1948–1952. Instrumental in building Israel's economy.

Kasztner, Yisrael (Rudolf, or Rezso in Hungarian). Transylvania, 1906–Tel Aviv, 1957. A jurist and publicist, a Zionist leader in Hungary and Rumania. As a member of the Aid and Rescue Committee in Budapest, 1943–1945, negotiated with the Gestapo for rescue. Emigrated in 1948. Became spokesman for the Ministry of Trade and Industry, a senior official in the Information Department of the Prime Minister's Office, and was in charge of press and broadcasts in Hungarian, 1949–1954. Was accused in 1954 of collaboration with the Nazis. His trial, 1954–1957, shook the country. Was found guilty by a district court, murdered under the impact of the verdict, and acquitted posthumously by Israel's Supreme Court in 1958.

Katznelson, Berl. Russia, 1887–Jerusalem, 1944. The spiritual leader of the Labor movement. Emigrated in 1909. A founder of Mapai; the Histadrut;

Davar, the Labor movement daily (which he edited until his death); and Am Oved, its publication house.

Klarman, Joseph. Poland, 1909–Israel, 1987. Secretary general and vice-president of the Revisionist movement in Poland, 1934–1939, and its delegate to the Zionist congresses. Emigrated in 1940. Member of the Rescue Committee (1943), an emissary of the Revisionists in Turkey (1944), and an Aliya Bet organizer in the Balkans (1944–1948). A publicist and editor.

Klinger, Chaika (Chaya). Poland, 1917–Israel, 1958. A leader of the Hashomer Hatzair youth movement in Poland and of the armed underground in Będzin. Escaped at the end of 1943, after the revolt and the liquidation of the ghetto, reached Slovakia, and in March 1944 gave full and shocking reports in Palestine. Joined the kibbutz Ha'ogen and raised a family. Committed suicide on the fifteenth anniversary of the Warsaw ghetto revolt.

Kollek, Teddy. Vienna, 1911. Emigrated in 1934. A founder of the kibbutz Ein-Gev. An emissary of Hechalutz to Europe, 1938–1940. As a member of the Jewish Agency's Political Department, 1940–1947, handled contacts with the British army and intelligence in Palestine and Istanbul. Director general of the Prime Minister's Office, 1952–1964. Mayor of Jerusalem since 1965.

Kook, Hillel. Lithuania, 1915. Emigrated in 1925. Joined the Haganah in 1929 and Etzel (the Revisionists' armed underground) in 1937. In the U.S.A. established the Committee for a Jewish Army (1941) and the Emergency Committee for the Rescue of European Jews (1943). Took the name Peter Bergson to keep his late uncle's name (A. I. H. Kook, chief rabbi of Palestine, 1904–1935) out of his activities. In 1944 helped found the Hebrew Committee for the Liberation of the Nation. Member of the Knesset, 1949–1951.

Korczak, Ruzka. Poland, 1921–Israel, 1988. A leader of the Hashomer Hatzair youth movement in Poland and a member of the armed underground in the Vilna ghetto, 1942–43. Left the ghetto with her comrades in the summer of 1943 and fought as a partisan in the forests. In December 1944 was the first to reach Palestine from the areas east of the General Government and to bring news of the Holocaust there. Joined the kibbutz Ein-Hachoresh in 1946. An educator, active in kibbutz committees and in Moreshet, the Holocaust documentation center of Hashomer Hatzair.

Kovner, Abba. Lithuania, 1918–Israel, 1987. A leader of the Hashomer Hatzair youth movement in Lithuania. Commander of the underground in Vilna and of Jewish partisan units in the forests of eastern Europe. Among the initiators of the Bricha, the movement of survivors to the south and out of Europe, 1944–45. Fought in the war of independence, 1948–49. A poet (winning several literary prizes), an intellectual, builder of the Diaspora Museum in Tel Aviv, 1978, member of the kibbutz Ein-Hachoresh, 1946–1987.

Levin, Yitzhak-Meir, Rabbi. Poland, 1894–Jerusalem, 1971. A founder of Agudat Yisrael in Poland. A member of the first Jewish council in the Warsaw ghetto; escaped and reached Palestine in 1940. Member of the Rescue Committee, 1943–1947. Head of Agudat Yisrael in Palestine (1947) and of its World Executive (1954). Member of the Knesset, 1949–1971. Minister of welfare, 1949–1955.

Levinsky, Akiva. Switzerland, 1918. Emigrated in 1934. Member of the kibbutz Ma'ayan-Zvi since 1936. A emissary for youth immigration in Germany (1939), Istanbul (1943–1945), and Europe (1945–1948). Chairman of financial, educational, and kibbutz institutions. Treasurer and member of the Jewish Agency Executive, 1978–1988.

Lichtheim, Richard. Germany, 1885–Israel, 1963. An emissary of the World Zionist Organization in Turkey, 1914–1917. A member of the Zionist Office in London, 1920–1923. Representative of the Jewish Agency in Geneva, 1939–1945.

Lubetkin, Zivia. Poland, 1914–Israel, 1978. A leader of the Hechalutz youth movement in Poland, of the Warsaw ghetto revolt, and of the survivors after the war. Emigrated in 1947. A founder of the Ghetto Fighters' kibbutz. Head of the Jewish Agency Executive's Youth and Pioneer Department. Active in kibbutz committees and the Histadrut.

Magnes, Judah-Leib. San Francisco, 1877–Jerusalem, 1948. A rabbi in Brooklyn and Manhattan, 1904–1912. Chairman of the Jewish Community Executive in New York, 1909–1922. Emigrated in 1925. Chancellor (1925–1935) and president (1935–1948) of the Hebrew University. A founder and leader of Brit-Shalom and Ichud, groups for Arab-Jewish cooperation.

Meged, Aharon. Poland, 1920. Emigrated in 1926. Member of the kibbutz Sdot-Yam, 1939–1950. An emissary of Hechalutz to the U.S.A. and Canada, 1946–1948. An editor of literary periodicals, an author and playwright, winner of several literary prizes.

Meirov (later Avigur), Shaul. Russia, 1899–Israel, 1978. Emigrated in 1912. A main leader of the Labor movement and the Haganah; instrumental in acquiring arms and establishing secret intelligence services. During the war, head of the Mossad for Aliya Bet (the illegal immigration) and the Bricha, the movement of survivors to the south and out of Europe. In the 1950s and 1960s handled clandestine contacts concerning Soviet Jewry.

Minz, Benjamin. Poland, 1903–Israel, 1961. Emigrated in 1925. A member of the Rescue Committee, 1943–1945. After the war worked in the survivors' camps in Europe. The leader of Poalei (workers of) Agudat Yisrael, who advocated cooperation with the Zionist movement. Member of the Knesset, 1949–1961; its deputy speaker, 1949–1959; Minister of posts, 1960.

Myerson (later Meir), Golda. Russia, 1898–Israel, 1979. Lived in the U.S.A., 1906–1921. An active member of the women's Labor Council and the Histadrut bodies, which she occasionally represented abroad. Member of the Zionist Actions Committee and the National Council. Minister to the Soviet Union (1948–1949), minister of labor (1949–1956), foreign minister (1956–1966). Prime minister, 1969–1974; resigned because of the Yom Kippur War.

Neustadt (later Noy), Melech. Galicia, 1895–Israel, 1959. Emigrated in 1926. An active member of Mapai, the Histadrut, and the Zionist Actions Committee and secretary general of the Mapai World Union, 1931–1952. Handled contacts between Mapai and the Histadrut and members of affiliated movements and parties in Nazi-occupied Europe.

Nusbacher (later Palgi), Joel. Hungary, 1918–Israel, 1978. Emigrated in 1939. Parachuted into Nazi-occupied Europe in 1944, reached Yugoslavia and Hungary, organized rescue and relief work in Budapest. Deputy director of El Al airline, 1949–1960; director of civil aviation, 1960–1964. Ambassador to Tanzania, 1964–1966. Member of the board of the Histadrut Sick Fund, 1966–1978.

Plotnicka, Frumka. Russia, 1914–Poland, 1943. A leader of the Hechalutz youth movement and the Jewish fighting underground in Nazi-occupied Poland. Infiltrated most of the main ghettos to bring news, help, and arms. Organized the revolt in the ghetto of Będzin, in which she was killed.

Pomerantz (later Hadari), Venia (Ze'ev). Poland, 1916. Emigrated in 1933. Joined the kibbutz Ramat-Rachel, 1933. A rescue emissary in Istanbul and Bulgaria, 1942–1946. Worked for the Mossad for Aliya Bet (illegal immigration) as an assistant to Meirov in Paris, 1946–1948. A founder of the Israeli Nuclear Research Center and of Ben-Gurion University, where he is professor of nuclear engineering.

Posner (later Pazner), Chaim. Poland, 1899–Jerusalem, 1981. Head of the Palestine Office in Danzig (1934–1938), its cochairman in Geneva (1940–1945), and its head (1945–1949). After the war represented the Jewish Agency and the Israeli government on fiscal and monetary matters in Geneva, South America, Scandinavia, and Israel. Member of the Yad Vashem (The Holocaust Remembrance Authority) Executive (1966) and its vice-chairman from 1970 until his death.

Rabbi Benjamin (pen name of Yehoshua Redler-Feldman). Galicia, 1880–Jerusalem, 1957. Emigrated in 1907. An editor, author, and publicist. An initiator of new settlements and suburbs. Active in groups advocating Arab-Jewish cooperation.

Reiss, Enschel. Galicia, 1886–Israel, 1984. Emigrated in 1926. An active member of Mapai, the Zionist Actions Committee (1929–1984), the World Jewish Congress (1936–1984), and the Rescue Committee. Delegate of the Rescue Committee to London, in contact with the Polish government-in-exile, 1943–44. Active well into old age in the World Jewish Congress and organizations of Polish Jewry.

Remez, David. Russia, 1886–Israel, 1951. Emigrated in 1913. Leader of the Labor movement, a founder of the Histadrut, and its secretary general, 1931–1944. Chairman of the National Council, 1944–1948. Minister of transportation and of culture and education successively, 1948–1951.

Riegner, Gerhard. Germany, 1911. Legal secretary and director of the World Jewish Congress's Geneva office, 1936–1945, member of its executive since 1948, and its secretary general since 1964. Active in Christian-Jewish relations.

Rubashov (later Shazar), Shneur-Zalman. Russia, 1889–Jerusalem, 1974. Emigrated in 1924. A central leader of Mapai, the Histadrut, and an editor of *Davar,* the Labor movement daily. Minister of culture and education, 1949–1950. Member of the Jewish Agency Executive, 1952–1956; its chairman, 1956–1960. Third president of Israel, 1963–1974. A writer and a poet.

Sadeh, Yitzhak. Poland, 1890–Israel, 1952. Awarded a medal in the Russian army in World War I for extraordinary courage. Emigrated in 1920. A leader and commander of the Haganah. A founder of the Palmach, the Haganah elite units, in 1941, and its commander until 1945. He was largely responsible for the special spirit of the Palmach, characterized by informal relations between commanders and privates, and whose members were viewed as a combination of soldiers and agricultural pioneers with a national mission.

Schmorak, Emil. Galicia, 1886–Israel, 1953. Emigrated in 1938. Head of the Jewish Agency Executive's Trade and Industry Department, 1938–1947. Treasurer of the Jewish Agency, 1947–1951. A leader of the General Zionists, a jurist, and an economist.

Schneerson, Fischel. Russia, 1885–Israel, 1957. A writer of Hasidic stories and a psychiatrist. Cousin of Menachem Schneerson, "the Lubavitcher," a famous rabbi in New York. Developed a new school of psychology, "the science of man."

Scheps, Shmuel. Poland, 1904. A Zionist leader in Poland. Member and head of the Palestine Office in Basel (1933–1939) and Geneva (1939–1945). After the war, a businessman and economist representing Israeli interests and companies in Switzerland.

Schwalb (later Dror), Nathan. Poland, 1908. A member of the Gordonia youth movement in Galicia, 1925. Emigrated in 1930. Member of the kibbutz Hulda, 1930–1938. An emissary of Gordonia in Prague and Bratislava (1938) and of Hechalutz in Geneva (1939–1945). Since 1956, a delegate of the Histadrut to Europe on special missions.

Schwarzbart, Ignacy. Galicia, 1888–Israel, 1961. An active Zionist since 1921. Member of the Polish Sejm (1938–39) and the Polish National Council in London (1940–1945). Worked for the World Jewish Congress in the U.S.A., 1946–1958.

Senesh, Hanna (Szenes Anna in Hungarian). Hungary, 1921–1944. A poet, from a Jewish Hungarian family of authors, poets, and musicians. Emigrated in 1939 at the outbreak of the war. Joined the kibbutz Sdot-Yam in 1941. Joined the British army in 1943, parachuted into Yugoslavia in 1944; was arrested upon crossing the border into Hungary, tortured for five months, and executed. Her courage throughout this ordeal inspired authors and playwrights.

Sereni, Enzo (Chaim). Rome, 1905–Dachau, 1944. Member of a distinguished Jewish Italian family. Emigrated in 1927. A founder of the kibbutz Givat-Brenner, 1928. An emissary to Jewish youth in Germany (1931 and 1933) and Iraq (1941). In 1944 parachuted behind enemy lines, was captured by the Germans, and was executed in Dachau. A philosopher, scholar, and labor leader. His widow, Ada, became one of the main organizers of illegal immigration from Italy.

Shapira, Moshe (later Moshe Chaim). Russia, 1902–Israel, 1970. Leader of the Religious Zionist party, or Hamizrachi. Emigrated in 1926. Deputy member and member of the Jewish Agency Executive, 1935–1948; cohead (with E. Dobkin) of its Immigration Department, 1935–1945. Minister of immigration, health, interior, and religion and welfare successively, 1948–1970.

Shertok (later Sharett), Moshe. Russia, 1894–Israel, 1965. Emigrated in 1906. An officer in the Turkish army in World War I. Studied law and economics. A leader in the Labor movement and member of the editorial board of its daily, *Davar*, 1923–1931. Head of the Jewish Agency's Political Department, 1933–1948, he was in fact the informal foreign minister of the Yishuv. Foreign minister, 1948–1956; prime minister, 1951–1955. Chairman of the Jewish Agency, 1960–1965.

Shind, Ze'ev. Lithuania, 1909–Israel, 1953. Emigrated in 1929. A member of the kibbutz Ayelet-Hashachar. On immigration missions in Poland (1935–

1939), Istanbul (1942–1944), and the U.S.A. (1946–1948); took "Danny" for a clandestine name. Director general of Zim (the Israeli shipping company) (1948–1950 and 1953) and of the ministries of Transportation (1950–1951) and Defense (1952).

Shostak, Eliezer. Poland, 1911. Secretary general of Betar, the Revisionists' youth movement, in Poland, 1931–1934. Emigrated in 1935. Secretary general of the National Labor Federation (the Revisionists' workers' union), 1936–1976. Member of the Rescue Committee, 1943–1945. Member of the Knesset, 1951–1988. Minister of health, 1976–1984.

Shragai, Shlomo-Zalman. Poland, 1899. Emigrated in 1924. A leader of Hapoel Hamizrachi (the Religious Zionist workers). Head of the National Council's Press and Information Office, 1929–1946. Member of the Zionist Actions Committee and the Jewish Agency Executive, 1946–1950. Mayor of Jerusalem, 1950–1952. Head of the Jewish Agency's Immigration Department, 1954–1968. A writer and religious scholar.

Silberschein, Abraham. Poland, 1882–Geneva, 1951. An active Zionist in Poland, a lawyer, and a member of the Polish Sejm (1922). During World War II in Geneva he established the Relief Committee for War-Stricken Jews, which sent letters, food, and documents to Jews in Nazi-occupied areas.

Sprinzak, Joseph. Russia, 1885–Jerusalem, 1959. Emigrated in 1908. A founder and leader of Mapai and the Histadrut; secretary general of the Histadrut, 1945–1949. Chairman of the Zionist Actions Committee, 1943–1959. Member of the National Council. Speaker of the Knesset (called "Father of the Knesset"), 1949–1959.

Suprasky, Yehoshu'a. Russia, 1879–Israel, 1948. A Zionist leader in Russia. Emigrated in 1920. Chairman of the Tel Aviv–Jaffa Jewish community, 1925–1932. A leader of the General Zionists. Member of the National Council and the Zionist Actions Committee, 1932–1945.

Szold, Henrietta. U.S.A., 1860–Jerusalem, 1945. A writer and educator. Founded Hadassah, a Jewish women's welfare organization, in 1912. Emigrated in 1920. As a member of the National Council and other committees from 1931 on, organized welfare activities in the Yishuv. Called the "Mother of Youth Immigration," which she headed from 1933 until her death.

Tabenkin, Yitzhak. Russia, 1887–Israel, 1971. Emigrated in 1912. A founder of the kibbutz Eim-Harod, the Histadrut, and Mapai. A Labor spiritual leader, especially of Hakibbutz Hameuchad (the United Kibbutz), affiliated with Mapai. A close friend of David Ben-Gurion and Berl Katznelson. Member of the Knesset, 1949–1951 and 1955–1959.

Wallenberg, Raoul. Sweden, 1913–? Member of a distinguished Swedish family, volunteered to organize and head the Department of Humanitarian Affairs in the Swedish embassy in Nazi-occupied Budapest, June 1944. In this capacity rescued tens of thousands, perhaps 100,000, Jews. Arrested by the Russians in January 1945, and his fate since is still unknown. Became a worldwide symbol of personal courage and human compassion.

Weissman, Yitzhak. Turkey, 1892–Israel, 1970. A businessman in Cairo, Vienna, and Berlin, whence he escaped in 1937 to France. In 1940 fled to Portugal, where he organized, first individually and then within the World Jewish Congress, extensive rescue work. Honorary consul of Guatemala in Israel, 1948–1968.

Weissmandel, Michael Dov-Beer. Hungary, 1903–U.S.A., 1958. An Orthodox rabbi, scholar, and teacher. Son-in-law of Rabbi Shmuel-David Ungar, leader of Orthodox Jewry in Slovakia. A rescue activist, especially as a member of the Working Group in Slovakia, 1942–1944. Sent to Auschwitz in 1944 with his wife and five children, jumped off the train and continued rescue work. Emigrated to the U.S.A., 1946, where he established a yeshiva (a talmudic high school). Strongly objected to the establishment of the state of Israel.

Weizmann, Chaim. Russia, 1874–Israel, 1952. An initiator of the Balfour Declaration of November 2, 1917. President of the World Zionist Organization, 1921–1931 and 1935–1946. First president of Israel from 1949 until his death.

Wise, Stephen S. Hungary, 1874–U.S.A., 1949. Ordained as a rabbi, 1893. A founder of the Federation of American Zionists; its secretary, 1898–1904, and its president, 1936–1938. Cofounder and head of the World Zionist Congress, 1936. Cochairman of the American Emergency Committee for Zionist Affairs, 1940–1945.

Ya'ari, Meir. Galicia, 1897–Israel, 1987. Emigrated in 1920. A founder of the kibbutz Merchavia. For decades a leader, with Y. Chazan, of the Hashomer Hatzair youth movement, its affiliated settlement movement (Hakibbutz Ha'antzi), and the Mapai party. A founder of the Histadrut and delegate of Hashomer Hatzair in its committees. A Marxist theoretician.

Yehieli, Tzvi. Rumania, 1905–Israel, 1970. Emigrated in 1925. A member of the kibbutz Givat-Chaim. An emissary of the Histadrut to Europe, 1930–1936. An activist in Aliya Bet (illegal immigration), 1942–1948. A member of Zim (the Israeli shipping company) Executive, 1948–1967.

Zaslany (later Shiloach), Reuven. Jerusalem, 1909–1959. Member of the Jewish Agency's Political Department, 1936–1948. Headed the secret cooperation between the Haganah and the British army during World War II, including the parachutists' mission. A founder of Israel's intelligence services. Minister in Washington, 1953–1957. Political adviser to the foreign minister, 1957–1959. An expert on Middle Eastern affairs.

Zuckermann, Yitzhak (Antek). Lithuania, 1915–Israel, 1981. A leader of the Hechalutz movement in Poland. Volunteered to return to Nazi-occupied Warsaw, 1939; wrote and edited underground publications in the Warsaw ghetto. Founded the fighting Jewish organization in Poland. Second in command to Mordechai Anilevitch, commander of the Warsaw ghetto revolt. A leader of the survivors after the war. Emigrated in 1947. A founder of the Ghetto Fighters' kibbutz, where he established the Ghetto Fighters' House, a center of Holocaust documentation and study.

Zygielbojm, Szmul (Arthur). Poland, 1895–London, 1943. An active member of the Bund party; its delegate to Belgium (1940), the U.S.A. (1940–1942), and Britain, and its representative on the Polish National Council in London (1942–1943). Committed suicide because of the world's indifference to Jewish plight.

INDEX

Linton, Joseph, 218
Lisbon, JDC in, 100
Lithuania: refugees in, 9, 13, 101; an-
nexation of, 18; aid to Germans, 31
Livne, Eliezer, 253–254
Łodz ghetto, 23, 38, 148, 219
London, 8, 10; JAE office, 2; WZO office,
12
Lubetkin, Zivia, 42, 123, 241–242, 314
Lublin, 9, 32
Ludin, Hans, 186
Lutz, Charles, 133, 237

MacClelland, Roswell, 215
MacDonald, Malcolm, 14, 15
MacMichael, Sir Harold, 6, 24, 59; and
"merchandise for blood" proposal,
192, 199; and immigration operations,
234
MacPherson, John S., 20, 21, 149, 161
Mafkura, 232
Magnes, Judah-Leib, 248, 314; and rescue operations, 95, 100, 125
Mantello, George, 215
Mapai, 2, 7, 22, 26, 61, 68, 252; World
Union, 7; policy-setting, 11; and Revisionists, 11, 60–61; on German invasion of Russia, 19; on Baghdad pogrom, 20; on Molotov's letter, 23;
delegation from Jordan Valley to, 25;
on Polish refugees in Soviet Union,
27–29; on public mourning, 54; and
rescue operations, 84, 95, 126; and
child rescue operations, 149, 150, 155,
156, 157; and ransom plans, 168, 171;
and "merchandise for blood" proposal,
209, 211; and Yishuv fighters' proposal, 221
Maritza, 230–232
Marks, Sir Simon, 105–106
Masada, 32, 242, 243
Mauritius, refugees sent to, 16
Mayer, Saly: and Europa Plan, 176–177,
179, 181, 183–184, 187; and appeal to
bomb Auschwitz, 218
McCloy, John, 217, 218
Meged, Aharon, 25, 314
Meir, Golda. *See* Myerson, Golda
Meirov, Shaul, 15, 123, 134, 136, 243,

252, 314; and rescue operations, 83,
88; and Yishuv fighters' proposal, 222,
224; and immigration operations, 231–
232
"Merchandise for blood" proposal, 148–
149, 186, 188–211
Merlin, Shmuel, 171
Military plans: appeal to bomb Ausch-
witz, 206, 208, 212–220; parachutists,
220–228
Milka, 230, 231
Mills, Eric, 132, 233–234
Minsk: pogroms in, 26; *Einsatzgruppen* in,
32
Minz, Benjamin, 314–315; and Rescue
Committee, 65, 69
Mitrani, Yitzhak, 124
Mizrachi (Religious Zionists), 149, 247
Mobilization and Rescue Fund, 81, 83–
92
Mobilization Fund, 73–74, 77, 80–81,
89–90, 156, 261
Moeller, Gustav, 116
Molotov, Vyacheslav, 23
Morgenthau, Henry, Jr., 182
Mossad for Aliya Bet. *See* Aliya Bet
Moyne, Lord Walter, 201, 209, 225
Myerson, Golda, 43, 315; and public re-
sponse, 57–58; and rescue operations,
79–80, 82–83, 86, 97–98, 104, 156,
159

National Committee for Rescue from
Nazi Terrorism, 140
National Council (Vaad Leumi), 7; and
public response, 50–55, 57–58, 68;
and Action Committee, 64–65; and
Rescue Committee, 66; and Mobilization Fund, 74; and rescue operations,
75, 79–80, 96, 108
National Jewish Committee, and rescue
operations, 82, 128
Nazis, 1, 2, 12; need for Jews as work
force, 30; extermination plans of 1942,
34–35; ideology, 186, 254
Netherlands: German occupation, 10;
deportations and exterminations, 23,
26, 32, 78; rescue operations in, 113;
confirmation-of-immigration permits,

Teheran, 233; Dobkin's mission to, 29–30; refugees in, 98
Tel Aviv, 7; on deportation of Warsaw Jews, 32
Temple, William, 140
Theresienstadt, 29, 238; rescue operations in, 127–128
Tito (Josip Broz): and "merchandise for blood" proposal, 203; and Yishuv fighters' proposal, 225
Transnistria, 21, 165; rescue operations in, 128; and child rescue operations, 153, 172–173; ransom plans, 164–174; mutual aid, 243; immigration operations, 248
Treblinka, 32, 36, 38, 186, 213–215
Tripoli Jews, and exchange plan, 148
Turkey: Polish refugees in, 9; and *Struma* entry, 24; Rescue Committee emissary to, 69; immigration through, 96, 106, 120, 229, 230–234, 236, 246, 249; rescue operations in, 120–126; and child rescue operations, 154–156, 158–163; and ransom plans, 167; and "merchandise for blood" proposal, 193–194; and appeal to bomb Auschwitz, 216. *See also* Istanbul emissaries
Tuval, Meir, 124

Ukraine, 128; aid given Germans, 31
Unger, Eliezer, 87
United Rescue Committee of the Jewish Agency, 65
United States, 254–255; on Jewish resettlement, 16; and public response, 32, 53, 55, 56; learns of extermination plans, 34; on Yishuv delegation, 52; and Bermuda Conference, 57, 140–144; Etzel activities in, 60; State Department, 78, 144, 148, 154, 169, 196, 208, 215; funds contributed by, 91–92, 94; anti-Semitism in, 96; financial aid to Nazi-occupied areas, 98–99; JAE appeals to, 137; and exchange plan, 144, 148; and child rescue operations, 153–154, 159; and ransom plans, 167, 169–170; and Europa Plan, 182; and "merchandise for blood" proposal, 191–192, 195–196, 200–201, 203,

207–209; and appeal to bomb Auschwitz, 212, 216–219; knowledge of Auschwitz, 215; and Yishuv fighters' proposal, 222; and immigration operations, 233, 235–237. *See also* Joint Distribution Committee; New York
United War Appeal (South Africa), 98, 101, 102, 103
Uzbekistan, Jewish refugees in, 27

Vaad Leumi. *See* National Council
Vašek, Anton, 177
Vatican, 119, 132–133; and "merchandise for blood" proposal, 202; knowledge of Auschwitz, 215
Vilna, 23; exterminations in, 26
Vittel transit camp, 32, 147–149
von Thadden, Eberhard, 147

Wallenberg, Raoul, 116, 133, 237, 319
War Refugee Board, 99, 125, 215, 236; and appeal to bomb Auschwitz, 217
Warsaw ghetto, 38; deportations from, 32; destruction of, 42; revolt, 42, 57–58, 82, 89, 144, 219–220, 240–241, 262
Weissman, Yitzhak, 19, 319; and rescue operations, 113, 126
Weissmandel, Rabbi Michael Dov-Beer, 175–180, 184, 187, 196, 319; and appeal to bomb Auschwitz, 216, 218
Weizmann, Chaim, 2, 61, 71, 255, 258, 319; 1939 report on Poland, 8; on Britain, 15; and rescue operations, 105, 153; and ransom plans, 170; and "merchandise for blood" proposal, 191–192, 195, 199, 201–203, 205–206, 210–211; and appeal to bomb Auschwitz, 216–217; and immigration operations, 236; and Ben-Gurion, 250–252
Welles, Sumner, 34
Whittall, Arthur, 159
Winant, John G., 32
Wise, Rabbi Stephen S., 7, 34, 45, 52, 215, 319; appeals to Eden, 141; and ransom plans, 171; and Europa Plan, 182; and appeal to bomb Auschwitz, 216, 218

DATE DUE

MAY 3 0 1995			
JUN 16	1995		
APR 1 9 1999			